Sterling A. Brown's
A NEGRO LOOKS AT THE SOUTH

Sterling A. Brown reading from
his *Collected Poems*, ca. 1980

Photo credit: Courtesy Roy Lewis Archives

Sterling A. Brown's

A NEGRO LOOKS AT THE SOUTH

Edited by

JOHN EDGAR TIDWELL
and
MARK A. SANDERS

OXFORD
UNIVERSITY PRESS
2007

OXFORD
UNIVERSITY PRESS

Oxford University Press, Inc., publishes works that further
Oxford University's objective of excellence
in research, scholarship, and education.

Oxford   New York
Auckland   Cape Town   Dar es Salaam   Hong Kong   Karachi
Kuala Lumpur   Madrid   Melbourne   Mexico City   Nairobi
New Delhi   Shanghai   Taipei   Toronto

With offices in
Argentina   Austria   Brazil   Chile   Czech Republic   France   Greece
Guatemala   Hungary   Italy   Japan   Poland   Portugal   Singapore
South Korea   Switzerland   Thailand   Turkey   Ukraine   Vietnam

Published by Oxford University Press, Inc.
198 Madison Avenue, New York, New York 10016

www.oup.com

Oxford is a registered trademark of Oxford University Press

Library of Congress Cataloging-in-Publication Data
Brown, Sterling Allen, 1901–
Sterling A. Brown's A Negro looks at the South /
edited by John Edgar Tidwell and Mark A. Sanders.
p. cm.
Includes bibliographical references.
ISBN-13 978-0-19-531399-4
ISBN 0-19-531399-2
1. African Americans—Southern States—Social life and customs—20th century.
2. African Americans—Southern States—Social conditions—20th century.   3. African
Americans—Southern States—Biography.   4. Oral history.   5. Country life—Southern
States—History—20th century.   6. Community life—Southern States—History—20th century.
7. Southern States—Social life and customs—20th century.   8. Southern States—Social
conditions—1865–1945.   9. Southern States—Race relations—History—20th century.
I. Tidwell, John Edgar.   II. Sanders, Mark A., 1963–   III. Title.
IV. Title: Negro looks at the South.
E185.86.B698 2006
975'.00496073—dc22   2006012377

1   3   5   7   9   8   6   4   2

Printed in the United States of America
on acid-free paper

The editors dedicate this book to the memory of
Daisy Turnbull Brown,
Sterling A. Brown's beloved wife, "Roseanne."

Acknowledgments

With the publication of *A Negro Looks at the South*, an important part of Sterling A. Brown's aesthetic vision comes to fruition. In his absence, this book has benefited from the contributions and collective goodwill of the following institutions, colleagues, friends, and family.

John L. Dennis, the adopted son of Sterling A. Brown, has understandably been a strong advocate for this project as well as a vigilant guardian of its integrity. We are grateful that he has entrusted us with the task of making this project available to the public.

To Thomas C. Battle, Joellen El Bashir, and the Moorland-Spingarn Research Center at Howard University, we wish to express our gratitude for working so closely with us in bringing this important aspect of Brown's writing to completion. In this same spirit, we can only begin to thank Michael S. Harper, who, with perspicacity, encouraged us to investigate Brown's papers for this unpublished material; Henry Louis Gates, Jr., who saw, in the earliest draft we compiled, the poignancy of Brown's extraordinary writing; and Joanne Gabbin, whose germinal scholarship provided the sturdy foundation on which we build.

Adequate financial support is crucial to the completion of any extensive project, especially one that seeks to make disparate parts coalesce into a meaningful whole. We would like to thank the University of Kansas General Research Fund, Glenn Loury and the Institute on Race and Social Division at Boston University, and the Center for Humanistic Inquiry at Emory University for their generosity.

Collegial support is also a necessity in a project like this one. For their wonderful words of advice, their time, and their financial and other kinds of assistance, we thank our supporters in the University of Kansas Department of English, particularly the Ad Hoc Committee on African American Literature; the chancellor of the University of Kansas, Robert Hemenway; the College of Liberal Arts and Sciences; Victor Bailey who serves KU as director of the Hall Center for the

Humanities; and the members of the Department of African American Studies and the Department of English at Emory University.

Thanks are due also to colleagues who wrote letters of recommendation, read drafts of the manuscript, and offered unfailing encouragement in those bleak moments we experienced: William L. Andrews, Lawrence Buell, Rudolph P. Byrd, Deborah L. Dandridge, Elizabeth Davey, Leroy Davis, Frances Smith Foster, Cris Levenduski, Ethelbert Miller, Arnold Rampersad, Steven Saltzman, and John S. Wright. If by chance an error or two have accidentally crept into our work, the fault lies with us and not with their generous assistance.

The physical preparation of a manuscript is never an easy task. We are fortunate that Paula Courtney, Pam LeRow, Gwen Claassen, the late Lynn Porter, Arneta Allen, and Elizabeth Simoneau undertook most of this work for us. Part of this preparation owes to a group of very bright student assistants, who are now scholars in their own right; we gratefully acknowledge the work of Rachel Bateman, Ayana Free, Robert Patterson, Nathan Poell, Vibha Shetiya, Shirley Toland-Dix, Cara Van Nice, Renee Watson, and Andrea Craig Gruenbaum.

Rose Marino, associate university general counsel at Kansas University, was truly unselfish as she provided cogent and timely legal advice, despite her demanding work schedule. For her moral support and her abiding commitment to carrying on Sterling Brown's legacy by making his house her own, we thank Marcia Davis. We also wish to extend a warm thanks to Tina Dunkley, director of the Clark Atlanta University Art Galleries, and to Corrine Jennings, director of Kenkeleba House, for their invaluable help in procuring the artwork that graces the cover of this book. And to Shannon McLachlan and Elissa Morris, our editors at Oxford University Press, we offer our sincerest gratitude for their diligence and perseverance in shepherding this project through to completion.

Finally, and most important, we reserve our most heartfelt gratitude for members of our families. We are grateful to Verlean Tidwell, Carmaletta M. Williams, Linda Calvert, and Cornelius Tidwell; Earl and Arthrell Sanders, Claire Sanders and Burton Balfour; Rose Wallace, Raymond Wallace, Christopher and Kimberly Hall Wallace, Gregory Wallace, and Jeff Weiser; and Kimberly Wallace-Sanders and Isaiah Anthony Wallace Sanders for their patience, their understanding, and especially their prayers. They provided so much more than support; they gave us the freedom and luxury of thoughtful reflection in the safe harbors we call home.

Contents

A Note on the Text

In the early 1940s, Sterling A. Brown earnestly began collecting materials that would expand the brief representation of African Americans in the region that Jonathan Daniels impressionistically described in his *A Southerner Discovers the South* (1938). Brown studiously examined published texts on the matter, and, more important, he personally explored the region with a poet's eye, absorbing African American customs, mores, life, language, and lore. As he encountered more and richly diverse experiences, he complained to his wife, Daisy, that there was too much. The Southern landscape's legacy of awesome beauty and its anguished tragedy were aesthetically and emotionally overwhelming. He nevertheless wrote in different expressive modes to capture and present the breadth and depth of the experiences he embraced. The results are preserved in his body of papers and manuscripts collected in the Moorland-Spingarn Research Center at Howard University.

To organize the disparate pieces to this project, Brown created six different tables of contents. From them, we infer Brown was troubled by the challenge to discover an organizing principle and to bring coherence to the flood of observations and feelings that showered him with fresh insights into the complexity of black Southern social and cultural diversity. To that extent, we have endeavored to complete what a penchant for comprehensiveness and perfection prevented Brown from doing: making the difficult editorial choices that would allow the many parts to coalesce into a cohesive whole.

First, we had to decide which essays to include and to exclude. We were naturally drawn to the completed, unpublished essays in his manuscript collection and to the previously published ones, which appeared in such periodicals as *Survey Graphic*, *Phylon*, *The Record Changer*, and *The South Today*. Our next decision was how to arrange the different pieces topically. In making these choices, we used his tables of contents as guides in creating six sections for the book. In two instances, the sections that Brown proposed contained only two or so short essays.

Thus we combined these obvious fragments into logical wholes, grouping the essays most related to each other. Brown provided no prologue for the collection, so we created one that would assist the reader in understanding the purpose of the text. However, "Count Us In," which Brown proposed as a coda to the volume and which first appeared as an essay in *What the Negro Wants* (1944), serves here as his intended epilogue.

To ensure uniformity and textual consistency, we made minor but necessary editorial changes to spelling, grammar, and punctuation. Many readers, we felt, might be unfamiliar with some terms deriving from a 1940s context. For that reason, "Annotations" contains a number of terms we glossed and placed at the end of the volume. In choosing them, we make no claim for comprehensiveness; we representatively selected ones that are likely to be most unfamiliar to today's readers and that are most crucial to textual understanding. Last, for easy reference, we created topically a suggestive index of important names, places, and organizations.

Sterling A. Brown's
A NEGRO LOOKS AT THE SOUTH

LOOKING AT STERLING A. BROWN'S SOUTH

An Introduction

John Edgar Tidwell *and* Mark A. Sanders

I

From their humble beginnings with Lucy Terry's earliest poem to Rita Dove's Pulitzer Prize–winning verse and Toni Morrison's Nobel Prize–winning prose, African American letters have laid claim, either implicitly or explicitly, to the same Enlightenment values and ideals shaping the founding documents of the American Republic: freedom, equality, justice, and, above all, universal personhood. Indeed, in eighteenth- and nineteenth-century contexts, where letters and the literary tradition often served as the demarcation between human and animal, free and slave, subject and object, the very assertion of literary ability was the assertion of being, citizenship, and democratic inclusion.[1] Thus a poor eighteenth-century black woman's chronicle of her community in Deerfield, Massachusetts, and a contemporary black woman's epic tale of slavery's (and emancipation's) trauma may serve as bookends to a tradition shaped by the African American struggle for full democratic access.

Sterling A. Brown, poet, essayist, literary and cultural critic, teacher, ethnographer, anthologist, and raconteur, is a pivotal figure in this two-hundred-year-plus tradition, a figure who culls from his literary and cultural past, from prosody, voice, and idiom, and reinvents them for his generation and those to follow him. A quintessential New Negro, Brown stood in the vanguard as his generation reassessed its literary heritage; indeed, Brown created a completely new artistic and poetic vocabulary, re-created the modes of conception and

1. Henry Louis Gates Jr., "Literary Theory and the Black Tradition," in *Figures in Black: Words, Signs, and the "Racial" Self* (New York: Oxford University Press, 1987), 25.

representation of the African American and blackness for a modern age, and, in keeping with the ongoing democratic struggle, asserted full and complex black representation in service to the New Negro claim to African American participation and citizenship.

On May 1, 1901, Sterling A. Brown, the last child and only boy, was born into the well-educated, middle-class Brown family of Washington, D.C. A former slave, his father, Sterling Nelson Brown, earned his B.A. from Fisk University in 1885, his B.D. from Oberlin Seminary College in 1888, his A.M. from Fisk in 1891, and an honorary D.D. from Howard University in 1906. He also served as pastor of Lincoln Temple Congregational Church while he taught in the School of Religion at Howard. Sterling A. Brown's mother, Adelaide Allen, also a Fisk University graduate (B.A. 1891) and a patron of the arts, helped to create a household where education, culture, self-improvement, and service to racial uplift served as the defining values of his youth. In short, Brown's parents—their determined rise from poverty to education and thus to professional standing and political influence—were children of Reconstruction in that they were able to take advantage of the educational opportunities newly accorded blacks. So, too, his parents witnessed the demise of Reconstruction, the nation's reneging on the new constitutional guarantees of the Thirteenth, Fourteenth, and Fifteenth Amendments. As a result, their professional and personal lives remained devoted to the struggle for full citizenship for African Americans. Of course, their struggle was not in isolation; theirs was a home that regularly hosted their better-known contemporaries—Frederick Douglass, Kelly Miller, John Mercer Langston, Alexander Crummell, and others—who were all deeply committed to racial uplift and political equality.

In a larger sense, the politics of Brown's parents and that of their generation largely shaped the ethos and political strategies defining the New Negro Movement. The New Negro generation, born after Reconstruction through the turn of the century, inherited both the promise of civil rights legislation under Reconstruction and the systematic exclusion from these constitutional guarantees. Furthermore, this generation witnessed one of the most dramatic transformations in African American history and culture to date, as unprecedented numbers of blacks moved from South to North, from country to city, and from being sharecroppers/tenant farmers to laborers/wage earners. As a result, the New Negro generation inherited the responsibilities of reconstructing the theoretical, cultural, and political contexts in which African American life and culture would be understood. Thus, a new sense of political self-awareness gave rise to institutions, political movements, and expressive arts all devoted to making palpable Reconstruction legislation. Organizations such as the NAACP, the Urban League, A. Philip Randolph's Brotherhood of Sleeping Car Porters and Maids, and even Marcus Garvey's Universal Negro Improvement Association (UNIA) reflected this new political self-awareness. This generation pursued, with renewed vigor, litigation challenging segregation, in particular the doctrine of "separate but equal," upheld by the Supreme Court in 1896. This generation aggressively campaigned for federal antilynching legislation and for equality in education, affordable housing, fair treatment by law enforcement and the courts—in short, for equal opportunity and full citizenship.

What we have come to call the Harlem Renaissance is better understood in the context of the New Negro Movement; as the artistic wing of the movement, New Negro artists responded to the overarching aims of black equality and justice through a comprehensive address of the ways in which African Americans were represented in American popular and expressive culture. Challenging the racist caricature of minstrelsy, vaudeville, and plantation tradition dialect (as well as in popular advertising and the new technology of film), New Negro artists explored a fuller range, depth, and complexity in black being within art that sought to expand a vision of black humanity. To be sure, Brown disagreed strongly with the ways in which some of his contemporaries approached this larger project. In Brown's opinion, for example, those who followed W. E. B. Du Bois's prescription for art that focused on black middle-class life simply substituted one set of reductive poses for another. And those who evaded issues of racial inequity altogether—the romantic tradition—Brown dismissed as "escapist" or "derivative." Brown even found fault with many in the smaller group of artists who explored and portrayed African American folk culture: James Weldon Johnson, Jean Toomer, Zora Neale Hurston, and Langston Hughes. Hughes's portraits, in particular, failed to discover the full range of psychic and emotional complexity readily available in the black vernacular. About Hurston, Brown voiced serious reservations about the lack of stoicism and bitterness in her portrayals of the folk. Nevertheless, Brown unequivocally affirmed the goals of the movement while going his own way to achieve them.

With a distinct sense of New Negro intellectual and artistic rigor, Brown embarked upon a unique political and critical journey into the black vernacular, into the folk and rural South, and thus into the blues, work songs, hollers, ballads, folk sayings, and more. Brown firmly believed that folk speech was fully capable of expressing the complex, often contradictory responses to the profound conundrum of black life in America. Thus Brown wrote poetry and criticism, edited anthologies, lectured, and taught courses all in pursuit of the critical and artistic acuity commensurate to the relentlessly complex humanity he found at the heart of modern black life. Much of Brown's keen awareness of the poetic possibilities inherent in folk forms resulted from the very best formal education available to a New Negro. In 1918, he graduated from the prestigious Dunbar High School, where he was taught by the likes of Jessie Fauset and Angelina W. Grimke, among others who had distinguished themselves as scholar-artists. He went on to attend Williams College (1918–1922), where he was elected in his junior year to Phi Beta Kappa, and he was the only student upon graduation to be awarded "Final Honors." He graduated cum laude with an A.B. in English. And it was there that he began to read contemporary literature under the tutelage of the irascible George Dutton and to explore literature's critical potential.

From 1922 to 1923, Brown studied for and earned his M.A. at Harvard University. While he was there, he continued to study modern American poets such as Robert Frost, Edwin Arlington Robinson, Edgar Lee Masters, and Carl Sandburg, poets who expanded upon the Whitman tradition for the twentieth century, conceiving the universal in the particular and the ordinary, crafting local and common speech into poetic metaphor. So, too, they reconfigured form not simply as a medium of thematic design, but as the very embodiment of the democratic values inherent in the celebration of the common and often overlooked voice. Indeed, Brown often commented on the importance of the maverick Harvard professor Bliss Perry and his instruction in contemporary American literature. He taught American fiction, prose, and drama, emphasizing the authors' critical reflections on material conditions and thus the ways in which everyday people struggle to live their lives.

After completing his formal education, Brown could have easily returned to Washington, D.C., and to Howard, where a job awaited him. Instead, he took the advice of his father and that of Carter G. Woodson and went South for yet another kind of education, one equally as informing. From 1923 to 1929, Brown taught at Virginia Seminary and College, Lincoln University in Missouri, and Fisk University successively. Using these schools as his base, Brown often went out into the surrounding counties, embracing African American folk culture, speech, and lore. He encountered Slim Greer, Mrs. Bibby, and Calvin "Big Boy" Davis, all of whom would become heroes in his mythmaking projects. On farms, in bars, and in juke joints, he interacted with the rural folk, an experience that afforded him an intimacy with patterns of speech, idiomatic expression, folkways, and, of course, the blues. Through such close contact, he became familiar not merely with form or gesture, but also with a certain philosophical approach to life encoded in the vernacular.

During this period, Brown wrote some of his most successful poetry and critical essays. Thus began his long and influential literary career. His first essay, "Roland Hayes," appeared in and won an award from *Opportunity* in 1925 for its poignant examination of the baritone's virtuosity, particularly his interpretation of Negro spirituals. This initial success was quickly followed by the publication of an experimental, provocative poetry in *Opportunity*, *Crisis*, Countee Cullen's *Caroling Dusk* (1927), V. F. Calverton's *Anthology of Negro American Literature*

(1927), Benjamin A. Botkin's *Folk Say* (Vol. 2, 1931), and the second edition of James Weldon Johnson's *Book of American Negro Poetry* (1931). For a young and unknown poet, being published in the leading black journals and anthologies of the day constituted considerable success in and of itself. But more important, these poems—including "Odyssey of Big Boy," "Challenge," "When de Saints Go Ma'ching Home," and "Long Gone"—dramatically inaugurated a new approach to the poetic representation of folk speech and forms. Perhaps the force of Brown's innovation is best expressed through the conflicted position his famous editors found themselves in. James Weldon Johnson had introduced in his 1922 edition of *The Book of American Negro Poetry* the claim of dialect poetry's bankruptcy; that given its manipulation in the overtly racist plantation tradition, it could now render only humor or pathos. Yet by 1931, in the second edition, he featured Brown's deft use of dialect, and the following year he wrote in his preface to Brown's first book, *Southern Road* (1932), what amounted to a most eloquent retraction, finally conceding the complexity of black life delivered in dialect:

> [Brown] began writing just after the Negro poets had generally discarded conventionalized dialect, with its minstrel traditions of Negro life (traditions that had but slight relation, often no relation at all to *actual* Negro life) with its artificial and false sentiment, its exaggerated geniality and optimism. He infused his poetry with genuine characteristic flavor by adopting as his medium the common, racy, living speech of the Negro in certain phases of *real* life. . . . [H]e has made more than mere transcriptions of folk poetry, and he has done more than bring to it mere artistry; he has deepened its meanings and multiplied its implications. He has actually absorbed the spirit of his material and made it his own; and without diluting its primitive frankness and raciness, truly re-expressed it with artistry and magnified power.[2]

Echoing Johnson's earlier reservations about dialect, Cullen introduced in *Caroling Dusk* the importance of standard English and free verse for young poets; yet he featured perhaps Brown's most forceful illustration, in "Odyssey of Big Boy," of idiom, language, and folk form's ability to defy racist caricature and to deliver a fully realized black persona.

Following quickly on the heels of these earlier successes, *Southern Road* reassembled many of the previously published poems and presented a corpus of new poems to create a collection that caught the critical eye of Alain Locke, who wrote,

2. James Weldon Johnson, "Introduction to the First Edition," in Sterling A. Brown, *The Collected Poems of Sterling A. Brown*, ed. Michael S. Harper (Chicago: TriQuarterly Press, 1989), 16–17.

"Gauging the main objective of Negro poetry as the poetic portrayal of Negro folk-life true in both letter and spirit to the idiom of the folk's own way of feeling and thinking, we may say that here [in *Southern Road*] for the first time is the much-desired and long-awaited acme attained or brought within actual reach."[3] So, too, the highly influential critic Louis Untermeyer reviewed the volume with cautious enthusiasm, noting, "The book [*Southern Road*] is not only suffused with extreme color, the deep suffering and high laughter of workers in cabins and cotton fields, of gangs and gutters, but it vibrates with less obvious glow—the glow which, however variously it may be defined, is immediately perceived and ultimately recognized as poetry."[4]

Riding the success of *Southern Road*, Brown approached several publishers about a second volume, *No Hiding Place*, but was rejected for reasons that remain unclear. He would not publish another collection of poetry until 1975 when Broadside Press brought out *The Last Ride of Wild Bill and Eleven Narrative Poems;* *No Hiding Place* did not appear until 1980, in *The Collected Poems of Sterling A. Brown*. Despite the long publishing hiatus, Brown continued to write poetry throughout the 1930s, and he pursued his larger cultural project through research and critical writing. Indeed, the late '30s and early '40s were equally if not more productive than the previous period, producing two volumes of literary criticism, an anthology, numerous essays and reviews, and contributions to major studies. For example, in 1937, Brown wrote two highly influential volumes addressing the representation of African Americans in American literature: *The Negro in American Fiction* and *Negro Poetry and Drama*. Augmenting the earlier work of William Stanley Braithwaite,[5] Benjamin Griffith Brawley,[6] and Brown's own essay "Negro Character As Seen by White Authors" (1933), the first volume examines the historical types used to define (and ultimately limit) African American literary representation. *The Negro in American Fiction* is the first book-length study of black stereotypes and their ideological import from a black perspective, laying the foundation for Ralph Ellison's reflections in *Shadow and Act* (1964), Toni Morrison's *Playing in the Dark* (1992), and the larger critical tradition addressing black representation in American popular culture. The second volume, one of the earliest African American literary histories, defines a tradition of African

3. Alain Locke, "Sterling Brown: The New Negro Folk-Poet," in *Negro: An Anthology*, ed. Nancy Cunard. 1935. Edited and abridged by Hugh Ford (New York: Frederick Ungar, 1970), 88.

4. Louis Untermeyer, "New Light from an Old Mine," *Opportunity* 10 (August 1932): 250–251.

5. William Stanley Braithwaite, "The Negro in American Literature," in *The New Negro,* ed. Alain Locke (New York: Albert and Charles Boni, 1925), 29–44.

6. Benjamin Griffith Brawley, "The Negro in American Fiction," in *Anthology of American Negro Literature,* ed. V. F. Calverton (New York: Modern Library, 1929), 237–247.

American poetry and drama, helping to make possible the flourishing of literary histories by the ensuing generation of black literary critics.

From 1938 to 1940, Brown also worked with Gunnar Myrdal on what would become the seminal study of American race relations: *An American Dilemma: The Negro Problem and American Democracy* (1944). The Swedish sociologist had been selected by the Carnegie Corporation to conduct a comprehensive study on the ongoing disparity between black and white achievement in American economic and social life. He admittedly knew little about African American life and culture and thus relied heavily on Ralph Bunche and Brown not only to provide pertinent information but to write major sections of the study.[7] For his part, Brown took Myrdal to Harlem jazz clubs, exposed him to the blues, and more generally explained to him the intricacies of African American folk culture. Brown also wrote a summarizing memorandum and an essay in conjunction with the study: "The Negro in American Culture" and "Count Us In," which he also envisioned as the anchor to an extended collection of essays about the black South.

During the same period, Brown, Arthur P. Davis, and Ulysses Lee compiled the unprecedented anthology *The Negro Caravan* (1941), a revolutionary assemblage of representative elements from across the vast array of African American expressive cultural forms. Not simply literary in a narrow sense, the anthology collected folk songs, spirituals, hollers, blues, and more created by unknown bards, along with poems, plays, and prose by noted literary figures. The most eclectic and representative anthology to date, *Negro Caravan* served as the model for *Cavalcade* (1971), *Chant of Saints* (1979), *The Norton Anthology of African American Literature* (1995, revised 2004), and *Call and Response* (1998)—all of which insist upon the interrelatedness of folk forms and literary art. The collection also responded directly to *The American Caravan* (first published in 1927), the annual anthology that professed to represent contemporary American literature yet excluded black authors.

From 1936 through 1940, Brown also served as national editor of Negro affairs for the Federal Writers' Project. Fighting for a serious address of African American culture in the tourist guides to Southern states that the Federal Writers' Project produced, Brown edited the editions of the guides to ensure the use of appropriate images to represent African Americans. He also wrote "The Negro in Washington" for that mammoth tome *Washington: City and Capital* (1937) and advised the Virginia project that wrote *The Negro in Virginia* (1940).

As if he didn't have enough work, Brown continued to write columns in the leading popular and academic black journals, perhaps most notably his regular

7. Walter A. Jackson, *Gunnar Myrdal and America's Conscience: Social Engineering and Racial Liberalism, 1938–1987* (Chapel Hill: University of North Carolina Press, 1990), 131–132.

reviews of contemporary literature and film in *Opportunity*. The final punctuation on this dauntingly prolific period came when Brown wrote and assembled
much of the material that would go into *A Negro Looks at the South*. To be sure,
Brown remained productive after World War II, as his papers in the Moorland-
Spingarn Research Center at Howard University well attest. Brown lectured and
gave readings at colleges and universities across the country, continued to write
scholarly essays, and ultimately inspired a generation of Howard-based writers
and radicals who would animate the Black Power and Black Arts movements. After
retiring from Howard in 1969, Brown highlighted the latter years of his public
life with lectures and readings that helped to launch the recovery project of which
this volume is a part. In 1973, Brown returned to his undergraduate alma mater
and delivered a legendary address that was recorded as "A Son's Return: Oh Didn't
He Ramble" and later revised for publication in *Chant of Saints*. And in 1980, the
year that his collected poems were published, he gave a reading at the Library of
Congress in which he reassessed his long career.

Aptly appraising a life and a career instrumental in shaping our contemporary
understanding of African American literature and culture, Michael S. Harper and
Anthony Walton view Brown as the central architect in the creation of a wholly
new way of representing African American life and culture:

> Brown strove to show that rural southern blacks in particular . . . had in fact
> developed a system of active strategies of encompassing the harsh economic
> and social situation in which they found themselves. . . . [He] distilled the
> rhythms of black speech and song, merging them with English form and
> rhetoric to create a wholly invented language that, as such, takes us both
> through and beyond history into myth, beyond the apparent face of things
> into the commonality of human hopes and ambitions hidden by social forms.[8]

Thus *A Negro Looks at the South* renders, in often lyrical prose, portraits of black
lives about the heroic business of self-assertion, self-expression, and self-possession.

II

In 1938, Jonathan Daniels, a North Carolina journalist, published *A Southerner
Discovers the South*, a book-length narrative and travelogue tracing his firsthand
experiences in which he confronts and embraces both the beauty and the horror

---

8. Michael S. Harper and Anthony Walton, "Introduction," *The Vintage Book of African American
Poetry* (New York: Vintage, 2000), xxix.

of Southern life. Driving a "well-behaved" Plymouth, he toured from Virginia to Arkansas and as far down as New Orleans to collect feelings, observations, and impressions that would enable him to understand the many changes occurring in the South. To Sterling A. Brown, Daniels's book represented more than a record of travel; it presented the South trying to free itself from the restrictions of its past. In part, Daniels's book disabused readers of the notion of a highly sentimentalized, undifferentiated region by presenting the South with a greater sense of complexity and variety, and therefore as a composite portrait. Brown saw Daniels's work as going much further than previous studies of the South, such as *I'll Take My Stand* (1930), in investigating the successes and the failures of a deeply racialized part of the country. Nevertheless, for Brown, Daniels's approach to black life remained underdeveloped. As he said, Daniels's "chats with Negroes are too few."

During the late '30s and early '40s, an exhaustively productive period for Brown, he never lost sight of the fact that he wanted to address the shortcomings of Daniels's study more directly. Fortuitously, Brown discovered a way. At the 1942 American Literature Symposium sponsored by the English Department at the University of Oklahoma, the National Council of Teachers of English, and the Rosenwald Foundation, he met Rosenwald's executive director, Edwin Embree. Through his presentation on "The Negro in American Literature" and in subsequent informal discussions with Embree and others, Brown created a strong presence and offered conclusive evidence of his thorough knowledge of African American literary and cultural life. Persuaded by Brown's command of the subject, Embree encouraged Brown to apply for funding, in part to collect material for a book about the black South.

Brown taught during summer sessions at Atlanta University from 1933 to 1937, and thus he had informally established Atlanta as his base of operation for his investigation and collection of materials of Southern black life. In 1942, prior to returning to Atlanta for another summer session, Brown responded to Embree's encouragement with an official letter of application to the Rosenwald Foundation, requesting funding that would allow him to remain in the South through the end of the year. On April 17, 1942, Brown received an official notification of a $1,500 grant to pursue his research. Brown's response to this award was to go "from Arlington to Alexandria [Louisiana]," from the Eastern seaboard throughout the Deep South in an effort to document the variety of blacks' experiences. In an era during which folklorists, literary historians, creative writers, and cultural critics were consumed with issues of the folk, common people, and, more polemically, the proletariat, Brown was drawn into this national conversation by persisting in his fundamental need to rescue the representation of black people from the clutches of racial stereotyping. *A Negro Looks at the South*, a racial portrait composed of disparate black voices, represents his most sustained effort in prose to invest black people with dignity, grace, and courage—qualities denied them by a history of misrepresentation.

Of the many artful deployments used to correct such misrepresentation, one that bears particular relevance for *A Negro Looks at the South* is the way in which Brown constructs the artist as witness and chronicler. As a collection, *Southern Road* ably makes the Southern road into a metaphoric avenue crossing the geographic landscape and affording the poet entry into the lives of its many black inhabitants. Traveling across the milieu, the poet witnesses the strife of life on the chain gang, the hard luck of floods and boll weevils, and the celebration of the lives of Ma Rainey's blues people and the unnamed creators of spirituals. In short, he captures a range of richly textured experiences. He astutely chronicles the response to hardship—the wit, the stoicism, the determination—as revealed through blues, spirituals, work songs, ballads, and idiomatic aphorisms.

Whereas *Southern Road* uses this particular construction of the artist poetically, *A Negro Looks at the South* reconceives this strategy for prose. Again, the artist, via trains, buses, and cars, traverses the Southern landscape in an effort to collect and recollect the diversity of Southern black life. Gathering these experiences required the artist to be, at times, subtle and cautious and, at others, less concerned about how he was perceived. Often he used an active process in which he overheard conversations, let knowledgeable people instruct him, observed the performance of stories and jokes, and allowed himself to be guided to particularly poignant places; he generally recorded these in three-by-five-inch spiral-bound notebooks. At other times, the process was rather passive: he read historical literature and guidebooks for background and context. As seen in many of these texts, the process of recollection is represented as stories embedded or framed within stories or as stories reconstructed from memory.

Brown worked steadily on this book for more than three years, constantly reworking the order and structure of the collection as he continually revised individual pieces. Pulling from a relatively disparate set of published and unpublished essays, sketches, and reportage, we have organized the collection around six points of view by which Brown observed black life in the South. Readers of "By Way of Autobiography" will find an implicit methodological statement about how Brown himself embarked upon the path of collecting these narratives. In revealing this information, he unwittingly tells us much about the life he lived but did not construct more formally in a longer memoir or autobiography.

"Jim Crow Journal" frames a discussion of the discrepancy between constitutional promise and national practice. That is, it records the view of what life is like when the law is used to deny people their constitutional rights as citizens. It also illustrates their response to this denial. With its historical focus, "Gone with the Wind" emphasizes the past and its effects on the present, as the section observes dimensions of the Old and New South, both black and white. "Academic Retreat" testifies to the significance of education for African American people and to the tenacity with which they pursued equality. Shifting the focus to the fine and performing arts, "Pursuit of Happiness" celebrates artists and their art forms as viable responses to the cruelty of racial segregation. In the final section, "Men of War" reminds the reader of the global politics necessarily affecting black life, as soldiers and civilians confront the paradox of struggling for democratic freedoms while working in a context in which those freedoms are actively denied.

We have framed this material with a prologue and an epilogue that articulate more broadly the central concerns of the collection. The first piece in the prologue, "South on the Move," responds directly to Daniels's *A Southerner Discovers the South*, offering an analysis of its strengths and shortcomings. Furthermore, this book review implicitly offers a methodology that Brown will modify for his own study. "Out of Their Mouths," the second piece in the prologue, responds to the question, "How do you feel about Negroes in the war?" In plural voices, it offers disparate perspectives on the war effort. Multiple and necessarily distinct, these voices challenge the assumption of black homogeneity and simplicity. Moreover, the piece serves as the first implementation of Brown's own approach to collecting and representing the material of black lives in prose. Completing the frame for the collection, the epilogue consists of Brown's seminal essay, "Count Us In," which answers the question, "What does the Negro want?" The answer, of course, is: "We want equality, and we want it *now!*" It's appropriate that the collection end with this piece as it makes overt the political implications of the preceding pieces. This broad polemic claims full political and civic participation for African Americans, indeed the fundamental human rights afforded a group finally accorded all the privileges of citizenship.

A Negro Looks at the South not only plays on the example Daniels provides; it also responds to a long tradition of African American writing about race in a Southern context. This tradition has employed a number of strategies to this end, some of which may include recurring themes of family, work, play, education, travel, and politics. Often, writers conceptualize their persona's experience of the South in terms of patterns: immersion and emersion, awakening and self-realization, or exile and flight. Though each text does not employ all of these patterns and themes, the tradition is largely defined by the construction of the South as paradox or conundrum. At once the site of family and community yet also the place of oppression, both the location of one's origin and the cause of one's alienation—in short, both home and hostile territory—the South is presented in this tradition as a deeply conflicted place, both physically and psychically. In one sense, it is the essential tension itself, the impossibility of reconciling oppositions, that drives many of these texts and thus the tradition as whole.

Beginning with David Walker, and including Frederick Douglass, Harriet Jacobs, and William Wells Brown, nineteenth-century African American writers have used their personal experiences of the South in order to critique American politics, to appraise the success and limitations of African American culture, and to construct a personal identity capable of controlling (or at least rationalizing) the harrowing dissonance between "certain inalienable rights" and Southern (ostensibly American) political practices. Needless to say, this critical tradition moves aggressively into the twentieth century, sustained by Brown's immediate predecessors including W. E. B. Du Bois, James Weldon Johnson, and his own father, the Rev. Sterling Nelson Brown. Du Bois's chapters on eastern Tennessee and Dougherty County, Georgia, in *The Souls of Black Folk* (1903), clearly inform Brown's personal accounts of rural Virginia and Louisiana. So, too, Johnson's early sections in his autobiography *Along This Way* (1933) and Rev. Brown's *My Own Life Story* (1924) produce echoes in "What Could Freddie Say?" a critical look at education in the South. Equally important, Brown would have been acutely aware of J. Saunders Redding's rendering of black life in the South in *No Day of Triumph* (1942). Similar to Brown's project, Redding's text overflowed with vibrant black voices; yet where his portrayal emphasized the debilitating effects of Southern racism (and thus held out little hope for triumph), Brown would strive to capture both the harsh realities of white supremacy *and* the heroic responses on the part of blacks living and thriving in the South.

But just as these earlier figures inform Brown's immersion into African American culture in the South, Brown's essays anticipate Ralph Ellison's work on Southern black music, particularly Ellison's highly personal address of blues and jazz, and his praise of performers such as Jimmy Rushing and Charlie Christian. Most obviously, Brown's meticulous attention to the specificity of the local looks forward to Albert Murray's *South to a Very Old Place* (1971), a rambling tour of legendary sites on the mythic Southern landscape; more recently to Anthony Walton's *Mississippi* (1996) and Endesha Ida Mae Holland's *From the Mississippi Delta* (1997), looking poignantly at the state made metaphoric for the entire South; and Deborah McDowell's *Leaving Pipe Shop: Memories of Kin* (1998) and Trudier Harris's *Summer Snow: Reflections from a Black Daughter of the South* (2003), continuing the tradition by exploring the compelling contradictions of the South through childhood memories.

Finally, *A Negro Looks at the South* serves as a crucial study that lends a voice to the voiceless and represents an emergent effort in oral history, a field that has recently begun exploring systematically the psychological truths of black life. Against Jonathan Daniels's appreciative but limited discussion, Brown's collection delivers a much greater variety of black voices and experiences and thus a more complex portrait of black life in the South. In so doing, Brown illustrates the Lakota tradition of "fierce listening," that is, listening with purpose, commitment, and responsibility—a responsibility to convey the story to the next generation. This personal investment in the lives of ordinary black people reveals a participation in what latter-day scholars have more formally conceived as oral history. Like them, Brown asked a number of questions that sought not just to elicit information. Rather, his probing enables us to understand the more crucial issues at stake in the stories he presents: how they work, what they do, and what they reveal about the storytellers. *A Negro Looks at the South*, therefore, provides fresh perspectives on the old problem of racial representation and anticipates the engaging work now being undertaken by a new generation of oral historians.

Prologue

"South on the Move" and "Out of Their Mouths" open the collection with a call and a response. "South on the Move" points specifically to the need for a more thorough examination of Southern black life in the 1940s, whereas "Out of Their Mouths" serves as one of the first responses representing the method of the collection. Unlike the formal responses of *What the Negro Wants* (1944) and the quantitative sociological analyses of *An American Dilemma* (1944), *A Negro Looks at the South* is a discursive record of ordinary folk talking and doing.

Brown found motivation for his research in an earlier project published by journalist Jonathan Daniels. In 1938, when Daniels published his *A Southerner Discovers the South*, Brown fully appreciated the effort Daniels made to represent more broadly than previous studies the variety and complexity of Southern life. Arguably more than any other study, the Daniels book expanded, if not downright revised, the Agrarians' rather narrowly construed view of Southern life as sentimental and homogeneous. Prior to Daniels, Brown had consistently challenged such representations via his regular book reviews in the Urban League's *Opportunity: A Journal of Negro Life*, a major venue for African American art and literature. In "South on the Move," Brown used his book review in *Opportunity* as a forum to applaud the richness of Daniels's insights and to anticipate in "Out of Their Mouths" a "fair sampling of current talk among American Negroes from a store of conversations harvested up and down the Atlantic Seaboard, from Massachusetts to Mississippi, but mainly in the Deep South."

Brown wrote "Out of Their Mouths" at the height of World War II, when the effort to preserve democracy both abroad and at home exacerbated racial tensions. Paul Kellogg and Alain Locke attempted to reprise their editorial relationship by developing another special issue of *Survey Graphic*. In their earlier collaboration, their interrogation of Negro Harlem became transposed dramatically into *The New Negro* (1925), the celebrated anthology of art, essays, poetry, short fiction, and drama that virtually defined the New Negro Renaissance. In 1942, *Survey Graphic*, a social welfare journal featuring graphic arts, was asked once again to perform important social labor. This time, the editors would turn their attention to assessing the ideas and attitudes of African Americans toward the war. For this issue, no better representation of the voices and outlooks of a cross-section of African Americans would be found than Brown's contribution, "Out of Their Mouths."

Although Daniels's observations, in Brown's view, proved more liberal in racial attitude compared to those of Daniels's white contemporaries, the treatment of African Americans nevertheless remained less than satisfying. This patient but still probing review, therefore, can be read as a methodological template inscribing the approach and meaning not only of Brown's "Out of Their Mouths," but of *A Negro Looks at the South*, too. For Daniels's careful attention to nuances of "talk," gathered in peripatetic travels, accorded with Brown's own immersion into a people's way of life. In this way, "Out of Their Mouths" represents the sine qua non of Brown's achievement.

A Southerner Discovers The South by Jonathan Daniels is a new kind of travel book. It is candid photography of a section, which until recently was sentimentalized. Deceptively written to resemble a casual jaunt, the book finally emerges as a composite of the South, too long and foolishly called "solid." From wide reading and long thinking, Mr. Daniels knew what to look for and what questions to ask. Symbolic incidents and speeches, bits of excellent description, humorous anecdotes, glimpses of tragic events, allusions to well-known books and places, contribute to a portrait that anyone knowing the South in whole or in part must recognize as real. Resembling a personal essay at the outset, *A Southerner Discovers The South* becomes valuable social commentary. The tone is affectionate, but irony and protest are present. Editor of the *Raleigh News and Observer*, Mr. Daniels knows how to disarm Southern prejudices. A few sharp cracks at Yankee meddling occur here and there. But the South is taken severely to task; tabooed subjects are brought out in the open as when he mentions Virginia gentlemen "breeding slaves for the Deep South," or refuses to howl over Reconstruction, likening the Ku Klux Klan to the Brown Shirts of Germany and the Black Shirts of Italy.

Mr. Daniels's well-behaved Plymouth carried him from Arlington as far West as Little Rock, as far South as New Orleans, and by way of Tampa and Charleston back to Raleigh. He sees Williamsburg, restored to its colonial past by the Rockefellers, and he sees the New South along Gold Avenue, a stretch of mill villages (some almost private towns) from Danville to Atlanta. Here John L. Lewis is thought of as a new, more dangerous John Brown, come to rid the South of a new slavery. Mr. Daniels sees the palaces of Coca-Cola and patent medicine plutocrats (wealth in the South coming chiefly from cheap luxury or cheap anodyne), as well as the mansions in Natchez of antebellum aristocrats, whose descendants throw open the hallowed doors for a much-needed fee. Chattanooga of the low wages and bustling Birmingham appear in contrast to Savannah and Vicksburg and the "ended towns" like Darien, Georgia, caught in the past. He looks at Norris, Tennessee, suspicious of its blue-print planning; considers the planned Dyess community in Arkansas to be "a toytown cut out of the jungle"; and is dubious of the Hillhouse cooperative struggling along on the "buckshot" earth. For TVA he has warm praise. He sings again the melancholy beauty of the Swanee River and the proud glory of Charleston, he marvels at the rich black loam of the Delta, but the wasted lands of the South are here too: the bone barren corner of Polk County, Tennessee, and the frightening erosion in southwest Georgia. Unimpressed by the manors on Paces Ferry Road in Atlanta, he heads directly for the not-so-distant slums. As a final instance of his unconventional tour he is struck on Beale Street, not by uproarious abandoned laughter, but by Negroes, lost from the Delta, staring through the store windows at food.

"It takes all kinds of people to make the South," but Mr. Daniels gets a goodly number of them into his book, finding them "high up the creek and close to Courthouse Square." He talks with governors and editors, economists and poets, café loungers and tramps, hopeful socialists and embittered mine-operators. He hears the mythology being created about the lost leader, Huey Long, and he hears attacks upon demagogues. He notices that attempts to better the lot of the sharecropper are labeled communistic. He hears Roark Bradford tell of a successful Negro foreman, who went all to pieces as a landowner because, according to Bradford, he needed the white man. He hears Donald Davidson reject industrialization of the South as a hateful "Yankeefication." He listens to David Lilienthal of TVA who urges a faith in the people if freed from overwhelming handicap; to the operator of a huge plantation who believes that only paternalistic capitalism can help the sharecropper, and to Sam Franklin who believes that white and Black men, by cooperative labor, can create security and well-being for all. Some of the best talk, however, comes from the untitled, the anonymous. One of these, rebelling at being penned up in a past "gone with the wind," cries out "Damn antique! I want to live." But all of the talk is good, pungently phrased, and thought-provoking.

Mr. Daniels's chats with Negroes are too few for this reader. From his earliest reference to a neighbor "as dignified an Anglo-Saxon gentleman, for all the little Negro blood in him, as I ever saw" to the last, Mr. Daniels is almost always fair-minded and sympathetic. He repeats again and again the idea that "the Negro was set free, in a manner of speaking," and he resents contemporary injustice and exploitation. At Chickamauga Dam he sees solemn Negro workers drinking out of sanitary paper cups; the departure from the much besung water-boy strikes him as humorously symbolic of TVA's efficiency. He records not only Negro company preachers, who keep their flocks in line for the bosses, but also the Negroes in the improvement of conditions among the sharecroppers. In Arkansas he shows that he understands the Negroes' mask of stupidity and cackling laughter; good union men, they know the wise thing to do is to lie low, like Brer Rabbit, and say nothing.

To Mr. Daniels, the South is on the move. But intelligent planning must begin at the bottom, among the people. "The tyrants and the plutocrats and the poor all need teaching. . . . All are in the warm dark, and whether they like it or not—white man, black man, big man—they are in the dark together. None of them will ever get today alone."

Mr. Daniels says that the derided phrase "forty acres and a mule" once seemed to him the only proposal which might have solved the agricultural sickness of the South. He is afraid now that it is too late. In *Forty Acres and Steel Mules*, Herman Clarence Nixon, a Southern economist, agrees. "The mule in the flesh must be adjusted to the steel mule, and both must be subordinated to the service of rural society."

Forty Acres and Steel Mules is modestly called a hillbilly's view of the South. It is obviously the work of a careful student, written with uncommon persuasiveness, but there is something of the hillbilly's drawling humor and gift for pointed anecdote. One hastens to add that it is written with serious intent and out of a democratic sympathy that one does not generally expect from hillbillies. As in Archibald MacLeish's *Land of the Free* and Erskine Caldwell and Margaret Bourke-White's *You Have Seen Their Faces*, photographs are liberally supplied, reenforcing and reenforced by the text. Some of Mr. Nixon's captions are epigrammatic: one reads, under a picture of a little Negro girl in a "romantic" cotton field: "The sight of the first cotton boll gave her a backache"; a second, under a page of pictures of white and Negro sharecroppers with their broods, reads: "Population has been the most consistent surplus crop of the South."

The author started his research into the rural South as a boy on an Alabama upland plantation, and continued as director of a Rural Rehabilitation Corporation and as a college professor. Once inclined to idealize the "agrarian" South, he is now convinced that the South is desperately sick. He knows the problems of sharecropping, the rural slums where a man fixing to move needs only "to spit in the fire and call the dog," having no other belongings after a lifetime of toil. He knows the relationship of tenantry to the exhaustion and erosion of the land: "The tenant skins the land and the landlord skins the tenant." He knows the merchant planter, charging exorbitant interest, bringing the tenant out behind by "blacksmith bookkeeping," but himself a victim of the banks, the tariff and freight rates. He sees the little towns, "dreary eyesores in sections where the one-crop system predominates." He sees absentee ownership with its attendant evils; he sees industrialization coming in with all of the abuses fought against in a more unionized North. He sees poverty and illiteracy closely tied up with the injustice of present race relations. Seeing all this he insists that something must be done: "Southerners can no longer ask to be let alone to solve their own problems and then not solve them."

Mr. Nixon does not believe the problems insoluble. Like Jonathan Daniels, he refuses to believe that sharecroppers and share tenants are humanly hopeless. Looking upon TVA as the strongest card in the New Deal, he believes that more education and statesmanship are imperative: "The South must plan for social action or resign itself to poverty and disintegration." Among some of the immediate needs, Mr. Nixon lists maximum cooperation with the Social Security Program, socialized or public medical service, democratic education beyond the school room, and governmental aid to get farmers on good land and to develop attractive farm villages. He concludes that the South will never escape exploitation or be a highly productive, educated democracy until Southern farmers and laborers, white and Negro, are freed from exploitation and accorded their full share of the gifts of democracy.

In the news of the week there is the report of a Southern Conference for Human Welfare in Birmingham. Among the many sponsors were Dr. Frank Graham, president of the University of North Carolina; Arthur Raper, author of the invaluable *Preface to Peasantry*; and the author of *Forty Acres and Steel Mules*. Over a thousand delegates were accredited. Two Negroes, John P. Davis and Mary McLeod Bethune, were elected to office, and the conference endorsed Federal anti-lynching legislation and deplored the segregation of Negro delegates. A "Greater Birmingham Committee" hastened to insist that the conference was not "representative of the South," and the cry of "communism" was raised. But the conference, like these two books, is a sign that the South is on the move. The hind wheel may be off and the axle dragging, but the old cart is a movering along.

⤳ OUT OF THEIR MOUTHS ⤶

The author of *Southern Road* draws this "fair sampling of current talk among American Negroes from a store of conversations harvested up and down the Atlantic Seaboard, from Massachusetts to Mississippi, but mainly in the Deep South."

He writes: "Whether in army camps or juke joints or dorms or offices or commissaries or cabins or Jim Crow coaches or bus stations, I naturally found more wartime grousing than beatitudes.

"A few were recorded on the spot at interviews; far more were bootlegged into many small notebooks, which sometimes got me into embarrassing predicaments and occasionally got me out of them. In their rendering, I found no better advice than Chaucer's, written six centuries ago:

> *Who-so shall tell a tale after a man,*
> *He must rehearse, as nigh as ever he can*
> *Every word, if it be in his charge,*
> *Although he speak never so rudely and large,*
> *Or else he must tell his tale untrue,*
> *Or feign something, or find words new!*

⤳ *I. The People Yes . . . Yes Indeed*

Deep South—*a Soliloquy:*

"Why do you reckon white folks act like they do? I sit home studying them. A cracker is like this. He will cut his own throat just to see a Negro die along with him. Further and more, they're fussing and squabbling among theirselves so much that a man can creep up behind them unbeknownst to 'em and hit 'em on the head.

"Take Talmadge, that narrow-minded rascal. All this trouble, war, soldiers being killed by the thousands, hostages being killed, bombs falling on women and little children—and all he can do is woof about 'coeducation of the races' or 'segregation.' Somebody ought to dump him on his head in some sea or other.

"This war now. It looks like they don't want you in the Navy, Army, or Marines. Just like before the war they didn't want you anywhere you could make a dime out of it. When those Japs first started out in the Pacific, I thought Negroes ought to thank their lucky stars that they weren't on those ships going down with the white folks. Then I got to studying and knew I was wrong. Onliest way we can get anything out of this war is to put all we can in it. That's my best judgment.

"The diffunce between the Northern and the Southern Negro is that the Northern is a freeborn-minded Negro, but the Southern is trained to say 'Yes-sir' and 'No-sir' all the time. That don't mean the Southern Negro won't fight, but he's just more kinderhearted. The gurvenment is exchanging them, sending one to the north and one to the south.

"These crackers will chase a Negro like he was a jackrabbit. There ain't no right in their heart or soul.

"Do you think they will elect President Roosevelt for a fourth term? They'd better, if they know what's good for the country. I don't wish him no hard luck, but I hope he will wear out in his job. But I hope that won't be for many a long year. Yessir, I hope he dies in the White House. But I hope he lives forever. He's the best friend the Negro ever had. Bar none, Lincoln, Washington, Teddy Roosevelt. And Mrs. Roosevelt, she's the greatest woman living today.

"The party—I don't give two cents for party. My question is who's gonna do most for me, my people, all the poor people. I'm a New Dealite.

"It's remarkable how the Negro continues to keep coming on. Right out of slavery, the Negro jumped into teaching college. Course he ain't perfect. Cutting, fighting, laziness. A lot of Negroes have gone to hell and destruction fooling around with numbers and that mess. But you can't fault the Negro for that. Not much diffunce between a man robbing you in the nighttime with a gun, and robbing you in the daytime with knowledge.

"The Negro's obstacles made a man out of him. Depression, lynching, all like that, the Negro kept coming, smiling and singing. They come on like the Japs before Singapore. You bend back the middle, the niggers (I mean Negroes) flow around the edges.

"I'm patriotic. I've got a boy in camp. Yessir, some of my blood is in the army. I love my country but I don't like the way they doing us down here in the South.

"I know all the professors. I guess I know more of the fine upstanding Negroes than any man in my field. I have seen 'em go from raggedy students to deans.

"I declare it's so hot today the hairs stick to your neck like flies to glue."

→→

Old Mose had made the best crop of cotton he ever made, but still he came out even. The landlord told him he had done fine, and that he could start the next year out of debt. Old Mose didn't say nothing, just sat there looking. Old Cracker kept on making admiration over the crop and how fine it was to be out of debt. Mose didn't say nothing. Cracker kept throwing out chances for Mose to talk. Finally his curiosity got the best of him. "What you thinking about Mose?" Mose just looked at him. Old Cracker banged his office desk and hollered, "What the hell you thinking about, Mose! If you don't tell me what you thinking, I'm gonna run you off my place." Mose said, "Oh, I was jes thinking, Mr. Landlord, jes thinking that the next time I ever say 'giddap' to a mule, he gonna be setting in my lap."

→

Store with newsstand, white operator, Negro neighborhood: "I lost eight sales on that *Ladies' Home Journal*. I wonder why did so many want that number?"

Magazine circulator: "Didn't you hear the governor's speech?"

Storekeeper: "No. Did they have an article on him? I read the *Saturday Evening Post* article."

Circulator: "No. He made a speech against the *Journal*."

S.: "What for?"

C.: "Well, they had some pictures in it of colored people. Four or five pages. High-toned colored people getting ahead. When the governor spoke against it, that made all the white people want to see it. And it was already going like hot cakes among the colored."

S.: "Why doesn't somebody tell me these things? I wish . . ."

C.: "We don't know what's in these magazines until we get them. How do we know which way Governor Talmadge is going to jump? . . . I can't let you have but two *Supermans*. We can't keep anymore in stock."

→

A: "Little Orphan Annie has joined up, too. Did you see where she discovered the Negro?"

B: "Indeed I did. Harold Gray got around to it at last. At long last, too. The Asp, Punjab, that Chinaman, and now the colored brother."

A: "You're never grateful for anything. He made the little Negro boy a sergeant, didn't he? And he showed that he was the one who found the car."

B: "Sure. But you never see him any more, do you?"

A: "Well, that was as far as he could go. Trouble with all you Negroes is you want little Annie to fall in love with that boy."

B: "Don't you put out that lie. Confidentially I think she's going to marry Daddy Warbucks when she grows up. Only reason I read the thing is for that."

→

"Uh-uh. Here it is. I see they have arrested Gandhi. He'll be a tough nut to crack.

"Used to make salt. Englishmen wanted them just to use English salt. Gandhi went down to the ocean and made salt out of the seawater. The English ordered him to stop making it. But he went right on making it.

"He's a man all right."

→

Negro union business agent: "In the early 20s, when wages went up to a dollar an hour, the clamor went up as today for industrial training. The whites took over the Booker Washington idea. Most of our schools slept through the whole thing. The whites learned so fast and took over the jobs that had been called 'Negro jobs' so fast that the colored workers couldn't believe it. Now the white Technical High School and Boys High are giving from 25 to 30 courses in various trades, but over at Booker T. Washington they are hardly giving any. I blame our educators in part for that."

↦

Negro bricklayer: "I know one local where whites and colored work together on the same scaffold, meet together in the same hall. They all kid and joke together. As a general rule there is brotherliness. Of course when the whistle blows, that just about ends. But the Negroes do have the whites' respect as good bricklayers."

↦

Negro trade unionist: "Lots of white people are willing to work on the job with you side by side. Others object, and sometimes they talk so loud they scare the fair-minded ones.

"Something about this working 'side by side' you ought to know. For instance, say I'm painting ceilings in here. The white man in the next apartment will be painting walls. But if I'm painting walls, he's painting ceilings. Just reverse and vice verse; I've seen it working both ways. Crazy ain't it?

"One trouble with the Negro worker, he doesn't know how to break into the union, he doesn't know what the labor movement is all about.

"Negroes and white workers just had to get together. Had to unite for strength. The smart white working men agree with that 100 percent. They want you on the job because you're entitled to it. They want you to get the same amount of pay. They're willing to go bargain with you. It's to their advantage. They wouldn't go out with you if it wasn't good business. But they don't play social equality. And most of them don't want you working side by side with them."

↦

A: "Did you see this week's *Statesman*? A *great* educator, one of *your* people, is reported to have said, 'We want a separate little university of our own.' "

B: "He's gonna get it."

A: "Then he says, I quote: 'We came with the shackles of slavery about our wrists, today we are clothed with the American ballot, which makes us citizens of the greatest republic on earth.' Unquote."

B: "He said that?"

A: "Here it is."

B: "I don't want to read it. All I can say is that if the Negro is clothed with the ballot, he most certain sure is going around with his butt raggedy."

↦

"The Negro starts out with two strikes on him."

"Well, it don't take but one to hit it."

➤➤

Old woman: "Son, you worries too quick. You gotta learn how to take the sad stuff easy."

➤➤ *II. Southern Traditions*

Southern white editor: "These fellows come down here and instead of doing the job with common sense, they go at it in a crusading way. They just blow open prejudices. So the dyed-in-the-wool traditionalist backs up, god-damning this and that to hell. The way these crusaders go about they hurt some real friends of the Negro."

➤➤

Negro journalist: "Some of these Southern liberals used to want to accelerate Negro progress. Now it seems that all they want to do is put on the brakes.

"A lot of white women are up in arms because they have to bring up their own children."

➤➤

Negro newspaper editor (backstage at Louis Armstrong concert, City Auditorium): "Did you see that? White boy said to the Negro 'You go ahead,' and then drank out of the same water fountain. There's the paradoxical South for you. He was by himself. When they come in threes or fours, they won't do that. Scared of being called 'Nigger-lover.' "

➤➤

Little redheaded girl (Negro): "Ethel and I got on the elevator in the department store. You know Ethel is lighter than I am, and her hair is straighter. A white man got on, looked at me, and especially my hair. I was looking at him out of the corner of my eyes. He wasn't sure, and finally he took off his hat. We burst out laughing. Right away he put his hat back on his head."

➤➤

On the train *Robert E. Lee*, headed South. In the Pullman washroom the whites had been neither hostile nor polite, but reserved. On leaving I overheard one say: "The price we have to pay for democracy!"

➤➤

"If it had to happen—"

"Don't finish. That's what I wouldn't want to happen to a dog."

"No more would I, but what I'm saying is this. If it had to happen, it's best it happened to a great man like Roland Hayes. Shows Europe and the whole world how even our greatest, our potentates, ain't safer than our least ones."

"Them peckerwoods up in Rome (Ga.) ain't never heard of Roland Hayes or Europe either."

"Well, Europe is gonna hear of them peckerwoods."

→→

Young Negro professor, working toward a doctorate in American culture, closes his narrative of how he was thrown off the train, and badly beaten at Tupelo, Miss. "He told me that I looked like a smart boy, that I ought to know better than to sass a white man in Mississippi. That he would fine me $5 for breaking the peace and $5.40 for costs of court, or else he would bind me over for the next court session. He advised me to pay the fine. After I paid it he said to me that he hoped I would profit by my experience."

→→

Dr. P. talking: "The road-cop pulled up and told me I'd been exceeding the speed limit, that he'd been pacing me on the whole trip. I told him the car wouldn't go much over 40. It was a red Chrysler with wire wheels, sorta fancy. I knew he didn't like the looks of it with me behind the wheel. Both of us argued back and forth. Finally he said, 'I don't know whether to shoot you or take you to jail.'

"I said, 'Well, it won't make any difference to me. One's about as bad as the other.'

"He said, 'You don't act like you're scared at all.'

"I spoke right up. 'Why you're the last man in the world I'd be scared of. You're the *law*. You're supposed to be my protection.'

"Man, that threw him off balance. He finally said, 'Well, Doc, you'd better watch yourself. There's a couple fellows in a pepped-up Ford (that's a Ford with a Frontenac head) on the road that are kinda mean. They'd like to pick you up in a car like this. So you take it easy now.'

"Then he growled at me, 'But you know damn well you were doing more than 40 miles an hour.' "

→→

White liberal: "This Negro soldier was sitting on a seat opposite to a white man. The bus was not crowded, and he wasn't sitting in front of any white. But the driver came back and told him to move. He refused. The driver shouted, 'I'm gonna move you.' The Negro took his coat off and said, 'Well I'm fixing to go off and fight for democracy. I might as well start right now.' And I want to tell you that bus driver backed down. It did me good to see it."

→→

Lawyer to Negro defendant who violated residential segregation: "You keep talking about the Bill of Rights. Do you know what the Bill of Rights is?"

Negro defendant: "I may not know exactly. All I know is that whatever it is, it's something the Negro ain't got."

‌→→

FEPC Hearings:

Investigator: "You were first employed by the company seventeen years ago?"

Negro shipyard worker: "Yessuh."

Q.: "You were upgraded for the first time within the past three months?"

NSW: "Yessuh. They made me a leaderman. . . . "

Q.: "Why would you say that there has been so little upgrading?"

NSW: "Most of the men do not feel themselves capable."

Negroes in Amen Corner (whispers, low growls): "Why he's just a pimp for the company! Hurry up and get rid of that Negro. Put him off the stand."

→→

Barber Shop. *The day that* Life Magazine *appeared with pictures of Paul Robeson as Othello with a white actress as Desdemona*:

A: "Some Negro's going to get his head whipped before nightfall on account of that picture."

B: "I'll bet Talmadge is writing his Friday speech for the radio."

A: "Yeah. Gonna make Shakespeare out to be a communist, or a Rosenwald."

→→

Young woman teacher (Negro): "Well the experiences I had were on the pleasant side. They used to set up a table for you in your space. But the porter came up and said they were going to serve me in the dining car. Had a sign on the table 'Reserved.' The steward pulled out my seat for me. The diner was full of white people; my table was right square in the midst of the car. As I sat down they put up the little curtain. But I could see the white folks eat, if I had been curious; and they could see me eat, if they were curious. And some of them were curious. The Pullman conductor tipped his hat when he came in the car this morning. Great day!"

Professor: "He must have thought you were Booker Washington's daughter."

→→ III. This Is War

Negro taxi-driver (northern city, early months after Pearl Harbor): "Man, those Japs really do jump, don't they? And it looks like everytime they jump, they land."

Passenger: "More they land, the worse it's going to be for you and me. How's your rubber?"

T-D: "I know it's gonna be a long war. But one thing you've got to give those Japs, they showed the white man that a brown hand could handle a plane and a machine gun too."

P: "Yes, Hitler believes that they're fit to be allies of the great Nazis."

T-D: "Well, I reckon one's bad as the other, but they still can fight, and they've already knocked out a lot of the white man's conceit. And that's something."

→→

Harlemite (shortly after Pearl Harbor): "All these radio announcers talking about yellow this, yellow that. Don't hear them calling the Nazis white this, pink that. What in hell color do they think the Chinese are anyway! And those Filipinos on Bataan? And the British Imperial Army, I suppose they think they're all blondes?"

→→

Negro foreman (big as John Henry), Tuskegee Flying Field, talking about the Negro contractor for the building of the base:

"Have I anything to say about Mr. X.? I don't know what to say about him. I just don't have any words to tell you. He's a great man, that's all. Only way he can get shed of me is to fire me.

"I'll tell you something. I'm pastor of a little church. When I heard about this job, got a letter from Mr. X., I asked my church for a leave of absence. If they hadn't given it to me I was going to resign. You know when a preacher is willing to give up his church, he really must have heard a call."

→→

Negro in charge of big government project: "The Negro has kept on saying: 'I can do it, I can do it.' But this is the kind of world where Negroes have got to say: 'Look, see what we've done!' "

→→

First Negro: "They can't win the war that way. And they keep on messing around, they sure gonna lose it."

Second Negro: "That's all I've been hearing, 'they,' 'they,' 'they.' We've got to learn how to say 'We.' "

1 N: "I said it on purpose. When they let us work and fight for the country as much as we are willing and able, I'll stop calling it *their* war."

2 N: "You've got a point. They are shortsighted, no getting away from that. But it's still *our* war right on. They've taken some slow steps: employment, navy, new branches of the service."

1 N: "Slow steps won't win this war for them."

2 N: "Nor for *us*, either."

→→

Civilian defense worker in a Southern metropolis: "This was the first black blackout, the rest had been white blackouts. (Only houses of whites got orders.) Man, guns were going off every place. Airplanes dropping sacks of flour. One Negro said to me, 'They just dropped that flour on white folks' town. Showered it on the crackers, dodged the Negro sections. We'll be lucky if that's the way bombs fall.' "

→→

In a small Southern town:

Buying bus tickets in drugstore. White boys and colored en route to camp. Warm friendly atmosphere. All were talking about whipping the Japs. One Negro draftee holds spotlight with his badinage. Asks soda clerk for a Coke. White boys drinking theirs look up. Noise and stir.

Soda Clerk: "Ain't got none."

Out front a truck is unloading cases on cases of Coca-Cola.

Negro: "You ain't got none? All that Coca-Cola I see and you say that? Now, that's bad stuff."

Clerk: "You want to make something out of it?"

The boy walks out into the street. The screen door slams.

→→

In a Barber Shop:

A: "I see here by the paper that Bob Considine says, 'The Little People fight on against Hitler tyranny.' All about the Belgian underground."

B: "What's that underground?"

A: "That's the way people get out of slavery. The name came from the Negroes here. A lot of slaves got away from the South by underground."

B: "Under the ground?"

A: "No. But under cover. At night time. Friends helped them. Some white folks, even."

B: "Never heard of it."

C: "That ain't all you never heard of."

B: "What do he mean by little people?"

A: "Frenchmen, Greeks, Jews—all of the little countries Hitler overcame and conquered."

B: "You got to be white to be little people?"

C: "You got to be white to be big people, too. You got to be white to be people. Period."

→→

A: "Well, Bob Considine's all right."

B: "Whatcha mean, all right. He's white, ain't he?"

A: "Man, sometimes you sound like a black Talmadge."

B: "Don't you call me Talmadge. And don't call me black."

A: "If you was white, you'd be as hard on the colored as a hound dog is on fleas. Everybody white ain't bad."

B: "I would expect an old handkerchief head like you to say that."

C: "Considine used to be a sports writer, didn't he?"

A: "Yes. He was fair, too. He really wrote good stories about Joe Louis."

B: "It's easy for white folks to write good stories about Joe. What else could they write?"

C: "Yes, even that Pegler can find something good to say about Joe."

A: "Maybe they'll get around to writing something good about *Negroes* fighting against tyranny."

B: "Maybe they will. Then I'll be *for* them, same as you."

➤➤

College purchasing agent: "I put a cracker salesman out of my office the other day. I was going to buy some stuff from him, $300 worth of it. He knew I was going to buy it, too. When I was just about ready to order he started getting confidential. He said, 'You know one thing. All this stuff was started by these goddamn Jews. We get rid of these Jews everything will be all right.'

I said, 'That's just what Hitler is saying. I believe I'm not going to buy anything today.'

'What do you mean?'

'I mean I don't want anything from you.'

"He got to stuttering. 'But—but you.'

'I'm busy today.'

'Well, tomorrow,' he said.

'Today, tomorrow, from then on, far as you're concerned, I'm busy. Now let me get to my work.' "

➤➤

A Negro bragging at a gas station: "I done regist. Expect to be called soon. That Hitler. Think he can whup anybody. I'm gonna capture Hitler. I'm gonna deliver him to President Roosevelt. At the front door of the White House."

The white bystanders applauded.

"Then I'm gonna fight for some rights over here."

The whites froze up.

➤➤

A: "Yonder goes a Negro knows more about electricity than the man that invented electricity."

B: "Yeah? What ditch is he digging in?"

➤➤

Folk Tales:

"They're telling the story that a cracker running a lunchroom at a railroad junction got a wire ordering lunches for 500 soldiers. He got together all the bread and eggs and chickens and coffee and stuff he could. When the troop train pulled in he saw they were Negroes. He ran to the officer in charge: 'You said 500 *soldiers*. Those are just Nigra boys.' The officer told him they were soldiers in the uniform of their country. Man kept on: 'You said *soldiers*. I can't serve those boys in my place.' The captain wouldn't budge. Finally the man said to the white officers, 'Well, y'all can come in and eat but I'll have to put their food in boxes. I reckon I can stir up that many boxes.'

" 'No; these men must eat hot food.'

"But that cracker wouldn't give in. So the boys went unfed. The story goes that all the townspeople went together and put in so much money apiece to save white supremacy and the lunchroom man's money."

↦

On a border city trolley, a strapping white sailor, in a spic-and-span white suit, jumped up from the seat when an old Negro woman sat down beside him. He stood scowling, looking around for support.

"Thank you, son," she said. "But I didn't need the whole seat. I spread, but not that much. You know, you sure look cute in that pretty white suit Joe Louis bought you."

↦

Taxi-driver, northern city: "One of the Negro soldiers came back on leave with his eyes blacked and hands all bruised and tore up. He said it was hell down there. You either took it or you fought back. Said a cracker yelled at him, 'You goddam nigger, get off the sidewalk down in the street where you belong.' Said everything, really lower-rated his mother. The soldier told me, 'I just couldn't take that. So I had to fight.' He could barely see out of his eyes but the skin was off his knuckles."

↦

A: "I heard that the crackers made threats that if a Negro aviator ever lighted in their fields they'd burn the plane and lynch the pilot. Is there anything to that yarn?"

B: "That's stuff. It's really been just the opposite. They tell the story of a cadet who got lost in Florida. Some of these details may be wrong, but when you meet him he'll vouch for the rest. He lost his way and landed in a Florida field. He says that as soon as he came to a stop, a little white boy stuck his head over his wing and asked, 'Are you a Jap?' But he proved to everybody's satisfaction that he was an American Negro.

"Since his orders were to stick by his plane whenever grounded, there he stayed. All of the people of the nearby town, white as well as Negro, looked out for him. The story goes that the next day when the lieutenant and the pilot found him, there was a picnic spread out on the wings of his plane: thermos bottle with lemonade, sandwiches, cake, everything. And some young white ladies were waiting on him. The boys at primary swear that the cadet brought back a lot of canned goods in his plane. They say they're still eating them."

↦

Attributed to Joe Louis by a public speaker: "There may be a whole lot wrong with America, but there's nothing that Hitler can fix."

By Way of Autobiography

The section titled "By Way of Autobiography" creates in the reader an expectation that Sterling A. Brown will present a picture of an examined self—a view not provided elsewhere in his voluminous writings. However, instead of the familiar autobiographical focus of self-discovery or of creative or imaginative engagement with the past, Brown's self-construction is more akin to memoir, where greater emphasis is placed on the self in relationship to past events, persons, and places. As this section reveals, the context created of facts, dates, and (re-)collected experience admirably locates Brown within a historical world crucial to understanding the motivation, the structure, and the methodology of *A Negro Looks at the South*, in its entirety.

Brown's review of Daniels's *A Southerner Discovers the South* implies that an appropriate methodology for such investigation is based on what folklorist Benjamin A. Botkin earlier termed "folk-say," a folkloric theory capturing people talking, doing, and describing themselves. Though Botkin intended this theory to denote the untitled, the anonymous, or "the people farthest down," Brown, for this collection, modified the notion to encompass black people of all stations representing themselves through talk. "Old Buck" and "Old Man McCorkle" present this spectrum.

Through his recounting of earlier personal experiences with Buckner, Brown retraces memories of his own life at Lincoln University, from 1926 to 1928. Buckner was then a student who not only studied under but also served Brown as an entry into the world of "The Foot," a section of a Negro neighborhood in Jefferson City held by some to be unsavory or undesirable. It is here that Brown was introduced to Old Man McCorkle, often called "Preacher" or, in a name preserved by Brown in a memorable poem, "Revelations." As suggested by his name, McCorkle was reputed to be odd, if not downright mentally ill; nevertheless, Brown found his view of the world to be incisive and his storytelling ability masterful.

"Bus Station" and "Club Car" carefully delineate two modes of transportation Brown used extensively on his tours of the South. Significantly, the bus and the train became for him centers of performance where passengers (re)enacted their various responses to "separate but equal" transportation modes. In these groups, where the drama of real-life Jim Crow was staged, Brown witnessed and chronicled the strength, the endurance, and the love of a people, whose representation by nonblacks often denied these powerful features. As a complement to transportation, "Roommate" adeptly recalls one such living arrangement to which Brown often had to accommodate himself.

Because Brown said comparatively little about the genesis and background of his poems, "Return of the Native" is especially poignant. Arguably, it frames Brown's personal, intellectual, and cultural-hybrid approach to art. Ostensibly, this title reminds the reader that Brown's trips to rural Louisiana were numerous and that the one recorded in *A Negro Looks at the South* was done expressly for this text. In five memorable poems in the "Frilot Cove" section of his *No Hiding Place*, Brown finds another venue for recording his aesthetic response to this milieu by alerting us to the specialness of Cajun and Creole life, as found in their language, customs, and mores. But the use of "Return of the Native," although muted, suggestively invokes an aesthetic legacy that has shaped Brown's theory and practice of art. Like Thomas Hardy's novel of the same title, Brown's "Return of the Native" resonates with a nuanced depiction of pastoral life; however, the world Brown represents differs from the Wessex don's in that the relative harmony of Louisiana rural life is disrupted by intrusive racism. So committed was Brown to the people of Frilot Cove that he made their quest for an African American priest into a cause célèbre.

Buckner telephoned the day after Christmas; he was on his way to New River, North Carolina, for boot training as a Marine, and he had a short layover. Yes, naturally, he would be right out.

I had not seen Buck for fifteen years. When I was teaching at Lincoln University, in Missouri, Buck needed money to get through school and I needed somebody for odd chores. The rambling old house that I had rented was not easy to keep straight, especially since I had started my hobbies of collecting theme papers, books, and phonograph records. Buck liked the records and was a curious reader of whatever books looked interesting. He was probably most indispensable, however, for the yarns he spun and the characters he guided to the front door. The two most startling madmen were Revelations, the garrulous preacher, and an escaped patient from Kankakee, Illinois. The latter told me a pitiful tale of how his foot had been purposely broken in the hospital. He talked so coherently that I had no suspicions of him; later I learned that he had been captured across the river and returned to the asylum as a dangerous lunatic.

Buck made the fires in the numerous stoves needed to warm the dark house. Saturdays and Sundays he insisted on cooking the breakfast and serving it to my wife and me in style. He was waiting evenings at the Hotel Jefferson, and he put on the dog as well as the sparse silver of newlyweds permitted. We soon discovered Buck's true reason for the weekend cooking. He always cooked too much, and student friends of his would drop by who were welcome to the extra food, to keep it from wasting. We finally caught on, but we were grateful for the unfamiliar luxury of breakfasting in bed. One morning my wife gave Buckner a bill and told him to go to the store and buy stuff for a real breakfast for his clan. Buckner returned loaded down with porkchops and potatoes, and the wolves descended.

After that, the porkchop breakfasts became something of a rite. It hurt the budget, but, I am certain, they helped my classroom teaching. All of these fellows had a sense of honor: they couldn't eat a man's porkchops Saturday mornings and flunk his tests on Mondays. So they even tried to master Emerson's *Nature* and Shelley's "Hymn to Intellectual Beauty." But I was repaid in better coin. They were a grand lot as I remember them: Reuben Benton from Kansas City, with wits sharp as a needle, a track man whose absolutely flat feet gave him, they said, an undue advantage in the dashes, a sort of kangaroo leverage; droll Roba Farr; "Fats" Green, the football star; Abe Lincoln, slightly ashamed of the honored name he bore, but coincidentally tall, stoop-shouldered, morose-faced with high cheek bones overhanging sunken cheeks; and Nathaniel Sweets, who never got his

37

diploma since he hadn't paid any money to get through college, and couldn't be so inconsistent at the end to pay for a diploma. "A foolish inconsistency in the hobgoblin of little minds," he misquoted loftily, abusing my teaching of Emerson. All of them liked porkchops and potatoes for breakfast, even cabbage, until I laid down the law about that.

They dropped by in the evenings too. I had a Brunswick portable phonograph with a full tone for those days. The fellows shared my zeal for Bessie Smith and Clara Smith and the jazz which was then getting righteous. Fats told me of a blues singer named Ma Rainey who sang up and down the Mississippi River Valley bringing the people out in droves. Roba and Reuben told me of a joint on Twelfth Street, Kansas City, where there was a piano player named Pete Johnson, famous for his walking bass. Not to be outdone, I mentioned casually that I had gone to high school with Duke Ellington (a slight inaccuracy, as we went to rival high schools, but it served). Our tastes ranged wide in the good records of that time: we liked Whiteman's semi-classic arrangements of "Among My Souvenirs," "When Day Is Done," and "Washboard Blues," as well as Jim Jackson's "Kansas City Blues." I believe our taste was right: there was a trumpet passage on "Mississippi Mud" that we would play over and over; somebody would lift the needle arm and precisely locate the passage, until I begged them not to wear a groove in the record. A dozen years later I learned that the trumpeter had a name, that he was the great Bix. Fats swore by two colored trumpeters named Charlie Creth and Louis Armstrong; and I brought out Duke's "Washington Wabble" and "Creole Love Call" as my exhibits A. But the blues got us all, without argument, and when Bessie Smith's "Back Water Blues" came out in that bad flood year of 1927, we solemnly agreed that this was the best.

"Back Water Blues" started a series of tales about floods. Fats knew the country along the Mississippi River and its tributaries—"The Big Muddy," "The Little Muddy," "The Osage"—and he was full of memories. "As long as those people can make three crops a year on that bottomland, they aren't going to move away, river or no river. 'River missed us one time, may miss us again' is their attitude," Fats explained. All of the boys were good yarn-spinners. Fats had worked on road-building gangs and knew many work-songs. He would holler in a voice high-pitched for so stocky a fellow:

> *"Pay day," Captain, "ain't got no soap!"*

or chant:

> *"Says to my Captain, Captain my hands are cold,*
> *Goddam yo' hands, let de pick and shovel roll."*

Abe Lincoln did not talk much. But I shall never forget one story he told in his stammering drawl of a lynching he had seen in Waco. He had been standing in a drugstore in the Negro section of town when the mob brought the body of the Negro there and burned it on a heap of packing boxes doused with kerosene. "There are some things you just can't forget, Mr. Brown," he said. "But talking about 'em don't do no good."

Buck and Sweets would tell stories of their experiences in hotel work. The Hotel Jefferson was the chief stopping place for the "white quality" folks who visited the capital city: governors, the warden of the penitentiary, drummers, politicians, racketeers, professional men, and high-class women of the oldest profession were among the many guests. Buck and Sweets kept their eyes and ears open. They were tickled when they read what Emperor Jones said about little stealing getting you in jail sooner or later, whereas big stealing landed you in the Hall of Fame, quoting with relish: "If dey's one thing I learns in ten years on de Pullman ca's listening to de white quality talk, it's dat same fact." Eugene O'Neill had something there, they agreed.

They told of greenhorn waiters and busboys run up a tree, of captains and headwaiters with itching palms and finagling tricks to get theirs, of chefs with tempers as hot as their ovens. The best tale teller of the hotel crew was named Slim Greer, and they told me a fantastic yarn about his experiences passing for white, though he was plenty colored. These fellows had to scuffle, waiting tables or busing dishes or hopping bells for long hours, yet as they told their yarns the hotel seemed less a bustling, rushing, prosperous establishment than a comic gallery. Buck told an anecdote of his bell-hopping. In "rooming" the people, he failed one day to provide soap for a bathroom. A woman rang the desk, raising Cain. Buck went up to the room, tapped on the bathroom door. "Madame, here is the soap," he said, and opened the door only wide enough to get his hand and the soap in. "Bring that soap on in here," the woman said. "You're nothing but a nigger." Buck obeyed. Buck said he kept his eyes averted from the woman in the tub, but he knew that she was just daring him to look. He got out of there fast.

I was remembering some of all that when the cab door slammed. Buck ran up the steps, breezed in, and took over at once. The cab driver had carried him over half of Washington, he suspected, delivering the other passengers. Washington cab service reminded him of the jitneys in Chicago and Kansas City, only not so good. At the Union Station all the Diamond Cabs had driven past him. "Not going *your* way, buddy," the drivers had said. Finally a Harlem Cab rescued him and the other marooned Negroes.

I looked at Buck, and he looked at me, and we knew the years had gone by. Buck's head of black curly hair had gray in it; the hairline had receded slightly. He was paunchier. But he was good enough for the United States Marines, he reminded me, and I know what the Marines ask for. He hadn't seen the gang for a long time. Reuben was in the Army; Fats was the principal of a school in a small town in Missouri and had several dependencies keeping him out of the Army; Sweets was the rising young man of St. Louis in politics, and editing a newspaper.

On the trip across the continent he had tasted another brand of democracy from that dished out in the nation's capitol. He had traveled in a tourist Pullman with a carload of white sailors and soldiers just back from the South Pacific. Soldiers were at the fore and sailors at the back end. Buck had the last bed, but it was uncurtained and definitely part of the barrack-like arrangement. Since Buck was not in uniform, they all wanted to know what he was doing in their Pullman. When Buck told them he had been inducted into the Marine Corps, they would not believe him until he flashed his cards, which he offered, I am sure, with a flourish. None had ever heard of, much less seen, a Negro Marine. He became the attraction of the whole car.

He told us how some of the boys would sit staring out of the window for miles on miles. We had the radio turned on to the Bears-Redskins football game. The announcer advertised that the game was being heard by our armed forces all over the world. "That's not what those fellows told me," said Buck. "They didn't mention listening to the radio. Just told me about sitting in muck, afraid to slap at the mosquitoes, just sitting there waiting. They were a good bunch of kids, tough as hell. They were willing to go through what they had gone through, but they just didn't want any ragtime." Ragtime, Buck told me, was a sailor expression, meaning the run-around, a lot of lies, gassing to fool somebody. "This guy's got more ragtime than an admiral" would be said of a scheming talker.

Buck said it gave him a funny feeling when the train would jolt and hang in the night and several of the fellows would jump out of bed grabbing for helmets that weren't there. One sailor from Tennessee came down to Buck's bed and talked a long time after the other fellows had gone to bed. "Said he just couldn't sleep. He had been on submarine duty at Pearl Harbor when the war started; he was a first-class Petty Officer now. He was a Southern boy, he told me, born and bred in Tennessee. 'You ever been in Tennessee?' he asked me. I said, 'No,' which was a lie; I've been all over Memphis, and to Chattanooga as well, but I didn't want any ragtime." Buck said he had been giving a lot of thought to the way Negroes had to live in the South. Had never thought about it much before, but after seeing

Negroes in Hawaii and the islands of the South Pacific, he had a different opinion of Negroes. He had seen them all around, none in combat troops, but in engineering and labor battalions, hard working, uncomplaining, good men. He had been struck by their bravery in bringing up ammunition. Buck explained, "I never got it clear from him where he saw this. Now he was worried about something he had been used to all his life. Really worried. He was a right guy."

Buck ran into a little ragtime, he told me, waving his fingers as if strumming a banjo, at Union station, where gents told him that there was no accommodation available for his governmental first class ticket to New River. I suggested that this was the Xmas season and that all space might be taken; but Buck said that inductees had priorities and he did not believe any train to North Carolina was full of nothing but service men. "Uh-uh," he said, and laughed. "I believe it's a little ragtime."

Plenty had happened to Buck in fifteen years. After graduating from Lincoln, he had gone into school teaching. He had been principal of a Rosenwald County Training School in a small town in the Arkansas cotton belt. Several of the Negroes there owned their places; a few had big farms, hiring their own help, and in the off-season selling milk to a creamery in Kansas City. But most of the Negroes were tenants on two big plantations. The superintendent of the school was a Negro, getting up in years. He didn't have many up-to-date ideas, Buck said, but he surrounded himself with people who did have. A good politician, he had powerful white friends in Little Rock, and he secured some Rosenwald and county money to get materials for two brick buildings to supplant the old one-room school. Negroes of the community, in spite of only a smattering of skill and experience, put up two adequate buildings. One contained classrooms and a good auditorium; the other was a Home Economics and Industrial Building for serving, cooking, canning, blacksmithing and other vocational subjects. "The superintendent had a cannery bug; he was always preaching to the people that they should can their food. He was in the Booker Washington tradition of letting down your buckets where you are. He wanted to teach the people to own their own property, to raise their food and can it, and to get hold of cash so that they could stay off the credit books. Reared in the South, he knew how to get things out of white folks. He wasn't any Uncle Tom; he got things without Uncle Tomming, but still he didn't put that Northern pressure on.

"Well, the old man built up something from nothing. At one time he had four or five buses running all over the county, bringing the kids to the school. Then the county white people, especially the plantation owners, got jealous and watchful. They accused him of stealing government property. Just as in all such cases, they found a few cans in the old man's home. He was judged guilty. He fought the case in the courts, and lost his school and all of his money fighting.

They crushed him all right; the last I heard of him he was working on a WPA project.

"I was teaching the same things the old man stood for, things I didn't think were dangerous at all. I also added higher education. There was one boy four-teen or fifteen years old who had a wonderful mind. I told him and some other promising students how easy it was to work your way through school, if you really wanted to. I told them they ought to get away, if it was nowhere but to Little Rock, and get started on a real education. I told them they could make it if they would try. I was much younger than I am now, and I would blow my head quite a bit.

"Well, the school was near to two big plantations. I never went there, but I could hear the bells ringing at four-thirty in the morning to feed stock. They didn't want anybody on the plantation who could read or write. In cotton season the man from the plantation weighs the cotton in, tells the Negro croppers how much, and always steals off what he can. Then the things they buy on credit in the off-season are figured in at the pay-up at the end of the year. And the croppers al-ways ended up owing something. The plantation bosses didn't want any figuring Negroes; they would figure for them.

"So one day a young white fellow, just about my age, he was educated some-where in the midwest, Kansas, I'm not sure, dropped past the school. He didn't come to me rough, but rather friendly. He didn't want it known that he had come to see me. He said, 'You know, you seem like a smart fellow. Well, if you want to teach school down here, *teach school*. And keep your mouth off of what doesn't concern you.'

"This young fellow died that same year. His father, a big man in the county, was really knocked out by his death. They held the funeral at a small church near the school. A lot of plantation Negroes were sitting on the fences around the little church when the funeral procession came out. The old white man looked at the Negroes and said, 'All of those niggers. Not one of them would have been missed and God had to take my son.' I wasn't there, but I heard the story over and over in about the same words from Negroes who heard it and I believe it is the truth. At any rate, that was the attitude toward the Negroes that I found in that part of Arkansas. Not one of them would have been missed."

So Buck left his principalship. He had been promised seventy-five dollars a month, but was getting only sixty, the top pay then in 1932. This pay was always in scrip, except for a couple of months. When he made up his mind to leave, a well-to-do colored woman of the neighborhood who had people working for her told him, "You need money. I can pay my taxes in scrip; the county issues it and the county has to take it back." She gave Buck the full value of his scrip; that was the first time he got it.

Buck returned to his native Hot Springs and became a chauffeur and house boy for one of the big men of the town. This was the middle of the depression and his pay was seven dollars a week and board. Buck went to the government-supervised bath house schools, and shortly after was employed as packroom helper and then bath attendant. Because of government supervision of the bath houses, Buck explained, Hot Springs is a piece of the North set down in the heart of Arkansas. Big shot whites and Negroes from all over the country come there; there is a racing season for thirty days every year and money gushes like the springs. After his apprenticeship, Buck preferred to work at the remaining Negro bath house: "An old time Negro can work in the white places. Mind you, I'm not saying all of those working there are old timey. Not at all. Laura Jones worked in a government bath house. She is one of those colored women who gets respect even in the South. When she walks in a bank in Arkansas, they all say, 'Mrs. Jones, yes, what can we do for you?' She was fired from her job and the government official insisted that she be rehired. Told the white man, 'She has forgotten more about bath house work than you'll ever know.' But as far as I was concerned I knew that in the summertime the Southern whites come for their treatment and you've got those insults and slams coming to you, and it takes the fight out of you."

In the off-season Buck worked as a Pullman porter or as a dining car waiter. He got over the country quite a bit: "I got to know all kinds of people. In Chicago, for instance, I knew everybody from the big shots in the First Ward to the hoodlums around Twenty-Second and Wentworth."

It was always Buck's way to keep in touch with the big shots, colored and white. He still had numerous anecdotes about them. He knew Andy Kirk when he was at the outset of his career playing in Oklahoma City with a young band. He remembered Basie before he became a Count. Basie had played the organ for a whole winter at the Bethel A.M.E. Church in Little Rock, because the Moten band of which he was pianist had gotten stuck. He knew many Negroes from Oklahoma on whose places oil had been discovered. One of these, whom Buck knew well, had run through fabulous sums of money in a short time; his friends had to take up money to bury him.

Well, the time came for the National Defense. "It happens that I like to pick up everything I can," said Buck, "and I took a course in welding. The teacher was a colored boy named Chester. He had been working for an old whisky-head who took him out on jobs. He was a better welder than the boss, but in Arkansas a Negro couldn't join the union and so he couldn't go out on his own. So the white man and his partner set up a three-way partnership, with Chester as the third partner. Then he became an owner working and the union couldn't bar an owner. They were fond of Chester, but they made him a partner not because of that, but because he was a *welder*. When he took the examination he passed the highest government qualifications. He taught every welder, white as well as colored, who came through that school.

"I took the course, but didn't finish. When I had my first Army exam, the board knew that I had been to welding school and had a good record, and told me I could go somewhere and work in a shipyard. The school gave me a recommendation as a tacker. Tacking is sticking something together until the welder comes along to weld it.

"I went out to Richmond, California. The United States Employment Office refused me a job as welder. A young fellow about twenty-four years old with a tongue as smooth as a Philadelphia lawyer gave me a soft story. 'It's awful, in times like this that the union won't let you in. Maybe when the war is over, unions will be done away with. They ought to be now, refusing you a job.'

"I went into the yard as a shipfitter's helper. When I told my story to the welder quarterman he had me transferred to the welding department. After my transfer and after I joined the union, I went back to that employment office and straightened that fellow out. In the meantime, he had given my brother the same spiel. I joined Boilermakers 513; they didn't have an auxiliary then; three or four months later they set up the Negro auxiliary.

"I got along fine. I told them about my school back home and showed them what I could do. I was the only colored on the gang. They all seemed to like me. I told them a lot of tall tales. Sixty days after I started tacking I was eligible to take the journeyman's test. I went on for four months, my salary increasing five cents an hour every sixty days."

When he left, he was getting the top salary of $1.20 per hour. Buck explained the three shifts: the day, the swing, the graveyard; the vacation with pay at the end of 1,200 hours, though workers are asked to continue at work.

Buck went on to tell the following story:

It takes good eyes, watching that puddle of steel. The work isn't hard, but nerve wracking. And it can get cold out on that bay. You may have to lie flat on your belly, or in a knot with your knees all up in your face, watching that puddle of molten steel all the time. If there's any welding to be done on the outside of the ship, they have a little rigging to let you down. If it's raining, you have your tarpaulin over you. When the ship rocks, you rock. You're out there sometimes with the waves licking at your feet.

If you're the least bit leery, you don't have to do it. Our gang was proud of its record and would go anywhere. I held back only once. They sent me to the crow's nest on one of those LST boats, one of the invasion barges.

When it's rolling the least bit down here, it's swinging plenty up there. I had to climb straight up a little ladder about a foot wide. I thought I'd see what it was like. That crow's nest took such a pitch, I pulled on my line and came down from there.

I never worked on an all Negro gang. I asked to be changed from my first gang when they put a West Virginia white fellow in as leaderman. He would always put me off by myself. I had been working with white girls; we all got along fine. Perfect camaraderie. One girl was of Mexican-Chinese descent. Another girl was from southern Missouri. They were as good buddies as any colored girls I've ever seen. I never had any trouble because of the women. It was "Gimme a cigarette, feller," "Hello, Buck." I was strictly business with them. No social stuff. We'd laugh and talk but I never got personal with them. With the West Coast girls it wouldn't have mattered; a colored man was just another man to them. That wasn't the way with the Southern girls, though.

Well, this West Virginian never pushed me around openly, but you can tell when you're being pushed. I'd always find myself set off on some job by myself. So I went to a leaderman I knew. "I'd like to work on your gang," I told him.

"Fine," he said.

My old leader raised Cain and tried to get me back. But I wouldn't go. He never spoke to me after that of his own accord. Sometimes we worked on the same ships. We lived in the same housing project (no, not the same house; colored and whites live in separate houses). Sometimes I'd get devilish and make him speak to me.

There was another Negro on this gang, named Herby. The gang was mixed: people from Minnesota, Arkansas, Wyoming, North Dakota, Missouri. I had all kinds of experiences. None of those fellows ever knew I was from Arkansas. The first question a white Southerner want to know is, "Where do you come from?" If I had said Arkansas, he would have started, "Arkansas, well I swar. You know I used to know a lot of good darkies from down in Arkansas."

So I always answered snappily, "Milwaukee. Ever been there?"

"Uh-uh," they would say. That Milwaukee lost them. They knew I knew Arkansas, though.

Those Arkies and Oakies are despised by the West Coasters. They never call Negroes Arkies and Oakies, though. When the Bay Area opened, and wages were five or six dollars a day, there wasn't any strong union. The Arkies and Oakies, living in tent cities, would sign up for three or four dollars a day. So the tradesmen and labor men hate them for bringing down wages.

Then they don't like the twang of their voices, and their noisiness. It seems to me that people from the South, white and colored, make the most noise on the buses and street cars. Seem to want to make themselves heard.

I didn't have any trouble. One day an electrician said to me, "I got a good story I'd like to tell you, but it's about your people and you might get mad."

"Yeah," I said; I knew from his twang that he was from the South. "I might. I get mad easy, and I'm hell when I'm mad." He didn't tell me the story and we were good friends from then on out. Another day a pipe-fitter yelled at me: "Hey, boy, come here. I got some tacking I want you to do." I pulled my line up to him. "Say, pipefitter, what part of the South are you from?" I said.

"I'm from Texas. How'd you know I was from the South?"

"Because in the South, colored people never grow up," I said. "They're always boys." From then on he always called me Welder. But some colored people from the South wanted to fight all of the time on the least excuse. They got so angry they couldn't do their work.

Buck told me another story, this one of a white shipfitter from Duluth with whom he was on a job:

One day he came in just laughing. He laughed all the morning until about eleven o'clock. When you're working with a man who's laughing all the time, you wonder what's wrong with him. Think he might be off his nut or something.

"What you keep laughing at? You batty?"

"Something happened on the bus this morning. I'd like to tell you about it, but you might get mad." I told him I wouldn't get mad.

"Well, can I use the same words they used?"

"Sure," I said. "Shoot the works."

"Well, the bus was crowded this morning. I was in the back. A big red-faced Oakie or Arkie, I don't know which, walked in, and stood in the aisle, looking around. Then he said, 'Ain't none of you niggers gonna get up and let me sit down?' Nobody paid any attention to him, so he repeated it two or three times. 'Where I come from, niggers don't sit down where white men are standing.' A big Negro jumped up at that, with a grin on his face. He scraped and said, 'White folks, you want to sit down?'

" 'Sure, nigger, of course I want to sit down,' the Oakie said.

"The white fellow sat himself down. Then the Negro's expression changed; he pulled out a big knife with a shiny blade: 'Now you got a seat, and now I'm gonna get me a seat.' And he sat down on the white fellow's lap."

The shipfitter could hardly tell the rest for laughing: "The colored fellow held the knife against the Oakie's neck. He cursed him all the way from town to the shipyard. He sounded like he was crying. 'All this kind of thing's gotta stop,' he said. It looked like tears were running down his cheek.

"Two or three white men started toward the back of the bus. The colored fellow said: 'You tell those fellows if they take a step further, I'm gonna cut your damn head off.' He held his knife around that guy's neck, sitting on his lap (he was a big fellow, too) until we got to the yard gates. He walked off the bus, holding the knife against the fellow. I got off right behind them. Then he said, 'Now let this be a lesson to you,' and disappeared in the crowd."

And then the guy from Duluth started laughing all over again.

"On a job like that," Buck continued, "somebody's always dropping out, going to the Army. Our leaderman joined the Seabees. The other Negro, Herby, a combination electric and acetylene welder, had been trained by the NYA. He was a good welder, but I could never get him to take the certified test. Well, they gave the job of straw to a white fellow named Joe who wasn't as good as Herby or myself. Joe was from Arkansas, but I never met a fairer fellow in my life, certainly not from Arkansas. He knew what Herby and I could do. Herby was disappointed, I could see that. If he had come into that yard a white fellow with two hundred hours of electrical and gas welding, maybe he would have got the job. Or if he could have talked more. Herby was from Oklahoma, and a lot of those boys don't have much to say. I don't mean they won't talk up; when they get mad, they will raise hell. But I mean they won't assert their rights without blowing their top.

"There are some colored men there who are ship's engineers, walking around with blue prints in their pockets and white collars on. But I never saw any Negro leadermen over mixed crews in the skilled crafts. Herby took it hard. He didn't say anything, but he went over to the graveyard shift almost as soon as Joe was made leaderman. He just said he wanted to make more money, that he had a wife and a couple of kids. Yet he had worked eighteen months on the day shift, and had always told me he liked the day shift best.

"They treated me fine after Herby left; Joe was O.K. One thing that stung me, though. Every fellow in the gang who left for the Army or Navy got a present, except me. We'd take up ten or twelve dollars, get a serving kit or little bag or shoeshining outfit. I'd always chip in. But when I left, they didn't give me a thing. Said they were sorry I was going and all that, but no present." Buck laughed. "It didn't make me feel bad. I've learned from experience what to expect and what not to expect."

Buck found that Filipinos and Chinese were just a little above the Negroes in chances to rise; they don't get to be leadermen much faster. He found the Filipinos cordial. They held his hand, teaching him the fine points of welding, which Buck likened to Palmer penmanship. They taught him how to hold the rod close to the puddle so as not to make "wasp's nests," one of the flaws in welding. Buck found that most of the Negro welders wouldn't teach another Negro a thing; they were "too high up on the hog for that." Buck didn't know as he blamed them; some of the Negroes didn't want to learn from Negroes. Buck passed by a colored girl one day, dropped his hood down and said, "Say, pal, you're doing it wrong. Try a downhand with your machine a little cooler; you'll get along better." "I know what I'm doing," the girl snapped at him. Buck had merely wanted to be helpful; he knew what he had come through.

Buck found that whites, even Southerners, will come to anybody to show them how: black, green, white, red, it makes no difference. "I can't get my machine fixed. Can you help me?" (The trick in welding, he told me, is getting the machine fixed, to get good penetration.) Oddly enough, Buck found the Chinese to be snooty. Once when he had gotten a "flash" in the eye, a dangerous exposure to the fierce light, he had gone to a Chinese nurse, who acted up and didn't want to give him the first aid service.

Buck found many Negro workers satisfied, but one group quite militant. Most welcomed the FEPC as a righter of discrimination. "Being from the South doesn't mean you accept discrimination. As a matter of fact, many of the workers from the South are ready to start cursing and squabbling. Then a lot of others like to cut them down easy." Kaiser is tops with the men personally; he pays top prices. He isn't blamed for the inside stuff that Negroes and many whites don't like. Kaiser just wants to get the ships out.

Buck praised the CIO because it had no auxiliary unions. "If you're a member, you're a member. But the CIO was slow in getting to the West Coast, and found itself tied out." Buck belongs to the Committee Against Discrimination in the yard, a committee open to anyone opposed to discrimination and in sympathy with the effort to break up the practice of Negro auxiliaries in the Boilermaker's Union. The Boilermaker's was the largest offender; the committee figured if you break one, you break the others. Buck used to carry around petitions. A Negro counselor in the yards, employed by the company for morale, was hot against the petition. "Stirring up trouble," was what he called it. Buck didn't think much of the counselor. He had got his job because "It's not what you know in the yards, it's who you know." This counselor would tell the Negro workers, "You're making more money than you ever made before, you know that. You get to fooling around signing those petitions, you'll find yourself without a job."

"Ragtime," said Buck, pretending to be strumming a banjo.

Buck's wife was director of recreation in one of the housing projects. Negroes and whites lived in separate apartment houses but all in the same project. The big hall and the small club room were for everybody to use. Across the street were the new dorms built by the Kaiser Company; they had no provision for recreation. A hillbilly band was organized there by a fellow named Tex. One night Tex and his band and a group of white people wanted to dance and asked to use the dance hall without authorized permission. Buck's wife refused and closed the building. She had her orders. The supervisor upheld her. The next day a delegation of the whites met with the supervisor.

"Last night," they said, "you took sides with a colored person against white people. We're from Arkansas; we've been trained that their place is in the kitchen and the field." The white supervisor, a woman from the midwest, flew all over them. From then on, Buck's wife has had no difficulties to speak of. Tex, the hillbilly bandsman, always calls her Mrs. Eden. Some, however, Buck admitted, won't call her anything; they just say, "May we have the ping pong set? May we have the basketball?"

Buck also mentioned that there is no racial line in the poker pool. This game is played by using the serial number of your check as your hand. Thus 22414 would equal two pairs. Zeroes are wild. Five numbers are considered; if the serial number has six or seven figures, the first one or two are cancelled. If hands are equal the pot is divided. Any gang can organize a pool; sometimes they run to twenty-five or thirty in the same pool. It was a very useful pastime, Buck found. He had been fairly lucky. But it was really unskilled gambling.

On two calls to the Army, Buck was deferred because of his welding job. Then the third call came.

"I got to figuring," he said. "Bud was dead in Sicily, and Jesse was in the South Pacific, dead or alive I didn't know. So I decided I was going in." Both were old buddies. Bud was a younger fellow whom Buck had looked out for in Hot Springs. "He was a well liked old boy. I tried to give him the kind of help I got all along the road, at Lincoln, for instance," he said, looking away. "Bud used to come to me when he was in trouble or need. 'Lemme have four dollars, Buck, I want to get a pair of shoes.' That boy really hated to go to the Army. He wrote me from down in Florida. They were being trained to tear into the swamps with cats and bulldozers, dig in, and have a airfield ready when the airplanes got there. I got a V mail letter from him in North Africa. Then the news came home that he had been killed in action. Invasion of Sicily. Before Bud went to Florida I guess he hadn't been farther from Hot Springs than Memphis.

"And then Jesse. Jesse was a fellow I met on the coast who went into the Navy. Last time I saw Jesse he was telling me of a racket he had. Jesse was a born gambler. He had a buddy on the shore patrol, or whatever is the same thing in the naval barracks. When Jesse was winning and wanted to leave the game, he'd go to the window and sneak out a signal. Then his buddy would break into the barracks and yell, 'Break it up, fellows. No gambling.' And he and Jesse would split the winnings." Buck didn't know what kind of ship Jesse was on: "He isn't a mess boy. I believe that he's an able seaman. I hear they've got colored seamen on everything now from an ocean-going tugboat to a battle wagon. Of course, that may be ragtime. Anyway, nobody has heard from Jesse for a long time.

"I could have got another deferment but I handed it back to the man. I went down to the office and they asked me what branch of the service I wanted. I told them the Marines." He tried to sound casual, but pride was in his voice. "And here I am on my way to New River."

When Buck left the house, I kidded him about the tough boot training he was about to face. I reminded him that he was no longer the young man he was at Jeff City. "Well," he said, "working in that shipyard wasn't any bed of roses. I can take it; it's all in the knowing how." And he swung down the steps.

I guess that soon they'll be having Buck sing:

> *From the Halls of Montezuma*
> *to the shores of Tripoli.*

He will sing it with gusto, I know. The only thing that he will ask, I figure, is that they leave out of it all traces of ragtime.

→→ OLD MAN McCORKLE ←←

It was over ten years ago that he stalked out of the past up the walk to my house. He wore a greenish "jim-swinger" coat, pipe-stem trousers a bit too short, large heavy-soled shoes, a piece of cloth folded around his neck, and a crushed old felt hat. His dark brown face, fringed with gray, had what some would call an aristocratic cast. He looked a little like Jefferson Davis. His hair was frizzled gray; his slightly receding mouth was nearly toothless. In gestures and manners he was truly aristocratic. He walked so erectly that he seemed to be about to topple backward.

He had come to Missouri from far away North Carolina. We soon got to be friends. He announced himself as "an arrow in the quiver of Lord God Jehovah's power," and he was eloquent enough for such. After we had won each other's confidence, he did not resent, he even welcomed, my taking notes on his talk. He ate heartily for all of his near toothlessness, stripping a pork chop with ease and neatness. He was a great drinker of strong coffee.

He was eighty-four years old. He boasted that long before freedom he could read, learning partly from his mother whom his memories reconstructed into a superior person, partly from the questions in the catechism, partly from the grandson of the McCorkles, who were "kind to their colored folks." Most of the other slave owners whom he recalled were hardly "rickommendable."

He enjoyed telling us of how his family worked at night for themselves, hoeing up patches in the woods for gardens, making baskets of splits. Church was five miles from their cabin, and in order to get there, they had to take a "bateau" over the river. He chuckled remembering how, when they were stealing back after the long nightly meetings, they woke up the man who ferried the bateau.

Most of the people were kind to him, because even early he had the gift for speech. His master used to send him for apple brandy. "Maybe," he chuckled, "because I wouldn't uncork the demijohn."

The leading question, as inevitable from Negro youngsters hearing his tale as its converse from whites, brought a start to him.

"Was they ever cruel!" he repeated indignantly. "They was always cruel," he said simply. His voice sank low when he talked of cruelties; he never lingered long upon them.

He did tell of Uncle Logan. "Uncle Logan," he spoke with satisfaction, "was a great man for praying. The man he belonged to was a sinner, and told Uncle Logan not to pray. But Uncle Logan would pray anyhow. So the white man strung up Uncle Logan. Buzzards soared over the spot until white folks and colored folks found him and cut him down. Though nearly done for, Uncle Logan survived and lived to have children. But his master one day put a big pistol .to his head and blew out his brains."

Whether Uncle Logan's was a true tale or a derivative of *Uncle Tom's Cabin*, or part of the folklore by which *Uncle Tom's Cabin* was sustained, there is no doubt of the simple sincerity with which the old man recounted it. To him it was an instance of "the dispensation of time."

There was no overseer on the McCorkle place. "Our people would not have stood for it." The Negroes on the McCorkle place and on the Schiffer place were upstanding fellows. Overseers he called "no account." The patterrollers were hard boys to get around when you got caught without a pass. One patterroller, a poor-white named Ike, wanted to come between a slave named Munday and his wife, but without much success. As a matter of the truth, Munday's wife laughed at Ike and told Munday about him. So the patterrollers were very hard on all of the males of the Munday family.

No Negroes were ever put in the jail. That was the place for poor whites. If a Negro got caught stealing he was given forty-and-nine with a leather thong, or thirty-and-nine with a braided cow-hide with the end loose. They wouldn't put a Negro out of commission when they beat him anymore than they would a horse. If the skin split they would wash the openings in brine. Always at our expressions of distress he would carefully explain that salt and water kept mortification out of the wounds. When a Negro got too bad they would put him in the drove and send him down to Alabama, Mississippi, and New Orleans. Speculators paid good money, especially for a good woman.

A poor white named Bartley overseered one time on a neighboring farm. He came from across the river where his large poor white family lived in a peeled pine, mud-daubed cabin "worse'n we slaves lived in." Mr. MacDowell, the owner of the place, left to practice law in Mecklenburg. At harvest time Bartley abused the Negroes, who forthwith left.

"How did they get away?"

"Oh they had ways and means. They got away all right. And some for good."

Bartley lost his half of the harvest. And Bartley's mother with her brood of children across the river went uncared for. Mr. McCorkle seemed satisfied.

"Po' whites always the worst enemy nigger got," was one of his dogmas, based on kind memories of the McCorkles, Abernethys, MacDowells, and Schiffers. "Po' whites never would work with niggers. They would cut and drag ditches, split fence-rails and logs. They spised us, and we spised them right back."

The slaves he remembered with respect did superior jobs to ditch-digging and rail splitting. "Uncle Abner could build a four-horse wagon, wheels and all. And yit he never had been taught the trade."

"Niggers made furniture, beds and chairs, coarse furniture, naturally, not like these fancy chairs we setting on now." They also were great makers of coffins. The coffins they made for the white folks were made of walnut or cherry and painted or varnished; those for Negroes were pine, stained with a dye made from maple-bark. They were all right nice coffins.

One of his stories was about a bright-skinned coachman, one of the best servants of the neighborhood. The daughter of the household took a hankering for him. He drove her, wherever she wanted to go, on long rides over the countryside. They loved each other. When she got in a fix, the white folks wouldn't mob him, but they sent him away. The child was put out to nurse a long ways off.

He seemed to relish informing us that this wasn't so scarce a happening. That is how come the "free ussues," he said. "Some folks calls them the 'gray eyes.' If a black man and a white woman have a child it's born free: free issue. If a white man and a black woman have a child, it ain't nothing."

White families gave free issue kinfolk something, a horse and saddle each, something like that, never much. They were lucky of course to be given anything. But there were more of them than you might figure on, back in the old days.

He told the same stories over and over again, remembering new details sometimes, never altering the main facts. He told them simply and eloquently, relishing the rapt attention of my family and friends, a seemingly forlorn but really proud walker out of a far land and time. He was a good dramatist. He must once have been a first-rate preacher.

He had no praise for the past of slavery, no special blame, but a horde of memories vivid and sure. He had very little, however, for the present and for the younger generation to do, always excusing us. We sympathized with him, especially since we knew where he was living. It was a poor rooming house in the section well-called "The Foot." We hoped the landlady would respect him as a man of God, but the place was unsavory.

It turned out badly for him. He came to the house one day, breathless, sputtering, his eloquence, his sway-backed dignity, his calm pride gone. He was pitiable, denouncing the scarlet women of the house and their drunken men. They had not seen in him a man of God but a funny-looking old fool in mutt-legged breeches and a green jim-swinger. They had scorned him. "Eyes have they and they see not," he mumbled. We did all we could to quiet his wrath. When he left us he left his blessing with us. I remember him after long years, stalking down East Miller Street, still so erect that he was leaning backwards. He was one of the best teachers I have ever had.

⤜ BUS STATION ⤛

The bus for Macon was due to leave at 2:45 P.M. I had been unable to get a cab; Frank finally picked me up and by driving his Pontiac like a red ball through hell through all the back streets and alleys, he had got me to the depot at 2:43.

The station was white, new and cheaply imposing. I ran up the steep incline to the colored entrance, swung through the glass door with its chromium bars, and wove through a crowd of folks to the barred off ticket window. There were two lines ahead of me, one of Negro employees of the company, and the other of passengers.

A lanky, ruddy-faced clerk was taking his time, cashing the checks of the employees. When the fellow abreast of me came up, the clerk scrutinized him with gimlet eyes.

"What's the matter, James?"

"I been sick, Mr. Doyle. That's the reason I didn't make much time. I had to lay off two days."

Doyle grunted suspiciously, looked at the back of the check, and paid out a few dollars.

The white woman waited on the last customer before me, and then was long gone. I don't know why; maybe it was because I had a suit and a tie and was smoking a cigarette. But she turned away as I got there, and rushed to the white folks' window which we could see through the office.

The lank clerk had business with a lot of stubs. I waited. I watched the electric clock jerk its hands, 2:47, 2:50. The room was close and sweaty, packed with soldiers, some asleep, and a number of mothers with their babes in arms and little children.

I waited, staring at the clerk's sweaty back. Finally I said, "I'd like a ticket for Fort Valley."

The cracker turned sharply and glared at me. In spite of being weak-mouthed, he tried to look stern.

"Is the Fort Valley bus supposed to go at 2:45?" It was 2:52 then.

"Yes," he snapped.

"Has it gone yet?"

"I don't know."

"I'd like a ticket for Fort Valley," I said, pulling out my wallet.

"Somebody will wait on you as soon as they can." He looked at the cigarette drooping from my lip, a curl of smoke winding through the bars toward him. I didn't move it. He returned to counting his stubs, slowly, laboriously. It seemed too big a job for him to be doing, all that reading and adding.

I spoke to the soldier next to me. "They announce the buses when they're ready, don't they?"

The soldier looked unhappy. "I reckon they do. I don't know much about it myself."

"I've got to get to Fort Valley, and I heard this is the last bus. I can't afford to miss this one. I've been waiting here all this time—"

The tall cracker snapped his head up and glared. A whine and tremble entered his voice. "I tole you once," he said. "I'll wait on you as soon as I get done what I'm doing."

"Well, I don't want to have to wait so long that I'll miss the bus. I was told it was to leave at 2:45."

"It's still about there. By rights it should have gone before you got here. You came to the window after leaving time."

"Oh, no," I said. "I was here in time, if I could have got a ticket."

He threw his face forward and glared at me; the soldier looked surprised too. I knew he wanted to come through those bars at me. Well let him come, I thought. I tried to play it cool, and I looked squarely at him.

He went back to his reading stubs and ciphering.

"Can I pay on the bus for my ticket?" I persisted.

"No. You got to buy your ticket here."

"So that's that," I said to the waiting room.

The loudspeaker announced departing buses. I couldn't make out the words. The bus company is trying hard to play choo-choo, with parking and loading places marked "track eleven," etc. The loudspeaker imitated the railroad announcers' fog-horn jumbling. "And Chatthooga," blared the brass. Well, that one wasn't it, anyway.

Finally a floridly pink woman, reddish haired and husky, came over to the window. I started, "I want—"

"He wants a ticket to Fort Valley," said Lanky.

While she trotted away, I asked him, "If the bus has gone, and if this is the last one, can I get my money back?"

"Yes," he snapped. "But it ain't gone yet."

Ticket in my hand, I rushed out to the platform. I nearly ran into a white woman and her child who were bouncing about. A Negro porter, sweeping up, threw his eyes up in mock horror as he saw me throw on brakes. Then he winked solemnly. But I was shaken in nerve; the ticket agent's anger hadn't troubled me, but rather stimulated; however, knocking against a white woman and child was something else again.

Mine was the bus for Miami. A swarm of white people were about the door. There were a few farmers, a large number of soldiers. About eight of the Negroes stood on the fringe of the swarm. The doors finally opened. The swarm of whites more than filled up the bus; the back seat, our only chance for riding, was taken over by soldiers. A few white people were left out and of course all of the Negroes. The doors closed, and the bus slowly rolled off.

They obviously didn't want me and mine on that bus. We Negroes looked at each other. Somehow I felt relieved; I remembered momentarily the many tales I had heard of Negroes being thrown off of buses and beaten within inches of their life. This was the time of rising tension in the deep South; Talmadge had warned white women to be on guard; and strange, foreign, trouble-making Negroes were supposed to have descended on the South like locusts. When I saw those sunburnt red-clay crackers troop into that bus—the soldiers looked full of devilment and the ordinary travelers looked just ordinarily mean—I did not fancy being cooped up in that crowded space for four or five hours.

I looked over the crowd, packed and jammed on the loading platforms. It was a hot, steaming day. A few Negroes huddled together, but the crowd was mainly Aryan. Most of them seemed poor and harassed. A few girls, flaunting finery, got off of incoming buses; some of them told the drivers goodbye sentimentally, affectionately. There were a lot of kids. A few of the people seemed fresh and spruced, but most of those who came in after long hot rides seemed beaten out.

I waited for a long time for the second section that, it was rumored, would take the overflow. The dispatcher knew nothing of such an extra section. I finally returned to the ticket window to get my money back.

There was another woman there, as indifferent as the first.

"Have you tried to get on that special they're making up? There's another section. You try to get on that. It's an extra fare bus though."

"Do I pay that here or on the bus?"

"You pay the steward."

I wove back through the crowd. The dispatcher knew little about it—maybe in fifteen minutes. I went back into the station and asked the colored girl behind the soft drink counter for smoking tobacco. She didn't have any. "You go through that door, you can get them at the white newsstand." I stood there ten minutes waiting. "I'd like some tobacco," I said. The white girls kept their backs to me; I know they heard me.

I rushed back to the platform. The bus was ready. The people got aboard slowly, paying the extra fare to the steward, a big-nosed fellow. A little colored girl was ahead of me. He looked around her at me. He couldn't quite make me out. If I had been a white gentleman I should have stepped in front of the girl. Maybe I was a Yankee, though, not used to the Georgia way. He said to her brusquely, "This is not your bus. Your bus will be along later." I smelled the rat then. As I handed my ticket to him, I said, "I was told that I should pay the steward the extra charge."

"That's right."

Fumbling for my change, I said casually, "I'm colored. Do I ride this bus?"

He stared at me, confused, as if he had been wronged. "Wait a minute," he blurted.

He called a fat burly man, who, in his dark gray shirt and dark breeches with a stripe down the side, and black puttees, made me think of Mussolini. He had the Gibraltar jaw and the pout and the bugged eyes all right, but instead of the Caesarian dome, he had cleanly parted, plastered black hair.

"This man says he's a nigra," Ciano reported to Mussolini. "Can he . . ."

"No, he can't ride this bus," said Il Duce.

I took my ticket back. The young one said, "There'll be another bus along." They clambered on board the bus, slammed the big door, backed out of track 3, swung around, and roared away. They were in a big hurry; the bus was only two-thirds full; there were many special seats for me empty at the back. There could have been a quarantine region of about three seats between me and the whitefolks.

A Negro sitting on the rail said to the young girl and me, "He just talking. Ain't no more buses to Macon today."

I went back to the ticket window, told the man, a new one now, that I'd been told that if I couldn't get on the bus I'd be able to get my money back.

"When did you get your ticket?"

"About two hours ago. Around three o'clock. They wouldn't let me on the limited section."

He didn't seem surprised.

"You were going to Fort Valley, huh?"

"That's right." (I was going to die before I said "sir.")

"Who'd you get it from?"

How do I get out of this? I wasn't going to say lady, not then; and to be honest, I wasn't going to say woman, either.

"From—I don't know her name."

A woman came up, saved my face, and redeemed the ticket. I didn't say "thank you."

I went over to the counter to get a drink, and bought a couple of swallows of ginger-ale in a paper cup for a nickel.

One of the white newsstand girls was standing there, querulously talking about some matter of book-keeping.

The colored girl's voice was taut. "Yes, if today was Tuesday. But it's Monday." She was slow and calm.

"That is raght," said the white girl. "It plum slipped my mind. So you're raght about it after all, Ellie."

"When you get through with my book, I wish you'd be kind enough to bring it back to me," said Ellie evenly.

Ellie sort of inspired me. I told her my troubles.

"They're getting awful," she said. "They always fill up with white folks first. Any seats left, the colored can ride, sometimes, on some buses. No real telling. They just don't want the colored to ride on these buses. You was lucky to get your money back. Most often they make you write to the management up in Chicago. They figger won't many colored people do that. So much red tape. You be glad you got your money back."

→ CLUB CAR ←

It was a slow train through Northern Alabama, stopping, as a fellow traveler put it, "at every pig path." I got on at midnight, and had at least an eight-hour trip to Atlanta. There wasn't to be any sleeping I discovered: the porter and brakeman saw to that by continually slamming the door between the baggage compartment and the Jim Crow smoker. They had to work; why should anyone sleep? This wasn't a Pullman anyway.

I had the choice seats, the two facing each other on the side with the toilet. The conductor's "office" was across from the toilet; in the two other seats, one of which had been turned, two fellows sprawled facing each other. I put my feet up on the opposite seat and smoked myself into a semi-daze. I caught a few phrases from the talk of the fellows who were less curious about me than I was about them.

One fellow gave his name as Young. His little daughter was asleep in the first seat of the main part of the Jim Crow coach. She came into the smoker once for a drink of water. Ever so often Young and his fellow traveler would get up and go look at her.

Young was just crazy about that child, he told the coach. Her mother was dead now. Died when she was a baby. He had taken out a good insurance. "So if I peg out, she won't want for nothin'." Every pay day he put so much money in the bank for her education. He hoped to send her to some good college, like Spelman in Atlanta. She was real smart now, leading her class. She asked a lot of questions about things he didn't know anything about. Then she answered them.

The other big fellow got up and looked through the glass of the door. "She still sleep," he said in awe. "Purty as a pitcher. Jes' look at her."

"You're doing a fine thing, sending her to that Spelman," he stated profoundly, as he sank down in his seat. "Yassuh, a fine thing."

Young had a quart bottle of whisky in a paper bag, in his carefully packed suitcase.

"Mmm-uhm," said the other fellow. "Mr. Boston Bourbon. Now that's whisky."

"I won't drink no rot-gut stuff," said Young. "Tear yo' insides out." They got paper cups and drank to each other, solemnly. Young admitted that he liked his whisky, that is good whisky. And a little sport too. Every now and then, that is.

The other fellow grew talkative as the drinks circulated. "Anytime you come to Anniston you ask for me. Just ask for Big Red. They'll all tell you they know Big Red. 'A big red nigger with a black spot between his eyes,' they'll say. That's me. They all know me in Anniston." He pointed, rather proudly, to the black spot on his forehead between his eyes.

Young spoke of some people he knew in Anniston. One was some kind of cousin to his wife. He didn't recall her name and not much else other than that she was a spare-made woman. Finally Big Red worked out who she was. "Man," he suddenly yelled, "you're just about in my family. Talk about a little world!"

It developed that this woman often visited his mother, in fact she would probably be coming over to his house that morning, shortly after he got home.

"Man, man. Put it there." They shook hands and took another drink together.

Big Red had found a new friend. "Man, I'm going to call you up Tuesday, after I see your cousin. There's a phone in the office that they let us colored boys use. Let me call anywhere, just so I pays. I'm going to call you Tuesday at lunch time. Let you know what she says when I tell her as how you and I done met."

When Big Red got off at Anniston in the early dawn he told Young to be sure and come to see him. "I'm going to find you some real sport. And you take care of the little girl." His voice was warm because of the bourbon and the new friend and his proud certainty that everybody in Anniston knew him, "the big red nigger with a black spot between his eyes."

The porter was kept busy. He had put on light blue pin-stripe work overalls over his porter's trousers, a dark blue bandana around his neck and a dark blue cap. He would go into the baggage car and bang the freight around, just before the short stops. Then he would swing off the car, unload the baggage, wave his lantern, and as the train puffed under way, he would be back again. It was getting near to daybreak: the people in the coach behind were mostly asleep, contorted in all shapes. I looked down at Young's little girl, curled on the seat and peacefully asleep.

There was a rough comradeship in the smoker. The conductor was sorting tickets in the first seat, which faced a wash bowl and the porter's pressed uniform coat on a hanger. The brakeman occasionally sat beside him. All of us, the porter, the brakeman, the conductor, Young and I, threw conversation about. The porter, whose name was Jerome, generally played lead.

The conductor was to be off the next night, and told of a fish fry he was going to. "I'm not going to bed tonight," he said. "Going fishing on the river. We're going to fry them right where we catch them. That's the way I like my fish, right out of the river, not off the ice." He walked out of the car, as the porter wished him luck with his catch.

The porter was going to be off too, but he was going to sport some that night. He wouldn't guarantee that he was not going to bed. Expected that he'd end up in bed all right. His round dark face split into a grin.

The brakeman cackled, "You're the godammedest lahr I ever did see anyway, Jerome."

The porter seemed a bit taken aback, with Young and me listening in, though it was evident that the rough kidding was an old habit. He started pulling off his overalls, and squeezed in front of the brakeman at the washbowl.

"This here soap is too strong," he said, jabbing the plunger in the soap container sharply.

"You're using it," said the brakeman.

"Well it don't hurt to use it one time," Jerome said, "but it's too strong. It's like lye."

"I reckon you want some kind of perfumed soap," said the brakeman. "What kind of soap you want the railroad to put in here?"

"I use Palmolive," said the porter. "You know. You been in my house."

"Palmolive ain't strong enough to cut that grease you got on you," said the brakeman, getting up to go.

After the door slammed, Jerome confided to us, "He's all right. He's a good fellow. He'd go back there now and mop up for me, but it's too close to Atlanta. He's willing to help me out, and I helps him."

An hour or so after daybreak we rolled past the shanties and factories on the outskirts of Atlanta. Young poured a wakening snort for himself and Jerome and the brakeman. The conductor entered during the ceremony. Young asked him, "Will you have one, Captain?" The conductor didn't care if he did. They offered me one, but I begged off; I needed some breakfast in my stomach, I told them. They all drank out of the paper cones. Then the mail clerk, a gun on his hip, came in. The conductor, brakeman, Jerome, and Young were smacking their lips and drinking chasers of water.

"Have a drink," said the porter. Young held out the quart bottle.

The mail clerk hesitated. "Aw, go ahead and take a drink. Everybody's done had one." The porter caught his quizzical glance in my direction. "He's all right," he said. "He just can't drink in the early morning."

The mail clerk held out his paper cup.

The Jim Crow smoker took on, for a moment, the guise of a club car. Three whites and three Negroes and the remnants of a quart of Mr. Boston Bourbon.

Later, discussing some of the taboos with a member of the interracial commission, I mentioned the episode.

"Whose whisky was it?" I was asked.

"A Negro's."

"That's it," I was told. "If whites need a drink and a Negro has one, they'll drink with him. But if the whisky had been theirs, they wouldn't offer him a drink."

But I wasn't sure, and I've heard from many others since, that such does not invariably have to be so.

I suspect that if any whisky is drunk in the mail-car or baggage or smoker of that train, Porter Jerome is going to get his snort.

⇥ ROOMMATE ⇤

The director of the Negro USO at Columbus, Ga., had called up the Y.M.C.A. and arranged for me to get a room. The old decaying shambles of a building seemed deserted. There was a dim light over the counter, but nobody to check me in. I waited awhile, then started exploring. One door led to a pitch-dark, damp smelling hole; I learned the next morning with a postponed scare, that the swimming pool, full of green water, was just a few yards from where I had groped in the blackness.

Finally, the old man who was in charge came in. As we mounted the steps he told me that he was really looking out for me, that my room had a bath. We climbed the shaky stairs, and then he knocked on a door. I heard a grumbling "Who's there?" and a click. Through the transom I saw a light come on. I was surprised at having a roommate; I was more surprised when he flung the door open and stood there.

He was a little old fellow, reddish bronze, with walrus moustaches, looking mean and mad. He resented being aroused from his sleep. From his looks and speech I suspected that he was a down-home farmer, but he was wearing the latest style jockey shirts and shorts. He looked funny standing there, a bandylegged little old farmer, caricaturing the magazine advertisements.

He was short in his talk, until I parked my bags and went out to get something to eat. I brought him back a chicken sandwich and a couple of bottles of Coke. He stripped the chicken bones neatly and practicedly. Then he warmed up.

He was a farmer from Waynesboro, Ga., and had ridden all day on buses to get to see his boy at Fort Benning. He was proud of being a good farmer. His son had been a good farmer too. Right after the draft, he had told his boy he'd buy him a mule so that he could go to farming on his own and stay out of the Army. But his son wouldn't pay him any attention. Then Uncle Sam sent him the letter.

"He came to me crying. But what could I do when Uncle Sam wanted him?"

His son didn't like it at Fort Benning. Too many men with pistols over him. He made it seem like a prison camp.

He talked on and on, welcoming the audience of a stranger in a big city. He farmed his own land, wasn't beholden to no man; had stopped cropping for others years ago. Everybody around Waynesboro, white and colored, respected him. He didn't gallivant around; this was his longest trip away from home.

The night was sweltering, and bugs of all sorts were flying and singing about the electric bulb. I was dead tired, and finally mentioned that I guess I'd put out the light so we could get some sleep.

"What for," he said, "we paying enough fo' hit." We were being charged $.75 each for the room. And his slow but intense autobiography continued. I was a new type for him, with a briefcase and magazines, and now that his suspicions had proved unfounded, he seemed to think it imperative that he tell me his story.

But finally he ran down. I got up and said I believed I'd put up the window for a little air. I didn't want him to think I disapproved of his sleeping arrangements, but I had to get some air in that stifling room. He said, "Go ahead. But hit won't do no good. Hit ain't no pane in it. The sash was down; what I had thought was a window pane was night air."

He woke me before daylight by clicking on the bulb. I watched him putting on a new crinkling green suit over the incongruous sporty underwear.

"Did you rest all right?"

"Too good," he said. "Nearly overslept myself. I guess I'll get me something to eat and go over yonder."

He had traveled a whole day to reach Columbus; he figured on seeing his son for a couple of hours or so; then back on the bus to Waynesboro. I told him not to rush so, to take a day off; if somebody had taken care of his stock the day before, he'd do it today too. Everything would be there, safe and in good shape, when he got back.

It was an idea that hadn't struck him before, and he thanked me much. Maybe he would. Maybe he would take in one of those moving pictures.

I told him maybe they'd let his son come in from camp and go with him.

No, he thought, that would be too much to ask. But he walked jauntily when he left me, a little bandy-legged figure of a man, with bristling moustaches in an ill-fitting, country-store suit, a big straw hat, and yellow, stub-toed shoes that all cried out their newness.

⇥ RETURN OF THE NATIVE ⇤

When I got out of the car that had brought me there from Baton Rouge, Gus and Abe and Alan ran down to the gate to greet me. They all talked at once: Abe about the hunting I had missed, Alan about his new family, and Gus about the gatherings and sports that had been his welcome home. The yard was full of children of all sizes and ages. Near the porch, in barrel-stave swings and comfortable chairs, on benches, on the steps, were the grown-ups, and every now and then another would appear out of the rambling old house. I asked Gus later how many of his kinsfolk had been at this gathering; he was never certain, but counted up near to forty. All close relations were there except two sisters and their families.

The clan had gathered because Gus, the second son, the junior, had come home. Over a score of years ago, a tall, green youngster, their hope, he had left Frilot Cove for Tuskegee. He returned home after his graduation, but had been away now for over fifteen years. Most of the relatives, his young nieces and nephews and cousins, he had of course never seen, but they had heard all about him. The youngsters tumbling around and yelling, the older sisters and brothers and cousins and in-laws chattering away, were mostly fair in complexion; nearly all of them would have been taken for white; some were olive-colored, some blonde, one in-law was a fiery red-head. A few were light tan—French, Spanish looking; only two were what could be called brownskin: Gus's stepmother, Indian-like, with coal-black straight hair, and Abe's wife, a recent addition to the family. Gus himself looks like a Frenchman.

Père Auzenne, an old patriarch with long moustaches, a sly twinkle in his eyes, a staunch set to his jaw, was sitting on the porch in a rocker, monarch surely of all he surveyed: his sons and daughters and the grands. I paid my respects to him, and then to his dignified, quiet wife; they both courteously welcomed me to what, by rights, I had no business barging into. And then the younger ones claimed me. I too was of that strange outside world where Gus had been so long, and they wanted to know me. I had made a couple of trips to Opelousas and Frilot Cove before. The old man and I struck it off well; I had got through his crustiness because I was Gus's friend. On one visit Abe had driven his father and me the few miles out to the old home place. The drive was long from the gate marking the beginning of the Auzenne property to the house where the eldest son Raleigh lived. The house was old but sturdy, spotlessly clean, the typical home of substantial farmers in St. Landry Parish. Of the old French planter style, made of cypress, it was not wide but ran to length; additions to the house recorded the additions to the family, though the long years now made it seem all of one piece and time. In the front yard were the usual cedars and holly bushes, and abundance of flowers. The womenfolk of the household had a hand for making beautiful things grow: there were princess plumes, roses, bridal wreaths, and what were locally called "little violets," unlike those I knew. Fat grunting hogs took their ease in a watering pond; a dirty ram strutted before several meek, inquisitive ewes. A band of geese and ducks and chickens rattled away. In a nearby pasture a few well-kept, wide-horned cattle were grazing. Tall bright cane rippled in the sunlight as the wind swept over it. The cotton was deep green, a good stand. Most of these long flat acres, extending to a fringe of woodland, were under cultivation. Raleigh was a tireless farmer and manager, but running this place was certainly full time work for him, his family, and the six tenant families who lived on the place.

Tall and raw-boned, with a yellowish brown—what the natives call *chatin*—handlebar moustache like the old man's, Raleigh showed us around, explaining to a greenhorn as well as he could. He showed me the old fashioned but serviceable cane mill and the pans for boiling cane. Raleigh ground and boiled cane for the entire community; the cans he has sent me prove that he turns out a good product. In a dark shed, he found a bottle of cane bière, from which he offered me a drink.

The yellowish and oily liquid did not look appetizing, but since I was under scrutiny, I took a couple of gulps. I gasped as it went down. I thought I had sunstroke. In that summer heat, with an early afternoon sun glaring down on the top of my head, I realized that drinking cane bière wasn't smart. The old man and his sons, however, tossed down good swigs of the stuff, and laughed at my misery.

On a small phonograph in the front room Raleigh played a few of his records. Most of his favorites were Cajun songs; they seemed to me to be hillbilly songs translated into French. Hearing them I thought of the musical oddity of French melody with Cajun words to Negro or hillbilly ragtime and Swiss yodeling thrown in for good measure, but my analysis may have been influenced by the cane bière. The singing was mournful. I bought a few of these records in Opelousas, where they were as popular as their hillbilly cousins in other parts of the South; even in the juke boxes in Negro places, Cajun bands jostled Louis Armstrong and the Mills Brothers.

We talked about farming, the threatening war, the South, Louisiana, and Gus. "You be sure to tell my son, Gus, now, to come back to see his old father," the old man ordered. "Tell him it is a long time now." He tapped the ashes out of his pipe on his heel. "What kind of Tobak you smoking?" he asked. I offered him my pouch. He looked at the mixture that was then my pride. "Humph," he said, scornfully. "Cocktail tobacco." He filled his pipe, and smoked contentedly.

I got to know Abe and Alan, the middle brothers, best. Abe took me on long rides over the parish: over the Teche Country, the Evangeline Country, from

Washington to Lafayette. I got many views of the Big Teche and the Little Teche; sometimes at night when the still, black water seemed sinister; sometimes in the daylight, when I could see the flowers, too lush, too beautiful, too perfumed, covering the oily, poisonous-looking blackness. The gloomy, ancient trees dripping moss were too often the roosting places of carencros. On the way to St. Martinsville I saw sun-swept rice fields and heard an obliging colored Creole farmer explain the methods of irrigation and drying. One of the sights of St. Martinsville itself was the Evangeline Oak. Local tradition has it that Evangeline and Gabriel finally met at this moss-hung live-oak; but, harsher than Longfellow's poem, the tale goes that Gabriel had found another love in those long years, and Evangeline became grief-crazy.

Folktales that I heard of the Cajuns convinced me that Longfellow's gentle peasants had also altered for the worse; I heard of the cracker-like prejudices of Villeplatte particularly, and when we drove through that town we gave it the once-over lightly. I was disabused of the prejudice that "crackerishness" was an Anglo-Saxon monopoly, for according to the tales I heard, poor-white Acadian French hated Negroes in the same manner and degree as did the poor-white Scotch Irish.

A dozen or so miles from Lafayette, we noticed the lights of a car weaving across the road, coming toward us lickety-split. Abe swerved to the shoulder of the road; the careening car struck our rear fender and wheels and went into the ditch. Abe stopped within about fifty feet and went back. A runabout Ford was on its side in the ditch. The road seemed full of Cajuns, jabbering their patois excitedly. There were ten of them, nobody badly hurt; the girls were in fluffy party dresses, the fellows in ordinary clothes. Soon several cars drove up and stopped. The Cajun spokesman, a ruddy blonde with crimpy hair, gestured and fumed, but in the glare of the headlights the slanting course of his wheels across the line to the ditch was unmistakable. Alan talked for us; he looked more like a Cajun than any of the rest, and he knew the tongue. The Cajuns, living near Lafayette, just coming home from a dance, were given lifts by passing motorists; soon they were all gone. We looked at the runabout; the rumble-seat was full of empty bottles of a cheap, native wine.

The highway policeman was kindly disposed to Alan and Abe, who were clearly in the right. He nodded his head when he saw the bottles. He was a strapping fellow, brunette and swarthy, like Abe. In his report, he said, he would certainly absolve Abe. He mounted his motorcycle, waved friendly to us, and was off.

Abe's car was unusable; the wheels had been knocked out of line. We pushed it to the shoulder, dangerously close to the vine-covered ditch. Abe and Alan decided to stay by the car; the rest of us were to get to Lafayette where a bus would take us along another road to Opelousas. A passing truck gave us a lift; I stood on the little step serving for a running board, with the wind beating my face, and watched ahead as well as I could to gauge the curves. All in all it was a wild night for me. In Opelousas I had to find and wake up Henri Lemel, an auto mechanic and a friend of ours, go with him to the house of his boss, and get the keys for the repair truck. We got no answer from ringing the bell, so we walked around the large yard calling. The watchdog, overlarge and overfaithful, charged us dangerously close, barking every time we yelled. Finally we got the keys, got the truck, and went to Abe's home. His people were to call Abe's and Alan's bosses the next morning to explain their absence. The mother came to the door, shading an oil lamp with her hand. She was sick with worry: the boys had been due back hours ago. She told me, plaintively, that she had been watching the clock; that first when she saw the little needle on two and the big needle on twelve, she had confused them, and then she heard the clock strike the truth: two o'clock. She blamed me somewhat, I knew, for their making the long trip, and though I told her that nobody was hurt, she was unconvinced. She knew something would happen to her boys that far away, that late at night.

Dawn was graying when our truck reached the place of the accident. When day cleared, we had the car hoisted ready for towing. Over a slight rise the road-cop appeared. He looked at Henri, who is light brown, and at me, then closer at Abe and Alan. He became curter, more officious than he was the night before. He went back to the runabout, muddy and rusty, its radiator jammed in the vines. "He'll never drive that again." He had said that he had been thinking about the accident and asking questions. Maybe our lights *had* been too bright. At any rate, we wouldn't get a penny if we sued; the young fellow driving the runabout did not have a quarter. Alan pointed out the slanting tracks and was inclined to argue. Henri said that Abe's car was badly damaged. The cop stuck his fingers in his black belt. "You'd better let the whole thing drop. It was good luck that didn't nobody get hurt." And he roared off on his motorcycle, authoritative, ponderous, martial in his gray uniform, leather belt and puttees and holster, one of Huey Long's proud cossacks.

I remember one other thing, however, quite as vividly. As we sat there, digesting the advice from the officer of the law, a Cajun farmer appeared across the road as if from nowhere. We could not see any house around. He walked slowly and carefully. As he came closer we saw that he was bearded, long-haired, roughly dressed, a typical poor farmer. He had a cup of coffee in his hand. He offered it to us, to pick us up, to keep us going. The cup was heavy pottery. All four of us drank a sip of the coffee, which was muddy, black, and oversweet, with a lot of chicory in it. It was not hot; in the trip from his invisible house it had cooled somewhat; but it was warming to the stomach and to the heart. I can still see old Frenchy brushing through the cane, on which the morning dew sparkled in the sunlight like diamonds.

Later I offered to pay Abe part of the repair bill. He flushed at the suggestion, and told me impatiently that I was his guest and that I had nothing to do with it. I could not get through his pride, though. I felt guilty that I could not. Both he and Alan, and from all I learned, the whole family, were proud and sensitive. Good, swift, Gascon pride. Alan's quick was probably most exposed. When I left, he shook my hand, looked away, and said, "Now you're going off just to make fun of us in your writing." Nothing was further from my heart and mind, but he couldn't know that.

Now after four or five years, I was back. They were warm in welcoming me to the family reunion for Gus. Much water had flowed under the bridge. Abe was now the district manager of an insurance company; he was married to a brownskin girl named Anita; definitely darker than any of the other in-laws, but a live-wire if ever there was one, charming, ambitious, and hard-working. The family had got over their color-prejudices in her case. Alan was the father of a bouncing family, and was therefore bouncing himself. The youngsters had grown up; one was in a Beaumont, Texas, shipyard, another was soon to go into the Navy, where Abe also is now serving. Gussie, the youngest daughter, had grown into a deep-eyed, beautiful young woman.

My schedule, like the train and bus schedules, was running late; I was a day overdue. I had missed an outing on the Atchafalaya River, where the men of the tribe had caught an amazing number of carp, barbus patasa, and a Louisiana trout. The hunting trip had been called off because of my lateness. They didn't like this; they bawled me out; they wanted me to bear witness to their angling and shooting skill in this country noted for fine game and fishing. But they made up with their fish stories, big ones, as expected. Gus described the river outing with descriptive detail unexpected in a public accountant. The way he spoke of the luncheon of courbillion cooked in moss made me hungry.

Well, I had missed out on the fishing trip, but Gussie and Anita heaped a plate with barbecue, potato salad, spicy tomato and celery salad, country bread, topped off with a mountainous slice of coconut cake. The old man watched me eat with complacence. In spite of my deficiencies it looked like I could put away a man-sized meal, anyway. He sat there rocking, clutching a squat bottle of King's Ransom Scotch whisky in his arms like a baby. It was one of the presents Gus had brought. The vieux pulled out the cork and let the younger men sample the aroma, briefly, then he corked it again. None of the young whippersnapper's *brigands* would even get to taste his treasure, he told us. It was a good day. Rolls of film were used up; the younger ones posing grotesquely, the old man posing like the handsome old codger he was, the little mother, sober-faced and tense, facing the camera as an ordeal. There were races; relay teams with each member running about a hundred yards from one end of the barnlot to the fence and back again, the young girls swift and graceful as gazelles. Nelson, one of the in-laws, stumbled on the uneven turf and fell, and the crowd whooped with laughter. When my team won I got no credit as the anchor man; my legs were so long, they told me, I ought to be able to run well.

As we walked to some of the fields near the house, the old man gravely discussed his problems: it was hard to get farm help; most of his sons had left the land. From the looks of his Poland China hogs—he snorted when I mentioned Berkshires which my father had raised—and his corn, cane, yam, and cotton fields, it seemed to me that his yield would certainly be a good one. But no; he had his worries and he wanted to talk with someone about them. His heart was in his land, but the hearts of most of his sons were not there.

Toward sunset, the kinfolk hugged and kissed Gus, shook hands all around, and wished me Godspeed. When the last young one was found and safely stowed away in the cars and the large truck with chairs in the bed, they drove off, with great yelling and blowing of horns. Gus's homecoming party had been a rousing success.

Gus took me around later to talk with many of his kinsfolk who had not been present at the homecoming. Way back off the main road we visited his Aunt Vèronique. She was old now, but there was little gray in her heavy black hair; one could see that she had been striking looking; she looked like a Frenchwoman. And of course she was. She and Gus were overjoyed to see each other. She had taught the pure French to Gus as a lad, not the Creole distortions, and Gus was a Dumas enthusiast because of the hours she had spent reading *The Three Musketeers* and *The Count of Monte Cristo* to him in the original. The glow from the lamp was not bright, but I could see and feel the fine old red bindings on the small library of French classics that she had there. With the two of them talking away in French, Gus less sure, Aunt Vèronique fluent and precise and musical, with the lamplight glinting on the highly colored crucifix and Catholic emblems on the white clay walls, it was easy to imagine that I was in a farm home in France rather than in the American South. I could only isolate a word here and there, my French of Williamstown and North Adams not serving me here. When Aunt Vèronique looked at me for response, I feebly said "Yes" or "No." I knew when they talked of me, however; I heard Gus advertise *The Negro Caravan* and heard him speak of this book that I was working on. She murmured, "*Ah, des Noirs, Des Pauvres Noirs.*" I was glad to hear her express such sympathy, but Gus told me later that she felt sorry for the victimized Negroes in America, but, true to the attitude of the older Creoles, certainly did not identify herself with them. She was speaking as a humanitarian outsider.

I also met an uncle, who was a character. Regretful at his lack of schooling, he had taught himself to read, and with some of the proceeds from his cotton had bought a set of the *Encyclopaedia Brittanica* from a traveling book agent. He had read it from cover to cover. Naturally, he could talk well on any subject, and he had memorized much of the teachings of the experts. He had laid this massive pile on a foundation of common sense and peasant shrewdness. His wife, however, quarreled with him because of his intellectual searchings, and he was forced to read his beloved *Encyclopaedia* in an outshed, by the light of a farm lantern. Father Hyland, one of the best-loved of the priests, had held him up to the people as an example. "If Jimmy Auzenne can do so much without a single day of schooling, how much more should you accomplish with schools and teachers available?" he would ask his laggards. But they considered Jimmy a sage and a miracle.

Jimmy's wife's hostility to learning was not peculiar to her. Père Auzenne agreed in a measure. He was not enthusiastic about his younger children's going farther in school than the Holy Ghost High School in Opelousas. The older children had gone to normal school or college, and they had left the land. I saw evidence of the tug-of-war, the old patriarch stubborn, the young ones in grim though not open-voiced rebellion. Gus was their ally, but the old man clung to his point. Gus did not know. Had he not been the first to leave the land? A young woman, now, had no need for college education; she should get married, keep a clean house for her husband, raise up strong sons to keep the ancestral fields joined together.

The old ones refreshed Gus's memory of the history of Frilot Cove, and he passed it on to me with the fervor of a research student.

Of the propertied Creoles in Opelousas, Gus singled out the story of Simeon Birotte. Birotte owned considerable land near the town and along the Bayou Teche, which tenant farmers work on halves. In addition, Birotte ran a dairy and a livery stable, but his chief source of income was a thriving store in the heart of the town. One late afternoon, Birotte dropped dead as he was closing the store.

The story then follows familiar lines. Birotte's right-hand man was Auguste Crouchet, a poor white of Cajun stock, with a shrewd eye for the main chance. He had started as a handyman around the barnlot and as a wagoner, but as Birotte's enterprises increased, his position improved. Birotte's widow, against the advice of her brothers, kept the store open, and Crouchet became manager. Shortly after, the Crouchet family, once humbly housed, erected an imposing dwelling. A few years later the Birotte store closed, but Crouchet opened a quite elaborate undertaking establishment and a livery stable. Even after the store failed, however, Madame Birotte still had large land-holdings and wealth. In her will she named Crouchet as executor of her estate. She wished first "que toutes mes honnêtes dettes soient payées." The substantial residue of her property, she bequeathed to her close kin. But they never got it. Instead, all of her property, both real and personal, was sold at auction. None of the heirs ever knew how much money was realized at this auction. None of them received a cent from the estate. Certain prominent townsmen offered their aid to force a settlement, but the matter was left undercover. But the descendants of the original heirs know the history and are rankled by the trickery and robbery committed with what they firmly believe was connivance of the law.

The people were glad that Gus had come home so they could express some of the thoughts and feelings with which their minds and hearts were brimful. They might accept an outsider like me as a friend, but their sensitivity to criticism kept them on the defensive about the church, the school system, the law. But Gus was bone of their bone, flesh of their flesh; he would never misunderstand; he knew what had conditioned them; he shared to a degree their prejudices and preferences. He had made good in the large outside world; he had a position of high responsibility; he had the power, then, and the knowledge to set about getting the long-wanted changes. Older men who had taught Gus how to ride a horse, shoot a gun, grow cotton, and grind cane, came to him humbly as to a father confessor. They told him what they would not tell their priests, even. And they expected him to do something about it.

So Frilot Cove and Opelousas were not as Gus remembered them; they had changed, and he had changed. Opelousas was still a drowsy, apparently peaceful town, but the sleep was not a good one. There were too many signs even more glaring than the "white" and "colored" on the drinking fountains and park benches, for instance; the streets and sidewalks where the colored people lived were never paved. If whites and Negroes lived on the same street, generally the whites lived on the side where paved walk was, or more accurately, the town paved the walk on the white folks' side. Even the few homes of the better-off Negroes, the doctor, the small shopkeepers, the artisans, were on unpaved, undrained streets, dusty in the dry season, treacherous in a slight rain, sloughs in a heavy downpour.

The only Negro school for the town was a two-story tinder-box, with a fire-escape from the front porch stressing the danger rather than seeming to be a protection. The school board rents an annex from the Colored Odd Fellows, but the school is still so packed that it should burst at the seams anytime. A small homemade drinking fountain with six pipes sticking out of what resembles a watering trough furnishes water for the hundreds of school children. "A good place to suck up septic sore throat," said the Jeanes teacher.

Charles S. Johnson and his associates had just published their findings on the Negro educational facilities in the *Louisiana Education Survey*. It was an objective, unanswerable report of a bad mess. Copies were not easily available, but Gus got hold of one, and pored over the shameful record with rising anger.

Gus went to work to prepare a supplementary survey of the educational situation at Frilot Cove. His summary was as follows: Frilot Cove is a community of seventy-nine heads of families who own their property and pay taxes. There are 132 children of grade school age whose educational facilities are a two-room schoolhouse and two teachers. Of twenty-seven pupils of high school age and preparation, only nine attend the high school in Opelousas, fifteen miles away, and three of these use bicycles for the trip. The forebears of the people in Frilot Cove were the original owners of the land. For nearly a century, the people of Frilot Cove have paid taxes to the State. They form a homogeneous, law-abiding community, with no members ever indicted or accused of any crime or misdemeanor. In six decades the total appropriation made by the Parish to the physical improvement of the public school at Frilot Cove had been less than $500. Yet, according to Gus's careful estimates, some individuals at Frilot Cove have paid taxes amounting to nearly $400 annually, and averaging taxes per head of families at ten dollars a year over six decades, the people have paid approximately $50,000 in taxes to the state.

Gus found the church situation also unsatisfactory. There was no church at the Cove. Father Cooney used the little school house, built chiefly at the expense of the community and by its labor, to celebrate mass on Sunday morning. Contributions are compulsory, and if no money is forthcoming, commodities must be. The people feel that their gifts are being used in Opelousas, fifteen miles away. Three miles nearer Opelousas, at Andrepont, a church has been erected for the white Catholics, who are outnumbered by the Creoles of Frilot Cove. Father Cooney accedes to many of the regional practices. In paying the colored teachers at the Holy Ghost School in Opelousas, for instance, he had the checks delivered by a boy student; on the envelopes there was only the first name of the teacher. Upon questioning, Father Cooney stated that he thought that the teachers preferred to be called by their first names, and without any title, and he refused to alter the practice.

One shocking revelation was the story of Father Carmen George Chacheré. Gus told it in cold anger, his usually rapid speech slow and restrained as if he did not want me to miss a detail. The story's ending was almost unbelievable. But a field investigator for the Carnegie-Myrdal study had written it up from an interview with the bedridden Papa Chacheré. Face to face with death, Papa Chacheré had probably brooded over his shattered hopes, and he talked frankly for a man whose long years had been obedient and faithful to the Catholic Church. Gus had pieced out the story from nearly whispered confidences here and there; he was certain that the interviewer's story from the dying bed was true. I could not have got the story, Gus told me; for all of my acceptance in the community, the people were wary of seeming to criticize the Church to one not of the faith. A friend of mine, however, teaching at Lincoln University, has heard the story, substantially the same, told by a student from Opelousas. It was part of a hidden local lore.

George Chacheré was an altar boy in the Opelousas Holy Ghost Catholic Church and the smartest youngster in the school. Papa Chacheré had high dreams: his boy George was going to be a *priest*. The Creole neighbors were skeptical: that was a good dream now, but so far from their experience. They had never seen a Negro priest themselves.

The family worked hard for their dream. The final money before George left for the Seminary came from the sale of two hogs and a mortgage on the small farm. While George was studying Papa Chacheré sold his farm and moved to Opelousas; from a farmer and landowner he became a butcher's helper, and Mama Chacheré took in washing for the whitefolks. They and the younger ones lived beside the railroad tracks off of Market Street, desperately poor. But for all the shabbiness of the clothing that the Chacherés wore to morning mass, Papa Chacheré was as proud as anyone there. His son was doing fine at school; it was like a miracle.

When George traveled to Rome to be ordained at the hands of Pope Pius himself, Papa Chacheré's happiness was boundless. Mama Chacheré rebuked him for showing off; a priest's father should be dignified, she thought. But there was great excuse. George, now Father Carmen George Chacheré, toured Europe with fellow priests; they were greeted by cheering crowds of the faithful, even in Nazi Germany.

America, however, was different. Though notified, no priests greeted Father Chacheré on his long trip home to Louisiana. But the young priest bothered less about Jim Crow than he concentrated on his sturdy hopes: he would have a clinic for the sick ones, hot lunches for the students, a nursery for the little ones. Like St. Francis, his ministry would be among the poor and the weak and the outcast.

The white priest of the parish was not among the excited Creoles and "American" Negroes and Cajuns and American whites whose curiosity and local pride brought them to the little Opelousas depot. It was said that the father was sick, or out of town; in either case he was very sorry. But the muttering of the people went on: "It was a damn shame de Good Father couldn't greet de only colored Priest dey ever had."

The people that confided in Gus were bitter about Father Chacheré's first direct snubbing. Reporting to Father Long at the Parish Home, he was kept waiting for forty minutes. There was no room at the Parish Home for him as yet, Father Long told him; he was sorry but it was irregular for the Parish Home to have a colored occupant; of course Father Chacheré wouldn't mind staying with his parents in their little home. So Father Chacheré went to live along the railroad tracks.

The real shock came on the day of Father Chacheré's first mass. From all over the parish, afoot, or riding mules or horses, or in wagons, trucks, and cars, the people came to see and hear their son hold his first mass.

The young priest's happiness was sharply cut across. At the church entrance, Father Long was demanding from the crowd that all who wanted to witness Father Chacheré's first mass should have their quarters ready. In amazed anger, Father Chacheré asked that no more money be collected, that in the name of St. Francis, his poor friends might be allowed to worship with him at his first mass without the extra toll. He was ordered to go to the altar; the matter of admission was not his province. Those who had no quarters Father Long turned away.

Father Chacheré's first mass was held on August 6, 1939; he died at his home August 15, 1939. The doctors said his death resulted from a heart attack. The people say that his heart was broken.

Gus showed me a prayer for the dead young priest that Father Long printed. It was a folded square bordered with heavy black; on the front is a picture of Jesus and Mary standing over a dying man. "Precious in the sight of the Lord is the death of His saints," reads the legend, taken from the Psalms. On the second page there is a photograph of the dead Priest. He seems light brown in color; his hair is close-cropped and curly, his eyes are deep set and brooding; the face is that of a melancholic, meditative boy, seeming younger than his thirty years. On the third page is the prayer: "In your charity pray for the soul of Rev. Carmen Geo. Chacheré, S.V.D." The last page is given over to *De Profundis*, beginning, "Out of the depths I have cried to Thee, O Lord, Lord, hear my voice." The people say that Father Long sold the prayer at the funeral for ten cents a copy.

I saw a snapshot of Papa Chacheré holding a picture of his son. The old fellow is handsome, sturdily built, but stooping slightly. He holds the picture as something precious. He is staring at the camera; the expression on his face is quizzical and sad. The young Creole who took the picture has written on the back: "Papa Chacheré ain't so gay as he used to be. Sometime he just stand and look quiet-like."

In telling Gus about all this, in overcoming their usual caution and timidity concerning the Church, his kinfolk had stressed that there had been good priests as well. Gus wanted me to know this, too.

When Gus's brother and sister saw him take the plane for Washington at the New Orleans Airport, they were saddened. They may have seen the roaring plane carrying their brother back to the North, back to his job, as a long farewell. But I knew that he had been upset; that he would be back; and that he was geared now to work for his people at Frilot Cove.

As he said later, "This is a matter more important than anything I have ever undertaken, and I cannot afford to fail." He has put at my disposal a stout black notebook in which his voluminous correspondence about Frilot Cove and Opelousas is carefully filed.

His first efforts were on behalf of the schools. He prepared a digest of twenty-five pages of the findings on Negro schools in the *Louisiana Educational Survey* and sent copies to interested parties, or parties that should have been interested. He wrote letters to Governor Sam Jones and to the Director of Public Schools for Negroes in the state of Louisiana, enclosing copies of the digest. He received no reply from either one; it's possible, he said, that the communication to the governor never reached his desk. After a conference with Archbishop Joseph Francis Rummel of New Orleans, he wrote him a letter expressing the belief that "the officials of the St. Landry Parish have systematically and continually ignored the educational needs of the people of Frilot Cove, in spite of repeated requests and their status as tax payers." He mentioned an earlier Rosenwald project to erect a school at Frilot Cove, to which the parish officials would not agree. In the past year these officials had required the school to raise forty dollars for the U.S.O. and the Red Cross, yet the total value of the equipment of the school would not exceed fifteen dollars.

But his efforts seemed to run up against a stone wall. After about a year of correspondence and a conference in Baton Rouge he heard from the state superintendent of schools: "I wish to assure you again that I appreciated your calling. We sincerely hope to bring about improvements not only in the Frilot Cove community but throughout the state as regards the status of education for children of the colored race." A representative of philanthropical agencies interested in rural education in the South promised to look into the situation at Frilot Cove. Not used to the kid-glove technique in handling state departments of education, Gus informed the state superintendent of the proposed visit. The representative felt that this jeopardized his usefulness. "To make it appear that I was coming to Louisiana in order to investigate the Frilot Cove situation is putting the matter in a very different light and I am sure now that somebody else could be much more useful to you in this matter." In spite of rebuffs here, indifference there, the necessity for "diplomatic dealings" that a novice in interracial techniques cannot understand, Gus remains doggedly hopeful.

His second determination was to get a resident priest for Frilot Cove. Since the state was so slow to act, the church, as it had done before, might aid educationally as well as religiously. He wrote letters to the Rt. Rev. Monseigneur Fulton J. Sheen of Catholic University; Father Lafarge, noted for his interest in Negro welfare; Saint Mary Frances, Dean of Xavier University in New Orleans; and Father Hylan, his friend of long standing. Advised to go through the proper channels, he wrote a letter to Bishop Jeanmard, of Lafayette, in whose diocese Frilot Cove was located. He told the bishop of a boyhood memory of one winter night when his mother lay on her deathbed and his father rode on horseback fifteen miles to Opelousas to get a priest for the dying sacrament. Today, he wrote the bishop, the condition has not materially changed: "Coupled with poor and inadequate school facilities, it has resulted in stagnation among the people of the community and to a great extent aroused a sort of suspicion of their faith in the Catholic Church. I say this with no intention of alarming; but there is no vision, very little hope, and above all, no leadership."

The Bishop's first letter advises Gus not to be so exercised: "There has been a great improvement in the educational and religious facilities offered to the people of Frilot Cove." At the school, for instance, mass is said once on Saturday, twice a month on Sundays. The Bishop points out that the priest found fifty-two, not seventy-nine, families in the community and "At no time did these good people make any move to build a chapel for their own accommodation." The Bishop sees no grounds for Gus's complaints; the fact is, he writes, "the colored people within the limits of the ecclesiastical parish of Opelousas have more priests designated to look after them and are receiving more attention than the white people."

Gus showed himself ready to argue about the number of families, and stuck to his guns in general, making use of Pope Pius XI's condemnation of racism. His people "had but two supports, the good earth (of which they owned little) and more important, the deep wells of Catholic faith. . . . Small wonder that the toll of time has made their land sterile and parched considerably the wellsprings of Faith. . . . There is very little that anyone outside the community can tell me about these people, their faith, the educational facilities, and the mission of the Catholic Church in our community."

Bishop Jeanmard replied that Father Cooney, who has charge of the people of Frilot Cove, would gladly undertake the building of the chapel, if the money could be found for this purpose. Frilot Cove, he believes, can contribute very little, $200 at most: "The Sunday collections bring between three and five dollars a Sunday, scarcely enough to pay for gasoline and the wear and tear of the car." The Bishop and Father Cooney wanted to know how much money Gus could collect toward the building of the chapel: "I beg you to believe that we are doing the best we can with the limited means and the limited number of priests at our disposal. All in all, Frilot Cove is faring much better than most communities of its size in the diocese. I must try to be impartial and give priority to those whose need is greater, as long as conditions do not permit me to provide adequate care for all."

In a sympathetic letter to Gus, Father Lafarge also urged the financial difficulties of the missions. Nevertheless, Gus believed that he had found a solution. He was confident that he could raise sufficient funds for the construction and equipment of a chapel. But a resident priest must be secured. The amount of local support would increase if it were known that there would be a resident priest; he would himself be reluctant to undertake the responsibility of raising funds to build a church unless the Cove was assured of one. He deplored the shortage of priests, but since the war had closed many foreign mission activities, he knew that several communities of priests had turned their resources to missions of the South. He quoted Pope Pius XI: "Why should the native clergy be forbidden to cultivate their own portion of the Lord's vineyard, be forbidden to govern their own people. . . . For since the native priest, by birth, temper, sentiment, and interests, is in close touch with his own people, it is beyond all controversy how valuable he can be in instilling the Faith into the minds of the people." Fortunately, Gus wrote, he had found such a native, one of the few colored students preparing themselves for the priesthood.

To Gus, the logic was simple and clear. Frilot Cove stood in great need of a resident priest; a native of the section could perform the best service; and a native priest would be available. But the Church Fathers did not see it so simply, as Father Hylan wrote Gus. By this time, Gus realized that he had to step carefully.

Bishop Jeanmard informed Gus that various religious communities were assigned given territories, and that Canon Law does not permit him to introduce a priest of another community in their territory without their approval and consent. To ask this consent could be interpreted as a reflection on their zeal and devotion: "In view of this I feel that it would be a loss of time and effort on your part to try to secure the services of a priest of another religious community for the Cove." If permission could be obtained, however, from the Provincial of the Holy Ghost Fathers, who were in charge of Frilot Cove, the Bishop promised not to stand in the way.

After a conference with the Father Superior of the Most Holy Trinity where the young colored priest was completing his studies, Gus was convinced that Father Superior would assign the priest to Frilot Cove, if he was invited. Gus then applied to Father Collins, Provincial of the Holy Ghost Fathers, telling him of "the native son from our own people who will complete his studies during the coming year." He requested an interview. Gus was much struck by the congeniality and broad-minded democracy of Father Collins, who listened with interest and left no question with Gus that he would willingly cede the territory to another mission if assured that it would be in good hands. Father Collins visited Frilot Cove afterwards, most cordially, according to letters that Gus received from home.

And then the well-laid plans somehow went astray. Father O'Keefe, Vicar of the Most Holy Trinity, wrote that his investigation revealed that "the mission of Frilot Cove was canonically assigned to the Holy Ghost Fathers," as Gus had known all along. Father O'Keefe had not intended to give the impression that he would appoint a "native son" to the work of Frilot Cove: "We could not promise to appoint any particular priest to the work." Furthermore, it "would not be right for us to make any advances toward, or consider any proposal for, placing one of our priests there. . . . The record of the Holy Ghost Fathers, particularly in this instance . . . speaks for itself. I am sure that, in God's time, your prayerful hopes for Frilot Cove will be realized. In accordance with the above mentioned decision, I have notified the Provincial of the Holy Ghost Fathers, Father Collins, that we could not further consider the matter. While this may be a disappointment to you, I trust you will try to see it as the will of God. Our work always is to seek and submit ourselves to that will which is made manifest to us through the Authority He has constituted in His Church. Be assured that we shall keep prayerfully mindful of you."

But for all his strict Catholic upbringing, Gus does not see this decision as the will of God. To him it smacks more of an ecclesiastical runaround. He is still determined, as he wrote to Father Hylan, "to provide the Cove with a spiritual center—a powerhouse—something they have always esteemed but never possessed—a Chapel of their own with a resident pastor and father of his flock." They were good people, his people, and they had been too long deprived. "If it's the last thing I do," Gus said to me solemnly, "I'm going to straighten that thing out." Meanwhile, the war has scattered one generation to all corners: in Texas and California shipyards, in the Army and Navy training stations, and on board ships sailing to places like Reykjavik and Buna that were not in the old geographies. When these young ones come back to Frilot Cove, if they do, they will have much to say about what goes on there.

Finis . . .

Jim Crow Journal

This section aptly demonstrates that Brown wrote with a sense of the original version of the U.S. Constitution in mind. The framers of our most significant governing document were forced to a compromise between Northern and Southern states' moneyed interests. On the issue of taxation, they finally agreed that African American slaves would be counted as three-fifths of a person. Even though slavery was eventually outlawed and the "three-fifths compromise" overturned, the spirit of the law lived on, kept alive by the practices of Jim Crow. For Brown, this legacy of a fractionalized existence was particularly disturbing. He was especially troubled when the Carnegie-Myrdal Study emerged with its infamous thesis about "victimized Negroes" and Negro culture as little more than a pathological condition of the general American culture. Brown set about refuting all of these claims. His "Jim Crow Journal" was intended to present a number of "entries" that, when collected, would present an entirely different version of reality from the prevailing one in American thought. In providing a collective portrait of black life "behind the veil," Brown presents a much broader racial portrait—one demonstrating rather remarkably the strength, courage, philosophical wit, and wisdom of a people.

Although not schematically drawn, much of "Jim Crow Journal" falls in one of two categories: humor or horror. "V for Victory," for example, recounts Brown's chance meeting with two Northern white naval cadets. Ironically, as the conductor kicks the cadets out of the Jim Crow railroad car, one flashes Brown the "V" sign. "Jim Crow Snapshots" and "Fats" come closer to the humorous tradition found in Brown's poetry. "Jim Crow Snapshots" appears almost tomfoolery in plot. The train conductor is the only white person in an overpacked car of African Americans. Behind his back, two blacks, forced to stand because of the overcrowded conditions, speak in a humorous double entendre. The unsuspecting conductor's discomfort rises as the misunderstood comments increase. He departs not knowing that he's been artfully manipulated by the skillful orators. "Fats" is very nearly out of the American tall-tale tradition made famous by Mark Twain. The Jim Crow railroad car is transformed into a performative environment, and Brown becomes the "greenhorn" or outsider whom the master liar Fats plays on and educates. In each of these instances, the exercise of humor becomes the exercise of control over the Jim Crow situation.

Counterbalanced by the humor, though, is Jim Crow at its worse: its potential for horror. In "A Harvardian Goes South," Brown creates a fictional version of himself to relate an incident that no doubt actually occurred. As the Southern white gas attendant pours gasoline over the car and Brown's shoes, the reader is forced to contemplate the frightening display of power that held black life to be dirt cheap. Black life is also treated as tenuous in "Georgia Nymphs," in which Brown and his guide are forced to acknowledge that their lives hang in the balance between a group of flirtatious white girls and a group of suspicious white men. In 1944, a black man expressing the smallest hint of interest in white women was, of course, sufficient cause for a lynching in this backwoods Alabama town. At the same time, any hint of reprisal at the jostling both experienced as they descended the stairs from observing night court would have provided enough incentive for their lynching, too. The feeling of powerlessness Brown re-creates here is matched only by the emotional intensity expressed so poignantly in his masterful poem "Old Lem."

In this setting, though, African American love does exist. Originally titled "Romance in the Dark," "Words on a Bus" is a poignant story of flirtation and courtship. "Separate but Equal" points to the efforts of black railroad workers to unionize and therefore improve their working conditions. Published originally as a short story, "And/Or" is a piece of reportage intended to highlight the tenacity of one man's efforts to register to vote. The first selection presented here, and one of the most hopeful pieces in this collection, is "On the Government," which concludes its discussion of Greene County in Georgia with "restoring the land, restoring the people." It affirms how the federal government, through its Farm Security Administration, can intervene in and improve the lot of poor black farmers, whose lives have been wracked by boll weevils, soil erosion, and poor farming techniques.

ON THE GOVERNMENT

When Eugene Talmadge campaigned in Greensboro, Georgia, his stock assault on the Rosenwald Fund was peculiarly ironic. Other sections of the state had profited from Rosenwald funds in education, but Greene County had an added debt. A Rosenwald fellowship enabled Arthur Raper to complete *Preface to Peasantry,* a thorough study of the county's possibilities and needs. This book attracted the attention of Will W. Alexander, a director of the Rosenwald Fund, and led to his interest in Greene County as Administrator of the Farm Security Administration. Because of this interest, the county has been "on the government" for four years, and all of the demagoguery in the world cannot destroy the facts of its progress.

Arthur Raper has written three works on Greene County, his doctor's thesis (1931), *Preface to Peasantry* (1936), and *Tenants of the Almighty* (1943) which traces the county's social history. Greene County was once fertile and prosperous, but concentrating on cotton after the Civil War, it slowly declined in fertility and wealth. Dairy farming in the early years of this century brought back something of prosperity, but another war, bringing in forty-cent cotton, returned the county to cotton farming and trouble.

Tenants of the Almighty ran weekly in the Greensboro *Herald-Journal* as *Greene's Going Great,* a careful, frank but sympathetic account that seemed to me to be unusual in Southern journalism. Raper's prose is familiar, close to the language of the region, studded with anecdotes. Prosperity meant: "Trace chains and mule collars, axes and hoes, bull tongue plows and scooters, overalls and brogans, meal and molasses, fatback and salmon, moved off the shelves faster than ever before. There were more sales for bedsteads and split bottom chairs, for guitars and phonographs, and for moonshine liquor, too. . . . Sally, those folks at Greensboro have convinced me I'm a rich man. Let's have fried chicken everyday." But though the boll weevil came to Greene a few years later than to neighboring counties, the land still wasn't "weevil proof." A shower was all right, but two or three cloudy days would mean additional young cotton squares on the ground. The cotton bubble burst. The small farmers' hopes of becoming owners were knocked out; it would not be easy for newspapers or a government agency to restore them. Thousands lost their farms; the chief export of the county was its people, and often the better educated of the people. Bermuda grass, crab grass, and weeds took the fields first. Then came the waving broom sedge. And then through the matted sedge came a million, million little pines, silent and green. The best soil washed away. Before the Civil War, one observer, standing on the Oconee bridge when the river was in flood, said, "See there goes Greene County under the bridge." "Yes," was the answer, "and it's too thick to drink and too thin to plow!"

The loan companies took thousands of the barren acres. About one-eighth of the county's acreage was forfeited for taxes or to creditors. Efforts were made to stem the tide of ruin. Goobers were introduced as a substitute crop, but soon that attempt failed. Marketing the thousands of rabbits shot and trapped in the broom sedge and pines brought in some money, and then a blight killed the rabbits as the weevil had killed the cotton. Sawmilling flourished briefly until a half century's timber growth was gone. The little pines kept growing. Distilling of bootleg liquor became big business and then government raids broke that up. An article on Greene County in *Collier's* called "Devil in de Cotton" was resented locally for "parading our poverty" and condemned by the grand jury as "scurrilous, unwarranted and unnecessary." But there was no hiding the collapse of cotton farming in this county.

One of the assistants to the farm management supervisor is a Negro, James Gay. He is a graduate of Georgia State College and for several years has been demonstrating and teaching scientific farming. He was solid, chunky, built like a football guard or tackle; he didn't talk much, but what he said was bluntly to the point. He was raised in this section, but he told me he knew a mean cracker when he saw one: "But nobody has known me to cut any corners yet."

Though busy (it was his afternoon for candling eggs), he was willing to drive me around to see some of his members of the project. All were not doing equally well, and he selected good, indifferent and bad samples. He talked to the people easily, familiarly, and they responded in kind. At the first home the four women folks were apologetic about the way they looked. But they were canning, and their pride in the gaily colored jars overcame their dismay at being mussed and sweaty. A few words of praise emboldened one of the sisters, who told us how hot it was working over that stove. Of course they all wanted to fill their quota: "But you know, Mr. Gay, I ain't had no vacation since Lawd knows when."

Gay told me as we drove off how strict FSA had to be for people unaccustomed to steady, incessant working. Some of the folks just would not keep up even with the minimum requirements, and after reasonable trials had to be dropped. Most, however, measured up well. In one house, a woman showed us happily a dresser she had just bought, with a large mirror. "You know how I bought that, Mr. Gay?" she asked, timidly.

"Yes," he said. "I'll bet you bought it with that money you made selling sour cream."

"I sho' did." She was tickled, she had profited by Gay's advice that selling sour cream was one way to provide the little extra money that they needed for the things that spelled home. He told her now to scrape the old flecked mirror with a razor blade to make it seem new again.

Gay pointed out to me instances of foresight, saving, ingenuity: pieced together chicken houses and hog pens; carefully designed garden plots; porches decorated with all sorts of pots, holding flowers.

"As soon as they get a feeling of belonging," he said, "they start fixing up. It's being on their own. They do things they never would think of doing, living on someone else's place, just cropping for someone else."

They dread having to move. One woman whose loving care was evident in her front yard, with two struggling peach trees and flower beds, her spotless quilts, her kitchen so clean it seemed polished, was unreasonably worried about having to move. "Don't let 'em move me away from here, Mr. Gay," she said. "I been drinking out of that spring for nigh onto thirty years."

The pressure cooker is called the "precious" cooker here with good reason. It is perhaps the best loved of the innovations, symbolic of the new life. Canned goods were strange to these people before they were urged to buy the new contraptions. They once put up little of anything, now they put up everything possible. Gay told me that the quota was between eighty-five and a hundred jars for each member of the household. At one home, the buxom mother of a brood of ten had put up eight hundred and fifty jars, and was working toward a goal of a thousand. Some of the men complain good naturedly that the jars are running them out of the houses, but they know how in the lean months of winter and early spring the food in the jars will stick to their ribs. A few of the men are expert themselves at canning. The pressure cooker, for all of its highly scientific action, works simply, and is just about foolproof. There have been few accidents; a steam whistle blows the warning when the pressure rises too high, and though the young ones may enjoy the whistling, they know the danger of the exploding steam and obey instructions with care.

The glass jars, filled with green snap-beans, butter-beans, cabbage, okra, peas, turnip greens, green-yellow succotash, yellow corn and squash, golden Georgia yams, brown slabs of veal and beef, and red tomatoes, are admired not only as a store of food, but also for their gay decoration of the bare shelves and walls. They are arranged with an eye to color symmetry. I was surprised to see the slabs of meat, even more so to see the jars labeled Irish Potatos. One favorite was the colorful vegetable stock for soup consisting of corn, peas, lima beans, string beans, okra, and tomatoes.

There is keen rivalry in filling or surpassing the quota. One good housewife hid half of her filled jars under the hay in the barn, out of sight of her neighbors, until the final day of reckoning. She was Miss Tortoise outsmarting all the Miss

Rabbits. In 1941, the champion canning family was that of Dock Miller, a Negro, whose record was 1,202 quarts. Negro families averaged 416 quarts; white families averaged 345.

At first, Gay told me, the canning was done because the supervisors urged it, not for eating. Canned goods weren't exactly to the taste of people whose food habits, enforced by need, were hard to change. For instance, these people, born and bred in the county, had to learn to eat spinach. Some had never, and most had seldom drunk any sweet milk. Milk was taken to mean buttermilk, which some of them got for churning at the landlord's home. But now the diet was picking up: squash, beans, corn, vegetable soup, beef, veal and pork, butter and eggs, and chicken.

At least one cow, some pigs and a brood sow were provided at the beginning for each family. Wheat is raised for flour; many of the farmers haven't bought a sack of flour since "going on the government." A dozen laying hens were also provided at first. Then baby chicks were brought in by the thousands, and kerosene lamp brooders were built in the vocational shops of the schools. The chickens introduced problems. There was resentment when the supervisors sent trucks for the cockerels in order to apply some money toward settling the purchase loan. Loan or no loan, chickens had been part of the family, sort of, before. One woman said: "I asked 'em not to give me them chickens 'cause I knew I'd get crazy about 'em. But they said they was mine. . . . Now they tell me to cotch up all my roosters 'cause a truck's a-comin' for 'em. If they come here after my roosters, I'll give 'em the pullets and the brooder, too. I don't want none of 'em."

Another problem arose from the conflict in the old and new ways in the raising of chickens. The brooder chickens, turned out to forage, did not know what it was all about and merely ran around after people hoping to be fed something to eat. Hen-raised chickens scratched for themselves. One woman said, "I ain't as proud of these brooder chickens as I am of my own. They didn't have no mother to teach 'em to scratch, and they ain't got as much sense." They were scorned as "government chickens"—there had to be some way of telling them from real chickens. But the moral of the story is not of the Horatio Alger variety: those "real" chickens that scratched for themselves laid only a few eggs, while the brooder-raised, mash-fed chickens laid eggs throughout the year.

Gay was all for the new scientific farming, but he taught indirectly. He asked one of his best managers, "Dog days? Do *you* believe in dog days?" When the woman murmured defensively, "Well, all the old folks say so," he showed surprise and pointed out how already the woman had improved on the ways of the old folks. He showed by doing as well as teaching; it was the only way to allay suspicion of the book farmer, he said. In the evening, after his duties at headquarters and his supervising, he worked in his own thriving truck garden. I watched him feed his pure-bred hogs and chickens; he discussed the various mashes and prepared foods with learning and affectionate respect. He talked to me about the Log Cabin Community in nearby Hancock County, originated by Zack, Benjamin, and Moses Hubert, and named the Camilla-Zack Country Life Center after their parents. Here on holdings of about 15,000 acres, seventy-five Negro families are successfully farming, and over half own their farms of from 50 to 150 acres. Gay's wife was then teaching at the Log Cabin Summer School. I ought to see that place. By all means, he said. He gave high praise to Tom Roberts, one of his teachers at Georgia State, now connected with the Agricultural Department in Washington. Roberts had been a regular fellow as well as a thorough teacher, relishing a good joke but quite able to lash out at sluggards and shame them into studying, an enthusiast for improved farming who had opened a new world to the Georgia boys who had come to college disliking the drudgery and hopelessness that the farm had meant to them.

He drove his dusty and worn car expertly over the winding, hilly roads. His talk showed me that his immediate trust for these people was in the project. It was a long way from perfect, but it was working. He praised the people. No trouble, he said, no drinking, no fighting. The girls did have babies early, he admitted; that was about all the sinning that went on. A few of the men were sorry and shiftless; one man took every excuse to ride to town, to get a Coke, to stand around talking, leaving his wife and the large family of young ones to tend the garden. But the churches and the school were giving good community service.

The next day Arthur Raper drove me over the county. He was full of the anecdotes and information that he was packing tightly in his new book. And he talked with the good, pungent, homespun quality of his prose. As a truck, hauling logs, careened madly toward us on a narrow road, he told me of the coming of the sawmills to the county. They had come in answer to the demand for cash, but they left the county poorer. In less than ten years the timber growth of half a century had been used up. There were still a few "coffee-pot" mills running and the truck that had just gone along hell-bent-for-destruction was serving one of those. There were plenty of pines left, but most of them were the "boll weevil pines, hardly big enough to saw." The pines, he told me, came by the millions: "They were not chosen, but were among Earth's greatest commoners."

Raper grew eloquent about the tragedy of the land. The "old" fields, once cotton acreage, had been abandoned to Bermuda and crab grass, the seedling pines, and the waving broom sedge, which was the county's greatest crop. Setting fire to the sedge and underbrush had been the farmer's improvident way out. To clear up a small plot, he often did not seem to bother whether he set the countryside afire or not. We passed several chimneys where cabins had once been that told the story. Careless and ignorant tilling of the soil had caused wide-spread erosion; on the red lands and the white, galls in the hills had deepened into gullies. He gave me a fine lecture on the value of proper terracing; he positively beamed as we passed fields that showed that the farmers had learned the art. Erosion had also been fought by the introduction of legumes such as lespedeza, and of the huge leaved kudzu, looking so much like earthbound grape vines. I told him of some farmers who had feared kudzu; even if it held the soil, it was dangerous to buildings on which it got its tenacious grip. It would knock a house down like lightning, once you let it get on, they had told me. Raper laughed. It would pull a house down, he admitted, but you can keep it off of houses. The main thing is that kudzu will actually go across a gully and stop it.

Raper was soberly enthusiastic about the success of the unified farm program. There had been and still was local hostility. The clients of the rehabilitation program were first called "Rehabs" and then "Arabs," and some of the derision has stuck. Many of the better off people of the county complain about the difficulty of getting wage hands and domestics now, and blame WPA and FSA for spoiling the labor supply. Some of the "government farmers" grumble at the new-fangled budgeting, planning, paying bills, and book-farming. Some just don't understand; one farmer likening himself to "a blind dog in a meat house about this program." Only twelve families, eight white and four colored, are Tenant-Purchase families, buying their homes and land over a forty-year period. The others are on an advance-rent basis; the landlord signing over a part of his rent for a five- to seven-year period. This amount is applied to improvements. That explained why, instead of seeing new houses, rural complements of urban housing projects, I saw so many old houses being used. But these had been renovated into sturdiness and comfort. Over half a million dollars have been loaned to FSA families in the county, but it had to go a long way in many directions. It is not such a huge sum when one realizes "how far back on the hog" so many of these families, white and Negro, had been.

It seemed to me to be a first-rate investment when I heard Raper talk of the improvements in crops, stock, soil, housing, diet, health, and education (for adults as well as children), of the basic human needs met by the program. Now these Arabs do not need to be wanderers and outcasts; they belong to something and something belongs to them.

One of Raper's most respected friends in the county, a sort of Exhibit A of the "good husbandman" is an independent Negro farmer named Jim Brown. He has made it on his own. Jim met us in his clean-swept front yard, before a comfortable white-washed home. There was a huge wisteria vine there, gnarled and twisted, the strong withes bound together forming a sort of summer house. Its thick roof of vines and leaves was not to be pierced by even the sun of Georgia. "That vine is older than you is," Jim told me truthfully. It was nearly a half a century old. Here Jim rested after his dinner, in the heat of the day. He was proud of his farm of one hundred and thirty odd acres. He even now owned two acres of an orange grove in Florida. It had meant work to get this land and keep it. "I worked hard as a hired hand with nobody driving me." He had raised a fine crop of children, too, fourteen of them, and sixty-six grandchildren. He had taught them to have manners, else there was whipping in the house. And he had taught them farming.

"The white folks living over there where that chimney is said to me, 'Jim Brown, you'll perish on that o' land.' " That had been long years ago. Now there was nothing over there but a chimney in a waste of brambles and broom sedge, scrub pines, and sweet gums. He had stuck it out here.

Raper pointed out to me that the huge bell on a tall pole, a relic of the old plantation of slavery days, was symbolic to Negro owners. They all seemed to want one. There was no need of it now, however, to call Jim's sons in from the fields. Jim's handsome reddish-brown face saddened when he told us that of thirteen of his children, whom he had raised on the place, only one remained to help him farm and hold these one hundred and thirty acres. Most of the boys were on "public works." "There is just nothing to hold them to the farm," Raper said briefly. "They want to go to town, to see a moving picture, to see young people, to get about the world. It is so all over the country."

Jim showed us proudly over his fields. He was a good farmer, one could see that. His cattle and mules were sleek and well kept. The manure seemed a foot deep in the barnyard; Jim certainly was not going to need much of the factory-made stuff.

Jim mentioned the ease with which he got credit at the banks in Greensboro. His dealings with the banks stretched back even before the days when they "went dead" in the depression. He had many white friends. They had even now told him that if he wanted to, they would let him vote. But he didn't vote. "Tell us why not," Raper asked. The old man was disturbed; he finally said, "You know why. You can tell me."

His sons might have deserted what he had planned and near about slaved for, but as he stood there, ruddy and erect for all of his years, I realized that he was far from beaten. There was meat in the smokehouse, flour in the bin, chickens and turkeys running around the yard, and fields of fertility unusual in his section. And after a hot morning's work, he could sit beneath the cool shade of the wisteria vine, dreaming perhaps. Still I knew that he would like to toll the big plantation bell, and see his tall sons heading toward the house.

"I'm sho' glad you all come by to see me," he said. I was glad myself.

On the roads I had seen occasionally one of those signs reading, "You May Meet God Around the Next Curve" and "God Is Your Only Help." Raper told me how many of the people on the project linked God with the Government: "I don't know what would have come of us by now if it hadn't been for God and the Government." Proof of this feeling came from the last home we visited, that of Louisiana Thomas. Mrs. Thomas is something of a character on the project; a hard working wife and mother who writes poetry in her few off hours. Raper took the title of his last book, *Tenants of the Almighty,* from one of her poems.

She was out when we called upon her; she was doing some washing for a neighboring white farmer. Her home was a typical blue and white old house, set up on slabs of some kind of sandstone. Before the house there were broadly sweeping fields of corn and sorghum cane, and lines of trees. It was a good vista for a poet. Far off we saw a woman coming toward us with a shock of fodder under her arm. We hoped it was Louisiana, but it wasn't. It was a younger girl, black and handsome. Josh stared at us as we stood there talking with Mr. Thomas. He didn't know when Louisiana was coming back. He took us through the house; two of the beds were old fashioned, one bedroom suite was modern. On this bed there was a black cat doll with beaded eyes glaring. In the fireplace there was a Black Sambo game for children. On the unsealed walls were several pictures, one by James Montgomery Flagg, with a football player on whose jersey was a huge "P," talking to wasp-waisted, long skirted belles carrying Princeton pennants; two of the others were pictures of Jesus. Mr. Thomas was proud of his home; they had bought the new furniture since going on the government.

Raper showed me several of the poems that Louisiana Thomas had written. One of them had these lines:

> Uncle Sam is my shepherd
> And I shall not want
> He don't make me lie down in green pastures
> He lead me down to the tin warehouse
> And give me a cotton mattress.
> He restoreth my cow and pigs
> And chickens and some eggs . . .
>
> Yea though I walk through the valley
> And shadow of death to stay here
> But as long as Uncle Sam hold everything
> No evil will I fear.

And a second tells that "a brighter day has dawned." It closes:

> *The houses was falling down*
> *And barns had long since gone*
> *Now stands in its place*
> *A beautiful little white home.*
>
> *We are tenants of the Almighty*
> *Entrusted with a portion of his earth*
> *To dress and keep*
> *And pass on to the next generation*
> *When evening comes and we must fall asleep.*

Riding back to Greensboro, Raper told, out of his deep knowledge of these people, of his great hopes for them, for the South, and for America. Restoring the land, restoring the people. From slaves and sharecroppers to self-respecting, independent human beings. "Straws in the wind," he said briefly. "Yes," I said. I found myself hoping that the wind would come up soon. And strong.

➤➤ V FOR VICTORY ◄◄

The first coach of the Dixie Flyer is divided into three parts: a long Jim Crow section; a cubbyhole which is the Jim Crow smoker, consisting of two seats that face each other on each side of the aisle; and a long section for whites.

The Dixie Flyer was hurtling through central Georgia. It was late at night, and alone in the smoker, I had snatched a doze when their voices woke me. They were in the khaki of naval cadets. I could tell from their accent that they were from the North.

They were criticizing the famed hospitality of the South. They had wanted to sit together, but nobody in the coach behind would move to another seat. A couple of fellows had refused a direct request even though they would have to sit beside a stranger in any case. Maybe the passengers detected that Yankee twang. So the cadets had come up to the Jim Crow smoker. One was dark-haired and short, looking a bit Jewish. The other was a tall blonde. As they scoffed at the local folkways, I ventured my question, "Where are you fellows from?" New York and Newark, they told me. I was just through an irritating experience at the Atlanta bus station and was hot and dog-tired. "God's country," I said.

"Where are you from?" the blonde asked.

"Washington."

The blonde told me that he had attended George Washington University. He answered my question, yes, he knew where Paul Pearlman's was all right; he bought all of his books there.

The chap from Newark wanted to know what I was doing down in the South. They were frankly curious. When I told them I was a teacher, they pretended deference, but I disarmed them by joking about my occupational questionnaire. There wasn't a solitary service listed, I told them, where I could be useful in the war effort. We got quite friendly. They were proud of their branch of service and their chance to fly. They talked a while of the war, and then they got on the race question. I think I started it by telling them, "They're not going to let you ride in here long. The conductor has already moved some fellows out."

"They're not going to move us out," the fellow from Newark said.

"Wait and see," I said.

They became explosive about race prejudice. George Washington wanted to be fair, after Newark had bitterly denounced the injustice. George Washington had been looking around. Apologetically he said that Southern Negroes seemed shiftless to him; they wouldn't take advantage of schools and things.

I told him a little of the lack of chance and incentive. They were unwilling to believe some of the facts I dished out about the schools. They said that I seemed to know a lot about those things; I told them I was working on a book. George Washington disclaimed prejudice. There was a fine colored couple working for his parents in New York, he said, but the Southern Negro did seem shiftless to him.

Newark admitted that the North wasn't much better for Negroes. To his knowledge there weren't many job opportunities: "But at least they recognize the Negro as a man, and don't herd them off."

He told me of a friend and schoolmate of his in Newark, a good athlete and piano player. He couldn't think of his name right then, but he had remembered that this friend got his license to fly before he did. I told him that I probably knew the fellow. "It must be Jimmy Plinton," I said.

"That's the guy!" he burst out, and together we said, "It's a hell of a small world, isn't it?"

Jimmy Plinton was his good friend. When had I seen him? I told him I had met him only recently at Yates and Milton's Drugstore, a sort of crossroads in Atlanta like Seventh Avenue and 135th Street in New York.

We talked of the Tuskegee Flying School where Plinton was stationed. They were deploring with me the scant opportunity of Negroes to learn to fly when the conductor entered.

"You fellows will have to move," the conductor said.

"What for?" Newark spoke up quickly.

"This here is the colored coach."

"We're satisfied," said blonde George Washington.

"Don't make any difference whether you're satisfied or not. You'll have to move. Colored and white can't ride together down here."

Newark burst out, "I think it's the most narrow-minded thing in the world the way you people down here kick Negroes around. Here we're in a war for democracy—"

The conductor's face turned red, but he spoke slowly, and quietly, "It's the law down here."

The New Yorker said, "We're not going to move."

"Oh, yes, you are," the conductor said. "It's the law in Georgia."

Surprisingly the New Yorker seemed to think his next words carried weight: "You can't move me; I'm a citizen of New York."

"Well, you're in Georgia now," the conductor drawled. That was unanswerable, but they continued arguing.

Finally the conductor, breathing heavily, his face flushed to his white hair, pleaded, "Listen fellows. I didn't make the law. I just have to enforce it. And the law says that colored and whites just can't ride in the same coach."

The cadets finally surrendered. They swung through the door grumbling, but hardly had the conductor got to the door when I heard a noise and they were back. They had come back, they said, to tell me good-bye. Each held out his hand. The conductor looked uncomfortable as we shook hands.

They scribbled their names on an old envelope, with the address of their flying field in Florida. Then they wished me good-bye and good luck. "Send us a copy of your book when it comes out," George Washington said. "We'd sure like to see it," Newark held up his fingers in a "V" salute as he turned to the white section of the coach. The conductor stood by helplessly. He looked as if he thought something should be done about such carryings on: "*A Negro.*"

➤ JIM CROW SNAPSHOTS ◄

The conductor had ordered all the Negroes who were deadheading to go on up to the head car. Still the coach was packed and jammed when the trio got on at Waxhaw. It was Sunday night and they were chirped up by liquor and their togs. They looked all around the coach, and then pointedly at the conductor who was taking up two seats with his tin box, bag, papers, and tickets.

"Well," sighed one dolefully, "I suppose we'll have to sit on the floor."

"I didn't pay my fare to sit on no floor," said another.

The first one got a seat by squeezing in beside an ample woman who lifted her child to her lap. His luck pleased him and he started agitating, "You'll grow tall standin'. Little man like you is."

The big fellow looked hard at the back of the conductor's head. The conductor was busy rustling papers, obviously getting ready to check out at Monroe.

"Ain't you done yit?"

The conductor turned around, but the big fellow was studying the water cooler.

"Wanna drink of water?" he asked the third fellow.

"Yes, I'll just take a sit," the other answered. "Kyah, kyah."

"Only sit you'll get on this train."

"Oh, no, let me pour hit for you," the big one said with mock courtesy. "You gets service on this train. I hopes you are enjoying your ride."

The third fellow took careful aim and threw his paper cup, only half emptied, on the already sloppy floor.

"I done paid my fare. And I done stood up ten miles."

"Oh, don't leave yit. Get every bit of your trip. You got a little mo' ways to stand."

The conductor rose, and stooped over to pick up his papers. The third fellow went into swift pantomime. Head, shoulders, arms all made the pose of a football player about to punt. It wasn't lost on the rest of the coach. Some, including the agitator, laughed aloud.

The conductor looked around sharply, and saw only bland innocence. Red-faced, he grabbed his tin box and was gone. As he went out the door, one fellow tiptoed down the aisle, stalking him like an Indian.

The big fellow sat down hard, banging his feet in the seat opposite.

The third fellow came back. "Pardon me, but do passengers sit in this *here* seat?"

"I'll think about it."

"You will like hell."

The fellow sat down with ceremony.

⤞ A HARVARDIAN GOES SOUTH ⤝

He could not help speaking with the Back Bay Accent. He had been bred in Boston and educated at Harvard, majoring in the classics. Inevitably, of course, in order to get a job teaching he had been forced to come South. He was a good-looking, brown-skin fellow, slight of frame and rather aristocratic—Harvard-Yardish—in bearing.

So the odds were strictly against him when he stated to the gas-attendant that he had been short-changed fifteen cents. A Yankee was bad enough, but a brownskin Yankee was hated at compound interest.

The gas man, over his first shock, said to a loafing kid, "Hand me my black-jack." Then waving the ugly weapon, he said, "You get out of that car. Now unlock your gas tank." The loaded blackjack hovered, ready.

The gas tank was full. The attendant turned on the stream of gas, played it over the gas tank, over the rear of the fenders, over the spare. Some few drops struck the Bostonian's well shined collegiate shoes. When the figures on the meter read fifteen cents the hose was turned off.

"Now, nigger, you get in that car and get the hell away from here. The next time you say anything like that to a white man you're liable to get killed. Now get!"

Down the road, one of the fellows in the car said, "Prof, I sure believe in prayer. I was praying to God that if only he would keep you from saying another word to that cracker. And praise God you didn't."

⇥ SEPARATE BUT EQUAL ⇤

I had heard some low-pitched talk between him and the conductor, and then he came over to me. "Could I sit here with you?" he asked.

"Sure," I said. "Help yourself." I slipped my briefcase to the floor.

He was a meek looking fellow, probably in his sixties. As he sat beside me, a man and a woman, loaded with suitcases, got in his vacant seat.

"Did you hear what the conductor said to me?" He sounded aggrieved. I told him no. "Well, he came and said, 'I told you to move before.' I said he did not tell me to move. 'I told you to git up,' he said. 'You didn't,' I said. 'You must have meant to tell me.' 'Well, I'm telling you now. You move over there by that man (meaning you) and let these people have this seat. That man (meaning you) ain't got no right to all that room.' "

"I didn't know," I said. "I don't want more than my share of room."

"Don't you bother. Look back there in the coach. See that long seat back there? Ain't nobody in it. A body could lie down on it if he wanted to. That's seven seats a person could sit down in. But he did not tell me to move. This crowded train has just got him excited.

"The more we keep silent-mouthed," the old man confided to me, "the further back they put us." He was riding on a pass, he explained, deadheading. But that wasn't no reason why he had to be put upon. He had been railroading over thirty years. He was an officer in his local of train porters. As soon as he got up in his union, they had been picking at him.

"Looks like they think all we ought to say is 'Yessir, yessir.' All they can say is 'Do as I say, do as I say.' My blood is in the Army; I got a son fighting the Japs in the Pacific. I got the same right to talk as anybody else.

"Besides taking care of our coach, we got to do everything the conductor can think of. Take for an instance my last trip. I had to move all the conductor's stuff: a crate of eggs, his bags, and his big tin box. This porter today gotta take the conductor's grip around to the conductor's room when he gets to Salisbury, before he is considered off duty. Seems like they think that's in the trade. All we get is thank you, if that. But our beholden duty is to keep these coaches clean and make these people as comfortable as they can be.

"I been railroading a long number of years. I'm a big man in our union. I can give you a lot of information." Except for my briefcase I saw no reason why he thought I was seeking information.

"I see you got a scratch pad there. Let me have it." I took a notebook out of the brief case. He thanked me, and then painstakingly, mysteriously, with half glances over his shoulder, he wrote out for me the following:

I wishes that your would. report anniething you see. I thing here is
a smoker and the ant a thing to spit in—This is a though train to
Washington.DC—It should be cuismedo in the colored Smoker. there
is just one. Of caus we are In war & we are trying to win it and we
must win it and Just think from Washington to Atlanta.Ga. and from
ATLANTA to Washington, D. C. that ever Passenger get on your train
would spit on the floor. In the Smoker. It would be Dangers for Annie
one to go In the Smoker. Thank if you would look in to this at once for
my Race.

Address to Mr. _____ Vice President
Southern R. R. Co. Washington, D.C.

I could not help looking at the floor. It was splashed with water; here and there
were orange peels, apple cores, cigarette butts, and paper. At my feet were the
ashes where I had knocked my pipe out a couple of times.

"You see?" the old man said triumphantly.

⤞ FATS ⤝

The two fellows in the box of a smoker on the Georgia Central Railroad looked up when I came in, glancing distrustfully at my brief-case, and stopped talking. But after I had passed the time of day with them, with a word or two about the weather and the train, they opened up. One tall, fairly well-dressed chap went on with his complaining: "They tell me the Army is like a convict camp. Course I ain't never been on no chain-gang, so I wouldn't know. I wanted to be a Pullman Porter, now Sam is calling. I don't mind going, but I don't want it to be like no convict camp. One thing sure, if I ever get to be a free man again, I'll never live in the South anymore."

Several railroad workers got on at a flag-stop on the edge of Atlanta. They were too many for the box which had only two long benches facing each other, divided by arms into four seats each. Two of them tried to squeeze in one of the seats, with a lot of laughter. It was Saturday; the weekend off had already started; some were already feeling their liquor. They were riding a fellow they called Scrapper, who wasn't taking it so well.

Scrapper and his buddy, Blackie, according to the way I pieced out the story, had been drunk and noisy on a bus. The driver had put Blackie out of the bus and started off, leaving him there raising hell and threatening. Scrapper suddenly went up to the bus driver and asked him, "Please, suh, can I get off this bus?" The driver had said, "Okey dokey," and opened the door. But the bus hadn't come to a full stop, and Scrapper fell off the bus. His buddy's gun he was carrying to him, to back his big words, fell out of his pocket. Then Scrapper tried to calm his buddy down and lead him away, but "you know can't no drunk man lead no drunk." So the law had come up and both Scrapper and Blackie had to serve time for disturbing the peace and carrying concealed weapons.

Scrapper insisted that it wasn't no such lie. His tormentor, unafraid of the growl in his voice, kept asking him, "Do you mean to sit there and tell me that the law didn't take you and Blackie up for all that hell-raising?"

Scrapper didn't want to talk about it. "Well, that's the way I heard it," said his tormentor, as persistent as a horsefly.

It was a rough crowd, relishing the "dozens." They were curious about me. I had a sort of buffer next to me, a man whom I had given a pipeful of tobacco and a light for his pipe. I knew, however, that I was being watched, and when two fellows after some slipping talk about the women, grabbed their knives, clicked the switch-blades out in a flash, and rushed together, I knew they were putting on a show for me. I just laughed and they laughed too, and sat down again.

"Man, I coulda cut you three times all that time you took to get that knife out."

"That thing you got there ain't no knife." Several showed off their oiled switch-blades, and praised their fine points. I was properly curious, and impressed.

"Oh my Gawd," yelled one of them, "here's Fats." My buffer friend said to me, "He's the biggest liar in the state of Georgia."

"In the whole United States," said another.

Fats beamed. He was pushing two hundred fifty pounds, I reckoned. He was dressed in a trainman's cap and khaki; his shirt was soaked with sweat. He had a pleasant boyish face. "Anybody believes that, stand on his head," was his entering speech.

"Man here it starts." They wanted to hear the old stories, and by nodding, called his attention to me, the stranger, to start him off. Fats waved one of the younger laborers off the seat and sank his bulk down heavily. How his hindparts got in that confined space was a wonder.

Fats didn't need much prodding to tell his lies. Naturally I couldn't use a notebook, so a good part of them escaped me. But I remember his boasting of a hog that he raised that was "so fat it couldn't stand in this here smoker. It would bust the sides out. If you wanted to move him, you'd have to back him out." Then he once had a bull with an enormous whang; as he told the bull's exploits, the compartment roared with laughter, and the conductor who was walking by, looked in. Fats waved to him familiarly.

A farmer living near him had a famous breeded cow, a beautiful cow. Her barn had white walls and white floors. She was tended by white men only, no colored, and these white men all had to wear white suits and white shoes. Her calves were delivered in a hospital, by a doctor, a whole lot more service than a whole lot of people got, whether colored or white. Thousands of pounds of butter a season. Milk her three times a day. My gawd what a beautiful thing she was, after they had curried her down and washed her clean. "Someday I'd like to live in a house as clean as that cow's barn," Fats sighed.

"I'd like to live in that barn right now," suggested a hearer.

Fats told a story about an accident, which comes jumbled from the memory. One night he drove his Ford into a long pole extending from an Army truck: "Six inches lower, it would have killed everybody in the front seat; a little bit more, everybody in back. I got out to see the damages, and saw all those soldiers. I thought it was the law. They were all around me asking if I was hurt. I told them of course not; I wasn't scratched. They turned me loose. Man, I lit a rage, I mean I *flew*. I woke up in the Savannah Hospital. They said they didn't see how I lived. That pole had caved in my skull."

One of his hearers roared, "If I had a belt I'd hit you good for telling that big lie. You old lying scoundrel!"

Fats grimaced, "The truth is cowed. A man come in telling you God's truth and you say it's a lie. But you know good and well I'm a man of truth."

Fats hasn't missed a day on the railroad for three years. He has twelve children: "I got so many behind me a man have to keep at it. Ain't that right, friend?" He boasted, though, that everybody on the job works harder than he does.

He told of a brotherly meeting at church. Everybody had to give testimony, to get up and express themselves. Fats got up and said to the preacher, "You asking us for back dues. You say you want $7.50. And here I am without a pair of drawers to back into. And all my children without a sign of drawers."

The people at the church cheered him on, as did our crowd in the smoker. Fats said the preacher got mad and told the whole congregation to go to hell.

Fats went on, "I got so many children I don't know when they're all in at night. I just tell my wife to cook for them as long as they keep coming. I ain't sure how many children I got. They was twelve when I left home this morning. There's supposed to be a new one in tonight, maybe two, I don't know. I saw the sack wiggling, but I cain't tell."

The butcher came in with fruit. Fats looked at the deep red plums: "Those plums shore look purty. Sure would taste good this hot day."

They were fifteen cents for an envelope of two. I bought ten plums and passed them around. Everybody got one. The one that was left over I gave to Fats, for being the best liar in the state of Georgia. The crowd cheered, and made up over the gift as if I were a Rockefeller. Fats accepted his prize calmly as his due. "You ain't heard nothing today," he said. "But Fats ain't no liar. They is just some people cain't recognize the truth."

➤ WORDS ON A BUS ◄

The first one who got on was a little girl with a market bag half as large as she; then came a sturdy urchin, rubbing his eyes, pushed along by his young, small mother, carrying bundles and a sleeping baby. An old man, having told the driver he was just helping his daughter with her things, started stowing away a big suit-case. Fortunately the couple behind me got off at Fayette and a seat was vacant.

As this family entered, one of the wits in the Caucasian front of the bus had said, "Eeny-meeny-miney-mo!" Some of his mates tittered. He even looked back to our section for appreciation.

It was not long after the patch of light had left the old man standing there at the culvert that the talk began. Most of us were a little beaten by the jolting and grinding of the bus; many had drowsed off, waking only when the driver clicked the lights on at Lorman, Fayette, the culvert.

Before the lights went off again, however, one man had come up and sat him-self on the arm of the chair opposite the mother and her brood. He asked her where she was going. She told him that she was hoping to get off at the bottom of a hill near a gas station and soft-drink place just before the bus got into Natchez itself. The bus driver, *He*, had told her that he didn't know whether he could let off there or not, he didn't know the place that she was talking about and that she'd better go on to the Tri-State bus depot in mid-city. But she hoped that she wouldn't have to go there; she didn't want to have to carry all of that luggage and those children all that way. Not with them sleepy and crying. But if she could get off at the foot of the hill, it wasn't nowheres at all from there. Not nowheres, hardly.

The man told her that he knew the place, and promised to pull the string when they got there. "You ain't living where you used to, then?" he asked.

"Who is you?"

"You don't remember me? I remember you."

"Ain't you Amos?"

"Yeah, I'm Amos."

"Lordy, I ain't seed you for so long a time. Well, I declare. No, we moved from the alley. We live up on the hill, behind that big ole house where Mis' Fletcher live. Nowheres hardly from where I git off, do I git off."

"I'll see that you gits off, all right. All these chil'ren yours?"

They were that, she bragged proudly. And then followed some talk of the fam-ily. But my eavesdropping was stopped by the lights clicking on again, the bus's stopping, and the exit of one of the whites into the engulfing blackness of the Mississippi night.

"How is Lowrie?" she asked, tentatively, I thought.

"Watchu asking me for? I don't know how she is."

"Where is she?"

"I don't know. I mought as well ask you. You know I ain't seed Lowrie for two years."

"You mean she and you ain't livin' together no mo'?"

"She left me a year and two months ago, lacking four days."

"Well, I do declare. I always thought you all were gonna do better than that."

"Warn't no you all. It was her."

"That's what all you men says."

"Hit's the truth. She up and left me."

"Where the chil'ren?"

"Wid me. Where'd you expect? For going on two years. No mother in the house."

"What was the matter?"

"I rightly don't know. Lowrie, she disliked it so much down here she kep' on talking about how she wanted to see her people up North. She wanted to go so bad I bought her a ticket and gave her a trip to St. Louis. When she come back, she was mo' dissatisfied than ever. I did all I could for her, made her a good livin'. But she disliked it here.

"But I never knew what was up. Went out to work one morning, came back and found the house empty. She had taken all her clothes and gone. No word, no good-bye nor nothin'."

"What did she do with the chil'ren?"

"She had sent them over to my mother's for the day. I went over and got them. They told me that she had been all packed up even while I was eating breakfast. No sooner had I gone than she left too."

"Looks to me that they would have told you."

"She had made 'em promise not to. Said she was coming back soon. Sent me a postcard the first Christmas and some things for the chil'ren. That's all I done heard from her for nigh onto two years."

"Well, I declare that's a shame."

"So don't you say you all. It was her."

"Yas. Ain't no kind of mother to leave her chil'ren."

"No. But if she wants it that way, she can have it. If she don't think no more of her own flesh and blood than that, I ain't gonna go runnin' after her. Or beggin'."

"Where do they stay?"

"Home with me. They see my mom sometimes in the day. My boy is working; he weigh over a hundred pounds now. The little girl cleans and cooks nigh about as good as ever Lowrie did."

"You ain't got nothin' to worry about then. Good riddance."

"Not much. I don't irk my mind thinking about Lowrie. But," the arch whisper came over the back of my chair, "I do git tired sleepin' in the bed all by myself."

"You can git yourself another wife. Never knew you to have trouble findin' a woman."

"I don't know. How you and Tom making it? You still wid Tom?"

"Indeed I is." Laughing embarrassedly, "I loves Tom. He's a good man to me and a good father to my chil'ren."

"How many you got? These all?"

"These three and the biggest girl. I left her back in Fayette with her grandma."

"I always thought you was too good for Tom."

"No indeedy." She laughed gently, a bit coquettishly. "He too good for me."

"Stop that. You the kind of woman wouldn't run away from her husband. Now ain't you? You take care of the house. I know good and well you wouldn't leave your chil'ren behind you in an empty house."

"I'd die before I'd ever leave my chil'ren. I just couldn't do that."

"You de kind of woman I needs. I wish I could git me somebody like you. I got me a girl, but she don't seem to take to the chil'ren, or to house-keeping. Is Tom doin' all right by you? I didn't think you and him would been together this long."

"He doing fine by me. Anyway, hit wouldn't do you no good if I wasn't wid him. You know you and I is kin."

"I knows that all right. Yet and still I didn't know, till you tole me, that him and you was still together."

The lights clicked on. Two whites left the bus. The driver craned, looked in his mirror, turned around. "Can't you sit down in the seat and get off the arm," he spoke sharply. Amos slid into the seat. They talked a little more until he pulled the cord for her to get off at the bottom of the hill. I listened no longer; the romance was done for anyhow.

⇥ GEORGIA NYMPHS ⇤

Ed and I had been talking to J. C. all morning, and at noon he asked us to have dinner with him. He wanted to put the big pot in the little one for us, but we had agreed beforehand not to take advantage of J. C.'s bounty. It wasn't only or chiefly that his ailing daughter and her young ones needed the fat meat and the greens in the little pot. It was rather that J. C. didn't have a well, but filled his old wooden bucket from a spring. And on this side of the track the type of community planning seemed to be: house, pig-sty (where pigs were occasionally owned), privy, and then in the dip at the bottom of the draining slope, the common spring.

I had been told in Atlanta to drink no more spring water in the back country than I had to. Ed and I had been guzzling all the various Colas of the brood sired by Papa Coca until we felt natural off the water wagon. We told J. C. that we had messages for Widow Thompkins from her son up in Fulton Tower, and while he was suspicious and jealous, he remained the old Southern gentleman that he truly was.

In her own right, Mrs. Thompkins was nearly as much of a character as J. C. Her son was doing a little time in Fulton Tower for fighting—"he was a good son, jus' easy misled"—and I had carried his mother's message to him, and some cigarettes. Mrs. Thompkins was not doing so badly for herself. For doing the white-folks' laundry and odd jobs, she was allowed the use of a three-room clapboard cabin, with a little front yard where she had flowers growing in plots and tin cans. A flowering tree, I forget the name, sprinkled its blooms on the hard, cleanly swept yard. Under the inevitable chinaberry tree there was a bench where the widow could sit in the cool of the day, taking some sort of ease, remembering. In her larger backyard, fenced in with wire, she had a small garden: onions, collards, tomatoes, and more flowers. The red land up to her place was bare, gullied, untilled. The plot allowed her for washing and ironing was strictly defined.

The widow seemed to take her lonely living well, fortified by her belief in herself, and by the fact that in the six months of schooling in the community she boarded and slept the teacher. Teacher's room was clean and neat (as was the whole house); there was a colorful counterpane on the large bed, and pennants (Spelman, Lincoln, Prairie View) on the wall. Teacher had left many of her things there, even two photographs on the dresser.

But now, with teacher gone and not due back till October, loneliness was setting in, the widow told us, in happy gratitude at our visit. Both she and the white lady whose husband owned the place were afflicted with loneliness. So they would sit on the bank of the pond and fish. Sometimes they would talk, but often when the widow would say something out of turn, like praising "the culluhd," or when something wasn't just right about the laundering, or when things were unsettled up at the house, they would just sit on the bank a yard or so apart, two lonely women in bitter silent conflict, casting sidelong glances at each other or short words intended not for conversation but for belittling. The widow's speech grew salty at the remembrance:

"She think cause she washed-out white folks, she kin lord it over me. I tell her I knew her when."

When one of the Professors from Atlanta University came down in his long Buick, which had trouble in turning around in the gullied road that ended at the widow's house, the white family had come out staring. "They ain't got nothin' but a Chevy," Widow Thompkins said. "And that don't run good. The doctor— he was one of those learned doctors, not a medical doctor," she said. "Son, is you a doctor? You ain't? You look smart enough to be one." This doctor was a light brown-skinned man, with a goatee, a poise and accent learned in New England and Europe, really distinguished as all hell.

The white woman was as nonplussed as her young ones who were clasping her about the knees, peeking out at the stranger. The next day on the fishing bank she asked the widow: "Was that man in the big car a nigger?"

"I flew right off. I had been a-lookin' for her to ask about him, but that word nigger done it to me. 'You hadn't oughta call nobody nigger,' I tole her. 'You know good as me what the Holy Bible say. It say we all kin to each other. We all cerzins. That's what.' "

" 'Yas,' I said. 'He's a culluhd. You know,' I said to her same as I talking to you, 'there ain't nothing white folks got, that some of the culluhd ain't got, somewhere.' "

The widow told how afterwards they had sat for hours, almost to sundown and suppertime, not speaking, the white woman sulking, she gloating. She told of her gusto when one of the fish she hooked outweighed those being caught by the white woman: "I pulled in one big old cat and tried to land it right smack in her lap. Got our lines tangled. Wish it had been a eel. I kin catch mo' fish than she kin any day God sends."

The pond where they fished looked like it had been scooped out of the red hills. Reeds stuck up around the edges and even out in the middle of the reddish brown water. A piece of a pier, a few boards nailed on cross-scantlings and short posts, extended a dozen or so yards into the pond. Georgia pines shaded the bank; cushioning pine needles made it comfortable sitting. The pond was nothing more than an oversized swimming hole. They caught eels there, and the widow said there were many snakes.

This day the widow was glad to see us. The sun, directly overhead, was blazing, and our first act was to drop our bottles of Coke and our cheese and crackers on the front porch, and go around to the well in the backyard. Cokes or no Cokes, we wanted some of that cold, sweet water from the well.

When we reached the well we hard chattering and splashing in the pond. We looked over. Five white girls were there. A couple were in what might be called regulation swimming suits, sleek, shining dark sheaths plastered against their bodies. The other three were in brassieres and shorts, their pink and suntanned midriffs bare. Two were jumping up and down in the water; three stood on the pier. They were having a ball.

They saw us as soon as we saw them. Then they started: they whooped, yoo-hooed at us, laughed, and waved their hands. One of them yelled, "Come on in, the water's fine." The girl nearest to her said something to her, and laughed aloud. They tried to push each other in the water, wrestled on the planks, tottered, and then both hit the water with a smack. Cheers and jeers rose, and young girls' laughter. It wasn't a pleasant sound to my ears; I was certain the noise could rise up from that clay saucer and flow back into Federal City.

I looked at Ed; Ed looked at me. He was scared too, I could see. He shook his head. There was a drawn expression about his eyes and mouth.

"Yoo-hoo," they called. "Come on in." They had us where they wanted us, right in the middle. If we had stirred a hand it would have been too bad.

We didn't bother about the water. We let the bucket clatter back into the well; the clanking wheel spun. Without a word we went back to the front porch. We couldn't see the pool from there.

Mrs. Thompkins heard a yell, and went to the fence between her place and the pond. When she came back, she was flustered.

"Y'all will have to go out back," she said. "They're coming in here to change they clothes."

We walked on back. We didn't look, but we heard them coming, their chatter and laughing high-pitched and shrill.

We heard them moving about and talking in the house. Some piece of furniture went over with a bang. The largest, probably the oldest of the five, came to the back screen door. She was a strapping buxom blonde, in a scanty pair of trunks and a heavily packed brassiere. She looked us over coolly and then put on her act: a home talent variant of a Mae West grind, gentle bump and all. She tossed her head and rolled away with a curt laugh.

Only two put on their clothes; three carried them in their arms. They walked up the rise in the rocky clay road, laughing and looking back. The buxom one walked last, switching and swaying, still in her swimming garb except for her high-heeled shoes, her print dress in one hand away from her body, her towel knotted around her hips. At the top of the hill she said something to her companions, turned around, looked boldly at us, wiggled and laughed. The others chimed in with girlish laughter, enjoying the joke.

There was only one road in to the pond; only one road out. We didn't want to go skipping out, certainly not behind five sparsely clad young Dixie belles. We were uncomfortable. The Coca-Cola had got warmish; the crackers and cheese were dry stuff. Mrs. Thompkins was uncommunicative, a bit ashamed. There would be no good talk that day. . . . She said little of anything; she did work up to saying "them hussies." But she caught herself, looking at us to see if we had heard. We let on we didn't. "They use this house to undress and dress in," she apologized. "This is the onliest place where they can go swimming."

After an uncomfortable half hour or so, we started up the road. When we got to Federal City proper, what we had figured on seemed true. The town had heard about it. It was way past lunch time but the workers at the small basket factory were lining the wall. We walked side by side on the shoulder of the pike close to the concrete. I could feel the tension in the air: the shimmering heat before the likely storm. We did not look to left or right or at each other. I don't know how they looked, but I knew they were there, waiting for, begging for, one word, one swaying off the road's shoulder, one bodily contact, anything to give them a chance. All they asked was one good excuse. We walked the chalk-line back to the gas station–grocery store. We left the bottles and got our deposit. At first I felt glad to be in the store; but that didn't last. The dealer had been civil in the morning, passing the time of day. He was grim-lipped now and slid our deposit over at us. We were glad to get across the track to J. C.'s—glad to see the old gray-haired patriarch. His cackling talk was good. It was a sort of hiding ourselves in the bosom of Abraham. After all, he had lasted for over ninety years.

J. C. calmed us a bit. We had come down in order to see Night Court and we decided that we would stay to see it. The night story falls elsewhere in the book. What belongs to this story, however, is the curiosity that our presence in the court room summoned. We got there early, since J. C., as chairman of the precinct, was a stickler for punctuality. There weren't many people there. After awhile some crackers of the dangerous age (anything from six to sixty, of course, but these were in the lower brackets) glimpsed us over the heads of the "criminals." After some pointing and staring a couple of young Paul Reveres whisked out. When they came back a crowd came with them.

As we saw the sickening court session draw to a close (told of earlier) I said to Ed: "We've just a few minutes left to catch our bus. Let's go. Goodbye, J. C., we'll be seeing you." Ed and I stumbled over the feet of some of the Negro "criminals" and started out. The gavel of the town's Mayor banged as we got to the head of the stairs. We were caught in the white crowd. The other Negroes sat there, waiting their turn, in the order of things. Going down the narrow stair-case, wide enough only for three, Ed and I were jostled back and forth. It was a variant of the old high schools game, "Get off me." From one or the other we were pushed. I kept my elbows out, and fell rigidly from one pusher to the other, concentrating, making sure that my feet were hitting the steps. Again they were hoping for some excuse. . . . We gave them none.

At last we got to the bottom. I looked out. In the cone of light from the high swinging lamp, I saw a ring of faces, long, sallow, and cruel. I said to Ed, "Let's go." And arms akimbo we forced our way through the ring. I stepped off the curbstone into a mass of mud; I yanked my foot out. Luckily my shoe stayed on, though the goo sucked at it. Our pace was between a run and a walk. A frank run would have been invitation; a regular walk was too much to expect of us. My heart was going like a riveter's drill. But we got away. The bus had to be late. We stood at the curve on the pike, across from the gas station grocery, under the blue arc-light. One car carrying one of the Negro woman defendants and her friends back to Atlanta pulled up at the pike and then with a grating of gears was gone. We heard the rest of the Negroes as they went across the tracks; their whoopings farther and farther away. It was past eleven o'clock so none were due to come to the part of town where we were waiting. A few whites walked by and looked at us; then a Ford car, crammed with crackers. They stopped a few moments, and then drove on.

We stood in the blue cone of light. Gnats swarmed about it. Cars zoomed by occasionally, their tires snarling on the curve. No bus came. The gas-station operator put out his last light. Night settled deeper, and the quiet seemed ominous. But we felt a bit safer.

Soon the night court crowd was scattered. The risks were over, we thought. Then from nowhere, two little white boys stopped by the gas tank. One picked up the rind of half a watermelon. He took out a piece of the meat still left and put it in his mouth.

"Whatcha doing, Larry?" said the other. "Don't you know a dog or a nigger could have been eating that watermelon? You get sick picking up stuff like that and putting it in your mouth. Look, here's something we can do."

He split the rind and put both pieces about the width of a car's wheel base on the highway. A car coming around the curve might run over both of them. And there we stood. If a car were to hit them, I thought, and skid into one of the brick posts of the gas-station, here we are, two strange Negroes, the culprits. If we hadn't put them there, still we should have moved them. If we moved them, we'd have the two kids to whip and then a whole town to fight. A car zoomed around, missing both rinds.

"Shucks," said one kid.

A wavering set of lights, a lighted body, and then letters on a car front: "Atlanta." Ed and I saw it at once. "There it is," breathed Ed. "At last," I said.

We got on the bus; Ed headed to the back seat. I was so glad to see the bus driver that I wanted to say something to him. "How much is the fare?" He told me shortly. "I'm a stranger here," I said. He wasn't interested, but looked contemptuously at me.

This year, on my way to Alabama, I watched out of the car window to see Federal City stream past. There is a sign there: "While here be sure to see the Lakes." Maybe they've fixed them up now as something worth seeing; maybe they've cleaned them out and dredged them. Maybe. But not for me. I saw all I wanted to see of them one hot August day a few years ago. All I wanted to see, and more.

⤍ AND/OR ⤎

For safety's sake, though he is a lieutenant in the Army now and may never come back to the South, let us call him Houston. He was short and frail, with a dark brown, sensitive face. I first met him at the FEPC hearings in Birmingham when, on short acquaintance, he revealed to me how he was burned up by conditions in Dixie. To judge from his twang, he was Southern-born, and he was Tuskegee trained, but he had the rather dicty restaurant on edge when he went into his tirades. The brown burghers, some of them a bit jittery anyway at FEPC and especially at the influx of a bunch of young "foreign" and radical Negroes into dynamite-loaded Birmingham, eyed him carefully over their glasses of iced tea.

I ran into him again in the small Alabama town where he was teaching. He was still quite a talker, in his high-pitched voice with a quaver in it—though he didn't quaver in other respects. He was brimming over with facts and consequent bitterness, deeper than I expected in a graduate of Tuskegee. To him, as to so many college men, the Negro's great need was the ballot. He had made a thoughtful study of the disenfranchising techniques and political shenanigans of Alabama in general. He laughed sardonically at the Negro's being asked to interpret such "constitutional" questions as "What is *non compos mentis* when it is applied to a citizen in legal jeopardy?" But he knew also how deeply engraved was the symbol at the head of the Democratic column on the official ballot used in all elections in Alabama: a rooster with the words "White Supremacy" arched over its head, and the words under it: "For the Right." White supremacy was well symbolized by the rooster, he thought; and he was afraid that Negro purposefulness was too well symbolized by a chicken. And a chicken with pip, lethargic, gaping, and trembling. He was determined to vote himself, and he told me with gusto the tragicomedy, at times the farce, of his experiences with the county board of registrars.

Knowing the ropes, Houston's first strategic step to get the vote was to buy a radio at a white store and charge it. This was his first charge account in the town, but it meant a possible white sponsor to vouch for him when the polls opened. Two weeks later he applied to the Board of Registrars. He was asked, "Do you have three hundred dollars worth of taxable property?"

Houston said no, but added that he understood that the property qualification was alternative to the literacy qualification. He was told that he was wrong: he had to have three hundred dollars worth of property or forty acres of land. That seemed to end the matter as far as the Board was concerned. Houston waited a few minutes and then asked if he would be permitted to make out an application. He was granted permission with the warning that the Board would have to pass on his case, and that as he did not have the property qualification, the chances were against him. He was also told that he needed two residents of the town to vouch for his character. He named the merchant from whom he had bought the radio and a clothing merchant.

When approached, the first merchant said that he would be glad to go over and sign, but that he couldn't leave his store just then. He would go over late that afternoon. Houston thanked him. The next day he telephoned the merchant, who hadn't quite managed it the day before but would try to get over some time that day. Houston thanked him again. The next day the merchant hadn't seen his way clear, either, things being so busy, but he gave his word that he wouldn't let the polls close on Houston. Three days later, the merchant told Houston that he had just got tied up and the polls had closed. A week later, Houston went to the store and paid the balance on the radio. The merchant said that he was sorry; he just hadn't been able to get around to doing that little favor, but he gave his word again that he would be glad indeed to go over when the polls opened again. Yessir, glad. That would be just the next month, Houston told him.

When the polls opened the next month, Houston called the merchant, who made an appointment with him for "about 2 P.M." At the store on the dot, Houston was told that the merchant was out of town. Yessir, a quick trip.

Houston then applied to the second merchant, with whom he had had even more dealings, but on a cash basis. The runaround here was also efficient. He didn't know Houston well enough "to take an oath about his character," but he promised that if men at the Post Office and Bank said O.K., he would vouch for him. Every time the Post Office superintendent called, the merchant was out. Finally, the banker caught him, and the appointment was made.

"I understand you have an application for R. T. Houston, who has been working out at the school for the last three years or so." The board informed the merchant that investigation showed that Houston did not have either three hundred dollars worth of property or forty acres of land. The merchant said, "Oh, I don't know anything about that." He wanted to get out of there quick. Houston stated again his understanding about the alternative literacy qualification.

"It doesn't make any difference whether you graduated from Harvard. If you don't have the property, you can't register," the merchant offered. Houston remembered that he seemed to cheer up, saying it.

The merchant and Houston left the office, Houston thanking him for his time, and the merchant saying jocularly, "Well, you got to get your three hundred dollars worth of property or forty acres of land somewhere. What are you going to do?"

"I'm going to register," said Houston. "There is a provision in the Constitution for having your qualifications determined." Houston was partly compensated for the long runaround by the look of amazement on the merchant's face.

With two other colleagues, both acquainted with the law, Houston approached the Board again to thresh out the matter of qualifications. The registrar, a woman, stated that somebody else had asked the same question and that she had "marked it in the book." She was told that the property qualification was an alternative.

"No," she said, "you must have the property."

"When was the amendment passed making both qualifications necessary?"

This question was ignored. In triumph, the registrar read the second qualification: "owner or husband of woman who is owner . . . of forty acres of land, or personal property or real estate assessed . . . at value of three hundred dollars or more," etc.

She was then asked to read the first qualification. She complied, hesitantly. Another registrar horned in: "This board will have to pass on you, and we register who we want to register."

The first qualification set up the requirement of "reading and writing any article of the Constitution of the United States in the English language . . ." and of being "regularly engaged in some lawful employment the twelve months next preceding the time they offer to register . . . etc." The word linking this to the second qualification is *or*.

On being asked what the word *or* meant, the registrar said that it meant *in addition to*, based on an interpretation from the Attorney General. Houston and his colleagues asked for this ruling, but it was not produced. Instead the three troublemakers were shunted across the hall to the Probate Judge's office. The Judge was asked point blank if *or* in the state constitution meant *and*. The Judge replied point-blank that it did. "You must have both the property as well as the literacy qualification," he said. The registrars got their ruling from the Attorney General; the Judge knew nothing of any law that had been made. Questioned closely on whether all the list of voters owned three hundred dollars worth of property, the Judge hedged. He complained that his questioners were only trying to get him into an argument with the Board of Registrars.

"What steps should we take to get an interpretation of the disputed passage?" was the straw breaking the camel's back.

"Find out for yourself," the Judge yelled, and stormed out of his office.

A few hours later, while preparing papers for an appeal to the Circuit Court to clarify the problem of qualification, Houston learned that the Board of Registrars had been busy telephoning him. Another call, unidentified but "from someone in touch with the Judge," informed Houston that he would get his registration papers.

When he walked into the office, there was a decided stir. One of the women on the Board said, "Here he is now." The spokesman of the Board was polite. "We decided to let you register," he said.

"Thank you very much," said Houston. The certificate was signed and dated as of the preceding day, when the Judge had ruled on "And/Or."

Houston was told that it would be wise to get two good people of the town to vouch for him.

He named colleagues of his at the school.

"We mean white people," said the registrar. "Don't you know two good white people?"

"Nossir," said Houston politely. "I don't know two good white people . . . to vouch for me."

Gone with the Wind

Across the entire collection, but most acutely here in "Gone with the Wind," Brown poses American history, particularly the history of the South, as the most deeply conflicted issue vexing American civic and cultural life. Referencing with irony Margaret Mitchell and her romanticized treatment of the antebellum South, the very title of the section suggests the ongoing presence of that mythologized past, as well as its obsolescence. "Gone with the Wind" opens with Brown's lonely traveler, ostensibly Brown himself, visiting monuments and sites dedicated to the Old South, musing over what he sees, and reflecting on the antebellum period and its effects on his own time. This persona of the itinerant reflective witness, both a part of and apart from the South, sets the tone and tenor of this deeply critical look at the past and possibilities for the future in the South.

For the entire decade of the 1930s, Brown was preoccupied with countering mythologizers' blind nostalgia for the Old South. *I'll Take My Stand*, published in 1930, was a call on the part of Vanderbilt intellectuals for the South to return to its agrarian, antebellum roots. Guidebooks to the Southern states written under the auspices of the Federal Writers' Project were filled with willful distortions (which Brown labored to correct through his work with the FWP). And the novel *Gone with the Wind*, published in 1936, met with enormous popularity, as did its film version in 1939. Brown saw all these as desperate measures that betrayed the utter ruin of a romantic past that never was and yet demonstrated the seemingly endless resilience of the mythology. More to the point, the romance represented by Southern mansions and monuments to Robert E. Lee and Stonewall Jackson perpetuates a history largely defined by the subordination of blacks. If African Americans appear at all in the mythology, they appear in the role of service, their being reduced to an appendage in myths unwilling or unable to conceive of black being in and of itself.

"I Look at the Old South" opens the section by announcing Brown's deep ambivalence toward the South and its racialized past by recording his impressions of visits to historical sites in the South, especially in Virginia. "Gone with What Wind" intensifies his scrutiny, as he focuses on Atlanta and its more recent past. "Symbol of the Old South" and "A Tour of History: Old New Orleans" continue this more concentrated look, reflecting on Natchez, Mississippi, and New Orleans, Louisiana, respectively. Moving to the lives and history unaccounted for in the romance of the Old South, "Gee's Bend," "Low Cotton," and "Take Your Coat Off, Gene!" depict rural and small-town life in Georgia and Alabama from the perspective of the local folk. In a strikingly different vein, "Insurance Executive" and "Let's Look at Your Base" take a critical look at black progress in what has been touted as the New South. Ending the section, "No Ties That Bind" returns to a sweeping overview of the South, past and present, again raising the question of historical record and thus the future for African Americans in this conflicted region. In the context of the late 1930s and early 1940s, "Gone with the Wind" looks back at a decade of economic deprivation seeking escape to a sanitized past free of economic or social strife. As Brown wanders through the ruin of latter-day romance, these resulting essays bear the weight of mythology.

MONUMENTS, MEMORIALS, AND MARKERS

I am not much of a sightseer, but since I was born and bred in Washington, I know my share of monuments and memorials. There are some that call up for me the antebellum and Civil War past: the old homes of Georgetown ranging from such beauties as Dumbarton Oaks to the cramped brick houses hugging the sidewalks; the groundworks of Fort Stevens where Lincoln curiously awaited Jubal Early's raiders, Ford's Theater where he was shot, all of the Lincolniana ending with the Lincoln Memorial. I have seen the old blank hulks, most of them gone now, that were said to have been slave jails for the thriving interstate slave traffic. One was across the street from the White House; another a stone's throw from the Capitol. And I know neighboring Maryland: have followed the trail of John Wilkes Booth in the southern counties, have seen the window from which legendary Barbara Freitchie challenged Stonewall's army; and over where Maryland joins West Virginia, have stood truly moved before the scarred firehouse where the rifles of John Brown and his band of whites and Negroes spat angry defiance at the slave-power.

I know Arlington, too, where the stately Lee's Mansion is supposed to introduce the Old South. I always found it difficult to fit this imitation Greek temple into the American past, finding it easier to associate the mansion with the nearby cemetery than to people; with Custises and Lees and their slave retinues. The slave quarters in the rear, even though belonging to George Washington's adopted son and to Robert E. Lee, reminded me only of stables. Still they interested me more than the huge columns, the classic pediments, the charming furniture and chinaware. Mount Vernon struck me as more of a living place than Lee's mansion. I know the other shrines of the George Washington country: Christ Church in Alexandria and the restored church in Pohick where Washington attended services; the markers showing the taverns where Washington took his welcome grog; and the Rappahanock across which he threw a silver dollar to show the power of his arm. And I have seen Jefferson's Monticello, crowning the mountain, and at the University of Virginia have strolled beside the serpentine wall along the Long Walk to the Rotunda, seeing the realization in masonry of another Jefferson dream. And I have seen James Madison's graceful Montpelier and James Monroe's more modest Ash Lawn, set in a frame of green.

Fredericksburg boasts not only the colonial homes and taverns, but also the slave-block, used by the belles to mount their steeds before taking a gallop, and by the slaves who were to be graded before being sold South. The slave-block was for a long time more cherished than the neighboring law office of James Monroe, a small shabby house owned and dwelt in by Negroes and therefore allowed to fall into decay. Negroes still live in it, faithfully guarding the Louis XVI furniture, the desk where the Monroe Doctrine was composed, and the dispatch box that Monroe carried while dickering for the Louisiana Territory.

From Fredericksburg through Richmond, west to Williamsburg, south to Petersburg, the roads ran through much fought over, bloody ground. I looked at the relics in the National Park Museum, and at the markers recalling Sunken Road, the Bloody Angle, Seven Pines, Malvern Hill, the Wilderness to the west, Cold Harbor to the east; the death place of Stonewall Jackson, the Yellow Tavern near which Jeb Stuart was fatally wounded; and the rivers—North Anna, South Anna, Chickahominy—that once ran red. Here Lee, here Grant, and beyond Richmond toward Williamsburg, here Lafayette, here Cornwallis did thus and so. The markers reeled off the information like a rapid history survey.

With a sense of duty more than zeal, in Richmond I visited the Confederate shrine: the Capitol and the White House of the Confederacy, which has a room set apart for each seceding state, and guards the hallowed treasures of Lee's coat and sword, Stonewall Jackson's epaulettes and spurs, and Jeb Stuart's plumed hat. But more than these mementos and the pseudo-classic buildings, it was a few unpretentiously beautiful homes, Glasgow House especially, that called up for me the graciousness that was the boast of old Richmond.

In that city I caught a sense of the irony of history on visiting Poe's Shrine, with its collection of the poet's belongings so carefully preserved now and the vast library of books written about him, which multiply a hundred fold the few books that the poet owned. The garden, with its ivied loggia, its well-tended flowers, and shaded walks about the fountain, was a shocking contrast to the place where Elizabeth Poe, his mother, died, which now stands an ugly and wretched shack in the slums of Sophie's alley.

My friends in Richmond were uncertain whether or not I would be allowed to visit the famed manors and estates in the vicinity. Though most of them had lived in Richmond all of their lives, they had never seen Carter's Grove, Westover, Berkley, and Shirley. They were not curious about them, nor did they see why I should be. Some of the grounds were open only during Garden Week anyway. Roscoe thought that Negroes probably weren't wanted even then, since there were no facilities for segregation. He told how he and his party had been driven from the picnic grounds in restored Jamestown. "You should have come in a Dutch schooner, instead of that V-8," somebody said.

So my sole view of the famous manors, where Virginia social life reached its peak, was obtained from the Charles City Ferry as it plied the broad James River. I have often ridden down the Pocahontas Trail to Williamsburg, but I never turned into the by-road that leads to the beautiful estates. When the National Association for the Advancement of Colored People chartered the steamboat *Robert E. Lee* for a trip down the James River, I think we did not get down as far as Westover, and even so, my thoughts were not on the past that day. But I have seen enough of the manors and gardens of the Old Dominion not to feel at too great a loss. And of course I have seen Williamsburg.

The restoration of Williamsburg attracts thousands of tourists during Garden Week at the end of April. Rockefeller's twenty million have re-created the old colonial capital as far as antiquarians, architects, engineers, and gardeners can do so. Replicas of the Capitol, the Governor's Palace, Bruton Church and the other colonial buildings are faithful stage-props and sets for the departed drama. I strolled through the grounds of William and Mary College, seeing the restored original buildings. I belong to a fraternity that started at William and Mary—Phi Beta Kappa—but I didn't look up the fraternity house. I probably would have had the wrong grip.

I could not recapture the past in Williamsburg. I confess that I was more struck by the engineering skill and the obvious expense than educated, as the philanthropist hoped, in what the period was like. The buildings are beautiful, the boxwood gardens are dreams. But it was Rockefeller rather than colonial governors about whom my thoughts centered. And I was inclined to agree with Frank Lloyd Wright's caustic criticism of the architectural waste and misdirection. I could not take seriously the "atmospheric" business such as the hostesses in billowing hoopskirts and the Negro coachmen and footmen in sky-blue coats, cocked hats, knee-breeches, white stockings, and buckled shoes. I could not get the chance to talk to these eighteenth-century black ghosts. But in front of the colonial A&P store, I talked to a sharp-looking Negro who said that the coachman and footmen had a hard time when they came back to colored Williamsburg wearing those breeches and stockings. Yessir, they certainly were low-rated at first. Negroes weren't too enthusiastic about the project, he told me, except as it gave them jobs. A number of Negroes had owned their homes on the streets that were needed for the Restoration. The plan of "life tenures" by which the Restoration bought the property but allowed the seller to live out his life in the restored dwelling, without paying rent, didn't hold for Negroes. Instead of getting life tenures, they were moved out. That told me more about the past than the beautiful colonial buildings did.

⤞ SISTER CITIES ⤝

I have not been down to Charleston in Azalea time. Nor on any of my three trips have I climbed to the top of Charleston's highest building to look down on the historic spots, which, the natives tell me, outnumber those to be seen from any similar vantage in America. But I am acquainted with some of the memorials to Charleston's past: the long, double-humped Cooper River Bridge, venerable St. Philip's Church, whose chimes cast into Confederate cannon, were never replaced; St. Michael's Church, whose four-dialed clock in the steeple tells the time by which old Charlestonians go, regardless of what radio Bulova announces; the Old Exchange, the Dock Theatre, oldest playhouse in America. From East on High Battery, I have seen Fort Sumter, low-lying, surly in the gray distance. I have strolled the entire Battery and those other famed streets: Meeting, Broad, Church, King, Tradd, and Legare, which the natives defiantly pronounce Legree.

I remember the "single houses" set flush with the pavement, characteristically shouldering the street, fronting to the side as it were. Charlestonians told me how in this subtropical climate, galleries and piazzas were faced south to catch the winds from the sea. Like New Orleans, Charleston is a city of hidden gardens, walled in from the vulgar street. Sitting on their long piazzas, the aristocrats can revel over their flowers: wisteria, magnolias, azaleas in the spring; crepe myrtles, and oleanders in the summer; daffodils and camellia-japonicas in the fall and winter. I have seen several age-mellowed houses of the great: Miles Brewton's Georgian masterpiece, the homes of William Rhett, John Rutledge, and Manigault; the Rainbow Row with its houses of varicolored pastel hues. Of the many examples of famous iron tracery, I especially remember "Sword Gates" with their scrolls, spears, swords, and cross, and the Sass Iron Gates, unbelievably delicate. Behind that wrought filigree I imagined Herbert Ravenal Sass, the contemporary author, lost in reveries of what he calls "The Golden Age of a region of romance . . . leisure, culture, in general a high sense of responsibility for a dependent, helpless race." I thought how much a "helpless race" had brought to this civilization: the wealth came in large part from slave laborers in the indigo, rice, and cotton fields; and the beauty in large part from slave artisans, skillful beyond ordinary imagining in ironwork, bricklaying, carpentry, and gardening.

Charleston's history cannot be confined to the big houses and families. The poorer houses, frame, brick, or cheap stucco, high and narrow with steep slate roofs, sharp gables, and chimney pots could tell of the old times, too, though maybe unconventionally. Ancient of ancients was Pink House, the cramped, steep tavern on a street whose cobblestones came from Europe as ballast in the sailing ships. Near at hand was the Old Slave Market, which the guidebook author,

Thomas Petigree Lesesne, calls mythical since "nowhere in Charleston was there a constituted slave market for the public auctioning of blacks from Africa." I could not quite get Mr. Lesesne's drift, as the domestic slave-trade which he admits could have had use for a slave market too. At any rate, his authorities assure him that no slave trade flourished in Charleston. I wondered if his research included Frederic Bancrofts's carefully documented *Slave-Trading in the Old South*, which lists so many of Charleston's honored surnames as in the business of selling men and women.

A couple of blocks from the slave market in St. Philip's Cemetery is the grave of John Calhoun. Not too far away, the Shaw Memorial School recalls another kind of hero, the young Massachusetts colonel who died leading his Negro regiment against Fort Wagner on Morris Island. Shaw's family purchased the land and built the school. Since 1874 it has been part of the city school system, an example, according to the guidebook, of "Charleston's tolerance as a community." Talks with some old Charlestonians, Negro and white, convinced me that the city had examples of tolerance more real than that.

Noted for its fine houses, Charleston is also noted for its alleys. In backyards of the old homes, Negro servants still live in quarters a century old. Some white outsiders, enraptured by the romance of Charleston, rent abandoned servants' quarters and even alley houses, traditionally the Negroes'. Most famous of Charleston's alleys is of course Catfish Row. The guidebook told me that Du Bose Heyward got his suggestions from Cabbage Row, a renovated slum, which he renamed. After seeing the original, I understand the creativeness of Heyward and Mamoulian. A Negro friend informed me that there was a real Catfish Row, though not the setting that suggested the novel, but that Porgy's true haunts were in Cool Blow, another kind of slum. The guidebook warns: "It would spoil a reading of 'Porgy' to discuss him at length." From certain other hints I gather that Heyward created a new person out of an actual character whose real life might have jarred the romance. Heyward was within his artistic rights; he was not recording local history, and he wrote a fine novel. But the authentic Porgy now teases my curiosity.

I never got to see the world famous Cypress and Magnolia Gardens. But I saw enough columns, galleries, walled gardens, wrought-iron gates, mellow hued bricks and stucco, fan-lights, doorways, stairwells, flowers and trees, to convince me of the grace and leisure that the lords of the Low Country enjoyed years ago. I could understand how, cut off from the main arteries of trade, Charleston might grow old too fast. When I had to enter and leave Charleston from a station in North Charleston, miles away from the city proper, I learned that out of Charleston no road can lead southward. When I saw the difficult engineering problems posed by the Ashley River and Cooper River Bridges, I understood that the isolation was not only voluntary, but also enforced by geography. A symbol of the encroaching present is the village of Cool Blow, once the summering resort of planters, now a set of ramshackly tenement houses, with galleries and stairways swarming with Negroes, hard-driven for the petty rent. I knew the stories of how families richer in pride than purse have been forced to trade on the ancient glory.

The last time I saw Charleston it was astir with the bustle of World War II. Soldiers and sailors, laborers from the war plants, and farmhands from the Low Country plantations thronged King Street, with money in their pockets. Charleston was changing, trade was booming, but the natives I talked with were sad. Tourists were one thing, but these outsiders were another and, spending or not, were unwanted. Some of the outsiders returned the hostility. One night, after the theaters let out, I walked behind two sailors and heard their talk as they tried to pick up two Charleston girls. When they were rebuffed, they crossed the narrow street. One yelled over his shoulder: "And I hope you *stay* in Charleston until you die!" He spoke it as a dire curse, in what sounded to me like a Jersey accent.

Savannah is much like her elder sister, Charleston; larger, more with an eye to the main chance, but less assured, now clinging to the past and now striving to be up-to-date. Upon both is the stamp of the Low Country; the state boundary, the Savannah River, is no real separating line. Savannah and Charleston are more akin than Charleston is to Columbia or Savannah to Atlanta. I understand that neither city cares much for the kinship to be stressed, but to a stranger it is apparent in the grace and pride and mellowness.

I thought of these resemblances, strolling down Bull Street past the old buildings and through the flowered squares. Bull Street, named after the city planner, William Bull, is the central axis of a city that is geometrically laid off, in contrast to Charleston's crowded jumble. The long straight street broadens at regular intervals into rectangular parks where, the natives told me, from the wealth of magnolias, oleanders, gardenias, roses, and azaleas, some flowers would be found in bloom every day of the year. I remember the cypress, palmettos, and live-oaks, the shrubs aflame with color. These parks were originally intended for defense against the Indians; when I was there last, they were trysting places for soldiers on leave and their sweethearts, and for brown nursemaids with their flaxen-haired charges. At Forsyth Square is one of the most elaborate monuments to the Confederate Soldier that I saw in all the South. Around its base I followed a Negro private first class with a good-looking brown girl on each arm, a trio quite interested in the busts of the Confederate generals.

Oglethorpe is the chief hero of Savannah's past. The memorials of colonial and Revolutionary times seem more numerous than those of the Civil War. Out of its eighteenth century Savannah resurrects a pirate, John Flint, the model for Stevenson's *Treasure Island*, and three preachers, John Wesley, Charles

Wesley, and George Whitefield, whose shouting Methodism is being continued with a vengeance by the Savannah worshippers of Father Divine and Daddy Grace. George Washington, Lafayette, Mad Anthony Wayne, Count Polaski, and Nathanael Greene were tied to the city's part in the Revolution. I saw the monument to the Revolutionary hero Sergeant William Jasper, but I found no mention in any of the guidebooks of the black Haitian soldiers, Henri Christophe among them, who were part of Count d'Estaing's French forces that attacked the British captors of the city. I saw the boulder where the Yamacraw chief Tomochichi signed the pact with Oglethorpe, promising friendship to the forlorn settlers. And I saw Yamacraw, the site of the tribe's village. A new highway cuts through and a few houses have been added to the section, but the over-crowded, broken-down tenements are still there to recall the time when Yamacraw was notorious as one of America's worst Negro slums.

Charleston disdains Savannah, I have been told, because of its earliest settlers, to whom even the rector of Savannah's Christ Church said, "My poor friends . . . you are the scum of the earth." If convicts, these city fathers were not criminals; they came to Georgia from debtors' prisons and almshouses, not from robbers' cells or murderers' row. Nevertheless, the guidebooks veer somewhat from these redemptioners; more fitting ancestors seem to be tough Jacobite Highlanders, a few wealthy Englishmen on the make, and French royalist refugees from Santo Domingo. One of the wise features of the new settlement, the prohibition of slavery, lasted sixteen years. But though slavery was slow coming to Savannah, the African slave-trade lasted longest in this vicinity, for until just three years before the Civil War, slave-ships smuggled Africans along reed-hidden waterways into the coastal islands.

Once started, an aristocratic society soon flourished in Savannah, and is memorialized as devotedly as Charleston's. I saw the famous buildings: Christ Church looking like a Greek Temple; the Savannah Theater, younger than Charleston's Dock Theatre but still the oldest theater in continuous operation since it now runs motion pictures; Telfair Academy, formal and neoclassic; McIntosh House, the oldest brick house in Georgia; Pink House, much younger and more pompous than Charleston's; and those houses pointed out as pure examples of Georgian, Regency, and Greek Revival styles. Three houses caught my fancy most. Wetter House, now a female orphanage, has balustrades whose cast iron work reminded me of New Orleans; Scarborough House, once typical Regency, now much altered, is a school for Negro children. I wonder what they feel when their history teacher tells them that the portico, arched windows and hall columns are as they were when President Monroe was a houseguest here on his visit to Savannah to inspect the first steamboat to cross the Atlantic Ocean. I saw the part-French, part-Victorian Meldrim House, headquarters for General Sherman, who composed here his telegram donating the city to General Grant as a Christmas present. And I also looked through the open gateway on State Street where the owner built a fine carriage house and servant quarters, hoping to build a fitting mansion in front of them. When he learned how far he had exceeded his budget, he decided to live in the carriage house instead.

Savannah lost some of its very old buildings by fire in the Civil War, and never had so many as Charleston. Like Charleston, Savannah boasts that its inability to build immediately after the Civil War saved it from the ginger-bread architecture of that period. Its characteristic houses with high basements, high stoops with double stairways leading from the sidewalk, and fine doorways to be entered at what is really the second floor, the fan transoms, brass knockers, iron handrails, balustrades, medallions, and other intricate wrought iron, make one realize how Thackeray, visiting it, as a lionized guest, could praise the comfort and civilization of this "tranquil old city, wide-streeted and tree planted."

Savannah's local historians do not point with as great pride to Oglethorpe's opposition to slavery, as to the nearby plantation manors. I visited Wormsloe, so named for the silk worms that the founder hoped to cultivate, and its low-lying land. Old Negroes on the place knew my guide's family, and I was therefore allowed to ramble through the grounds without even paying the dollar admission fee. Wormsloe is one of the few plantations in America still owned by the family to whom it was first granted. The rambling frame houses, much added to, looms a gray ghost among the aged trees. It is no mansion; the much later marble library building has the ornateness that the legend associates with the Old South. At the rear of the house are several walled gardens where the azaleas and camellias are famous attractions for tourists.

On many drives in the country around Savannah, I saw other homes down long tunnels formed by the boughs of live-oaks, shaggy with Spanish moss. Some were deserted, in yards overgrown with underbrush, playgrounds, my guide told me, for rabbits and even deer. But the reminders of slavery were not only those of grandeur. A few miles from Thunderbolt, where Georgia State College faces the present, is Lazarette, facing an ugly past. Here the slaves who became ill on the middle passage from Africa were quarantined. For the many that died, there was a convenient graveyard nearby.

Savannah's past has not been so tied up with the planters as has Charleston's. I find it symbolic that Hermitage, Savannah's famed mansion, is no longer even a ghost, that Henry Ford has used its "Savannah Grey" brick for his home on the Ogeechee River, that two of its slave-huts, restored, are on display in Dearborn, Michigan, and that a large bag plant now occupies the site. The old red brick buildings of Factor's Row, with their balconies overhanging the river front, and the iron bridges spanning the cobblestoned ramps slopping to the docks, are as typical of Savannah as the colonnaded facades and double stairways. Savannah has long boasted of its vast exports of naval stores, cotton, tobacco, sugar, lumber, and turpentine. It now has over two hundred varied industries.

But many traditionalists do not want the city to grow too commercial. They look, perhaps enviously, to Charleston rather than Atlanta. In the evenings in Savannah an odor hangs heavy on the air. The natives attribute its sourest components to the fertilizer factory, or to the pulp mills making paper and bags and rayon out of the slash pines of the region. I unwisely mentioned that I had heard that the smell came from the marshlands, after the tides ebbed. My host, a Negro of an old Savannah family, was vexed. The smell of the marshes, he told me, is a salty tang, bracing and pleasing, a distinctive excellence of the old Savannah. It is the newfangled factories that are smelling up the place.

⇥ GONE WITH WHAT WIND ⇤

In Savannah, I had several talks with a patrician lady who was working on a book about coastal Negroes. Our talks led to recent fiction, finally to *Gone with the Wind*. She cavalierly dismissed my criticism that the novel was sinister in its implications about slavery and Reconstruction. "You musn't be so sensitive," she advised me. "That's the way things *were* then. What I object to in *Gone with the Wind* is that Margaret Mitchell centers it about Atlanta and makes a heroine out of the upstart daughter of an Irish immigrant."

To Savannah and Charleston, Atlanta is as much an upstart as Scarlett O'Hara. Atlanta is not bothered. After all, to a money-minded metropolis, the payoff is that Atlanta's novel has outsold any about Charleston, Savannah, or Natchez. To the drugstore literary trade, Peachtree Street has become more famous than Savannah's Bull Street and Charleston's Battery. It was from shops near Five Points that the craze for antebellum hats and frocks (somewhat streamlined, of course) swept the nation. As the pert hussy, Scarlett, strode brazenly past her more retiring older cousins, so Atlanta. From low beginnings as Marthasville, Atlanta became the industrial capital of the confederacy, and is now capital of the largest state east of the Mississippi and the busiest railroad center in the South: "Look, we have come a long way, in spite of fire, hurricane, or Sherman!"

True to its go-getting spirit, Atlanta is not so enamored of the past as other cities. Sherman's attacking and Hood's departing armies (forerunning the "scorched earth" tactics) rid the city of what antebellum mansions it had. I saw decrepit houses, taller than the surrounding Negro slums but no prouder. They may have looked antebellum, but they merely aged too soon. The fancy scrolls and curleycews on their porches and gables dated from the General Grant period. Their favorite gray was overcast with soot from the soft coal burned in Atlanta's furnaces. The elegant Southern style manor-houses, my friends told me, were of the twentieth century, built by the Coca-Cola and other dynasties who lived in Druid Hills, or along those winding drives like Paces Ferry Road, with strips of rolling woodland shutting out the prying passers-by. Statues of Henry Grady, advocate of an industrialized South, and of Tom Watson, populist champion, are respected in Atlanta as much as any statues of Confederate heroes. Both seemed to me to be caught in unfortunate poses: Grady looks as if he is reaching beneath his arm for a pistol as he faces the New South at Five Points, and Tom Watson as if he has just tossed a ringer in a game of horseshoes on the Capitol lawn.

But let no one be confused about Atlanta's attachment to the Lost Cause. An anecdote tells of a woman in Ohio who was told that she could not collect insurance for her husband, because the policy did not pay off on suicides. She insisted that her husband had been murdered in Atlanta by parties unknown. "No, madame," said the adjuster. "Anytime a Yankee enters an Atlanta hotel whistling 'Marching through Georgia,' we call that suicide."

Markers and shafts of stone are not enough for Atlantans; they have a cyclorama of the Battle of Atlanta to recall the Lost Cause. With two friends, I visited the Cyclorama Building, a white terra cotta building with tall columns, set in Grant Park (named for a Confederate Colonel, not the General). At the rear of the building is the Rotunda, where in spite of the preview descriptions that I had heard, I was startled by the painting. It is 400 feet in circumference, fifty feet in height and nine tons in weight, the sole survivor of three Civil War cycloramas painted by a staff of German artists. In 1937, professional painters and sculptors continued the picture into the forty foot space between the circling canvas and the central platform. On this platform, reached through a tunnel and a stairway, observers could start anywhere, follow the vast canvas around, and return to the starting point. They could look into the muzzle of breechloaders, into the fixed glaring eyes of a charging Rebel, could almost reach over to parry the rifle-stock and bayonet being thrust at them. The plaster soldiers range from four feet to twenty-two inches, but so marvelous is the scaling for perspective that they look life-size. Clubbing, stabbing, shooting, yelling, dying soldiers, with bright red blood splashing their dusty blue and gray uniforms; corpses of men and horses, shell-shattered tree trunks, high-reaching Georgia pines, patches of bushes, weeds, and grass, log fences, cotton-bale barricades, wagon wheels, cannon and rifle smoke looking like bolls and wisps of cotton; guns jetting flame; all are done with immense realism.

My friend Anne, who directs dramatics, said briefly, "Belasco." Dickie, our companion, was carrying a chip on each shoulder, and wise-cracked not too softly as we slowly circled the platform. But even Dickie could smell out no particular Rebel bias in the lecturer's spiel. The lecturer, young, bespectacled, and Phi Beta Kappa, rattled off the information factually, fully, and a bit drily, as Dickie, a good actor but no historian, insisted. I told Dickie that he had probably been giving the same talk for years. I have wondered since, if after seeing the smoke-filled scenery of another kind of warfare in France, Dickie has ever thought back upon this recreated Civil War battle.

The painters and sculptors arrested one crucial moment in the important fighting around Atlanta. It was probably as close to the actuality as memory and photography could get—from the beleaguered Hurt House, red-bricked and spindly-columned, to the railroad painted on the canvas and then running a spur of real, though scaled-down rails, spikes, and ties across the field, to the picture on the other side. This railroad was a key point in this part of the battle. In the far haze are the city of Atlanta and Stone Mountain. *Gone with the Wind* has preserved on celluloid the scene of this furious defense of Hurt House, with the Confederates firing from behind cotton bales. It is likely that the paint and plaster of the cyclorama will outlast the celluloid. The amazing realism was produced not only by the artists' meticulous workmanship and knowledge of color, perspective, and lighting, but also by other factors like the tons of vari-hued Georgia clay which were packed into the field upon which one might jump from the observation platform. The blue or gray-clad figures—whether plaster, sculpture, or painted—look like living, breathing men; certainly at first glance they do. For some reason I did not care much for Old Abe, the Yankee eagle, fixed high above and trying to out scream the busting shrapnel. Otherwise, the Germans wanted thorough realism and they got thorough realism. A Confederate soldier charges a Yankee, both red-faced and moustachioed, grimy and sweaty, their uniforms caked with red clay, flecked with blood, their shoes worn out and muddy. Looked at too closely they seemed stiff and artificial, a bit like wax-works, as painted statuary always seems to do. Still I thought of Keats and the Grecian Urn. These warriors were fixed for centuries, I surmised, in murderous enmity.

Forever will they fight, and the guides drone on. I murmured to Anne. "Awful," she said. I did not know whether she was rebuking my bad line, or dreading the bad moral. But I drew no moral; the moral of permanent sectional estrangement is one that, Legend or no Legend, I refuse to accept.

Dickie was grumpy as we walked through the tall columns. "It's a tourist's curiosity. When it's no longer a shrine, and doesn't make money, it will close up," he said hopefully. I thought it would be a civic pride of Atlanta for a long time to come.

But if the plaster and canvas of the cyclorama fade, are destroyed, or are shut away, as permanent a memorial as man's ingenuity can devise has been planned for the granite of Stone Mountain. Of my several trips to Stone Mountain, the one that I best remember is the first, when I went with Mac, Windy, and Red. Mac wanted to see it, Connecticut Yankee that he was; Windy, a native Atlantan, had never seen it and did not want us Northern Negroes to have anything on him; Red went along for the ride, frankly indifferent. He had seen Stone Mountain from the Seaboard Railroad and that was close enough for him. "We couldn't get away from it. Looked like it was trying to keep up with the engine." I remembered how the Seaboard curved around it, keeping it in view for a long time.

Beyond Decatur, Stone Mountain hove into view, a gray bulge jutting out from the flat plain. "The Appalachians ran off and left it here," said Windy. From the curving roads we got different views: now of a fairly easy parabolic slope, but more often of a solid greenish gray wall. As we got close to it, we saw the glaring, light smooth gray expanse, without tree, shrub, or grass on its face.

We drove behind a small frame tourist shop and museum. Among the few natives and the tourists, Mac's new car and the four Negroes who got out did not occasion much interest, certainly no more than the Connecticut license plate. Our money was welcome in the store; descendants of slaves or not, if we wanted to buy the smoothed off blocks of granite with stickers of Lee, his entourage and the stars and bars on them, it was our own lookout. Other knick-knacks— tiny bales of cotton and little brown jugs—had Stone Mountain lettered on them. I bought a slab of granite, decorated with Lee and his generals, for a paper weight. Red bought up all the postcards that showed a pickaninny immersing his grinning mouth in a hunk of watermelon. He intended sending them to Harlem, he said, loud enough for the quizzical cracker behind the counter to hear him. But we knew better; he was taking as many out of circulation as he could.

Each of us got a Coke or Dr. Pepper to help against the scorching heat. Uncertain of the etiquette, Windy stood in the doorway, one foot over the threshold, one foot in, good interracialist that he was. Mac, Red, and I drank ours in the store. Nobody seemed to mind. We scratched our names with a faulty pen on the visitor's book, Red writing his with a flourish and, unfortunately, a blot.

Then we went out to see the mountain. It was, of course, stupendous. On the sheer face of it, we saw Robert E. Lee on Traveller, the outlined face of Jefferson Davis, and behind them Stonewall Jackson. I had heard in Atlanta that a breakfast party had been held on Lee's shoulder at the unveiling ceremony, that from the crown of Lee's hat to Traveller's hoof was the height of a ten story building. But the stickers and the picture postcards differed greatly from the dim scratching that showed on the face of the mountain. The likenesses were there: the Greek God Lee; Jefferson Davis, ascetic, stiffly proud; and Stonewall, Old Testament prophet. I was ready to recognize the achievement of getting more than conventional approximation into this granite. The height of the sheer drop and the massiveness of that granite formation were impressive without any doubt. But the majesty of Borglum's dream and Lukeman's continuation of it affected me less than the other evidence of man's handiwork there: the flimsy stairway and scaffolding and the spikes driven into the rock. I felt more sympathy for the men who had risked their lives toting dynamite and drills, timber and cement down those ladder-like stairs than I felt awe for the classic carving of the faces. It was so unfinished. A streak of rust ran down Traveller's flank; other streaks stained with bright gray. There was a heap of rubble at the foot of the drop, huge chunks in reality, but ordinary slabs from where we stood. Gray dust seemed to hang over everything in that heat; it lay heavy on the trees that, tall as they were, seemed just a fringe at the foot of the mountain. Buzzards soared in the windless air, not over the crown of the mountain, but against its face, still far up, however, above the tops of the Georgia pines. I thought that the Memorial Association would dearly like to have those omens away.

When we had looked our fill, we started back to the car. Mac was missing. Red and I found him in the museum gift shoppe. Mac had discovered another car from Connecticut, and was standing at the souvenir counter talking easily with two white couples from New Haven. He had not known them before but he knew some of their friends, and they had heard of him. They started rattling off names. I was afraid they'd wind up in the Yale bowl, at the last Harvard-Yale game, so I butted in. The man behind the counter was still indifferent, but a few crackers in the corner were alert and glum.

I jogged Mac's elbow. "O.K.," he said, "I'll be right out. Well, I'll be seeing you folks. Be sure to tell Anne Driscoll that you saw Mac. It certainly was good seeing people from home."

He shook hands all around, male and female.

"Folks from New Haven," he said to us as we passed the glowering crackers. "They know a lot of folks I know. Fancy meeting them in Georgia."

"Yes, at Stone Mountain," Red said drily.

We found Windy sitting in the back seat of the Dodge. He had picked up my copy of *The Undefeated* by Gerald Johnson, which tells the story of Borglum's carving, which was destroyed before this one of Lukeman's took its place. "Gentlemen, I give you the Lost Cause," he said. Then he intoned from the book:

> It is a doomed army that marches across the hill, a doomed leader that sits his charge in the foreground. The battles toward which they march are to be lost battles, the flags that flaunt above them are to be trampled in bloody mire. Yet on they must go, for they are caught in that trap of destiny against which the gods themselves strive in vain.

"Oh, shut up, Windy," said Red. Mac got in the car. "All those going back to Atlanta, get in. The rest of you can stay out here looking at the Lost Cause."

We piled in; Mac started the car and we were off. He had hardly meshed the gears into second when we heard a yelling and a clatter. A jalopy, packed with the young crackers we had just left at the shop, rattled alongside for a while, then shot across the front bumper. One cracker yelled back at us, "Get off the road, niggers!" Mac threw on the brakes and turned sharp off the pike to the shoulder. He yelled, but the jalopy was gone in a flurry of gray dust.

"The bastards," said Mac, slowly turning back onto the concrete.

"What do you mean, Lost Cause?" Red asked Windy. "How do you figure *lost*?"

I thought about this later, wondering since Stone Mountain Memorial is so unfinished how far the Lost Cause was truly lost. The United States Government accepted the memorial as a national undertaking, in the faith that idealization of Lee and Jefferson and other secessionists would make for union. Two Republican Congressmen sponsored the adoption and President Calvin Coolidge okayed an authorization to mint five million half-dollars to aid the project. These coins were to be sold by the Memorial Association at a hundred percent profit. Other vast sums were raised. But Stone Mountain Memorial is still far from the grandiose dreams. There were charges of fraud, continual bickering, misunderstanding, and buck-passing. Borglum destroyed his models and fled from Georgia into the mountains of North Carolina, where the Governor refused to extradite him. Borglum died embittered. Lukeman is now dead. The third sculptor, Julian Harris, has had to wait out the panic and the war years. But I am not sure that the tragicomic history of this memorial means that interest in the Lost Cause is in swift decline. Against the unfinished carvings must be set the fact that on the top of Stone Mountain, the new Ku Klux Klan sprang into being, with blazing crosses and all the fixings. And under whatever new disguises, in spirit if not in name, the Ku Klux Klan still thrives in Dixie.

For a gentler reminiscence of Atlanta's past, I went out to see "Wren's Nest," along with Griff Davis, a young photographer. This modest, typical old West End home, with many gables and gingerbread ornamentation, is known as a Mecca for American schoolchildren and their teachers, who want to see where the kindly Joel Chandler Harris created Uncle Remus, Brer Rabbit, Brer Tortoise, and Sister Cow.

Well, so did I; so I rang the front door bell. A little flaxen-haired girl answered. In response to my request to go through the house, she stood there with her blue eyes wide and, like Uncle Remus's Tar Baby, "she kept on sayin' nothin'." Then she skittered off. In a few minutes, her father, the caretaker, came to the door, hurriedly putting on a shirt.

I told him that we would like to visit the memorial. He started to open the screen door, and then noticed Griff. I had my hat on and he hadn't looked closely at me, but Griff is brown.

"Who's this boy?" he asked, staccato.

"He is Mr. Davis, of Atlanta University," I answered slowly.

"No," the man said. "Sorry, but I can't let you all come in. The Association has told me not to let in the colored."

I told him that I was writing a book, that at Harvard University in Massachusetts I had written research papers on Joel Chandler Harris, that I had a scholar's interest in Harris and his contribution to American literature, that Griff, Mr. Davis, was a serious student of photography, attempting to make camera studies of authentic Americana. I knew I wasn't going to get in, but I poured it on. I was thinking how the lonely lad, Joel, had hung around Negro cabins, none of them

shut to him, listening to every wisp of talk, storing in his memory all the anecdotes and tricks of speech and song, piling up a rich compost as it were to produce those fine flowers that made his fame and fortune. So I poured it on. His
mouth was hanging open when I stopped, and Griff was grinning.

"I didn't make the rule," he complained. "Far as I'm concerned, it wouldn't
make no difference. But the Association won't stand for it. They'd have my job."

He added that it would be all right to walk around the house, even to the
gardens in the backyard. We declined the honor, but stopped at the pink-marble
walk leading to the side of the house. Upon each paving stone is printed the
name of a Georgia author: Augustus Longstreet, Frank Stanton, Sidney Lanier,
Thomas Holly Chivers.

"Now, take Chivers," I said pompously to Griff. The caretaker was on our heels,
listening. "He was an unknown poet, of rare, eccentric genius, much like, and
quite influential upon Edgar Allan Poe. People in Georgia called him crazy, but I
do not know that he was any crazier than the rest of them."

Griff turned to the caretaker, and asked, "I suppose it would be all right for
me to take pictures?" The man thought it over, then, "I reckon so," he grunted,
and left. As rapidly as Griff focused the camera and worked those plates, he still
could get only the front of Wren's Nest and the capacious rear of the caretaker,
scrambling up the steps.

⇥ SYMBOL OF THE OLD SOUTH ⇤

I should see Natchez, I had been told, "where the Old South still lives." Here, I learned from the guidebooks, more of the old plantation homes were still maintained than anywhere else; here "the leisurely charm of the Old South has lingered long after it was supplanted elsewhere by the grim efficiency of the twentieth century."

My host and guide, bearing an honored French name, and as courteous as any Frenchman could be, knew his native Natchez thoroughly. He started our touring at Natchez Bluffs, one of the best vantage points in the city, or for that matter in the United States, for impressive scenery. The first monument he showed me was not out of the past, however. It was the neat stone shaft erected by the city fathers in memory of the numerous Negroes who were killed in the notorious Natchez dancehall fire in 1940. Two of my host's cousins were named on the crowded bronze plaque.

From that grim reminder of our times we turned to the river view. The cluster of toy houses opposite formed the town Vidalia; stretching beyond it for miles I could see the flat plains of Louisiana. The Mississippi curves grandly at Natchez. My host pointed out the new cutaway that shortened the course of the river eighteen miles, an engineering feat, aiding flood control, lessening erosion, and inviting the renewed day of barge and steamboat traffic. My eyes followed the old course until it was lost in the blue mists; then I looked up the canal where it met the river again. The bluff on which we stood—one of a chain extending all the way to Vicksburg—had been background for much pageantry, I knew. Across the river on Louisiana sandbars, Natchez gentlemen had settled their points of honor with dueling pistols; around its swinging curve had steamed the floating palaces; and where that one rowboat seemed immovable, flatboatmen had roared their lusty way to New Orleans. I thought of the dandies and belles, the gamblers and tricksters, quadroon fancy girls, and river rousters; I remembered Mike Fink, the greenhorn Mark Twain learning a trick or two of piloting at this wide curve, and Fate Marable beating out the new jazz on the piano while Louis Armstrong lifted his small gay horn toward the hill. From the bluffs this day the scene was quiet; the ferry was moored and the sawmill below, while busy, sent up only tiny puffs of smoke and noise.

We drove down a steep incline to Natchez-Under-the-Hill. On this narrow shelf of land there was little to see but old ramshackly houses, the saw-mill, and a few other industries. Year by year, the *batture* was cut away by the river; now, at last, it is protected but the history is gone. There was little to recall its wild past of lust and ferocity in the rake-hell dives, of sudden yells and curses in the dark.

It was easy to imagine that dirks, or their twentieth-century descendants, could be wielded expertly now on some stranger, caught there alone after nightfall; but for all that it was merely a beaten-down slum for poor whites and Negroes, exiles now as always from the glamour of the hill above. It was hard to imagine the flat-boats tied up to the bank in long rows while the half-alligator, half-men swarmed over the sides to the brothels and saloons. Time, tornadoes, and the river had washed away this indisputable part of the Old South as effectively as the romancers expunged it from the Legend.

But the river has been no kinder to the glamour of Under-the-Hill. The century old Magnolia Vale is settling too, with famed gardens of boxwood hedge and gardenias and japonicas that the travelers admired from the steamboat decks. On the hill, however, preservation, restoration, and embellishment of the Old South has been a flourishing business. Showing me Connelly's Tavern on Ellicott Hill, my guide told me that Aaron Burr prepared his defense in one of its rooms; he rolled off the name of Blennerhasset so easily that I was ashamed of my ignorance. We looked at King's Tavern, a sturdy timber "blockhouse," considered to be the oldest building in the section, with its heavy door pock-marked with bullet holes. Both taverns were simple and unpretentious, obviously built to last, but undistinguished beside the great houses.

I noticed the many styles of these: the Greek revival of Choctaw, the "grand manner" of Dunleith, the "Southern Planter" style of The Briers, and what I learned was the Irish Manor style of Cherokee. I saw so many that a welter of impressions remained with me rather than clear-cut distinctions. But I remember the exceeding beauty of Dunleith, set back in a grove of beautiful oaks, its tall white columns two stories high, spaced around the railed-in galleries. Variations in the columns struck my untutored eye; D'Evereux, a late Greek revival, had massive fluted columns across its white front; Melrose has four columns framing its doorway; the Linden has many slender columns across an admirably wide porch. I was less struck by Dunleith, D'Evereux, and the classics, however, than by some of the other homes. The "grand manner" was beautiful, but it had no element of strangeness in it; I had been here before, I felt. I learned why later: D'Evereux, for instance, was used by Hollywood for the picture "Heart of Maryland." I had certainly been surprised when I first saw that picture, since I had been brought up in the heart of Maryland. I realized how the Legend, by using them over and over, really did injustice to the undoubted beauty of such mansions as these. D'Evereux, Dunleith, Belmont, Melrose, Auburn, Monteigne, Stanton Hall, and the few others were never common in the past; they should be left as they were: exceptional magnificence that briefly was achieved in those flush times along the Mississippi when the planters' wealth and the architects' genius were happily met.

The unpretentious "Southern Planter" style, which has so many representatives in Natchez, struck me as more significant. I could believe that people lived in these homes; I had wondered just what kind of life could go on in the Greek temples, the colonnaded museums. Cottage Gardens, Glenfield, Hope Farm, The Burn, and The Briers, birthplace of Jefferson Davis's wife, Varina Howells, are charming examples of these story and a half dwellings, whose beauty is no less sure for being modest rather than grand. Here are verandas instead of porticoes, wooden pillars instead of Greek columns, steeply sloping instead of flat roofs. Some of the antebellum houses that I saw—Belvidere and Hawthorne, for instance—seemed definitely of our own times.

I saw the famed fanlights and classic doorways, the well-tended lawns and profuse gardens, the delicate grill work, and I realized that they deserved even the rhapsodies of the guidebook poets. But I had to take on faith the descriptions of the marble mantels, the spiral stairways, the massive poster beds, the Hepplewhite and Sheraton, the serving table "from the Duke of Devonshire," the mahogany and rosewood furnishings, the china and silver, the handmade wax fruit under a glass globe, all the luxury that made Joseph Hergesheimer nearly swoon.

All of the classic doorways were not closed to me. Stanton Hall, for instance, as elegant and imposing as any, is open to the public, and in Natchez I could qualify as a member of the public. My host informed me that it was possible to enter some of the other mansions, and his mother, quite informed on the whole business, assured me that such was true. But I stayed outside. I knew in general what I would find. And I felt more in line with history, staying outside.

Later I thumbed through the picture books of Natchez. The hoopskirted belles posed on the verandas of Connelly's Tavern, or sitting at a spinning wheel, or standing framed in the beautiful doorways, seemed doll-like and unconvincing. The Confederate ball that the Pilgrimage held annually also seemed like play-acting; I could not take it any more seriously than I could the singing of the Negroes who needed dimes and quarters for the shoes, robes and harps they sang about. These brought back no history to me. Tourists are regaled with the tragedy of Longwood. The story goes that at the call to arms of the Civil War the workers left their tools where they fell. Now the curious can see, for a price, the paint brushes stuck in paint that has hardened in the seventy-five years, the saws and hammers and nails lying where they were abandoned. The workers were in one big hurry, certainly. Treasured as a symbol of the shocking ending of the antebellum dream, Longwood strikes me instead as a symbol of the determination to cling to the exact past, regardless of absurdity. From the pictures, Longwood is pompous and ugly; if the interior matched the completed exterior, the workmen should have left earlier.

The society matrons and belles in flowing dimity and muslin representing the *grand dames* of the past, are of course more beautiful than Longwood. But they can bring back little of the past even to the unprejudiced. Quite as many of the old mansions are owned by newcomers as by members of the original families, and some of the owners are even Yankees. Nor do the participants in the Pilgrimage Week have their eyes set backward at the phantom past; many are in all likelihood concerned with the urgent present. In *Deep South*, the first rate cultural study by the Davises and Gardners, I read that membership in the Natchez Historical Club is a rather "hard nut for the upper-middle-class woman to crack." In lieu of membership, these women offer their services as guides, or their homes as rooming houses for visitors. Sometimes they serve meals with Negro servants in traditional antebellum costumes. Some even become assistant hostesses in an "old home," wearing hoopskirts for a week, and lecturing on history and architecture.

But there is more than prestige involved. The connection of pageantry and cash, which should never be forgotten in considering the Old South, is here too. The cleavage in the Garden Club was well covered a few years ago in Southern newspapers, and my host's mother added details, siding with the older group, the seceders. The first club had set aside one-third of the proceeds from the annual week to the club for preservation, beautification, and restoration of the homes and two-thirds to the homeowners; the new Pilgrimage Garden Club gave three-fourths of the net to the home owners and one-fourth to civic purposes. Snobbishness, or if you will, family pride, also entered into the angry controversy. At any rate, there are two pilgrimages now, each one to its own preserves of antebellum houses.

Tourists to Natchez are guided also to the inglorious past, to the shameful and revolting Goat Castle where tourists can hear an eccentric hermit play his antique piano for twenty-five cents. The once fine mansion is in shambles, where chickens, ducks, geese, and goats have the run of the place. The curious visit the place in droves, since sex and murder and abnormality were played up when the old man stood trial for murder a few years ago. Goat Castle is the Gothic horror amidst the classic calm; the guidebooks are careful to state that the inmate's father was a Yankee.

We drove up to the gate which had a sign on it: Keep Out. My host told me that we could get in easily enough, but I was uninterested. I merely wanted a good view of the house. I felt no tourist's curiosity about the old man and his guardian; it seemed a bit obscene to ferret them out. Let them alone with their past, too.

What was the place of Negroes in this restoration; what was their role in the pageantry? I remember that the main highway skirted Dunleith, and then shortly afterwards passed a line of Negro shanties, well preserved and painted, but still shanties. Skilled Negro carpenters had built the glory crowing the hill; perhaps some of their descendants lived in the shacks at the bottom. Otherwise the role of Negroes was the expected one: they tended the gardens and the manors; during the Pilgrimage Weeks a few extras with good voices could sing spirituals in costume; a few servants could wait on the tourists, and a few mammies could prepare barbecue in the spacious grounds.

In the homes that were open all the time, faithful old retainers still served, with inverted pride in their quality white folks. I learned that for a long time the owners of Melrose took care of ancient ex-slaves whose primary duty was pulling the punka during meals. Most significant of the Legend, however, is the picture of Old Wash, the only Negro included in any of the guidebooks that I saw. His woe-begone face, the handkerchief wrapping his head, the worn hat, are used to illustrate a Natchez custom "of placing coins in a box for old darky beggars . . . a thoughtful, good-natured gesture to the needy Negro from his 'white folks.' Uncle Wash is a 'regular customer on Penny Day.' " He may be free, he may be wretched, but the Old South looks out for its own; his needs will be cared for by the pennies.

The last Negro relic of the pageantry that I saw was very different from Old Wash. Outside of Natchez, as a come-on for tourists, is the Mammy Gas Station and Barbecue Stand. With clean-cut features, a trim waist, and an elegant hoopskirt, a tall, erect statue of a Mammy stands there, fronting the highway so proudly that her bandana seems out of place. My host explained why: the yarn goes that she was intended to be a Southern belle, but when the bodice was poured, the bust filled past all planning. Natchez objected to the breasts being so pendulous, and the statue's complexion was colored to a deep chocolate. Hoopskirt and waist and features still belong to the belle, but it is a colored girl, Egyptian-like, who welcomes the tourists to Natchez and invites the white natives to barbecue. The skirts cover quite an expanse, and a dining room was built therein. It is said, however, that the place is not popular; that the doorway in the hoopskirt opens less and less frequently. Pageantry has not paid in this venture, and the crude monument may soon be destroyed.

In one antebellum home in the vicinity of Natchez, I was a guest, not a tourist. Its history held great interest, increased because it was of a kind omitted from the guidebooks. A Negro family, "people of color," to use the distinction preferred around Natchez, owned this place. The father of the present owner had been thrifty, industrious and intelligent, and though a slave, had piled up a tidy sum, hoarding the dollars he earned by hiring himself out, until he finally had enough to buy himself. After the war, when the plantation was put up for auction, he outbid all others. It had been a rundown and mismanaged tract, but the new owner soon made a prosperous go of it. Making things click was no novelty to him. He had been a capable manager in another's interest; now he used his brains and brawn for himself. It was not an instance of bottom rail on top; it was proof that this rail should never have been laid on the bottom.

As we crossed a rickety wooden bridge we got a full view of the house, set well back from the road. It was of the French Planter type, a story and a half tall with a gallery extending across the spacious front. The barnyard was a compact unit of barn and stables, slave kitchen, corncribs, tool buildings, and the rest. Antebellum in age, they were contemporary in use; they housed gleaming modern tools alongside slave heirlooms. Fat hogs browsed around the foot of fodder stacks or nursed the heap of pinders on the porch of the barn. Chickens and ducks were everywhere under foot; the son cracked his long whip, discouraging the brash young steers. A very old, very black woman, her teeth about gone, was sitting in a cane-bottomed rocker stripping peanuts from the vines. She was surly at first until, watching closely, she saw that her mistress was friendly to us. Then she opened up slightly. She was born on a neighboring plantation and had never been many miles from it.

She seemed as much a part of the history of the place as the substantial brick kitchen (the slave waiters had had to carry the trays up the long back stairs, no cooking in that house). Old iron utensils and other relics were still hanging there. There were several fine old trees, festooned with Spanish moss. A crumbling brick house well over a hundred yards away at the end of a dim patch, was pointed out as the antebellum toilet. An earlier curiosity was satisfied.

Our hostess was busy, but more glad to see us. An old friend of my guide, she conducted us graciously through the house. But I could see that her natural pride in antiques was mingled with the pressing problems of running this big place with little help. The plantation may no longer be as flourishing as once it was under the father, but the daughter seems to be doing as good a job as possible in a time when so many farmers are taking a rude beating.

Five long doors, one for each of the front rooms, let onto the broad veranda. The rooms were large and high-ceilinged, with floors and woodwork of cypress. There were many heirlooms: solid heavy furniture, old coins, really valuable pictures (our hostess rather indifferently mentioned how collectors plagued her for some of them). I was glad to see some old pictures of Negro Reconstruction legislators, and a bust of Frederick Douglass. I saw two fine old tester (teester) beds, quite the equal in age and craftsmanship, my guide told me, to more publicized beds in Natchez. And at last I saw a punka in action. As a youngster I had had the job of sweeping the flies away with a brash of leaves over my elders at meals, but here was the real thing. I gave the twine a slight pull and the graceful wooden sweep started swinging. In this high dining room it had kept the breeze and the flies from circulating over many different kinds of heads.

The back rooms, less spacious than the front but still good sized, had once opened on a minor veranda, but that was gone with the years. Whoever had built this place in the old days had certainly got himself a commodious, sturdy, dignified home. The builders had used the means close at hand; dowel pins, for instance, had been used for nails, but there was one bit of foreign luxury in the Italian marble steps to the veranda. A visitor had offered a tidy sum for this treasure, but our hostess told us she had preferred not to sell.

From the veranda the view was a grand one over the rolling hills, across the highways, to a narrow river, and brought up sharply by a sheer bluff. Cousins of the hostess owned a good-sized place over there. I imagined the old French-Negro-Indian patriarch sitting on the veranda in the cool of the evening looking over these wide acres. Once he had labored here; his kinsmen had been slaves here. Now it was his, fruit of his energy and saving.

One story of the house is that after the Civil War the family took in the old white ex-mistress of the plantation, since she had no place to go. It is not altogether a pretty story. Old mistis suffered a paralytic stroke and her ex-slaves and their children had to care for her. She sat there on the veranda in a large rocker, mute and drooling, but often attempting her former imperiousness. Once a young attendant, irritated at her lofty ways, boxed her ears. Perhaps they did take advantage of her defenselessness; perhaps there was callousness and even occasional cruelty. But they did feed her and shelter her in her weak old age. They did not put her out to starve. In short, they did to her what her grandfather allegedly had done to theirs, and what the Legend has boasted of as one of its graces.

➤ A TOUR OF HISTORY: OLD NEW ORLEANS ◄

The stretch along the gulf from Pascagoula to Biloxi to Pass Christian to Bay St. Louis to Mulatto Bayou prepared me for New Orleans. Old French bungalows in shady thick gardens; the crosses and Catholic shrines; the shacks propped on stilts at the edge of the bays and bayous; the oyster shell roads bending into lush wildernesses where the tangled elephant-eared or lance-like plants showed all shades of green; cypress knees hunching swollen out of the muck; flowers delicately hued or like flame or startlingly white; sluggish bayous set in green frames; bearded water oaks and willows; straight long-leaf pines; palmettoes; the blue waters of the gulf, dazzling in the sunlight—all were fit settings for easy living Latins. The beauty of crepe-myrtles and magnolias belonged here, but so did the littered beaches, briny and tangy, smelling of fish at low tide. Old Spain was here— the hanging moss went by the name of "Spaniards beard," and the yucca by the name of Spanish dagger. Old France was here in the houses, the cemeteries, and the people—Cajuns, Creole whites, Creole Negroes. It was hard to tell, looking at these olive, sloe-eyed brunettes, where one started and the other left off. The Indians had been here, leaving traces in the high cheek-bones and long, coarse, blue-black hair of many of the people, white and colored. But the Choctaws were gone; the grandsons of the Congo were here to stay.

From the singing river at Pascagoula to the stealthy Mulatto Bayou, from the drone and hiss of the breakers on the beach, or their slaps against the sea-wall, to the wind stirring in the pinetops, the refrain of the Gulf Coast seemed to be: "Tek yo' time, mon ami, tek it easy." The pinewoods give the turpentine and lumber; the swamps the game birds and beasts; scratch the black dirt a little so the yams, collards, and okra can grow; the close-by waters give the oysters, shrimps, flounders, and speckled sea trout; the deep waters give the Spanish mackerel, the pompano, and the lemonfish. So in comes the little money to make the pleasure, to make the good times, man. It was easy, traveling without purpose along the Gulf, to lose the perplexities of the present, to believe oneself back in a langorous timeless past. I was ready for the green city that Frenchmen, remembering Paris and Marseille, had created in Mediterranean America.

Her lovers have done well by New Orleans. Early grammarians criticized the city's name "Nouvelle Orleans" for its feminine adjective; the Duc d'Orleans had most surely been a man. But it is a woman that the authors have written of New Orleans: Lyle Saxon as fabulous enchantress; George Washington Cable as a strange beauty, not without flashes of cruelty and morbidity; Lafcadio Hearn as an exotic mistress that he came to detest. Herbert Asbury has described her more gaily than his bishop grandfather would have approved as a harlot. Grace King praises her as an aristocratic grand dame. They all intrigue the imagination.

The first person I talked to in New Orleans disillusioned me. He was an Irish cabdriver. "Misterr," he said in a rich brogue when I was expecting patois, "you arre in the sinkhole of the worrld."

He did not mean that the city was low-lying, built up from swampland, nor that the day was steaming hot. His point he proved by a harangue on the current battle between the gangs led by Huey Long and the Mayor. Neither one, he said, was worth a continental damn. Not worth a breakage of the wind in a tropical storm (these were not exactly his words).

As he drove he beamed at my confusion over "uptown" and "downtown." "It is a cockeyed city, mister," he said. "What you strangers want to rememberr is: Uptown is downtown and vizy-verzy."

After long figuring, I got used to going uptown or South, from Canal Street. But Canal Street does not run due East and West but southeast-northwest, so a large part of northern New Orleans is uptown too. Then there is the section known as "back of town," that many visitors enter first. In the French Quarter corners are not identified as northeast or southwest, but as "uptown river" or "downtown lake" (that is, toward Lake Pontchartrain, which borders the city on the North). I often went uptown to the river, although in almost every other city that I know the river is downtown. But the Frenchmen were, as they boast, logical: I understand that the city sloped gently but definitely upward from Canal Street toward the southern levee. When the river is full, it is several feet higher than the city. The logic of geography, however, escaped me. New Orleans lies on the east bank of the Mississippi, but one ferry to Algiers, on the west bank, goes east. The bridge across the river slants southeast. The Mississippi runs northward alongside much of uptown New Orleans; it also runs south and east. Most of the city is enclosed by the river in a rough semicircle; the French Quarter—the oldest part—is on the crescent from which the city gets one of its nicknames. Knowledge of the snaking Mississippi and a look at the map will clear up some of the above confusion. After I had worked it out, however, I was still lost.

But an Irishman's crusty garrulity and my slowness in catching on to the quirks of the layout did not make me believe that New Orleans was a crazy city. Instead I felt that the old Frenchmen planned the city the way they wanted it; their descendants for a long time ordered it the way they wanted. It was a city that just did not give a damn. Love me or leave me, cela ne fait rien. . . .

I liked that about it. And I enjoyed looking at the historic places of a city that had gone its own gay way under four different flags: those of France, Spain, the United States, and the Confederate States. A fifth flag would have flown over the

Cabildo, but for the grace of God and Andrew Jackson's battalions of Creole gentlemen, San Domingan refugees, Kentucky raftsmen, freemen of color, slaves, Tennessee sharpshooters, Baratarians, Lafittes' buccaneers, and Choctaw Indians—a
rabble of fighting fools.

So Jackson is one of the city's heroes, certainly the chief American hero, com-
memorated more than Lee or Jefferson Davis. In Jackson Square I looked at the
dour-faced hero, the new frontier issue of the medieval knight on his rearing
charger, doffing his hat, as debonairly as a democrat could. The proud stance of
his horse, I understand, is a sculptor's achievement. No iron rod props this lung-
ing steed; his own solid hindlegs support more than ten tons of bronze. Good
horse, good rider. On the base of the statue General Ben Butler had cut the words:
"The Union Must and Shall Be Preserved." Local historians dislike this vandal-
ism, another mark of the Beast. But I saw nothing wrong about the inscription:
those were Jackson's words, and they were good words. I know that Old Hickory
was a slaveowner and from all reports a hard one; I know that like a typical fron-
tiersman he was unjust to the Indians. But the Confederates cannot claim him.
And I remembered with pleasure some other good words that he said. After the
famous battle of New Orleans he spoke to his two Negro regiments:

> I invited you to share in the perils and I divide the glory with your white
> countrymen. I expected much of you. . . . But you surpass my hopes. . . .
> The President of the United States shall be informed of your conduct . . .
> and the voice of the Representatives of the American nation shall applaud
> your valor, as your General now praises your ardor.

I got this out of Charles Rousseve's *The Negro in Louisiana*, not from the many
guidebooks to historic New Orleans that I thumbed through. I should like to see
it engraved somewhere. Near the Pentagon Building maybe. Jackson is commemo-
rated in several places. I noticed a big sign advertising the Jackson Brewing Co.,
and on the back pages of a folder dedicated to the history of the St. Louis Cathedral and the Ursulins Convent I read an advertisement: "JAX, Best Beer in Town."
(Though of the modern, this may give a clue to historic New Orleans also.) Jackson Square is much older than Old Hickory. As the Place d'Armes, it was the center
of affairs of French and Spanish New Orleans. Here assembled the incoming
shiploads of early settlers from France, some of them as sound and heroic as any
pioneers have been. Many, however, as early historians attest with more Gallic
frankness than their filial descendants, were decayed gentlemen, aristocrats who
had run afoul of the law, and a goodly sprinkling of thieves, foot-pads, smugglers, confidence men, deserters, and pimps. Here also were gathered the "filles
à la casset" girls approved by France as wives for the colonists and given une

cassette of clothes and linen—truly a hope chest—as a parting dowry. There were also "filles de joie," prostitutes sent over from the houses of correction in Paris. These were not given cassettes by the government, although they surely needed clothes and linen as badly as their respectable sisters. A scene in *Manon Lescaut,* the 18th century novel, shows the pretty grisette Manon and her chevalier about to leave for New Orleans exile. According to Prevost the girls "were fastened together in sixes by chains around the middle of the body." Many of the girls were from hospitals and reformatories and some had been waylaid and kidnapped. They were shipped to America on a kind of middle passage for Caucasians. Like the early settlers from Africa, sometimes these girls revolted, attacking their guards. But once landed, they were grabbed up as quickly as the more respectable "casket" girls. Bienville had urged: "Send me wives for my Canadians, they are running in the woods after Indian girls." They were probably chasing the few slave girls too. In 1724 Bienville had to forbid the marriage or concubinage of whites, freeborn or manumitted Negroes with slaves. "Casket" girls, or trollops, all got their men and were married with the blessing of the church. "This merchandise was soon disposed of, so great was the want of the country," said city fathers, gratified.

Located at the heart of the French Quarter, or Vieux Carre (old square, meaning the old rectangular city), Jackson Square is a good place to start the round of historic spots. Facing the square are the St. Louis Cathedral, the Cabildo and the Presbytere, now housing the Louisiana Historical Museum. To the rear of the Cabildo are the old Spanish Arsenal and the site of the Calabozo (calaboose, prison). Thus, around Place d'Armes were built the institutions symbolizing civilization: the Church for worship, the Cabildo for government, the Calabozo for the sinners and law-breakers, and the Arsenal for war. The Cathedral still fills its early purpose, but the first building was destroyed by fire, and the second has been so repaired and altered that only the lower part remains as it was in 1794. The interior is ornate with frescoes, paintings, and statuary, too rich in color and meaning for my liking or understanding, an American correspondent, I imagine, to the medieval cathedrals. The Cabildo, a year younger, teaches history even in its architectural style, for Spanish-Moorish arches and French balconies are characteristic of it. Here was consummated the Louisiana Purchase, Jefferson's Folly then, Napoleon's since. But a great deal of pleasanter history for the Creoles to contemplate had centered in the Cabildo before the Americans came.

I walked through the Quarters, hunting places that had housed such history. I saw where other needs than civic and religious were satisfied. Flanking Jackson Square on two sides are America's oldest apartments, the Pontalba Buildings, whose galleries, extending over the sidewalk, are noted for graceful ironwork. Not far away—the entire Vieux Carre is only a dozen streets long by six or so wide, an oblong of less than a hundred squares—I saw the remodeled French Market, recreating the older style and probably the turmoil and smells on the former site.

> *I thought I heard Buddy Bolden say*
> *Thirty days in the market, take him away,*
> *Give him a new broom to sweep with, take him away.*

Passing Antoine's Restaurant, I read its advertisement in the tourist circular of "a particular atmosphere which enhances the artistically prepared dishes and develops to the highest degree the gastric fluids." It was housed in a fittingly old building, but was younger than some other cafés in the quarter. On Royal Street I saw the Café des Exiles, where refugees from the French and San Domingan revolutions had done their plotting and drinking. On Royal too was Old Sazerac House, birthplace of the noted New Orleans cocktail. On Bourbon I found the Old Absinthe House. Noticing the coincidence, I marveled at the hardihood of the colonists.

On Bourbon also is the Blacksmith Shop where legend has it that the Lafitte brothers, master pirates, used an honorable craft as front for "blackbirding," that is, the slave trade. Even so long ago they were in approved New Orleans fashion, using respectable fronts for shady businesses of smuggling, bootlegging, and selling "hot." The facts of the smithy are dubious—smuggling slaves in had to be almost as secret as the Underground Railroad out. There are even doubts as to which shack was the real hangout, one circular placing it four blocks from the one that is marked by a plaque. As I looked at the squat smithy, the dormer windows still seemed to enclose something mysterious and sinister behind the closed blinds. I could easily imagine black ivory lying in the small attic, after being run in through the devious bayous under the very noses of the Federal cutters. There is no doubt of the age of the peeling plaster and the bricks showing beneath, sandwiched between solid timbers. Today the smithy is a café serving tourists, not smugglers; the pirates dispense the food and the drinks.

Near at hand were many of the houses that Cable's magic kept alive. I thought how blessed New Orleans had been (Chamber of Commerce as well as History Societies) in having such an artist as Cable to record the city's romance, before he was exiled because of his decency to Negroes. New Orleans still uses him, discreetly of course, for the romance, not the revelation. I saw Madame John's Legacy, a ramshackly brick and frame house, the oldest, say the researchers, in all the Mississippi Valley. From that gallery between the slender colonnettes, pirates and gentlemen, ladies, loose and otherwise, had looked at the world passing below them. The most famous resident was Cable's John who left the house as a legacy to Zalli, a quadroon, called Madame John, and to Tite Poulette, her octoroon daughter. Not far away is "Sieur George's House," the "first skyscraper" of New Orleans. Its original three stories were considered too heavy for the soft soil, and when the fourth floor was added, people felt that the good Providence was tempted too far. I saw the imperial Haunted House where Dolphine Lalaurie, sweet and elegant at her soirees, tortured her slaves sadistically in their dark, gloomy quarters. When the scandal of her neurotic cruelty broke, a mob drove her from the city. Romantic also was Le Prete House where a Turk is supposed to have lived in secret enjoyment with his harem of beauties until one morning all were found murdered.

The Haunted House is now a welfare home; the Turk's harem is now a bank. A couple of blocks away from the latter is the old Orleans Ballroom, the chief scene of the "quadroon balls." It is now the Convent of the Holy Family, a community of colored nuns. Conveniently close for Quadroon Balls and often the cause for quarrels between the hot-blooded, jealous Creole aristocrats is St. Anthony's Garden, an early dueling site. Far off from the Quarter, across Bayou St. John in City Park are the gnarled massive dueling oaks, more favored by the gentlemen when opposition to dueling arose, and the civil authorities became watchful. Though I saw these places by sunlight, no feat of the imagination was needed to conjure up the young gallants, vain almost to the point of sickness, facing each other in the chill fog, their brains, their thumping hearts confused with honor and bravado and fear and murder.

The glamour of New Orleans was only part of the story. If some of the galleries were decorated with iron lace, hand-hammered by gifted slave artisans, if they were so deep that they shaded the streets, others were mere catwalks, protected by iron railings, nothing much to look at. Doorways were both classic and frontier in style; the wide blinds, the long shutters on windows and doors were sometimes things of beauty, sometimes merely battens contrived on the frontier to fend off the elements. Some of the houses were elegant with their Spanish gateways and fan windows; others quite as historic were starkly plain, built of cypress and moss and plaster to endure, not to charm. If the patios were carefully tended refuges of rainbow-hued beauty, the vagabond blooms and weeds along the canals and gutters were as lush and lavish. I knew that the layout of the city, with each block a moat surrounded by a draining ditch, had been a health hazard. Time and again the fever of Yellow Jack had ravaged the city. I knew that all the firing of cannon to dispel the miasma, the cold water cures and the onions placed about the sick-rooms, the cry of "Bring Out Yo' Dead" was as much a New Orleans refrain as "If [sic] Ever I Cease To Love," or "Danse Calinda, boum, boum!":

Oh, de hammer keeps ringing
On somebody's coffin
Good Lord, I know my time ain't long . . .

The city advertises its water as the purest in the nation, because of engineering and chemical advances. But I knew the battle for sanitation that had to be waged on this built up swamp, with water only a few feet below the surface of the ground. My friends told me unsavory tales of a folk-figure—Zizi the Bucketman—whose bucket brigades and wagons were needed since sewers were rare. In the flowered cemeteries the dead are not buried but are stored away above the ground, in vaults that the candid folk call "bake ovens," sometimes like marble file-cares. In the first St. Louis Cemetery, I saw the grave of Marie Laveau, the famous voodoo queen, but praised on the stone as bonne mère, bonne amie. In the second St. Louis Cemetery, a second simpler resting place for Madame Laveau, her voodoo followers, colored and white, believe this grave to be the authentic one, for it is here that they mark their red crosses and deposit food and small pieces of money. Two graves for the Madame. And her voodoo goes marching on.

I have neither eaten at Antoine's nor seen Mardi Gras ("New Orleans's biggest business") so some natives will say that I should not write of New Orleans. But as much as an alien can, I have done my best, on several trips to the city, to lose my ignorance. Much that I was taught in New Orleans of Creoles, the Catholic Church, the schools and of Basin and Rampart Streets, for instance, falls elsewhere in the book. Even to the historic spots, however, I feel no longer a perfect stranger. I was not kept on the outside of the showplaces here as I had so often been elsewhere in the South. My swarthiness was no bar; people swarthier than I may once have owned these places. I saw beautiful patios, lavish with the reds, yellows, and purples of the flowers and the greens of the climbing vines, yuccas, scrub palms, and large leafed banana plants. I saw the stairway masterpieces, the luxurious furnishings, the beds where the great are supposed to have slept. I can understand, with good reason, how New Orleans is a gourmet's delight, a place of enchantment for the artist in love with the soft patina aperitif that the years have applied to the frame and stucco; and to the lovers of the past.

But to more purpose in dispelling my outlandishness, I loafed on park benches, inviting whatever thoughts would come; rambled through narrow streets and cobblestoned alleys, purposely lost; browsed in antique shops and bookstores; and stood on street corners to see the pageantry flow by. Ferd conducted me on one tour of the French Quarter. In one of the art shops in a dusty corner I found a picture of a nude, a quadroon I guess they would have called her. The large canvas showed two-thirds of the body. From a rather lifeless background, the woman's color seemed to spring; a light brown, a sort of tangerine coloring—I recalled Hearn's phrase, "statues of gold." Maybe the artist recalled it too, for the woman was statuesquely proportioned, though much warmer than any statue. Her hair was gleaming black, her eyes seemed to smolder, the expression about her full lips was quizzical, her breasts were firm and proud. From his really wide knowledge of art, Ferd criticized the technique as indifferent. The proprietor had forgotten what art student had left it with him. But I was struck—not by the arrogance—slight, only suggested, but there—of this handsome, provocative woman. I think the painting told something—a great deal—about the past of New Orleans. Maybe about its present too, for all I know.

In a cluttered bookstore that was run by canny booksellers who knew the value of their old, torn, penciled, dog-eared volumes, I bought Lyle Saxon's *Fabulous New Orleans*, Grace King's *New Orleans, The Place and the People*, and a volume of Gayarre's lectures, out of a broken set. A friend loaned me Perry Young's *Mystick Kreive*, the flavorsome history of Mardi Gras. In my host's walled-in yard (he laughed at me for calling it a patio), sitting in the slanting sunlight of Indian summer, I turned the pages idly. I picked up stray facts about Mardi Gras, how Carnival is thought by some to mean—Meat (carne); farewell! (vale!); that one of its mottoes is "If More of Us Would Live, There'd Be Fewer of Us Dead." I learned about Rex and Comus and the Zulu King's celebration, which seemed to have started partly in derisive envy, partly in derisive parody of the white folk's gaiety and ended as one of the most original and attractive of the Carnival's joys. I learned what a melting pot New Orleans had been: of the Chicksaw chieftains who could not keep their eyes off the beautiful ladies at the ball, believing that they "were all sisters . . . descended just as they were from heaven," of Le Moyne and Cadillac and the other Frenchmen; of Miro and Ulloa, the Spaniards and O'Reilly, the Spanish Irishman—Iberian Hiberrian; of John Law, the Scot, and his German pioneers who were amazed that, though they lived among savages and Frenchmen, they were in no danger. The river bank for a long way above New Orleans is called German Coast, after the settlers. Their own names were lost, as Saxon points out (his name may be one that survived): Weber became Fabre; Schneider became Shexnaydre; and Zweig became Labranche. The Italians came later than their Latin cousins, and did not climb to aristocracy. The Irish came in to dig the drainage ditches (labor too risky and heavy for the more valuable slave) and to populate the Irish Channel, another of the city's hell-holes. In the "Deep South" issue of the *Saturday Review of Literature,* which was not out, I read with pleasure Roark Bradford's anecdote of the Professional Southerner who sneered at "literary trash written by poor white trash": "I'm from Oklahoma," George Milburn put in, "but I come from the best blood in the South, by God, suh. I'm a descendant of Moll Flanders." I thought, reading of Manon Lescaut and her legendary grave in New Orleans, about Moll Flanders and her Latin half-sister, Manon: one from the streets of London, a grandmother of Tidewater Virginia; the other from the streets of Paris, an ancestress of proud New Orleans, and both novelists' figments though they were symbols of authentic history.

And I read, of course, of the darker ingredients in the gumbo that was New Orleans. Lyle Saxon tells fine tales of the sophisticated people of color, such as the mulatto Basile Croquere, who could not fight a duel with whites but who could cross swords with them in his studio where, master fencer that he was, he taught the deadly art of the rapier. I read of the "tignon" decree in 1788 of Governor Miro, who fretted over the fifteen hundred "unmarried women of color, all free, living in little houses near the ramparts," made it a misdemeanor for them to walk out of the house in silk, jewels, or plumes, and allowed them as headdress only the madres handkerchief, or turban, or tignon (fancy name for bandana, in Georgia). I have read in Tinker's *Life of Lafcadio Hearn* that Rose, an octoroon, showed Hearn the ways of tying the tignon for variety, adornment, maybe for shades of meaning, just as Hester Prynne embroidered the scarlet letter of her shame. My fancy roved to current feminine styles: along Canal Street in the French Quarter, or at Five Points in Atlanta, or on Broad Street in Richmond. I have seen white girls with gay bandana handkerchiefs to hold down their unruly hair or to flaunt a bit of color. Their faces, bare arms and legs were tanned by the sun or cosmetics to quadroon or even darker hue; some were brown as berries. Come to think of it, their naked toes stuck out of sandals, too. After more than a century the styles had come full circle.

Saxon told of the primitive slaves, too, the wild dancers, shouters, and drum-pounders of the Place Congo, Congo Square. Many times I had walked past the place, now known as Beauregard Square, but from the dust grass no frenzied leapers and shakers rose in the Bamboula and the Calinda. Saxon and Herbert Asbury have brought to life something of the famous square, the sea-bed of jazz, one of the nurseries of those roots of tribal song and dancing that survived the transplanting from Africa, and which now have spread sturdy tendrils over much of America.

Men like Oscar Dunn, C. C. Antoine, and P. B. S. Pinchback, governors of the state, and J. H. Minard and Charles E. Nash, Negro Congressmen, figure in the histories I read only briefly, if at all, and then as symbols of shame. For their stories, still too brief, I had to go to Charles Rousseve's book. Charles, his brothers Ferdinand and Alvin, took me on several rides. We crossed or drove along many of the streets with names that writers from Hearn to the present use to illustrate the complex history and nature of the city. Hearn tells how the devout had to go to church by way of Craps Street, but we could not find it. But we found streets named Desire (next to Nun Street), Love, Pleasure, and Piety; Tchouopitoulas, Cherokee, and Seminole; Royal, Dauphine, Bourbon, and Burgandy, Bienville,

Kerlerec, Glavez, Claiborne, Jefferson Davis, Beauregard, and Henry Clay; St. Louis, Peter, St. Ann, and Homer; Socrates, Ptolemy, Shakespeare, Dante, Rousseau, Poe, and Hawthorne (and I wondered what that New Englander was doing in this galley!); Calliope, Enterpe, Dryades, Melpomene, Terpschore, Urania, and Julia. The last is not a classic damsel, but a remarkable free woman of color, about whom the rest is silent.

What the back-country Negroes—or whites for that matter—could do with some of those names, Ferd told me, was a caution. There is a legend in New Orleans that Champs d'Elysses Street was changed to the Elysian Fields because of the murderous tongue-twisting it got. Socrates and Sryades are marvels to hear, varying in different sections, or even in the same section. Calliope is the Americanized Kalliope; Felicite becomes Filly-city (characteristically); other words get Classic Greek, French, Anglicized, or Americanized pronunciation. And who cares?

"I live out on Tawn-teye Street."

"Where?"

"Tawn-teye, man."

"How do you spell it?"

"T-o-n-t-i."

"Oh you mean Tonti."

"I mean Tawn-teye. Like I inform you. You gonna tell me where I live, mon?"

I remarked that Industry Street did not seem so important a thoroughfare as Religious and Pleasure and Independence Streets. But I was told that I should not draw any inferences from the wisecrack. Canal Street skyscrapers typify New Orleans far more than Madame John's Legacy or even the Cabildo. Driving toward the old Spanish trail to the northeast, we saw such neighboring places as Milneberg, the early resort whose joys were celebrated in the jazz classic, and Shushan Airport, one of the most streamlined fields in America. We waited at an open drawbridge over a canal (the Industrial, I believe) while gray landing craft nosed along on their way to the Mississippi, and up perhaps to Normandy or the Philippines. Their builder, Andrew Higgins, belonged to history, too. New times, new wars. The last sight my friends showed me was the mammoth Huey Long Bridge, the only bridge across the Mississippi below Natchez, a monument to the lost leader of so many Louisianians. I was to learn in the back country parishes that Huey Long's name meant far more than those of the Parisian or Creole cavaliers, the Spanish hidalgoes, Old Hickory, or Pierre Gustave Toutant Beauregard. The farmboy from the red hills of up-country Louisiana had left his mark plain.

Across the river lay the major part of Jefferson Parish. I should like to have seen the romantic fastness of this parish, but access at best is difficult and time and chance did not favor me. I saw only the sections along the river. But in a printshop where I had business I picked up copies of the *Jefferson Parish Yearly Review*. Though the official publication of the Police Jury, they are illustrated with imaginative photographs of water hyacinths, drowsy willows, lanes between live oaks, streaming with silver-green moss, cypress trees, swamp cabbage palms, bayous creeping into jungles, Indian shell mounds and Grande Terre and Grande Isle, the farthest island, that bar the Gulf of Mexico from Baratania Bay. Through these passes and jungle-like waterways Lafitte and his pirates steered their vessels with enormous bravado.

Lyle Saxon, Lafitte's biographer, contributes essays on the traditions of Jefferson Parish; the boosters tell us that Jefferson Parish promises present charms and future cash dividends. Beautiful girls in abbreviated swimsuits are posed before romantic backgrounds. Shown in their pirogues in the narrow shallow canals are the trappers, sons of the original "muskrat ramblers." All steps from the trapping of the muskrats to the finished coats for milady are pictured. Even the Spanish moss, symbol of ancient quietude, is described as a money crop; to be ginned, processed, and baled for pillows, mattresses, blankets, and horse collars, about a three million dollar industry. *The Review* attends to the history of Grande Terre, but is also concerned with the modernized sewage system, and the waterworks. It demands improvement of the bottleneck on what it calls Parish "Burma Road," because it is an industrial life line for the oil derricks and refineries, the bagasse mills, the host of other industries, now going at furious speed. For the post-war world the men of Jefferson want a ship canal to be dredged almost due South from Gretna to open sea, which would halve the roundabout distance between New Orleans and the Gulf. Inviting capital to come and bide awhile, the boosters say: "Wages are lower here than in the northern and eastern states, but that is because the cost of living is lower. . . . Labor in this parish is yet generally unspoiled by the infusion of alien agitation." And however charming were the illustrations of Lafitte's domain, I knew that I was back in the twentieth century.

⤙ GEE'S BEND ⤚

"Man, what you want to see is Gee's Bend," B. T. said in Atlanta, and went on to tell me how far back the place was both in the sticks and in customs. If I could get in, that is, because if the water was high I couldn't; and if it rained while I was there, I couldn't get out. There was no guarantee, he added, that I would get out even in dry weather, if I made any missteps while down among those people. At Tuskegee I heard that the inaccessibility of Gee's Bend had been exaggerated. But the legend of the wildness of the natives was current. The tall waiter at the lunch-room said, "Man, they say the folks are rough down there. Live like wild people. Whenever somebody up here at school doesn't know how to act they tell him, 'You must be from Gee's Bend.' I'd sure like to see that place."

I had read accounts of Gee's Bend; one had made the *New York Times*; and I had planned definitely to see it, even before I heard the legends. Over at the Veterans Hospital, Dr. Peters expressed a long standing interest, partly professional, in the community which he had heard described as quite primitive. He wanted to go along. So did Max Bond of Tuskegee, but under the pressure of securing teachers for the coming school year, he couldn't manage the trip. Nevertheless, with typically generous hospitality, he put a station wagon at my disposal, and Pete, and Moore the driver, an old friend by this time, and I set out one early Saturday morning.

It was a grand trip down. Pete was in fine fettle, and the anecdotes popped off one after the other like a string of firecrackers. His quick eyes missed little, and his pithy commentary smacked of the countryside, more than the laboratory.

Coming from Indiana, he was critical of the bare and wasted acres: "Look at that land. So poor a rabbit wouldn't run over it." He was sharp on the farmers near Tuskegee who wanted fortunes for the worn-out farms which the government intended buying for the Tuskegee Air Base: "They charged prices steep enough to bust the treasury. Their cotton crops were going to bring in more money than you could shake a stick at. Seems they had planned encasing the cotton bolls in cellophane to keep it from the evening dew." We ran over a crushed snake on the highway, a long rope of black hide and squeezed out bloody pulp. "Humph. That's not a long snake. I'll bet there are snakes around here longer than I've been at Tuskegee."

Even the taciturn Moore opened up. After a crazy driver, twisting all over the road, had zoomed by, he said calmly: "I don't know whether that man was asleep or drunk or what. Some drivers take too big a chances. A car is a thaing not to be meddled with."

Two white hitchhikers raised their hands and jerked their thumbs. As we got close enough to be made out, they snapped their arms down, almost as by a military command. Moore looked at them in the mirror as we sped by. He told about some white hitchhikers whom he had picked up once below Montgomery: "They tried their best to make me take them to Selma. I told them I had to turn off onto another road. They tried to arger me into going there. Then they got rough. I didn't pay them no mind. I had a wrench under the seat and I felt around for it. When I got far as I was going, I stopped and took holt of it. They saw I meant business, and got out, just a cussing. I didn't say nothing, but slammed the door and drove away. So that's why I've been slow ever since about picking up white folks."

He gave rides to several Negroes on the hundred mile trip; three fellows who were on "public works" had never heard tell of "Gee's Bend." Below Selma, however, we got various directions, some confusing, and warnings that we might not be able to get into the Bend. At Atlanta, which we drove a mile past, not recognizing it as a town, we met our best guide. The winding road to Gee's Bend was soft dirt and we could imagine what heavy rain would do to it. We stopped by an old woman, a snuff stick in her mouth, a small sack balanced on her head, two buckets in her hands.

"Are we near Gee's Bend?"

"Yes. Jes keep on a-goin." Her mouth was toothless, there were two yellowish brown stubs showing.

"Could we give you a lift?" The buckets looked heavy for her withered arms.

She looked carefully at the station wagon, a bit suspiciously at us: "No. I'm nigh about where I'm going. I thanks you kindly just the same."

The next person we passed was quick to ride with us. He was of Indian type, red in color, gentle in speech and manner. He was a renter (he wanted us to know that he was a cut above sharecropping). His daughter was the only one left on the place with him; his other children were in Mobile.

"I don't zackly know how far hit is to Mobile. Somebody tole me but hit slipped my mind. Some people used to drive hit in two and a half hours, but they've cut down on the limit now, and don't let you go so fast. I ain't seen my children since they left here."

White folks owned the land he rented. He was good white folks, a kind man. "I never heard him speak an oath to anybody on his place," the renter said. But it was hard making ends meet; he didn't know how he was going to make out this year. He had been on this place nigh about all of his life. He pointed to his home, a small house of logs, sagging somewhat up a gullied road. A chinaberry tree shaded it, and there were a few flower bushes in the yard, but it was little enough for a life's work.

"That sun is so hot I wouldn't of taken anything for that ride wid yawl," he said, his hat in his hand. "How much you charge?" We laughed that off. "You all stay over for the Big Baptising tomorrow," he said warmly. "Lots of people will come here from all around. Be coming in all today and tomorrow morning."

We told him we'd see and were off. A few miles farther on and we asked another farmer about Gee's Bend. "You'se there now," he said simply. "Yon hit is." Around a curve in the road we saw a sign:

U.S. DEPARTMENT OF AGRICULTURE
Gee's Bend Farms

From the crest of a hill we saw a scattering of neat houses, glinting in the sunlight, a windmill, a wide schoolhouse and, to the right, a large red building and a cotton gin with its stack puffing smoke.

The crowd of men around the cooperative barely acknowledged our greetings, but stared at us and the station wagon. Pete broke the ice by identifying himself as a Tuskegee doctor. Shortly after the farm supervisor came up. He introduced us to a guide and promised to be with us himself in an hour.

An old bearded fellow at the weighing platform of the cotton gin greeted us affably. He had been "bred and bawn here." "We trying to get over de fence, now," he said in answer to our praise of what we were seeing. "We been behind de fence so long, we trying to get over hit now. I'm an old man. But I don't git back. No. I keep on forward. How old do you reckon I am?" I ventured in the sixties.

"Seventy-four years old," he snapped, his eyes bright.

"How do you manage to keep so young?" Pete asked him.

"Well, I always stayed at home. I lost one wife and borrowed another one. I got seven children living, all of them on the project. I got grandchildren older than my youngest one. Yes. I stayed home and worked hard." He grinned at us; his teeth were all there, absolutely firm and white.

"That's our injuneer."

The engineer, greasy, sweaty, and happy, took us through the hot engine room and the rest of the building. Over the war of the machinery, the flying wheels and belts, the gasping of the large pipe sucking in the firm small bolls, the creaking and slamming of the bale-presser, he spoke his words of loving praise for the gin and his job. He knew plenty and gladly taught us.

We watched the pressing of a couple of bales. All of the workers were Negroes except for one white man who was marking the sacking on the bales with letters, figures, and a huge V. He was tow-headed, grimy, and his hands were stained with the purple ink; he stared at us, inoffensively, and went back to his marking. The two Negroes stripped to undershirt and overalls, who worked the pressing machine, dragged a couple of bales with their cotton hooks to the lading platform. One was well-muscled, and explained, grinning to us, boasting that he could do and had done every job about the gin; the other was gloomy-faced and surly. But he was willing to have his picture taken, and after a while relaxed and put in his word too.

When we went to the commissary for lunch we were met with level stares from the thirty or forty men, sitting alongside the large commissary or sprawled on the steps and floor and the railings of the store porch. Some returned our hellos, others just looked. A few followed us into the store. Our appetites probably did not hurt our reputation; we were nearly starved and we easily got rid of a can of salmon, two small cans of Vienna sausage, a loaf of bread, a store-cake apiece, and three of those oversized bottles of pop. We wolfed those sandwiches of pink salmon in huge pieces of bread, dripping oil on the brown paper that the shop-keeper laid on the back counter. It was about as satisfying a lunch as I've had. We probably became more acceptable as they saw how we could eat. The store-keeper was not a native of the Bend, but came from an Alabama town; his daughter was a Fisk student and asked us questions about Tuskegee and Howard.

Waiting for the supervisor who promised to show us the place, I scanned the government mimeographed bulletin on Gee's Bend. The geography and history go somewhat as follows:

The Alabama River, twisting and turning on its way to the Gulf makes a sharp horseshoe curve in southern Alabama around a tract of about 10,000 acres. Over a century ago, two slaveholders from North Carolina named Charles and Sterling Gee purchased this fertile land, which was thereupon named Gee's Bend. Their nephew, Mark Pettway, bought it from them and left it to his son, John, who managed it until 1900. It was a profitable plantation.

Gee's Bend was nearly isolated then. The slaves who were brought in seldom if ever got out. Traces of what may be African languages are still to be found there. After freedom, many of the Negroes took the name of Pettway from the owner. This caused confusion when children were christened with their parents' names, but by adding middle initials the confusion was checked. Thus Tom-o-Pettway and Tom-i-Pettway are names of two present family heads.

Even today Gee's Bend is difficult of approach. Camden, the county seat, is only about three miles as the crow flies and about eight as the road winds, but the Alabama River flows between. A ferry, little improved from antebellum days, is used to cross the river; the safer way to Camden is around a poor road forty miles long. The way we came in, by Alberta, on the same side of the river, had its difficulties too; there was a creek fordable when low but impassable by any vehicles when flooded. Gee's Bend is what the folks call "Plumb Nearly," plumb out of reach, nearly out of the world.

The supervisor told us that up to six years ago most of the people of Gee's Bend had never been to Camden. As a matter of fact, there were plenty of people seventy and eighty years old who had never been eight miles from the Bend. "A few years ago," he said, "if a station wagon like this one had come in here, there would have been a parade."

When John Pettway died in 1900, one of the families moved into the big house, and the community rocked along with ups and downs. A credit merchant in Camden provided the "furnish" against the crop. In 1916, a July freshet on the river flooded out the cotton crop in the low grounds, but the war brought back a measure of prosperity. In the Depression, however, five cent cotton spelled doom. The merchant advanced credit for three-years running. When he died, the administrators of the estate, without his paternalistic interest, conscious only of the "debt," sent wagons to Gee's Bend and hauled off every piece of household property, farming tools, mules, cows, poultry, everything.

Knowing no other place, unwilling to leave, the people of Gee's Bend were threatened with starvation. The owner of the land let them stay on, but could not supply "furnish." The Red Cross, the CHA, and the Alabama Relief Administration did what they could to keep the people alive. In 1934, the State Rural Rehabilitation Corporation began making loans; and then the Resettlement Administration, succeeded by Farm Security Administration, bought the land and set up the project. FSA supplies yearly credit and small loans each spring. A white man superintends the project, and a white accountant aids in the management of the cooperative store. The rest of the staff is Negro.

S. T. Haynes, the farm supervisor, had studied at Tuskegee under Booker T. Washington, and was an old friend of T. M. Campbell and Tom Roberts, Negroes who have labored strongly for the improvement of farming. Mr. Haynes had always been a great one for cooperatives; in one county he had preached cooperatives until his gospel spread like wildfire and he was in danger of being run out of the county: "If I hadn't had good white friends and good Negroes behind me, they might have made me some trouble. Then they transferred me in here and I was like Brer Rabbit in a briar patch."

He added color to the bulletins' history. He had seen so much of it. He satirized the old sharecropping: "The merchant and the landlord made sure that they would get back their advance. If you made forty, or if you made one, the merchant and landlord just got it. 'You did well, ole boy, you just lacked ten dollars of coming out of debt.' Sometimes they'd give a farmer who had done well twenty-five dollars for a Christmas gift." Interest on the "furnish" had always run high. He was coldly earnest when he talked of the destitute people after the foreclosure, trying to make it on berries and rabbits: "That woman didn't leave them a plough or a hoe, not even an axe to cut stove-wood with. They didn't own a thing in the world." It was a sorry picture of the past he painted; he shrugged his shoulders. There was a better present to see; and he led us to a central group of buildings, marked by a flagpole and a tall wind pump.

FSA built a fine community house but the Gee's Bend people insisted upon adding a steeple. To them it is still more of a church than a forum. In addition to the regular minister, there are among the eight hundred inhabitants fourteen lay preachers who take their turns in expounding the gospel. Two or three weekdays these men answer the call to preach; it seems to be the chief adult entertainment. Sometimes ice cream, cake, apples, and lemon water are served at church or union meetings. Some townhall features enter, such as voting on newcomers—they will vote on who's going to live next to them, or on community problems. But it is largely as a church that the sturdy, well-appointed meeting hall (reminiscent of New England) serves the people. The educational movies that have been shown were far less warmly received than the shouting of a neighbor whose ambition to preach they understood, and their own singing of the old melodies.

"To be fair with you," said the superintendent, "we're a bit back on entertainment. This is the first year for baseball. The church people fight it. If they found a member playing baseball, they'd turn him out of the church. Of course they might take him back in, but they will dead turn him out."

I recalled the story I had heard at Tuskegee of the basketball teams that an enterprising teacher had brought down to play a game for the folks. The teams wore their sweat shirts and slacks until time for the starting whistle. They then stripped down to their jerseys and trunks. When the women of Gee's Bend saw those ten men exposed in all their nakedness, they promptly rose in indignation, gathered their young ones together and shooed them out of the hall. They were not going to let their children be contaminated.

I asked the superintendent if the story was true. He laughed, and admitted that in large measure it was. Some womenfolk had been affronted for their children's sake by the nakedness. He added an anecdote of the Snow Hill Band, which was brought in to play at an entertainment. After the regular concert, the band played a bit of jazz. Some outsiders who had followed the band to Gee's Bend began to breakdown with a new kind of dancing, and the Gee's Bend kids joined in. The church people broke that up quickly. They turned all the kids out of church on Thursday, but took them back in Sunday, after they had got to work on them. "Yessir," he said, "They'll almost hang you for dancing."

"But they are the singingest people in the world," he went on. "It would do you good to hear them moaning out some of the old hymns." A man from the North heard about them over in Camden and came to hear the singing. From his description it sounded to me like John Hammond, and he believed that was the name. Then somebody from the Library of Congress had been down making records.

The schoolhouse was of one of the best I saw in the South for Negroes. It was a bright gray frame building with five rooms. Two large classrooms were separated by a folding door; a third room serves for home economics and a fourth for vocational training. There was a kitchen to prepare the kids' luncheons. The chairs and tables were modern; and the many windows made the rooms cheerful. There was a fine stove in one classroom; an old piano in the other. On the wall were pictures of Booker T. Washington, Dr. Will W. Alexander, Paul Robeson (on an advertisement of a concert at Tuskegee Institute and strangely for that gallery, an advertisement of a night spot on the Pacific Coast), and a picture from the *Pittsburgh Courier* of the three Joe Thomases of jazz fame. Benjamin Franklin's adages (in a sort of carbon copy) had been lettered on the walls: "Speak Little Do Much," "Be Careful," "We Are Always Prompt." Student drawings and cutouts were also on the boards: one student had pasted a picture of Abe Lincoln in a big red heart. On the blackboard had been carefully written:

> *I Pledge Allegiance To My Country*
> *And To The Production Program Which It Plans*
> *One Garden And Smokehouse For Each Family*
> *With Milk, Eggs, And Nutritious Foods For All ! ! !*

Together with the pictures of race heroes were beautiful pictures of first-rate cattle and Armour's Star Beef Chart. The masterpiece of this collection was a Polled Shorthorn Female Champion of the 1937 International. A Parent Teachers' Association functions, and, in addition, many of the older people are learning their three R's with a greater eagerness than the young ones. The supervisor, loyal student and friend of Booker Washington that he was, spoke glowingly of the practicality of the instruction. After the day's work, lessons were given in making scarfs, pillowcases, and slips from old sacking; and horse collars, floor mats, hats, and belts from shucks. Examples were surprisingly well made. He showed us the first dolls made on the project. "Many girls here, eighteen years old," he said, "never owned, never saw a doll before."

Gee's Bend was fortunate above most communities in the deep South in having an infirmary. The four rooms were spotless, organized for efficiency. Pete looked approvingly at the screened baby bed, Lesson One in health for the parents, and the operating room. A registered nurse had been serving Gee's Bend for several years, bringing needed science where herb-doctoring, superstitious practices, and midwifery had naturally flourished. Though illness had marked Gee's Bend, cleanliness had not. Lack of privies and drinking out of open springs brought on much sickness. "Eight people," the supervisor told us, "used to bathe in one tub of water without changing it."

Now for an annual basic fee of fifteen dollars a year, each family gets medical treatment. Two white doctors (the nearest Negro doctor is in far off Selma) come in for weekly clinics, serving a line of patients in a two-hour period. The nurse is kept busy with advice and visiting the entire community the other days. Everybody must take a medical examination and health is preached fervently. There is so much in the budget for dental work. When they "get him up fifteen or twenty patients" a dentist comes over, who because of the cooperation plan, charges fifty cents for extractions, which in town would cost a dollar and a half or two dollars each.

We sat in Mr. Haynes's office, talking it over. He had large albums filled with pictures, illustrating the "Before and After." The FSA had not exactly started all of the wonders, "it just latched on to what we had." A cooperative store, with seventeen members, was the parent of the present thriving cooperative. Eight men started the building of the houses. The authorities were dubious about the houses not standing up to requirements. "Just give us a trial," we said. "Don't persecute us. Give us three months. Then if we fail you, put 'em out on contract. They turned us loose. And there the houses are."

The "before" pictures showed splintery log cabins, two rooms and a runway (it was bad luck in the old days to join rooms together). Some of them had shutters on the windows, with a long prop to keep them closed. The roofs were of dilapidated shingles, and the chimneys were mud and clay. The only steps for entering the house were badly cut logs. The barns were bad; the animals might as well have been left outside. Where there had been toilets, they were merely dirty shacks.

Now each unit consisted of a house, a pump, a barn, a fowl house, a sanitary toilet, and a smokehouse. One of the pictures had the caption: "The oldest man on the Gee's Bend Project who has seen the wonders wrought and with his son sleeps and eats in an FSA Home."

From the famed Southern diet of the three M's (meal, molasses, and side meat, and sparse at that), the people had progressed to more varied nutritional foods. The "pressure cooker" was their friend, and they had stored their shelves with canned produce. They were even canning butter. Canning was one cause of the rivalry between the six sections of Gee's Bend. Each had its own thriving canning center. Mr. Haynes had his own shelves loaded at his office.

The supervisor's heart was in scientific farming. The long bottom right on the river was the cream of the land, but stood the risk of flooding. Most of the land was pretty rich. He admired Mr. Cammack, the project manager: "I give a man what belongs to him. He's a fine fellow." Since Mr. Cammack was an "Auburn man," a graduate of Alabama Polytechnic, they spoke the same scientific language. Mr. Haynes spoke lovingly of corn that grew eight to ten feet tall, of a good cross of Jersey and Whitefaced Hereford cows, of purebred bulls that served an unbelievable number of families apiece, of Poland China Boars. He moralized about a picture of two pigs of the same age, one round and fat, raised on crop pasture, and the other runted and scrawny from being allowed to run outside. He talked learnedly of replenishing the soil with kudzu, of compost fertilizer and droppings from livestock, of poisoning cotton with arsenic of lead to kill the boll weevil at the proper time, of side-dressing cotton with nitrate of soda, of the new type of cane Mr. Cammack had introduced.

It was not an ox-minded place. The Gee's Bend people had used them because they had to do it: oxen were cheaper to buy, could forage for themselves, and could be killed and eaten when worn out. But they couldn't make any speed. The place was definitely mule-minded.

So now there were many tight barns stored with corn, peas, peanuts, and hay; good harvests of potatoes and cotton; stables with good mules, horses, and cattle; canned goods on the shelves; clean drinking water; windows screened from flies and mosquitoes. He went on with a long list of blessings.

From impoverished, desperate, almost defeated people, they had come up, smiling and winning: "Now fourteen families don't owe us a dime in the world, and by the end of the current year, thirty will have paid out." Problems, of course, were not over. That of newcomers, for instance. They were allowed in only on five years' trial as renters; then if they proved worthy, they were allowed to apply the amount they had paid for rent to the purchase price. Another problem, that of relationships with white folks in the adjoining communities, was being solved interestingly. The community hires whites occasionally, to show what "the forgotten fellows are doing" and to show that they are not prejudiced but open-minded: "We stick them on the front even if they don't want to go there. We work 'em. You know you can get pretty close to a man when you work with him. Sometimes we take even the sorriest man in the county. He might be one of the scalawags but we give him a job, pay him well. It's a way of Christianizing. I'd be saying too much to say that relations are 100 percent. But there's a great improvement."

All of Gee's Bend people are not yet fully cooperative-minded. "A few stick their heads in the ground and go sell their cotton themselves. Sometimes it's good to let a man get out on a limb and learn for himself. One fellow said 'I don't believe I can do better, but I want to do hit for myself. I want to handle my own business. I want 'em to see what I've raised.' It's a little parade you know, when he can drive from house to house showing his cotton, eight miles to Camden. 'I want to go to town to meet those fellows,' one will say. 'I want to buy my fertilizer myself, and let them know I'm living.' The merchants slap them on their back, and charge them two dollars more than we do. But sometimes," he mused, "cents and dollars ain't all of it." Pete, who I fear is a rugged individualist, applauded this man with gusto; he was a good sign, he said.

Mr. Haynes definitely believes in his people. He said more than once that he has never heard a Gee's Bend man make an oath since he has been here. He was never bothered with the squabbling between man and wife; there wasn't any fussing all night, as in many places: "I never have a woman coming to tell me how her husband is throwing his money away gambling. And no switching or stealing of wives. No man with a family butchering up anybody. If there is any fighting it's seldom, and then always one of the boys. If somebody meddles with their girls, they would give plenty of trouble. They aren't cowed at all. They're game. But there's little fighting to speak of. But I want to give both sides. I'll be honest. Yes, the girls do have babies out of wedlock. They sure do. It used to be that few of the girls married who didn't already have kids. But usually they marry the fellow they have the kid by.

"There's no stealing. These people don't lock up a thing. The smokehouse may be full of meat, the crib full of corn, but they don't have locks on them. These people are honest as the day is long."

The last word in law enforcement, he told us, is a patriarchal Pettway: "Whatever he says is law and gospel. If anything serious happens, all he'd have to do is just go to the phone and call up the law. But he don't have to do that. The Council goes to the offender and tells him, 'If you don't do right, you're going to get off this project.' That generally works.

"Our folks are all right," he concluded. "Yessir. Just give 'em one-half chance.

"The next thing," he said, with what isn't so anticlimactic as it sounds, "we're going to have a barbershop and a shoe shop."

Since the trip, I have had a chance to read a master's thesis on Gee's Bend, done at Fisk University by Alice Reid, a graduate student in sociology. Like many of the students of Charles S. Johnson, Miss Reid has ability to win cooperation in her interviewing, and a quick ear for speech. Some of her quotations throw light on the history of the place. Some tell of the hard times "when that woman came and took everything we had." A woman recalled her house before FSA:

> Hit won't nothin'—jes' a dry weather house that I had. Look like hit leak outdoors and rained in the house. . . . Then I'd plaster the other one, everytime hit rained, de rain would blow de mud out. . . . The Lord and that good hearted government man, whoever 'tis, couldn't have done another better thing. . . . I ain't shame and I ain't scared to tell nobody I'se thankful.

Miss Reid found varying degrees of acceptance of the new institutions. The cooperative store is supported; cooperation being no new thing in the Bend. The infirmary is not unanimously approved; herb-doctoring and superstitions and ignorant carelessness are still to be found. All haven't been won over to the new diet. An old woman complained, "Dey say you got to put up six hundred jars jes' to keep 'em filled, but us don't eat hit after I put hit up. Food in them jars jes' don' taste right." The tradition of onions and collards, cornbread, and slabs of meat cooked over an open fire does not easily die out.

Many farmers will not admit that they have learned new methods of farming. One said, "I pretty much had good arts on farming before—ain't much to learn me 'bout dat—but jes' gimme de right things to farm wid." Another said, "I'm jes' fixed more to farm." But this is the old story of the practical "self-taught" man vs. the expert. The farmers adopt the new scientific ways though grudging in praise. And meanwhile, the farm supervisor laughs easily, seeing the improved crops and stock.

The school is too new-fangled; the old school teacher believing "that those teachers up there now, they don't come up to me"; and some of the parents fearing that "dem dat goes too far in school won't want to plow no more." The church remains largely as it was, otherworldly and dogmatic. The adjustment to a new way of life is by no means completed; the student likens it to "growing pains." There have been significant changes, socially and economically, the student concludes, but much remains to be done.

But we were filled with the supervisor's faith in the future of Gee's Bend when we pulled out to leave. "There are some Negroes who can do more with less, and some Negroes who can do less with more," Pete said sententiously. "These are the first." Moore expressed what was for him, an enthusiasm, "It sure is something. This has been one day." And I was thinking of a favorite blues line: "You take me to Kirkwood, I'll make St. Louis all by myself."

On the way out to the ferry we stopped at one of the older but renovated cabins. Two women were quilting on the porch. Mr. Haynes told them he had brought us by to see their quilts. "How many spreads do you have now, Mrs. Thacker?" he asked.

"You know I ain't gonna tell you that," she said pertly. The other woman laughed. They brought out several from the house, as brilliantly colored as the patches of flowers in their yard. Pete and I made selections. "How much?" I asked.

"Six dollars apiece." Mrs. Thacker spoke up promptly, without batting an eye. I think ours batted. It was take it or leave it. We took a quilt apiece. Mrs. Thacker counted the twelve dollars as if the transaction was an ordinary five minutes in her life. But when we got into the station wagon, I caught them looking down at the money. "Yawl come back again," the second woman called after us.

A light shower fell as we headed toward the ferry. Around the shoulder of a hill we came to the steep incline to the river. It was already muddy. The brown

Alabama River was high that day, swirling, quite active. We saw the dinky ferry being pulled over by the cable. It touched the steep bank; some youngsters maneuvered a Ford runabout onto the road, got about ten yards up in a dangerous spot where there was a sheer drop to the river, and stalled. We labored ten minutes more, baking and grinding, pushing, chocking wheels, to get it past the station wagon. The old ferryman watched our efforts. Then he told us he couldn't take us over. It was even more slippery on the other side. If we made it to his ferry on this side, we most certain sure couldn't get off it on t'other. We thanked him for that news.

"What was the name of that ferryman in the old stories, Brownie?" Pete asked. He was spattered with mud.

"Charon."

"Carried people over the river of death, didn't he?"

"Something like that."

"Well, I'm glad old Charon doesn't want any parts of us today."

I was glad too. That frail cable and wheel and that stack of lumber looked pretty weak to be pitted against those muddy waters.

We went out the way we came in. A few miles from the Bend in front of us we saw two lovers, arms around each others' waists. They turned their backs to us, and looked up at a tree, as we drove abreast. The man was older than the girl; the girl was a fair brown, powdered up and togged out. Always the candid camera enthusiast, Pete asked, "Do you want your picture taken?" The man said "No," flatly. A bit abashed, Pete offered a ride. "No," again. And then relenting, "I appreciate it." The girl was still curious about the tree. It might have been a sundown creep, we didn't know. But it might have been another instance of the self-sufficiency of Gee's Bend. They had a way of running their own business.

➤➤ LOW COTTON ◆◆

The plantation was a large one, on a backroad. Sandy, the young teacher, thought it wiser that we go there well after nightfall. He wasn't exactly sure how Mr. Cluttsby would take our visit. I was glad that he told Ulysses to dim the lights when the road wound around Mr. Cluttsby's big house. Though it was a hundred yards away, we lowered our voices too, feeling conspiratorial. Sandy said he knew the road as well as the back of his hand, and near the big house that was true. We stopped at the darkened commissary where the numerous families came for "furnish," and where, beside the watering pond, they exchanged news and kidding and tall tales. Sandy told us how he had gradually been accepted by the people. One of his stories dealt with his Christmas party, when he had introduced the plantation Negroes to Santa Claus. But the party ended nearly tragically. When Santa Claus appeared, in red suit and pink mask and white beard, the smallest children screamed in terror and fled to their mothers and fathers. They must have thought that Santa was old Satan. At any rate he was a strange white man. Even the peppermint canes and gumdrops and all-day suckers could not get the party to the proper Christmas spirit of good will to men, and Sandy did not repeat the experiment. Christmas is just another day to these kids.

Sandy did not know the farthest little traveled roads so well. Ulysses finally asked, "Are those weeds or cotton I'm driving over?" and in the headlights we noticed the green bolls. We were heading toward an old log cabin, and were in what should have been a yard, but cotton was growing to the doorstep. The cabin was deserted. Ulysses turned around as well as he could in the gray mire, and drove down what we had thought was a road but what was a stretch of low cotton. "I'll bet I've spoiled a bale of cotton," Ulysses said ruefully. Sandy's eyes were better in that pitch darkness than ours. "Stop," he said to Ulysses. Gathering shape in the darkness we saw him coming, black as the night. I had never heard his type of dialect before; it was a staccato mutter, sounding like a speech defect. But we gathered that the man we searched for: "He gone. He ain't there." That was all. Just gone. Nothing else was offered.

Sandy told us that these families were allowed to live in the log houses; the men received fifty cents a day, the women forty. Since they were not sharecroppers, they got no part of the harvest. Some might leave to go on "public works" (any job not on the plantation, such as sawmill labor for private employers, was "public works"). If they left, some member of the household must work or else the family had to get off the place. The man we were searching for had just gone.

We drove through long wide cotton fields on a barely perceptible road. At certain bends our headlights momentarily would catch gray houses, all seeming deserted. There were no lights. At one clump of blackness we stopped. Sandy got out and walked ahead, brushing through the cotton plants.

Ulysses maneuvered the car so that the lights shone full on the trees and shrubs around the house. Sandy hallooed. A woman's voice answered, halloo. We went up to the porch. Close to the house we could make out arrows of light escaping through chinks.

"Come on," yelled Sandy. In the car light they recognized him, were downright glad to see him.

"Watch those boards there," an older voice warned us. They did buckle and sway under our gingerly tread.

We went into the room where the light was. It came from a candle stuck in the top of an ink bottle. The flame waved dangerously close to the large black and gilt Bible on the table. On the sooty walls were pictures of the old man and of the old woman in oval gilt frames, but the features were too dim to make out in the candlelight. A musty smell of cooking grease and people hung in the air. On a large bed the quilts were thrown any which a way.

The old man, gray dignity, rose from the table where he had been writing a letter. He was grateful for the visit, happy at the "honor," embarrassingly so. He remained standing through our visit; beg as we might, he would not sit. Sandy asked about his affliction. He had been kicked by a mule over a year ago, and had rushed to put disinfectant on the injury. He was no better. In addition he had had a "mystic" in his ear, and another one, here, around his heart. His breathing was really gasping. He was by no means, he confided to us, the man that once he was.

His two barefooted daughters, surrounded by his grands, barefooted and in long dresses for nightgowns, were surly. One talked to herself, at us. Sandy was grudgingly welcome, not the other two. We soon were lost for words to say. Pretty speeches were worse than silence. The girls' husbands (or rather the husband of one, the other girl had merely borne children to her man) were gone, God only knew where.

Sandy asked them to sing. The surly daughter wasn't going to sing, she didn't know nothing to sing for. She just wasn't going to sing. The old man was pained by her unmannerliness, but retained his quiet politeness. From the door to the next room, the mother came with other grands hiding in the folds of her long shapeless dress. She spoke gently to the muttering daughter.

"Spirituals?" Sure they knew them, but they preferred to sing from the book. From a paperback edition of *Gospel Hymns*, Mr. Johnson read the line "Trust and Obey." "We will sing that for you," he said simply. The beginning refusal from the daughters he cut off in mid-flight: "All of you sing now." Patriarchal command edged into his gentle voice:

When we walk with the Lord
In the light of his word.

The harmonies were weird; the mother's alto beautiful. The old man weaved up and down around the melody. The daughters' voices were drawn in; they could sing. A boy's soprano rose, like a heartbroken cry:

What a glory he shine on our way
When we do his good will
He abide with us still
And with all who will
Trust and obey.

The silence was unbearable after the last wild harmonies. Mr. Johnson asked us to sing. We demurred, then finally rushed (to get it over with) into "I Shall Not Be Moved." They let us mangle it, and then they helped us out. They knew it all right.

Singing, perhaps the fact that we couldn't sing much, helped close the gap. The mother talked to us. Solomon was away at Fort Benning. He had been gone two weeks. They missed him, they needed his help so much. He had never been away from home before. Mr. Johnson vouched for him: "I raised my son right. He were a praying boy in church." The surly daughter spoke to me intently, "That my brother. He in camp now."

The mother's voice quavered in the doorway. "I dreamed of Solomon last night. I could hear him in the room just like I hear you. Heared him moving. I said, 'Son, are you back?'

"He say, 'Mamma, hit's me. Hit's Solomon.'

"I say, 'You got to go back?'

"And he say, 'Mom, I ain't gonna go back no more, not until August fust.' "

It was mid-September then.

The old man had been writing a letter to him, sending him a dollar and a quarter for cigarettes, soap, and things, since Solomon hadn't been in long enough to get any money. He was sending the change loose in the envelope. He didn't know what a money order was; Ulysses explained it to him and promised to mail the letter for him.

The mother talked on, increasingly tearful: "I hope no harm will come to my boy." "He'll be all right," I said brashly. "The Army takes care of the soldiers. Look," I said, yanking Ulysses over, "here is an Army officer. He'll tell you how they look after the soldiers."

They swarmed around Ulysses while I explained that here was one of our own, an officer in the Army. The old man was at the top of delight. "Honey, honey," he cried. "Those bars say that he's an officer," I told him. "Honey," yelled the old fellow, "let me touch them." He rubbed the bar on Ulysses' shirt collar like an amulet. The mother pleaded to Ulysses, "Look out for my boy. Don't let no harm come to him."

Ulysses took the letter; we folded a couple of dollar bills into the mother's hand. They forced a large green pear apiece upon us, the old man polishing them carefully with his hand. We sang one song, certainly the wrong one to carry in our memories: "God Be With You Till We Meet Again." I stumbled going out of the door onto the shaky porch, and fell against the surly daughter, striking her breast a really heavy blow. I was profusely apologetic. She listened to my stupid politeness (she had probably never been so apologized to before, for such a slight wrong). "You ain't hurted me none," she said shortly and finally. But her voice had friendliness in it. "Y'all come back," she said as we plunged into the darkness toward the car. One of the grands ran out into the headlights, his dress streaming behind him, and waved a long sleeve in farewell.

➤ TAKE YOUR COAT OFF, GENE! ◄

They were setting up an apparatus and trying out the loudspeaker when I got to the heart of the town. A steady stream of the inhabitants of that section of southeastern Georgia was already pouring in. Some had got off the train I rode; more were arriving in mule wagons, buggies, old model Fords, jiggling high above the ground, and other makes of cars, dusty and spattered. They found parking places and strolled the streets, truculent, suspicious, ready for a good time, spoiling for band music, oratory, liquor, and fighting.

The only white man I knew in town was an old friend, there on government business. I called briefly at his office. He warned me that an explosion was due, since Talmadge's chief of constabulary had broadcast his threat against troublemakers and his advice that Southern white women should arm themselves. The time was ripe, my friend told me, and I was quite the guy, obviously a strange Negro in the town, and probably northern. I tried not to appear too scared, and hoped to sound casual. "If I get into trouble," I said, "do I know you?"

"Sure you know me," he said. "I have some contacts here. The worst that can happen is that you'll be thrown in jail. They'll hardly beat you up, or anything like that."

When I got to the Negro side of town, however, I threw off any slight fear I had. All the Negroes I met were excited—it was like circus day—but none seemed worried about any "incident." "You'll be all right," said my host at the huge lunch he set out for us, "I'll tell them you're a cousin of mine from below Macon." He took it all easily; I fell back at ease. There were mean crackers in that section, but he didn't look for any trouble, that day.

We got to Courthouse Square well in time. A few Negroes were sitting on the curbstone of the lawn. Two were preachers, one Baptist and the other Methodist. They were glad to meet me. A flurry that might have perturbed me, save for their reassuring nonchalance, took place half a block away. A bunch of white men and boys ran yelling toward a building. Somebody at a window yelled out to them. "One of them sabatoors," said Baptist. I learned later that a soldier, AWOL and drunk, had been arrested. He had probably wanted to see the fireworks too.

We joined the rest of the Negroes who were naturally on the outskirts of the crowd, grouped round the statue to the Confederate Soldier with its legend "Loyal Unto Death." The crowd had four fairly distinct layers; one, the Talmadge rooting section, packed tight in the street before the flag-draped stand; the second, largely neutral from its cheering and demeanor (this country was "on the Government" and hence was waiting to see which way the cat would jump); and the third, a sparse scattering of anti-Talmadge-ites, critical and aloof. Drunks weaved in and out of the crowd, cracking wise, cracking foolish. Behind the clot of Negroes, some government employees sat in folding chairs; others looked out of the courthouse windows. A large number of the "Talmadge till I die" people were the wool-hat red-necks, burnt brick in color, light-haired, blue-eyed, large and gangling. Their womenfolks, in spite of their clean and starched finery, seemed invariably tight-lipped and worn. But liquor had loosened the tongues of the men. There were also the townsmen, in summer suits, collars and ties, and straw hats. They were shaking hands and slapping backs all over the place. Attractive town girls arm-in-arm, arms about each other, paraded the grounds in bright print dresses, really fluffed on out, and vari-colored socks and sandals.

They cut a few steps, shaking their shoulders, as the phonograph record of Talmadge's theme song blared from the loudspeaker. It was hillbilly in swing with a corny xylophone filling in the breaks:

> *The folks from Pabun Gap*
> *To Tybee's shining light*
> *Will put Gene back in office*
> *'Cause he stands for what is right.*
> *So let's elect Gene Talmadge*
> *And bring back once again*
> *The same administration of*
> *That red suspendered man.*

This song was played over and over; it was long the first time.

A roar told us that little dictator himself was coming. The meeting of the clan set the street resounding. Several Negroes (I was among them) stood up on the pedestal of the Confederate statue to see better. The governor was really something to look at: his broad grin as he shook hands all around belied his self-portrait: "Just mean as hell."

"I never figured he was such a little biddy man," said the Negro farmer on whose shoulders I was leaning.

Preliminaries immediately started. There was a long prayer from a sing-songy man who pulled out all the stops. One-third of his peroration asked for protection for Governor Talmadge's son with the Navy. As one critic said later, you would have thought young Talmadge was MacArthur.

He took seriously the second stanza of the campaign song which began:

Gene's only son, Young Herman,
Now sails the seven seas
To help defeat the Germans
And the Yellow Japanese.

I also heard later, how reliable it is I do not know, that the preacher was known as the town drunk. One leading citizen who was to introduce the governor showed up much later, on the outskirts of the crowd. The insurance agent who did introduce him was fulsome, praising the governor for paying the teachers their back salaries and for doubling the old age rolls in the county. A young man from the University of Georgia denounced his fellow students for burning the governor in effigy, promised to deliver the University to the governor, and read a bad poem, a sophomore's imitation of Eddie Guest. He turned out to be the son of one of the Governor's officials, sort of a relative of the governor's, from the governor's home-place, whom the governor had known since he was "so long."

The governor started easily. He had the most voluble part of his audience in his hands and he knew it. He played his voice like—like the old trouper he was: now "giving gravy" like a backwoods preacher, now slangy and raucous, now pompously constitutional. His early discussions of finances left the audience cold; this breed of hearers was obviously not mathematical. "Take your coat off, Gene!" one minion yelled, and a gale of happiness started when he shed his coat and snapped his red galluses back and forth. At last!

He would pause to listen to some cry from his gang, as if he didn't know what they wanted to hear. He was a vaudevillian, ready to act out any of his few skits on demand. Somebody reminded him of the education fight. "Oh yes, that," said the governor as if he'd forgotten. So he told the admiring throng the tale he repeated every week on the radio. He had to go way back to educator Cocking's being born and raised in Iowa, where they have the co-education of the races, whites and the blacks together. Then he attended Columbia University. Then he was brought to Georgia where he started administering the Rosenwald Fund and messing up in general.

"A white lady, the daughter of a Confederate kunnel came to my office and said that Cocking was advocating the co-education of the races. I was amazed. I asked her (don't cheer till I'm finished) 'Would you swear to that statement?' The good white lady swore it; I looked her in the eye, and I believed her. I knew I could not trifle with this; I knew the gre-a-a-te danger of this, there was something here that would destroy traditions dear to us down here in Gawgia. Wait a minute. Let me go on.

"Those Rosenwalds wanted a nigra on the Board of Regents in the Chancellor's office. The men he had driven out had said that nigra and white teachers should be paid the same. No one of them has ever denied it to this day. All the evidence he had offered to the *Atlanta Constitution* and the *Atlanta Journal* they would not print as news, but they carried anything else that would slander the good men of the state, whom they called 'stooges, trained seals, and puppets,' all for protecting the tradition of Georgia and our children."

He loved the University of Georgia as much as any alumnus. His grandfather, his father, and he all went there. He sent his only son there. And those two Atlanta papers dared to have that grand old university unaccredited. But wait until after September 9th. It would be accredited then because it would be a white man's college again.

Gross cheers from the woolhats, few of them graduates of elementary schools.

Did they want to hear how he had "stacked" his board of regents? Hell yes, they did. He told how he, the farmers' friend, had bearded the big city feller, Clark Howell, in his den. Howell promised that if the governor would write him a letter requesting him to resign, he would write one back resigning. So the Governor wrote one right there on Clark Howell's stationery, using Clark Howell's typewriter and signed it on Clark Howell's desk with Clark Howell's pen.

"That's the way I got rid of one of 'em," glowered the governor to stentorian applause.

"Mixed picnics, some Tennessee nigras had come down to Athens, nigras and whites at the same picnic (and all of you know what a picnic is). Nigra advisers on equal terms with white people in Washington, under Clark Foreman, Clark Howell's nephew, another administrator of the Rosenwald Fund. Oh it's pitiful. White girls visiting Tuskegee, a nigra school. Didn't stay three days but did stay one night.

"What's this other? Naow, you good ladies present listen good to this. I remember when I was a child at my mother's knee how my mother would read to us out of the *Woman's Home Company* . . . what's the name—*Ladies' Home Journal*. And now, in the last issue, there are eight pages building up nigras, encouraging nigras to want social equality. Oh the pity of it! When the nigra newspapers call me and Governor Dixon of the gre-a-a-te state of Alabama upholders of white supremacy, I'm proud to accept that title and honor."

Commotion in the crowd ceased only when a burly redneck demanded the chapter on the Rosenwalds. The governor enlarged on the theme song:

> *Gene saved our college system*
> *From all the Rosenwalds*
> *Who sought to end traditions*
> *Which we know are dear to all*

We don't want all their millions
And neither their advice
On how to educate our youth
We Southerners think twice.

First he took up Ralph McGill, who received a Rosenwald fellowship. What is a fellowship, friends? It's nothing but money. While McGill was spending Rosenwald money he was also, the governor said sadly, receiving state checks. His man Friday bustled up with the papers, and Talmadge waved checks above the heads of the crowd. There were checks cashed on shipboard, in England, France, Germany, Copenhagen, all those foreign countries. At Copenhagen the crowd groaned.

Ralph McGill, now his enemy, had fallen hook, line, and sinker for the Rosenwald Fund propaganda, which advocates amalgamation of the races. Here was a book written by Embree, the head of the Rosenwalds. He waved a book with a lurid yellow jacket and box-car letters at his panting audience. *BROWN AMERICA*! "Who is this man Embree? I'll tell you, confidentially. Embree is the author of *Brown America*, and in this book he explains how he intends to turn this South of ours into a m'latter South!"

"Not in Gawgia, he won't!" boomed a large cracker at the front of the bandstand. Laughter of relief, not curses, followed this outburst. And then Gene Talmadge really went to town, pointing his accusing finger, glaring from behind his black-rimmed glasses, transfixing his hearers with hypnotic gestures and Svengali glares, shaking that long hank of black hair over his face. His voice trembled as he gave out the hokum, and the crowd loved it.

All except the Jim Crow section. I looked carefully at the Negroes there: the town doctor, intent upon Talmadge's platform mannerisms; numerous farmers, in blue denims and reddish brogans. All of their faces were set stolidly. When the crowd laughed at Talmadge's witticisms, their masks retained that set of not exact passivity—but stolidity, grim disapproval. Only their eyes, staring glances at each other at some of the worst insults, at the use of the word nigger—it was oftener nigra or black—those only gave their feelings away. I know that they were angry and ashamed. The most expressive face was that of a youngster seated on the rear of the base of the statue. He stared at his sandaled feet. His face showed him to be in pain. I learned that he was the schoolteacher of a nearby community.

The sky was clear blue without many clouds. Three buzzards soared and circled, high up, then not so high.

I had a fairly easy time of it, caught up by the excitement of trying to follow everything. I had been stared at by some Negro farmers a bit coldly, maybe resentfully, but I had been so interested in the demonstrational debate of the two preachers before the circus began, that I was not accepted. Several whites had also stared at me fixedly; one drunk stopped squarely in front of me and looked me over a long time, insolently, before lurching off. I was startled when a finger dug into my side. I looked down into what I thought was a white man's face, but no white man would have grinned quite that way.

"Scared you, didn't I?" He was one of us, I knew then. "You see that white man, looking over here?" I did; the white man saw me too. "He asked me, 'Is those two tall ones yonder niggers or white men?' [One of the preachers was florid and pinkish tan.] I told him y'all was colored. He said, 'I wondered what white men would be fools enough to stand over with the niggers.' " My new friend was tickled at the episode.

I was stared at also by the village belles, who gave me the once-over coolly. One strutted back and forth, looking over her shoulder. "Lynch-bait," muttered one of my new friends.

I could have felt more comfortable, but there was no real bother. Tired of standing, I sat beside the young schoolteacher. The Methodist preacher found me there and told me that my host had left, but that he would get me back to my part of town. Suddenly we heard a woman's high-pitched voice. We stood up to look. A woman was on the platform, waving her arms. She was too far from the microphone for her squealing to be articulate, but soon we heard the governor answer her. The crowd yelled at the exchange.

"I'm ready to go whenever you are," I told the preacher.

"I'm ready now," he said.

As we got to the edge of the lawn, Talmadge had silenced the woman, and was intoning, "And in conclusion. . . . " When we turned into the street leading to colored town we heard the last stanza of the song blaring from the mike:

> Now let's elect Gene Talmadge
> To take the helm again
> For he's the one who helps our State
> In every way he can. . . .

➤ INSURANCE EXECUTIVE ◄

Though quite busy, E. M. Martin, secretary of the Atlanta Life Insurance Company, affably gave me much time, and proved to be a good talker. He is a sturdily built, sharp-featured man with shrewd eyes; his color is that of sunburned white Southerners; his thin, graying hair is straight. He is energetic and forceful, and from all quarters I heard that he was a resourceful business man.

One of his immediate concerns was an eight millimeter technicolor motion picture called "The Parade of Negro Progress" that the Atlanta Life Company had been exhibiting throughout the South. The picture took two years and a lot of money to make, he told me. The machinery belonged to the company and a photographer was employed for the filming and showing. Martin candidly admitted that the primary object of the film was to make money, but in a clean honest way, he said, "to build friendships, and to show others what we're doing. Many Negro schoolboys in their history classes learned only one thing pertaining to the Negro and that is that Lincoln freed the slaves."

The picture stresses the "highlights of Negro life," with such items as the Negro hospital in St. Louis, a commencement at Atlanta University, the new plant at the Tennessee A & I State College at Nashville, the celebration at Daytona Cookman Institute when Mrs. Roosevelt went down there on Mrs. Bethune's anniversary; Negro farmers in southwest Georgia with large mechanized farms, warehouses, fine mule and horse teams, well-fed cattle, and tractors at work in the fields; hair-dressing establishments; the bank in Atlanta; girls at the intricate statistical machines in the Atlanta Life offices; gas stations owned and manned by Negroes; Paul Laurence Dunbar's home in Dayton, Ohio; green troops marching in the camps; Negro pilots taking off at Tuskegee; Dean William Pickens selling bonds. And so the list went. "It would be an all-day proposition if we showed all the stuff," Martin said. So it was edited to meet local interest, with the school and church stuff varying according to the section. When shown in Texas, for instance, a few Texas churches and schools would be spliced in.

It was run off at churches and schools; Martin doubted if Negro theatres would be interested in some of the shots, and considering it to be advertising would want money to exhibit it. Martin believes the film to be worth thousands of dollars of advertisement to the businesses and colleges pictured, but he settles for good will to the company.

The picture takes about an hour to run, with the photographer and operator, J. Richardson Jones, explaining the scenes as the reels unwind. About ten minutes or so of the picture deal with the Atlanta Life Insurance Company. Then the state manager of the company makes his speech urging the people to take out policies.

The company was letting the picture ride for awhile, as "you can't use the same picture for two years running. . . . The cost had been way up yonder, but it was a good way to sell insurance."

Later on, I talked with Richardson Jones, the film photographer. He was a quick-jumping fellow, a go-getter if there ever was one, turning up, it seemed, at several places all at once. He was proud of the shots he had made, and wanted to give me a private showing of his masterpiece. An anecdote was told on Auburn Avenue about his absorption in his job. He had got permission from the War Department to take shots of a Negro tank unit while on maneuvers in the South. A sergeant with a detail of soldiers had been assigned to carry out Jones's every wish. The sergeant took his orders literally. Jones ordered a foxhole dug about shoulder deep; lowered himself into it with his camera; told the sergeant to let the tank come on; and readied his camera for a few feet of reel showing the charge of a tank. The juggernaut roared forward. Suddenly an officer ran toward the hole, yelling and swearing. The tank rumbled to a stop about ten feet away. "Get out of that hole!" he ordered Jones. The tank was signaled to go ahead, while Jones stood by, rueful at missing his dramatic shot. The tank roared into action and rode over the foxhole. Jones looked down at where he had been; the earth was packed tight as if no hole had been dug there; the foxhole could have been his grave. The sergeant and the detail stood by, nonchalantly. They had obeyed orders.

But Martin told no such anecdotes. He took the picture in all seriousness. His office contained added evidence of the company's pride in race progress. An Atlanta Life Calendar was devoted to pictures of Negro inventors. Martin reeled off the achievements of Robert A. Pelham, the inventor of a pasting machine and a tabular device for the compiling of statistics, and of Norbert Rillieux, whose invention of an evaporator for refining sugar was so useful to his native Louisiana that his statue is now in Cabildo. Martin was proud of these men and of the company's broadcasting their place in the world of commerce and finance.

It was with relish that Martin told me the story of Alonzo Herndon. I thought idly that two Negroes who had become heroes for different segments of their people had been named Herndon, one Alonzo and one Angelo, and both had been closely connected with Atlanta. Not far away, a mile or so, probably, from the shining marble and mahogany of the Atlanta Life Company that had housed Alonzo Herndon's enterprise, were the granite and steel of Fulton Tower, hunkering, sooty, ugly, and dismal, where Angelo Herndon had been jailed. I wondered how many Atlanta Negroes in Beaver Slide or Darktown knew of either Herndon, or, for that matter, how many whites at Five Points or in Druid Hill. Undeniably, however, both had made their marks: Alonzo, widely held to be the greatest Negro financier;

and Angelo, the symbol of working class protest and unity. And both had started from scratch.

Alonzo Herndon's story (I have pieced it out from other sources) sounded like a plagiarism from Horatio Alger. Born a slave on a farm near Social Circle, Georgia, in his youth he worked as a farmhand and developed a knack for barbering in the colored settlements in the hamlets roundabout. He opened his own shop in Jonesboro and became well known for his skill and tact, before leaving for the bigger world and money of Atlanta.

In Atlanta, a kindly disposed white man allowed the ambitious, thrifty youngster to open a shop in his hotel. This was the Atlanta of Henry Grady, Joel Chandler Harris, Frank Stanton, and Clark Howell. The serious, courteous, nearly white barber became the favorite of prominent white Atlantans, and his shop became a meeting place. Herndon was the model master barber. Though, according to a later partner, Herndon boasted that he had only been as far as Baker in the *Webster's Blue Back Speller*, he spoke with care and polish. No dialect. He neither smoked nor drank. An early partner, Bill Betts, was a good barber, but preferred hunting and fishing and spinning yarns. In those days, barbershops were open only on Wednesdays, Saturdays, and Sundays. Bill grudged even the three-day week, but his partner made and saved, made and saved.

Two of Herndon's shops burned down, a rather high mortality, that certainly did not result from Herndon's carelessness. It may have resulted from his race. The burning of the second made Herndon determined to put up the finest shop in the world. He traveled over Europe for ideas. Soon he owned three Atlanta shops, employing seventy-five men. His place on Peachtree Street became nationally known. Herndon's later partner, an old gentleman in his sixties named Howard Pitts, stated that the landlord wouldn't stick Herndon for rent; but after he died and his heirs sold the property, the rent started jumping. For a long time it had been $255 a month; at the time of Herndon's death it was up to $1,200 a month. Herndon died before he fulfilled his promise to give the shop to his barbers, but his wife and son fixed up the papers and gave the shop to the thirteen barbers who had been with Herndon longest. When the lease ran out, these associates bought a place on Broad Street, corner of Peachtree and Poplar, and moved "everything not nailed down—all the marble and plate glasses—across the street." The shop is still doing well, with a board of directors, although the white barber unions try to exert pressure against "nigger" barbers. It is, of course, in the white business area; several blocks down Auburn Avenue the Negro business section begins. I have given the shop several quick look-sees; it always was busy.

Before Herndon died, his influence defeated a bill introduced in the Georgia legislature making it illegal for white people to have their hair cut or their beards shaved by colored barbers. This bill was reportedly instigated by Herndon's disgruntled white competitors.

Well, the money came in and Herndon knew how to put it out again. According to Martin, he took a number of namby-pamby church benefit societies and welded them into a strong unit. Several associations that were too financially weak to comply with the Georgia insurance laws were taken over and reinsured by Herndon's Atlanta Mutual Company. In 1922, the company was named the Atlanta Life Insurance Company; it had been developed by sound, conservative business practice and its future was assured.

When Alonzo Herndon died in 1927, he was praised by Negroes and whites for his business shrewdness and Christian character. Fuzzy Woodruff, a columnist in the Atlanta *Georgian* wrote: "Thousands of Atlanta's colored citizens passed the ball and gazed with awe and reverence on the features of the man whose life had pointed them the way out of darkness. . . . Hundreds of the best white citizens [were] there to mourn the passing of a man whose life had told the story of how a Negro could achieve eminence and retain the friendship and regard of every kind and class and creed in his community."

I was, of course, not convinced that Herndon had shown Negroes the way out of darkness. That was too much to ask of one man. But I realized that Herndon was a striking representative of the handful of Negroes with foresight and shrewdness who had laid the bases for thriving Negro businesses, generally insurance companies.

I asked Martin why so many wealthy Negro families and businesses had started from successful barbers. I was thinking of men like John Merrick of Durham, William Johnson of Natchez, and Clayborne Pride of Lynchburg. "Here's the story," he said to me. "Negro life in slavery was stratified. The ploughhand did the dirtiest, coarsest work, where he didn't have to think. A large group of white people were down as low as slaves. The more intelligent slaves were trained as wheelwrights, carriage makers, painters, and tinkers. They carried on the necessary industrial life of that time. My granddaddy was a carriage maker. Then, of course, there were the house servants, who did the cooking, laundering, anything else the big bourbons wanted of them. Those bourbons lived like princes.

"It was advantageous to the South to make use of the smart Negroes. But in the adjustment period, after the Civil War, dirty work became Negro work. The artisans lost out. But barbering was not closed to Negroes; it was a field of personal service that he did well in. Nearly every town had a barbershop for whites run by Negroes. Recently there was a drive to run Negroes out of barbering white folks. I remember when cards were passed out with pictures of black hands on white faces. When bobbed hair came in, Negro barbers decided automatically not to cut white women's hair, but to stick to men's and children's. The women might get fresh or cute or scared. So the young people left barbering, or wouldn't learn it. But the older barbers had made hay while the sun shined."

Martin then started talking of his own career. He had attended Atlanta University: "The missionary schools wanted to develop preachers and missionaries. They stressed the 'spiritual' and a little culture along religious lines. They were run by good people, but their vision didn't reach out to industry and commerce. When I started in insurance, Truman Gibson offered me fifty dollars a month and board. When I decided on insurance, the missionary people deplored the fact that I was going out to make money. Well, it certainly wasn't money that decided me.

"Booker T. Washington was wise so far as industrial training goes, but he was all wet in telling the Negro to stay out of politics. He was wrong in social matters too. The Negro will never be anything but a serf until he has the right to free movement in public affairs. Whites call that social equality. I call it civic equality. In social life people are bound to pick their friends. I do. So do you. Booker Washington—he and the South—set the race back fifty years. In some ways he was just a front man for the white capitalists. Northern capitalists thought the Negro was not worth the ballot. So they set up a hell of a compromise, delaying the progress of the Negro. The South's progress too. Negroes will never have anything until they vote. No vote, no economic opportunities; no economic opportunities, we're in one hell of a fix.

"We pay taxes; there's a basis of equality there. Yet we're only one-tenth of the people, and the poorest of the poor. We're shut out, at the mercy of the nine-tenths. We're circumscribed from opportunity. The Negro as a race is an economic factor only as a laborer. That's a hard thing to say. But of the billions of capital in America, we're just on the fringe. The North Carolina Mutual and the Atlanta Life are our biggest institutions. A few more concerns are making money, but as far as big money goes, where the hell are they? No sir; it's a social problem all right. The Negro will never get to be a man, a free man, until he can go where's he's got the right to go. The race will never get out of the barrel until we have business equality, the right to go into public places. I don't call that social equality. Philip Randolph and some of those other young leaders are on the right track. The only thing is that we'll all have to pull together."

In Martin's opinion, one weakness of the Interracial Group, of which he is a member, is the insistence that "each race was cut out for certain specific things." The Negro, they said, was especially adapted to teach spirituality. And he had a sense of politeness and docility. Martin snorted. He told a few chestnuts about the Negro's excessive politeness: the Negro bellboy who, seeing a white woman nude, murmured "Excuse me, sir"; the Uncle Tom at the courthouse who took off his hat, kidded, bowed, and scraped unduly much, telling the Negroes who low-rated him, "Sure, I'm taking my hat off, but I'm doing it for money"; the head waiter who refused to answer when the guest asked for the head nigger, until the guest waved a ten dollar bill, when he walked up and said, "Oh, you want de head nigger? Well, I'se de head nigger here." "Politeness Humph," laughed Martin, "that's business tact."

Martin was a bit sore at the concept that all Negroes can sing and dance. "Anywhere they see the Negro, on the chain gang, in the street, anywhere, they expect him to give them a song and a dance. Then they figure that in the better class, every Negro can preach. That's a hangover from slavery. The slaves who could sing and dance got special treatment, the best medical attention and food. To keep them healthy cattle. The preacher got special treatment too, as long as he would preach 'Jesus and Him Crucified,' and 'You Take the World and Give Me Heaven.' So naturally we have a lot of preachers, singers, and dancers. Too many."

Well, he had decided on a business career. In his early years of insurance work he had had some tough experiences: "It used to be, yesterday, that no outside Negro could go into Monticello, Georgia, unless he was a minister. And even then it wouldn't be too safe. Monticello was in Jasper County, one of the meanest counties in Georgia, the county where Williams had his notorious peonage farm. You must have heard of it. Monticello was just a handful of houses, a block of stores. If a strange Negro came in, they'd pick him up for vagrancy and fine him fifty dollars. When the Negro couldn't pay, he'd have to go down on the plantation and work his time out. They kept the local Negroes in line. An old jackleg preacher was down there, bootlegging insurance. One day a white man came to him: 'Hello, Uncle Ike. How's Aunt Martha?'

'She's all right, I reckon.'

'She gets a little unruly sometimes, don't she?'

'Well, I reckon she do, sah. Yassah.'

'Well if she gets too unruly, we'll do her like we done Leo Frank.' Then the white man made a half circle with his finger around his throat. He wanted to tell Uncle Ike that he had an eye on him.

"When I went down to see Uncle Ike on insurance business, the sheriff came up. 'Hello, preacher,' he said to Uncle Ike. He just looked me over carefully. I walked around with the preacher and the schoolchildren followed us yelling, 'Nigger and a white man, nigger and a white man!' I stayed around until five o'clock before the preacher thought it wise to go visit prospects. 'What did you bring me down here for?' I asked him, but he convinced me that writing policies on Negroes in Jasper County was a sundown job.

"While there, I visited a Negro doctor. He had as many white patients as colored. He was making good money, but he didn't have a fine house. As a rule, the successful Negro in a place like that, won't buy too good a house. No need in incurring the enmity of the white people. Most of them get their money all right. They're treated somewhat as exceptions, things apart, as long as they do their work and stay off the race issue. Stay off education and better pay. That's crossing into social issues, and is dangerous.

"It's better now in Jasper County after the government went in to expose the Williams case. But it still can be rough down there."

The hostility of Southern whites to Negroes in the insurance game was an old story to Martin: "Folks who are in business can see the manipulations, the chicanery of the old Bourbonic South. For instance, in Mississippi, a group of Negroes went to the commissioner of insurance. They told him how they wanted to give the Negro a stake, that they wanted Negroes to develop into dependable farm workers, with some incentive to save their money. The commissioner said 'Well, boys, what you said about the farm is O.K. But I'm not going to grant any insurance license to niggers.' So business had to be bootlegged. A law was set up to discourage bootlegging business. It was a good law, but the real object was to get rid of Negro business. The Ku Klux Klan worked behind the scenes to keep Negroes out of insurance. Before 1912 this was the attitude: 'If those goddam niggers get $100,000 capital stock, we're gonna make it $150,000. If they get that, we're gonna make it $200,000.' Old man Herndon at the outset couldn't get a license. He had to sell his business up in Kentucky.

"Now, they can't make laws hurting one without hurting the other. There are a lot of things behind the scenes. Burial societies, out of which insurance companies grew, are not purely racial. There were a lot of white ones. Those societies, white or colored, did not have the reserve to guarantee the public the same as insurance companies. When laws are passed to kill them off, it's not racial, it's just big business killing off little business. They couldn't pass the law without hurting the little white man as well as the Negro. But in the administration of the law, that's where the damage was done. Big business wanted to destroy all Negro insurance. Negro insurance caught it both ways. For instance, the Mississippi Life was stolen from Negroes.

"The Negro is still a disadvantaged group in business, with his whole economic outlook determined. They can tax you out of business. Take Mrs. Malone of Poro College, St. Louis. They put up such a tax on her that she couldn't live under it. Georgia, now, is one of the cheapest states to do business in. The old law was running all of the capital away. Even Coca-Cola was having a hard time. That law was repealed for a more reasonable law, and now capital is coming back to Atlanta.

"Most Negro banks, insurance companies, and so forth, were started by unlettered men, ignorant of the laws of business. Take Rutherford. What did he know about business? He had only been in the fish business over in Memphis. What did he know about investment? Any eighth or ninth grade student in Atlanta would know more than he did when he started. What did Heman Perry know about insurance in the large? Negroes were ostracized, shut off from the councils of state. How in hell could they know anything?

"Well, old man Herndon believed in intelligence. He encouraged Truman Gibson to go off and study, and Gibson went from Atlanta University to Harvard. He insisted that young Norris Herndon should learn business administration. Now the company employs over two hundred college graduates. The key men are all college men, from Harvard, the University of Pennsylvania, Amherst, Atlanta University, Fisk, Morehouse, Howard."

Martin led me into Alonzo Herndon's office, now occupied by his son. I studied an advertisement that had appeared in the "Georgia Prosperity Issue" of the Atlanta *Constitution* for May 12, 1914. This gave an interior view of Herndon's shop that extended from 66 Peachtree to 65 North Broad Street. The advertisement was in the familiar Booker Washington pattern:

> Anyone who can "pull" a razor without cutting a person's throat can OPEN a barbershop. It is the man who "knows how" to CONDUCT a barbershop that keeps his place open.

The advertisement boasted of "cleanliness and workmanship," clean and sharp tools, and sanitation.

> Every barber changes his white linen suit daily. Every barber sterilizes his hands four times a day in a medicinal solution. Every towel, razor, comb, brush, and shaving brush is sterilized before and after using. Compounds, calculated to kill any possible germ, are used in washing the floors in Herndon's Barber Shop. . . . These are the reasons why Herndon's Barber Shops are known the country over as the finest establishments of their kind in the universe.

An interior view of the shop showed the leather seated barber chairs, the massive spittoons, the bottles, mugs, instruments; it was of old-fashioned elegance, a sort of O. Henry setting, but it must have been something in its day.

We walked through the marble corridors of the Herndon building. The Georgia marble in the old building, the Alabama marble in the annex were as spotless as Herndon kept his palatial shop. The recreation yard also showed the continuance of the passion for order and cleanliness. Crepe myrtles were in flower then, and Martin assured me that the shrubbery was of various sorts so that there would be all year round blooming. The pleasing rock work in the cleanly swept yard was done by colored people. Generally, corners are left junky, Martin said, but one order of the yard was "to keep tidy the places that do not meet the eye." In the recreation hall were a dozen or so bridge tables, a ping-pong table, a radio, and a Coca-Cola stand. A picket fence, by no means ordinary, I was assured, but made of French saplings, nailed with cooper nails, enclosed the yard. It shut out a bad-looking, littered area. I thought that this garden closet, with its protective fence, a stone's throw from teeming Auburn Avenue, was symbolic.

I was shown the printing department where all the necessary matter except policies was printed, the officer in charge, Pap Conley, whom I had been especially advised to see, was on vacation. Much of the real work, Martin told me, was done in the tabulating department, where girls were busy at the clicking, roaring tabulators and sorting machines. One young woman interpreted the services of these machines. They were too precious to be bought, Martin told me, so the company had to rent them. They were absolutely the best, however. I could well believe that; the process that they performed of sorting by names, states, agents, districts, struck me as amazing. They performed with superhuman accuracy and speed the tasks that ordinary humans once performed, but they were Greek to me as I heard of them, and in reviewing my notes they seem even more Greek. I visited several of the clerical departments; the people in charge explained the layouts carefully. They were used to curious visitors, I knew. "Who is the new kibitzer?" seemed to be the attitude of some of the girls. I could see that this was a growing concern; I did not need to read the credentials, framed like diplomas, on the walls of the board of directors room to assure me of that.

Back in his office, Martin handed over to me a pep-letter from the Director of Agencies to the Managers to be passed on to the seven hundred agents in the fields. Clipped to it was the 1942 *Dunne's Insurance Report: Analysis of the Atlanta Life Insurance Company*. Dunne had rated the company as A+. Facts that were stressed were that for each $100 of Liabilities, the average assets for the twenty largest companies in America was $105.12, whereas the Atlanta Life Insurance Company's average was $145.96 (nearly forty dollars over New York Life and Metropolitan, for instance); the average surplus per $1,000 insurance in force was $14.39; Atlanta Life surplus was $25.21; the average liquidity of assets was 60.23 percent to Atlanta Life's 84.49 percent; the average net interest earnings was 3.42 percent, whereas Atlanta Life's was 3.48 percent. There was a surplus of $1,685,438. "This type of report should enhance our opportunities to produce more business and earn more money," wrote the Director of Agencies.

Well, I thought, this is a long way to come from a barber shop in Senoia. But Martin, for all of his pride in his organization, in its sound business sense, did not want to leave too roseate a view of Negro business.

"The white powers that be don't like to see the Negro get but so far in business. The Negro has got so little at present, not enough to worry about. The crumbs from the table. But if the Negro got so that he was a threat, an economic power, then you'd have the same spirit as toward the Jew, only more accentuated. Right now, however, there's not enough wealth to worry them. The business field is wide open. Any kind of business if it's half way run will make money down here in the South.

"But it is a mistake to speak of Negro capitalists. They're just pseudo-capitalists, token capitalists. They're shut out from the Chamber of Commerce, from the law making bodies. They aren't in a place where they can even peek into what government and business are all about.

"My heart," said Martin, seriously looking at the cigarette smoke curling over his head, "is in the race problem." He was sharp against the half-hearted friends of the Negro: "They call a Negro sane when he is taking low ground. They call cowardice meekness. They've worked out a technique of adjustment, of finesse in compromise. It's not the poor whites the Negro has to look out for; it's his so-called friends, his fair-weather friends.

"Now you take Aza Gordon. He is a quiet, inoffensive fellow but he has spunk. Well he wrote newspaper columns attacking the failure of white folks to say Mister and Miss when addressing Negroes; and he favored equalization of school teachers' salaries. I ran into a fellow on Auburn Avenue, who said to me 'You know old Gordon is gone. He might as well have handed in his resignation when he wrote that piece.' He was teaching at Georgia State in Savannah, but Hubert didn't make any fight to save his job. He also lost his job in the U.S.O. These folks never let up on you when you've got in bad once. They cut you off economically."

Martin was bitterly convinced that if a man takes a stand on any issue, he is "just burnt up in any school system of the South, he just can't hold a job." Incidentally, he told me that no bright skinned Negroes were wanted as teachers in the rural counties. "The general belief is that bright Negroes have got more fight in them." Early in his career a white man told him of his prejudice: "The m'latter seems more bitter," he said. But Martin mused, "The white South is mixed up on whether the mulatto wants to be white or wants to be a man."

He was unenthusiastic, as so many old Atlanta University people were, about the merger, in which his old college lost its identity and became a graduate school. The old Atlanta University had stood like a rock against segregation; its charter stating that it was a school for youth, not Negro youth. He recognized that nothing in the new charter did away with the "original intent and purposes of the University" but he wasn't sure. And many old A.U. people felt the same. Some were inflexible. "Better not have a merger than sacrifice principle," they said. They felt there was too much compromise, too many palliatives, too much "suave talking behind closed doors." There was a moral effect, Martin said, in "so many of the old Yankees leaving here." But Northern philanthropy seemed to line up with Booker Washington's ideas about segregation. When things came to a showdown, to an issue, too many race diplomats took the lateral, not frontal approach. Martin shook his head sadly. "They can cut out the funds if you don't toe the line; they can get you at the source. Or if you get the money, they will manipulate it." Some Negroes, at whom the powers can't quite get, may make a strong stand. But three Negroes, E. Franklin Frazier, Howard Thurman, and Rayford Logan, had been forced to leave the Atlanta University system. "In the deep South," was Martin's studied conclusion, "no Negro of guts can stay in a big school position."

A brother-in-law of Walter White, Martin is a staunch NAACP worker. The Interracial Committee went too gradually; the white members, working for increases of Negro rights, and the few Negro members, working for equalization, couldn't quite hitch. Many Negro leaders in the South faced a dilemma. If they took a manly stand, they got in bad with the Interracialists. If unmanly, they got in bad with Negroes. Well, as an executive of a thriving Negro business that had made it on its own, Martin had definitely solved his dilemma and had taken his stand.

➤➤ LET'S LOOK AT YOUR BASE ◄◄

He comes naturally by his spunk. He and his sister told me tales of the family proving that. Their grandmother Ellen was their pride. Her slave master found places for all the good-looking slaves to work in the house, and when she came to Louisiana from far off Virginia, a fine looking fair woman, he put her to work in the house too. Old Mistis didn't like her as well as Master did. Once when they were having a big party, Ellen made some mistake, and she was threatened with a whipping after the party was over. When the time came, Ellen was made to take off every piece she had on. At the third lick, however, she flew through the yard and sat on the front gallery on the base of one of the columns: "Stark bark naked" was the phrase her grandson used.

Ellen was still young, but she was the mother of a child. The white children made a great fuss, yelling, "Look at Ellen, stark naked!" Mistis got all upset and ordered Ellen around to the back. But Ellen would not leave her perch until assured that she wouldn't be whipped. Every time after that when Ellen was threatened with a whipping, she would dutifully strip and then go around to the front gallery, stark naked, to wait. Ole Mistis got sick of seeing Ellen walking around naked in front of her children and menfolks, and soon Ellen was no longer whipped. She had made a front porch affair out of what was supposed to be a back door matter.

Ellen's master gave Ellen's firstborn child to his daughter for a marriage gift. This child was old enough to work in the kitchen so they just took her without a word to Ellen. Accidentally, while washing a valuable dog, she got soap in its eyes. For this she was whipped severely and kicked into a creek. Smart and brave, the child made her way along the levee on Bayou Fourche from Thibodeaux to Napoleonville, around eighteen miles. She was about done for when, with weariness and fear, she reached Ellen's place. Ellen was then the cook at the big house on the huge plantation and had her own cabin.

In the daytime the child was hidden in the cool weedy darkness under the house, which was built off the ground on brick columns. In the evening Ellen would shake out a quilt or some other large cloth and the child would take the food put there for her, or would crawl out and scurry into the house. Her master tried to make Ellen talk, even forcing her to haul wheelbarrows of earth for seven days to break her will. But Ellen wouldn't tell. She didn't deny knowing the child's whereabouts, but she said they could whip her until she died before she'd tell where she was. Every day the child would cower in the darkness under the house; every night Ellen would manage to get her into the house. Ellen kept her child safely hidden until the Yankees came.

All the tales her grandchildren cherished showed Ellen's unbroken spirit. When she combed and brushed her mistress' hair, she'd pull on it until it hurt, and then apologize blandly. Her mistress wanted to marry her off to a bad buck of the plantation. Ellen reminisced, "If they had give me to old Black John, I'd a killed myself. I'd a jumped in the bayou. I swear I'd a done it."

The man she favored was a free Negro, their grandfather. Finally old master had said to him, "If you work hard and save your money I'll let you buy Eleanor." Grandpa bought her, and thereafter any child was his. Some of their uncles, therefore, were never slaves. Grandma and grandpa got married after emancipation, having a distaste for the ceremony that had been performed when Ellen was a slave.

This grandfather was a wheelwright by trade and made good money, which he never banked, but used to keep about the house, sunning it ever so often to keep it from mildewing. The family judiciously bought a large amount of property in Napoleonville.

Their father was a contractor, who taught himself the trade. He built a couple of houses "that looked right good" and people started hiring him. Then he built up quite a prosperous business. He was a member of the Louisiana state legislature, getting eight dollars a day. At the end of the century, he was deputy clerk of court in Napoleonville. In the turbulent times, when the whites were driving Negroes out of power, threatening some Negroes, beating up others, buying from some the right to vote, he was offered big money to get out of politics. For certain records and lists he was offered $4,000. He refused to sell. "I have plenty of money," he said. "I've lived honest all these years; I'd like to die honest." The white politicians were surprised; many Negroes had sold out or been run away and they thought this deal was in the bag. They lost patience and called on the Ku Klux Klan which was then vigorously rampant, battling the Knights of Labor. The Klan threatened him with a lashing.

He knew what he was up against; the grim, determined reckless white men in their long white dusters, big hats and masks. He told them calmly, "This is where I live, this is what I've tried to make home. I built this home to live in, and this is where I intend to live. If you come after me, this is right where you will find me. If you kill me I'm not going alone. I'm satisfied I'll take somebody else along with me."

He got rifles and bullets from a friendly white man, a big supply, enough for two days, and sat there. The Klan never came, his children told me proudly.

They had other anecdotes of spunk. Their brother was beaten by a white boy one day and came home crying. He said that he hadn't fought back. The father said, "If you ever let a white boy beat you again without fighting back, I'll beat you myself. I mean it."

It was this tradition of spunk that helped to strengthen Alvin's backbone. Without any bragging, he told me that he had played end on Columbia's football team with Lou Gehrig in the mid-1920s. He hadn't played football in the Louisiana high schools he had attended, and at Columbia, he said, he didn't do much but study like hell. But he was strong and rangy, and some of his white friends persuaded him to go out for the team.

He assured me that he wasn't a star. But some of his adventures bear repeating. Head line coach Crowley one day called him "Smoke."

"I knew he was talking to me. I didn't look."

"What the hell's the matter with you, Smoke," Crowley said. "Didn't you hear me tell you to come in?"

"I'm sorry, coach. I didn't know you were talking to me. I heard you say Smoke. Didn't think you were talking to me."

Crowley ordered him to go turn in his uniform. Walking off Baker Field, he was stopped by Head Coach Haughton, "Where the hell are you going?" He explained the flare-up. Haughton called the entire squad together.

"This is Percy Haughton," he barked out in his usual introduction. "I'm the coach of the Columbia team. Now, goddamnit, there are no goddam smokes on my team. That man's name is Jones. Call him by it. That go for everybody. Now go to work."

"If that man had told me to run through a brick wall after that I would have tried it."

At West Point, the Army was set against Alvin's presence. At first they didn't want him to eat in the dining room. That's where the boys raised hell. "What difference does it make to you," they said to the West Pointers, "he's going to eat with *us*, isn't he?" That settled out all right. Then Haughton ran Alvin out on the first team. The cry really went up then. Army announced they couldn't play against a Negro.

"Goddamnit, this is Percy Haughton. *I'm* the coach of the Columbia team and I say who's going to play on it. I'm goddamned glad you told me you won't play; we've just got time to catch the next train for New York."

The stadium was fairly crowded, and the Army had to beat a retreat.

Alvin ran up against much dirty playing. Oddly enough, the end coach who taught him how to protect himself was Reynolds, from Georgia Tech: "One tackler kept hitting me behind the headpiece and my ear with the heel of his hand. Reynolds knew all about playing dirty. He told me to throw my arm up fast, elbow out. That tackle hit my elbow point with the heel of his hand. He grabbed it and wrung it, then pretended it was all right, but I knew it wasn't going to be much use to him."

Often down in the scrimmage he'd hear them saying, "Get the nigger, get the nigger." Alvin would crack back with whatever came in his mind. He had protectors, and one of them he remembered proudly was a big husky named Lou Gehrig.

He showed me a clipping from a New York rotogravure of himself, Gehrig, and a couple of other players talking to Percy Haughton. He showed it modestly. "I'm no great ex-athlete," he said, but I could see he cherished the brown clipping, nearly twenty years old, which showed a stringy but well built young Negro on equal terms with two of the greats of the American sports world. His people's spunk that they had shown on Bayou Fourche, on a sugar plantation in Napoleonville, he had carried in some measure to Baker Field.

Therefore I was not surprised when in a collision with a white man, Alvin was calm, polite but unbending. The white man had inclined to bluster, but Alvin pointed out with cold logic exactly where the white man had been driving against the law. There was no soft-soaping; it wasn't white man against colored man; it was man versus man; and one man, not Alvin, was in the wrong. I went with Alvin early one morning to the voting booths. As he entered the curtained box, I noticed the whites in charge looking and whispering. But Alvin acted as if this were nothing out of the ordinary, as if he voted every morning.

He is a trained statistician, and is called on for community studies. For the Carnegie-Myrdal Study he made a careful study of the racket of policy playing. He is not making an analysis of the economic cost of segregation, of the dual system prevailing in New Orleans. His figures on the costs of so many screens for so many New Orleans streetcars are coldly reckoned and presented, but the totals as he announces them cause warmth in the public conferences. He is himself not cold in pointing out the absurdities of the segregation practices, but he points these out, with canniness in terms of economic waste. I thought idly, while listening to his long arrays of facts and figures and costs and losses, of his grandfather sunning his paper dollars, distrusting the banks; of his father's buying real estate in reconstruction Napoleonville. Alvin himself is well-fixed financially. He repeats over and over that the Southern white man listens to arguments of dollars and cents more than of abstract justice.

The Negro needs to learn some economic horse sense, he insists. He told scornfully of some New Orleans Negroes who had a protest meeting, and did a whole lot of heated talking "down at the big gate." Afterwards they formed a committee and met with some white officials of the city.

"The white men talked politely. They showed figures that proved that they had given the Negras a 60 percent increase, while limiting the white increase to 25 percent. The increases were accurate. 'So you can see what we're trying to do for your people,' the white representative said, giving them a sort of pat on the back and getting them out fast. The Negroes were flattered by the nice white folks, and were going out, glowing and glistening. Then I broke in, 'Let us look at your base. In this instance, a 60 percent increase for Negroes raises one dollar to one dollar and sixty cents. A 25 percent increase for whites raises one hundred dollars to one hundred and twenty-five dollars. Before we can be grateful for what you say you are doing, we first must have a look at your base.' "

►► MEEKNESS IN BRONZE ◄◄

In Natchitoches, Louisiana, at Washington and Lafayette Streets, a famous statue was "Erected by the City . . . in Grateful Recognition of the Arduous and Faithful Service of the Good Darkies of Louisiana." An old Negro, clad in a prince-albert, stands on a flower-decked pedestal. His shoulders are bent by age, his knees by servility; his head is bowed like Chesterfield's valet; his misshapen hat is in hand, doffed politely. My Natchitoches friends were somewhat ashamed of this civic pride, and they took me to see it only at dusk. I repeated to them the folklore of the *Louisiana Guide* that "Plantation Negroes, inebriated after a spree in town, go to the statue to ask the way home and the Good Darky never fails to tell them the right direction."

"No such lie," a friend, born and bred in Natchitoches, told me impatiently. "They are more likely to wake up Dr. Johnson or John C. Lewis. And borrow bus fare or a dollar or so."

From Virginia to this farthest South, I had seen the souvenirs and statues of the ex-slaves, or the preserved relics themselves, who were supposed to charm the tourists with tales that ran on like deep-grooved phonograph records. And I suspected, as in this instance my Natchitoches friends insisted, that much of the business was no such lie.

The old darky's posture did not lie; that goes without saying. Many in the past could have been found to whom it was second nature to fall into the pose that this statue immortalizes in bronze. Too many in the present could be found willing to assume the pose, though in better clothing than the rusty jimswinger and baggy breeches, doffing an Adams or Knox hat rather than the crushed lid. Nor did those ex-slaves lie who earn a few dollars soliloquizing in Richmond, Charleston, and Montgomery, dredging good times out of a carefully diverted stream. Books like *Old Massa's People* do not lie in the separate entries; they just do not add up to the correct total. Too many other items are not entered. Thomas Nelson Page was not lying in his eulogy of the mammy:

Who may picture a mother? We may dab and dab at it, but when we have done our best we know that we have stuck on a little paint; and the eternal verity stands forth like the eternal verity of the Holy Mother, outside our conception, only to be apprehended in our highest moments. . . . So, no one can describe what the Mammy was, and only those can apprehend her who were rocked on her bed, fed at her table, were directed by her unsleeping eye, and led by her precept in the way of truth, justice, and humanity.

Page's feeling is honest if childlike. I am sure that he loved his mammy to death. And I am perfectly ready to believe that she loved him right back. But E. C. L. Adams also reveals honest truth about the mammy when he reports the overheard conversation of his unlettered but philosophical farmhands:

> Ole mammy ain't nothin' but a ole ooman wid a han'k'ch'ef tied 'round she head. Dere's all kind er ole 'ceitful niggers gittin' dey self called ole mammy— more'n you can shake a stick at. Dere's all kinds er white folks runnin' 'round lookin' for ole mammys wuh been in dey fam'ly an' tooken care on 'em ever since dey was born—an' afore.

Sprawled on a really superior antebellum bed in the high and wide front room of a Natchitoches home that always stands open to visitors like me, I explained to my host and the friends he had gathered why I had wanted to see the statue. I led the talk around to something I had been digging out recently. I mentioned an essay on Calhoun by Christopher Hollis, who goes out of his way to prove that "there is very little reason to think that the Negro race has at all benefited by the abolition of slavery." For proof, he writes:

> I have heard Negroes spontaneously appealing back to "seventy years ago"— the end of slavery-time—as to one "when de niggers all was good," and contrasting it with the evil present "when de devil, he go up and down in Montgomery County."

I did not have the exact quotation then, but I had the substance correct.

Though long residents in a parish above Aleck (i.e., north of Alexandria, La., where the white folks run tough and nasty), my friends were still amazed at this contemporary defense of slavery.

"He said *that*? Is that the only argument he gave?" said my host.

"No," I admitted. "He also pointed out that white and black babies no longer play together freely."

"Damn," said one. "I'd like to see that in print. Where could I find it?"

"In *Approach to Literature*, a college text by Brooks, Purser, and Warren," I told them.

One of the company, not a college man, broke in. "You mean they teach that in a *college*?"

"Yes," I answered. "Not far away. At Louisiana State University, I'm reasonably sure. All three editors taught there when the book came out."

"They teach that in *our* colleges, too," he went on, "down at Southern University?"

"I doubt it," I said. "I hope not, anyway."

"Damn," said my newly found friend.

This spirit of skepticism I found as prevalent among Negroes in the South as among whites I found the feeling of sentimental attachment to old aunties and uncles. Negroes notice the straight contrast: whites are idealized for dashing courage, self-assertiveness, and rebellion against injustice or subjection; Negroes are idealized for loyalty to others, humility, and uncomplaining acceptance. Sweet and glorious it is to die for one's country, honor, liberty (if white); sweet it is for Negroes to live for their white folks. Well, the Negroes I found, whether illiterates or booklearned, were not being fooled. So protest in a white skin is heroic, and protest in a black skin is impudent, incendiary, unnatural. "Damn," said my newly found friend.

➤➤ NO TIES THAT BIND ↤↤

I saw other historical cities: Lynchburg, Virginia; Augusta and Athens, Georgia; Nashville, Louisville, Montgomery, Mobile, and Vicksburg. Although called a "valley of humility between two mountains of conceit," North Carolina still cherishes its old homesteads like its neighbors. In New Bern I saw the well-preserved homes and churches that resembled those of far-off Salem, Massachusetts, with whom the town traded, more than they do those of nearer Williamsburg and Charleston. In the Salem part of Winston-Salem, the compact and rugged dwellings and churches, graced with the hooded entrances that the Moravian settlers brought down from Pennsylvania, had a warm dignity that pleased me more than the ostentatious homes of the tobacco barons in the suburbs of Winston.

Throughout the South almost every town had one or two showplaces. Sometimes on a back road an old columned big house would suddenly loom at the end of an avenue of cedars or out of a grove, or from high grown scrub pine. I saw many houses falling to pieces, the paint peeling or gone, the floors sprung, the roofs sagging, the blinds askew. In the towns, several decaying mansions took in poor whites or Negro roomers; I found two that were colored Y.M.C.A.s, and one that was an old folks' home.

I saw the many styles that varied so from the hackneyed idealizations. I saw homes more beautiful than Hollywood sets, but I also saw the gimcracked ornateness that Mister Big, Major Huge, and Colonel Vast needed to bolster their egos. Many of the most imposing colonial mansions were those recently built by the South's new rich on the outskirts of the cities. And I saw a large number of old homesteads that were merely overgrown farmhouses, some of them with incongruously pompous columns in front of frame structures that would hardly be noticed as anything special elsewhere. I saw some Georgian masterpieces, but I also covered many states. I knew that there were many more examples than those I saw, that big houses were off the beaten highways, and I allowed for the destruction of the Federal armies and the long years. But I also am sure that mansions were not the chief features of the antebellum landscape. Even if they were as numerous as the legend counts them, they were still the graceful, charming homesteads of the few who were on top of the heap.

Looking at old manors and baronies is not the same as looking at the historical Old South. I sensed quite as much history on seeing the sooty brick buildings of the Tredepan Ironworks on the canal at Richmond; the dirty aged but still busy tobacco warehouses at Lynchburg; Factors Row and the docks of Savannah, Cotton Row, Augusta; and the wharves at New Orleans.

And even more a part of the historic landscape I knew were the notched log houses. If climate dictated the piazzas of Charleston, the balconies of New Orleans, and the high-ceilinged spacious rooms of Nashville, climate and material also dictated these homesteads of the poor: the single cabins, or those enlarged into double, as the family or the income grew, by building another shack and roofing over the runway between them. When that was finally walled in as a hall, a porch might be added across the front with posters that sometimes grew into poor-man's columns. Time and the advertisers have of course not been kind to the older log cabins of the modern descendants; battered and weather-beaten, but numerous, these soft gray and brown [relics] merging with the worn-out land, itself a legacy of the antebellum South.

Slave markets and quarters were also part of the architectural distinctiveness. Some have been preserved or restored to advertise departed glory. In Fayetteville, N.C., the city fathers will not consent to the removal of the old slave market house even though it creates traffic jams because of its location at the juncture of four main streets. And one of the few points of interest that I was directed to in Louisville, Georgia, is the slave market, praised as one of the last standing in the South. The slave quarters that I saw throughout the South certainly left me few illusions about slavery. I could understand their being preserved as London might preserve Newgate Prison or Baltimore might preserve a prison ship. But it is beyond my understanding how these wretched mud-daubed log-huts, or even the brick houses which at their best resembled ovens, could be preserved as witness of a chivalrous past. The pride that vibrates in "Look, my people once owned slaves" I cannot get; it needs a different wave-length from mine.

I could not see this historical romance through the eyes of the Daughters of the Confederate Veterans, the Chambers of Commerce, the organizers of Garden Clubs, the keepers of the Gift Shops and Tea Rooms. I was ready to believe that many of these were people of goodwill, and I wondered if they knew what the thing really was that they wanted restored. A Southern white liberal advised me not to be concerned about it. They don't want restoration of the past so much as a thriving business in the present. "The South is poor," he said, "and the people need this money."

I realized that the worship of the past had its commercial aspects, some of them unsavory, outdoing even the maligned Yankee of the Legend. I knew the rather sordid story of the fiasco on Stone Mountain, with charges and counter-charges of fraud and bad faith. I had read about the battle of the two garden-clubs in Natchez, and money was the root of that evil. I knew the commercial slant of the Boosters Clubs' folders and postcards and billboards. It may have taken General Grant a long time to conquer these parts, but Babbitt made a swift, more infiltrating advance.

As my memory unveils, I find that I have glimpsed many of the places named in Southern history. I have seen the several oldest houses of Saint Petersburg, Florida, and have paid my quarter for the green bottle of water from Ponce de Leon's Fountain of Youth. I have seen reminders of Indian warfare: the little South Carolina whistle-stops called Yemassee, the Chickasaw-Choctaw country along the Natchez Trace, the beginning of the San Antone Trace at Natchitoches. I have crossed and recrossed the storied rivers: James, Roanoke, Savannah, Santee, Pedee, St. Mary's, Swannee, Chattahoochee, Clinch, Cumberland, Alabama, Tennessee, Ocmulgee, Black Warrior, Tombigbee, Peal, Yazoo, Red, the little Muddy, the big Muddy, and the Old Man himself. I have visited presidents' homes from Washington's Mount Vernon to Andrew Jackson's Hermitage. I have seen many of the river towns from Red Stick up to Mark Twain's Cairo and Paducah. As for the Civil War sites, I have seen Fort Sumter where the first shot was fired and Appomattox where Lee surrendered, along with various battlefields: those around Richmond, those of the Shenandoah Valley, Lookout Mountain, Missionary Ridge, Kennesaw Mountain, Atlanta, and Vicksburg.

In Montgomery, the old silver-haired lady at the First White House of the Confederacy told us as we were going out of the door of the museum, that visitors were supposed to leave something in the coinplate for looking at the relics. "But you don't have to do it," she added graciously. "I know your feelings."

She sensed correctly. The war relics, oil paintings, and the table upon which Jefferson Davis wrote his autobiographical *The Rise and Fall of the Confederate Government*, those were not our past. We thanked her, graciously too we hoped, and left the cool darkness for Montgomery's sunlight.

I made some attempt to discover my links to the past. I had a natural curiosity about the birthplaces of my mother and father. Once I made a layover in Gallatin, Tennessee, between L & N trains and wandered about the sleepy hamlet. It was here that my mother was born, but I knew that asking questions was fruitless, as it had been long ago, and my mother had been carried to Nashville as a baby. I knew that her childhood had been spent in the shadow of the state capitol, where her aunt had reared a large family of her own children, nieces and nephews, on the earnings of a first-rate seamstress. But Aunt Mercy's cottage had long ago been torn down to make way for progress. The landmarks that I think mother may have known were the homes of her cousins: dark-red brick dwellings, narrow-fronted but long because of frame additions with long side porches, high-ceilinged rooms, and the odd fronts decorated with the gingerbread ornaments of Victorian Nashville. And of course Fisk University, truly an Alma Mater for my mother, since she attended all the classes there from graded school through college. The somber magnolias on the campus looked old enough to have been there when my mother, a young fair-haired slip of a girl, recited a poem at the laying of the cornerstone for Livingstone Hall.

I remember driving through Roane County, in Eastern Tennessee, the birthplace of my father. Coming down off the mountain into Rockwood, one gray daybreak, I remembered with a warming at the heart that it was here that my father, even as a young man, had been boss molder of a brick kiln, earning and saving money to attend Fisk University—so far away in those days. That morning, with the Rockwood foundries going full blast under a pall of smoke and haze, it seemed a tough place to make a living in. I knew it had been tougher fifty years earlier, and I grew proud, visualizing my father's doing a man-sized job even as a boy. "So this was where it was," I said to myself, as we drove around the horseshoe curves.

With that sort of past I had links. But with much of the past celebrated in the guidebooks I found no ties to bind me. I could not people the broomsedge and pine barrens near Richmond with the young fellows in blue and butternut gray slogging it out for four bitter, bloody years; nor could I people the better preserved forts, breastworks, redans, and redoubts, sapworks and trenches at Vicksburg National Military Park. I knew that important battles in an important war for me and my people and America had been fought over these grounds. I was impressed, but my imagination did not spring.

I confess that less renowned memorials quickened my fancy more. One was Negro Foot, so-named because various members of the bodies of offending slaves, runaways and the like, were displayed there as gruesome warnings. Negro Foot is not far from Hanover, Virginia, and is the section famous for Patrick Henry, the Nelsons, and the Pages. While Roscoe Lewis was working on *The Negro In Virginia* he drove me to Cross Keys, where Nat Turner began his slave revolt. We retraced Nat's route down to Jerusalem, now Courtland, in Southhampton County. We saw the swamp land along the Nottoway River where, after his mad ill-fated stab for freedom, Nat hid safely for six weeks, from over three thousand searches. In an old brick-house, blackened with age, in whose heavy doors were bullet holes, we talked to a Negro tenant family. They were raising peanuts on shares for a big white farmer. The father knew nothing about the tradition associating his bullet-scarred house with the uprising. He recollected some kind of wooden marker at the crossroads, but it had long since been used for kindling sticks. He had heard something about Nat Turner; he disremembered what. We told him of Nat's march on Jerusalem. "So he fought to be free," the fellow said: "Well . . . " He hadn't been long in these parts, he apologized; really, he came from up around Emporia, about twenty-five miles up the big road.

In Florida I visited Apalachicola, where Seminole Indians, halfbreed Seminoles and Negroes, and runaway slaves fought so gamely against Federal troops, in one of the earlier wars against slavery and aggression. I should like to have visited Brackettville, Texas, where Kenneth Porter tells me the descendants of these Seminole Negro warriors still cling to their proud traditions. I have visited the Crater at Petersburg where Negro soldiers proved again at terrible cost that they were fit to fight in America's armies, which the Revolutionary War and the War of 1812 should have already proved, and which it seems must be proved periodically in every war. I did not see Fort Pillow where General Nathan Bedford Forrest ordered the captured Negro garrison to be indiscriminately massacred.

The Dismal Swamp in lower Virginia and upper North Carolina also stirred my imagination. We drove around its edge from the western rim to the outlet of the Washington Canal that links up with Lake Drummond. The swamp—consisting of the Big Dismal and the Little Dismal—is vast in spite of the recent drainage. A guide born and bred on the fringes of the Swamp led us a short way into its tricky fastness. The peat was spongy and soggy underfoot; oxen could walk on it, our guide told us, but no horses or mules. The streams in which large tree trunks lay water-logged were amber-colored, and ran over reddish-brown beds. "That water's got juniper logs sunk on the bottom," the guide explained. "Makes it good for what ails you. Juniper is what they makes gin out of." It was not long before we were in rank undergrowth, our faces stung by lashing twigs, our clothing caught by briers, our feet tripping over roots or sloshing into waterholes, even through the built-up peat. Cypress knees bulged out of still waters and the blackish streams became more and more serpentine. In two senses, I feared when our guide pleasantly told us of cottonmouth moccasins and rattlers he had seen, as thick around as his muscular black arm. Even though we had not penetrated far, it was not difficult for me to imagine a runaway Negro lurking in these wilds, marooned on one of the myriad hummocks, fighting off the froth-mouthed blood-hounds with a stolen rifle, or up to his neck in water and ooze as that fugitive of whom the slave-hunters reported: "Seeable but not come-at-able."

When we left the swamp, we stopped at the shanty of an ex-slave named Henry Milteer. He knew the swamp-lore, and told us of the whitened human bones found so often, the numerous lost travelers (a pair had been lost only recently) and the gaunt, haggard outlaws and fugitive slaves. These last had fled for freedom's sake into those dangerous morasses, had grown as wild and savage as the swamp bears and cougars and rattlers they met up with and would die before they would be retaken. He remembered how, during his boyhood, runaway slaves had slunk out of the Dismal to make forays on the corn-shocks and smokehouses of neighboring farms. Milteer's family had been free Negroes, who sometimes set out food for the outlaws. "But we had to be mos' keerful," he said. "Efn de white folks had found it out, we would have fared right common."

I realized that these reminders of Negro revolters, maroons, and fugitives are of exceptions in the past of the Old South. But so are reminders of wealth and glamour. For me they recall thrusts for freedom, as so many Old South memorials and monuments do. Insignificantly marked, most of them along byways and back roads, they are a welcome relief from the only Negroes allowed on the picture postcards and folders advertising the Old South. I collected many of the latter. A few will indicate the type: "The Home Stretch," which shows a young blue-black buck straddling an alligator, both grinning toothily; "Negro Heben," with four kids about to douse their brown noses and gleaming teeth into slices of watermelon; "A Coon Trees a Possum in Dixieland," where a gray-haired Negro is about to grasp a possum by his tail; and "A Darkey's Prayers," where an alligator grasps a praying Negro by his hands; "Sitting Soft in Dixieland," where a cute kid sprawls on a heap of cotton; and "Working Hard for the Family Dinner," where three boys fish drowsily and successfully from a wharf. And, of course, ex-slaves are allowed in the advertisement if only they are sufficiently grizzled and gracious, beaming relics of the good old days.

Academic Retreat

"Academic Retreat" not only records exemplary teachers and educational institutions, the section also traces unwavering commitment to education, a vehicle for attaining a social status long denied African Americans by a history of legal and social barriers. About this history, Brown writes eloquently in "The Little Gray Schoolhouse," "If the little red schoolhouse is a symbol of the American way of yesterday, the unscreened, unpainted, leaky, decrepit gray schoolhouse symbolizes a present disgrace." The narratives collected in this section speak loudly to efforts to achieve educational parity at a time when racial disparity was the order of the day. Some, including the persistent effort to equalize teachers' salaries and educational facilities, have a contemporary resonance. But even these efforts demonstrate how differently African Americans felt about the most effective way of bringing about change. For example, juxtaposed with the principled fight of Lutrelle F. Palmer to hold high the banner of academic excellence for his Negro students in Richmond, Virginia, were those teachers and administrators who "out-bookered Booker."

The narratives preserved in this section therefore represent the variety of takes on education and the differing meanings of literacy. "The Path to Alcorn" is an homage to the dogged determination of tiny Alcorn College to keep its doors open when so many other small, historically black schools were forced to close. "And Gladly Teach" reverses the stigma often attached to teaching ("those who can, do; and those who can't, teach") and testifies to the earnestness, the commitment that honors teaching as a profession. From the vantage point of Freddie, a schoolboy, Brown, in "What Could Freddie Say?" tempers a sense of hopelessness with a determination to succeed. "One Language, One People" is an ironic commentary on the National Council of Teachers of English's practice of "making provisions for Negro participation" in its annual conference. "Vicious Circle" asks the question, "When do you certify marginal teachers, who possibly inflict more ignorance on to students, and when do you draw the line and say 'no more'?" And "Signs of Improvement" points with some optimism to changes occurring in Southern education.

"Academic Retreat" participates in one of the oldest traditions in African American literature: the pursuit of literacy as a means for securing freedom. For African Americans, the notion of literacy took on special meaning beginning with the Age of Enlightenment in the eighteenth century, when men of letters, philosophers, and scientists urged the view that the ability to reason was the exclusive province of those who were supposedly "cultured" or "civilized." Because these thinkers further argued that people of color were incapable of being cultured or civilized, this "logic" became the foundation for denying the humanity of colored peoples. As misplaced as it was, it created a simplistic binary opposition between certain whites as rational beings and blacks categorically as emotional or irrational. To counter such racial denigration, African Americans sought to demonstrate fully and persuasively their abilities in literacy.

From Phillis Wheatley's efforts to prove her mastery of eighteenth-century English versification to Frederick Douglass's *Narrative of the Life of Frederick Douglass* (1845), arguably the most celebrated of the slave narratives, black writers were consumed with the passion to claim their own and to reclaim the race's humanity by using the written word to prove their excellence. As the post-Reconstruction ended and the New Negro Renaissance unfolded, writers such as James Weldon Johnson interpolated the quest for literacy into a broader claim: that a people is only as great as its literary and cultural production. Following the era of the New Negro, yet another interpolation of literacy took place. As more than one historian has written, the concerns for literacy shifted into a more generalized focus on education. Therein lies the importance of "Academic Retreat": it extends the pursuit of literacy and academic excellence into a much longer historical quest made by African Americans for their humanity.

We slowed up by the school. It was small, weather-beaten gray, with a squat belltower. The roof sagged slightly and a few shingles were off. A pole in the beaten, grassless yard had a barrel hoop fixed against it; another hoop was on the stock of a pine tree from which the lower branches had been cut. These were basketball goals. Roots stuck up as extra hazards for the players. Two outhouses were in plain view about twenty yards back in the loblollies.

Bullock glanced over at me. "So that's the school," I said, noncommittally.

"That's not one of the most bad ones," he said. "At least it's a building, and it has outhouses. There are plenty that don't have them. I've got the statistics in the office at Atlanta."

As we drove off, he told me how often Negro elementary schools had to be housed in churches and fraternal lodges of the Negro community. His voice droned on as the gray concrete sped under our wheels.

"So they went to the county commissioners and asked for a school. The head commissioner told them 'no funds.' They pitched in, fixed up a schoolroom on the upstairs floor of their lodge hall. They paid the teacher's salary, such as it was. When winter came, they went to the commissioner again. They wanted a little money for coal to heat the room. You won't believe what answer they got."

Oh, yes, I would. "What was it?" I asked.

"The commissioner got hot as blazes. 'What in hell do you mean coming here asking for money for coal? Do you think this county is going to pay to heat a building that don't even belong to it?' "

Back in Atlanta, Bullock reeled off, like a man pressing the nearly exposed nerve, a list of percentages that should have staggered me: In Mississippi (taking the worst instance), 38 percent of the Negro schools were housed in churches, lodges, garages, tenant homes, and privately owned buildings; 91 percent were without toilets; 73 percent without water; fifty thousand Negro children had no high school facilities; and the value of school grounds, buildings, desks, blackboards, and books per Negro school child compared to that per white was something like one cent to ten dollars. But it was a thrice-told tale to me; I have heard the dreary and ugly record as Horace Mann Bond, Charles Thompson, Doxey Wilkerson, and other statisticians have told it. My own sampling provided for me the brick and lumber structures to embody the figures of the experts. If the little red schoolhouse is a symbol of the American way of yesterday, the unscreened, unpainted, leaky, decrepit gray schoolhouse symbolizes a present disgrace. Throughout the South I found the state of the schools to be the indignity at which my friends seemed most ashamed. "Look here upon this picture [the fine red-brick trimmed consolidated school for whites] and on this [the one-room shack]"—became a ritual.

I was in Baton Rouge shortly after Charles S. Johnson published his hefty *The Louisiana Educational Survey,* a mimeographed report on Negro schools. My hostess, dynamic and civic-minded, had memorized passages of the study almost by heart. With three attractive youngsters of her own to be educated, she found the report striking close to home. She had marked pages from the introduction all the way to the recommendations. Coldly scornful, she read the Tulane University professor's prefatory comment, "It is sufficient to say, without going into historic details, that the South has always been in favor of Negro education." It was not sufficient for her. Swift in her anger, she thumbed through the pages to statistics showing the average cost of $54.95 for white elementary pupils to $15.33 for Negro; $111.32 for white high school pupils to $47.69 for Negro. She read me quotations from white superintendents who found scant time to visit Negro schools, leaving that to Negro Jeanes teachers. One superintendent did not even know what Negro schools were in his district. She was sarcastic about the Negro teachers whom the interviewers caught in revealing statements:

> I got my bachelor degree. I would rather teach in town because you don't have to work hard. I don't have no problem. I try to get the children to do right [i.e., not write each other dirty notes]. . . . The white superintendent, he come once, year before last.

Mrs. Huggins's laugh wasn't a good one when she read about the smaller children snipping pictures out of a Sears Roebuck catalogue in order to learn about the world. Nor when the older students, who were "having language," listened to a group of words, yelling "S" or "NS" to answer the teacher's "Is it or isn't it a sentence?" Nor when the teacher was quoted: "Now I gonna make the assignment for tomorrow: it's gonna be a test and you better know all of this that we been over or else you'll flunk." And to the tots: "You gonna have a test too so you better learn the names of the New England states. Now we gonna have health. We gonna say the chart for health. We should take a bath at least twice a week. Do we do that?" Echo answered yes. Echo lied, I told my hostess. She laughed ruefully.

There were bits of grim humor throughout, as when a teacher defined: "correspond, as to write people"; "examination—sometimes we have *yes* and *no,* that's examination"; "tennis, that's a game"; and "ninety, counting from one to ninety"; "all right, that's your spelling." Or when a student, asked to name her favorite actor and actress, answered, "My mother and father," and opened up an imaginative vista. Or when another student gave his life history: "I hafta cut wood, feed hogs and chickens, make fars." Or when a boy, while a girl was reading "What Does My Home Mean to Me?" burst in with a rhapsodic cry, "Jessie Mae, you got a lot!"

But Mrs. Huggins saw nothing to laugh at. She was not near to crying, as she is a fighter, not the crying sort, but she fumed at the dismal story of poor kids from broken families and getting an education as flimsy and makeshift as the rickety pine shacks where they get it. She did lay the heavy blame on the teachers; so badly prepared, underpaid, and heavily overworked, they could hardly have done much better. The recommendations—as sound as they were, calling for better salaries, less crowded classrooms, a curriculum more meaningful to the students—did not cheer her. For cold water was flung on her hopes by a recommendation by the white director of the overall study that "Congressmen and Senators from Louisiana should urge Federal aid for education *with no Federal control as to the details of the expenditure of the money,* but merely provision of the fields within which it is to be spent by the State Department of Education." She shook her head. She turned back to the underscored admission of a white superintendent: "We might as well be frank about it—all these years we have taken money from the colored children to educate the white. There's no use talking about how we did it or *why* we did it. We did it and we might just as well start there. I think it's mighty important to let the State and the Federal government see the picture as it really is, and if they want to do something about it, all right. But parish school boards spend money on white children first."

I was just as disheartened by a mimeographed survey of the Davis-Dyer community, a group of fifty-odd families living along the Dyer and Plank Roads in East Baton Rouge Parish, five miles from Baker, the nearest town. The people had decided that since their school was in a bad way, they needed a survey too. So somebody with a sociological yen estimated their annual income, how it came, and how it went. That wasn't tough. Then were listed the community's natural features and natural resources, such as the palmetto for making baskets, hats and mats, and clam and turtle shells for painted decorations. "The dominant mores of the community" are explained in one sentence: dancing and recreation were frowned upon; superstitions and mystical cures for warts and toothaches were still in favor. In "Living Men and Women of Opportunity and Achievement," the survey points with pride to "members of our community who have been fortunate enough to travel extensively in the United States, Canada, and Mexico, numbering six." The achievement of others is that they are living in Chicago, Seattle, and Los Angeles. The "creative individuals of the community" weave baskets out of thin strips of wood, horse collars and chair bottoms out of shucks, make beads out of chinaberries, and dippers out of gourds. In the business world, three are store-keepers, two are beauty culturists, and one sells chickens.

The most interesting part of the survey is the history: the hewing of the farm-lands out of the swamps, the battle against flood, fever, and such wild animals as bears, wild boars, wolves, panthers, foxes, muskrats, alligators, and skunks. White "bulldozers" scared off some of the new freedmen in the eighteen-seventies, but they returned. They soon had a church and a school.

The school today is a Rosenwald building of the one-teacher type. As usual, the enrollment slanted sharply from twenty-three in the first grade to four in the sixth and last grade. The average attendance was forty-five, with seats for only twenty-five. Two-thirds of the children had to walk three miles or more to school, as no transportation was afforded. The building needed painting; the two surface toilets were unsanitary; there was no water supply "on the campus." Textbooks, paper, pencils, and pasteboard were inadequate. The survey warily reached the conclusion: "That the teachers and parents deserve credit for progress under existing circumstances, but that the children deserve better educational opportunities." That hardly needed surveying. The recommendation was that "more efforts be put forth by patrons to secure the things necessary for better school and home life, by making contacts with proper officials and by continuing to help themselves, as they have done in the past."

I should like to have talked to one of the fathers of the community, sitting on his stoop at his home on the plank road, after a hot day at the Standard Oil Plant. I should like to know what he felt about the survey—if all he could recommend was "See Mr. Charley" and "Keep on keeping on"; and if in his book the "Living Men of Achievement" are only those who have hoisted stakes and gone.

I was to read all kinds of surveys (the dynamite sticks of their ratios warily bundled up in politeness and deference)—"Of course we wouldn't blame anybody but" . . . I found myself humming the more forthright folk-rhyme:

> Ought's a ought,
> Figger's a figger;
> All fo' de white man,
> An' none fo' de nigger.

Statisticians know the margin of error in the folk reckoning. Even so, it is too close for comfort. The surveys should not startle the white people of the South, though the act of surveying might. It is another sort of carpetbagging, if done by Southern whites, or smart alecky impudence, if done by Negroes. The way Negro schools are run in the South is the South's own business. So the principle of equal opportunity is violated. So what? That is the way it was planned. White apologists counter the glaring discrepancies with indubitable proof that the South is poor, that the education of the Negro was "the responsibility of a conquered and looted people," that the North or the West would not "have acquitted themselves any more handsomely, under like circumstances." But handsomely is hardly the word even though, as Southerners hasten to add, "the South spends a larger percentage of its wealth on education than any other region." Educational opportunities for whites in the South are far from satisfactory. Those qualifications are necessary. It remains true that dishonesty and injustice are rife. Stealing is no less stealing when the pot is small. North Carolina, the best state in the South for Negro education, spends for a Negro pupil less than two-thirds of a dollar for every dollar spent for a white pupil; the worst state, Mississippi, spends for a Negro pupil less than one-seventh on every dollar spent for a white pupil.

Uneasiness is spreading among Southern white liberals at the injustices. But the educational powers know what they are doing. Talking to an investigator, whose blue eyes, fair skin, and curly hair made her seem to be a white Creole, a parish superintendent explained that the only way they could have decent white schools was to spend on white children the money allocated to Negroes. "Yes, ma'am," he confided, "colored children are mighty profitable to us here in this parish."

Even if funds were more abundant, better Negro schools would not be welcome to many white Southerners. A Gallup Poll has shown that only half of the Southern whites believe that Negro school facilities should be equalized to those of whites. Words spoken in 1670 by Governor Berkeley of Virginia still ring too pleasantly today: "I thank God that there are no free schools nor printing; and I hope we shall not have, these hundred years: for learning has brought disobedience and heresy and sects into the world, and printing has divulged them." The difference is merely that the words are not today so applicable to poor whites as then.

Southern writers noted for their "sympathetic understanding" of Negroes have casually but quotably belittled education for them. In one of his less reliable moments, Joel Chandler Harris used Uncle Remus for his mouthpiece:

> W'at a nigger gwineter l'arn outen book. I kin take a bar'l stave an' fling mo' sense inter a nigger in one minnit dan all de school-houses, betwixt dis en de State er Midgigin. . . . [Education] Hit's de ruinashun er dis country. . . . Put a spellin'-book in a nigger's han's, en right den en dar you loozes a plow-hand.

Harris does not state their Uncle Remus is a hat-in-hand old fool, instead of a quaint philosopher. And Thomas Nelson Page applauds one of his favorite old uncles who declaims:

You knows de way to de spring and de wood-pile and de mill, an' when you gits a little bigger I's gwine to show you de way to de hoe-handle, an'd de cawn furrer, an' dat's all de geog-aphy a nigger's got to know.

In our own time, Julia Peterkin, called by her publishers the outstanding chronicler of the black man's life, devotes only a few words to Negro schools in her book on the "colorful life of the American Negro of the South":

Free school starts after all the crops are gathered and ends when field work starts in the spring. The children seem precocious and learn quickly, but they are less concerned with learning to read out of books than with learning lessons taught by woods and fields, swamp, and river. The old people mistrust printed words. They fear that book reading may put foolish notions into young heads and dim eyes that need to be keen in dealing with wild creatures.

Mrs. Peterkin complaisantly sides with the old people who, with "no books or newspapers to read, no radios or moving pictures to entertain, have leisure to develop faculties of mind and heart and to acquire the ancient wisdom of their race." The children, happy "in spite of the dangers and hardships that beset them" [in dealing with wild creatures most likely] learn the valuable lessons "that bearing heavy burdens makes for strength and that life was meant to be enjoyed."

Of the education of Negroes in his beloved Delta, David Cohn writes: "It is more important for him to know how to earn a living than to be able to conjugate Latin verbs. [The planters] think education of this kind tends to unbalance him mentally and to lose a sense of the realities about him; or in plain Delta language, 'to get out of his place.'" That which pains Cohn chiefly, however, is that "the blackboards of their high schools are filled with diagrams of the Peloppenesian [sic] wars; they prattle of Pericles and of Crete." The fact that Mr. Cohn's state of Mississippi was then spending an average of $45.34 for each white pupil against $5.45 for each Negro pupil does not seem worthy of his mention. It is hardly likely that the discrepancy can be laid to the Peloponnesian Wars. Many Negro school-teachers would gladly surrender even Peloponnesus if only they could get blackboards. It is tragic sophistry to lay the blame for the inadequacy of Negro schools on unwillingness to sponsor the conjugation of Latin verbs. It is not that education of this kind "tends to unbalance the Negro mentally." It is that education of any sort for the Negro is widely considered to be dangerous. Learning to read the Constitution, and to check on the landlord's "figuring with a crooked pencil" is dangerous enough, even without learning such facts of the Peloponnesian War as that Pericles dipped into the treasury for Attic glory, and that haughty states in their jealousy for power destroyed each other and a great deal of civilization to boot.

Bad schools in preference to bad notions. And so in the severest ordeal of our nation's history, the Selective Service reported that "failure to pass Army intelligence tests primarily because of educational deficiency, has deprived our armed forces of more physically fit men than have the operations of the enemy." (As of May 1944). . . . Adequate educational programs and the enforcement of compulsory school laws during the decade before the outbreak of this war would have resulted in providing the equivalent of 15 additional divisions of fighting troops for the defense of democracy.

It was not a "Negro problem." Negroes had no monopoly on the bad schools, thus were by no means solely the rejected. As Martin Jenkins and others point out in *The Black and White of Rejections for Military Service*: "In 15 states the percentage of Negroes rejected is less than the total percentage of white rejections, and in 26 states the rejection rate for Negroes is less than the rejection rate for whites in 10 southern states." It was all a Southern problem. Nevertheless, the national percentage of Negroes rejected (since so many Negroes came from the South) is about eleven times the rejection rate of whites.

The cost to the nation of these bad schools has been enormous. And the cost to the kids is greater than the statistics can tell. Dispirited, beaten before they start, rotted almost as soon as they bulge on the branch.

"How do you like your school," to the barefooted, ragged kid on the edge of the road.

"Aw right."

"Is there anything about it you don't like?"

"Nawsur."

"Nothing at all?"

"Well." Looking carefully from under his lids at the strange questioner. "I don't like the blackboard."

"Why not?"

"I doan know. I likes to write at my own seat." (At the blackboard his mistakes were there for people to titter at.)

One of the large yellow buses partly filled with white youngsters rolled by, with a monstrous shifting of gears at the hill's rise.

"Would you like for your school to have a bus like that?"

"Oh, nawsur."

"Why not?" The questioner knew that the little fellow walked nearly five miles to school everyday.

"That's for white folks," the little boy said simply but finally.

⇥ THE PATH TO ALCORN ⇤

Alcorn College and its environs were steeped in history too. In July 1830, the trustees of the Presbyterian Church brought some of their slaves to clear a campus out of the thick woodland and to lay the foundations for a college for white young men. Because of the live oaks that they left in beautiful groves, the college was called Oakland, and was intended for general culture and the training of ministers. Its location was in the center of things then, only a few miles on a good road to the flourishing river town of Rodney.

Its first president, the Reverend Jeremiah Chamberlain, an eminent Presbyterian minister, engaged in a heated dispute about slavery in the college chapel, and was stabbed with a sword cane in the yard surrounding the president's home. This assassination was ominous of the later history of Oakland. After the battle at Fort Sumter, the young men of Oakland College left the shady groves for the bivouac. At the close of the Civil War, financially wrecked, the institution was offered for sale.

Since Negroes were so important to Reconstruction Mississippi, the state bought the school for $40,000 and established it as a Negro college. It was renamed for James L. Alcorn, then governor, a former slaveholder who believed in the "capacity of the colored people for well-ordered freedom." Alcorn College became the first land grant college in the United States; and its first president was a Negro, Hiram R. Revels, after his service in the United States Senate.

Many of the buildings at Alcorn date back to the days of Oakland College. The chapel, in Greek Revival style, red brick with huge white columns, is the chief historical pride. Next in interest is the president's home, where the murdered Reverend Chamberlain bled to death "right over where we are sitting," said the vigorous young president telling me the story. This home is roomy, unpretentious, but beautiful. Some of the brick buildings did not survive as well as these relics and two are condemned. In talking to students and faculty members, I gathered that to them the facts of chief importance about these buildings are not that they are antebellum, but that they are old and that a few new buildings would be welcome. The worn old benches in the chapel may have been sat in by Oakland aristocrats but that doesn't lessen their discomfort. The chapel is hard to hear in, and when I was there, hard to heat. So history may come high-priced. Alcorn is now too remote from main-traveled roads for many sightseers to come and look at the past.

✦ AND GLADLY TEACH ✦

Church was a graduate student at Atlanta University; he was writing his Master's thesis on some aspect of romantic poetry. Though young, he had taught in three Southern states: North Carolina, Mississippi, and Alabama. He believed that his experiences would make a good book, and this is the story as he told it.

His first teaching job was in a North Carolina community of about six or seven hundred people. It was in tobacco and cotton country, not really near anywhere, well the nearest place that might be known was Hamlet on the Seaboard. There were more whites there than Negroes. The cracker class was numerous and ignorant; the whites of power treated them as badly as they did Negroes. There was a beautiful school for whites in the community. The Negro school, though brick, was only fair: there were no lights, the toilets were open earth, and a pump furnished the water.

In the community itself only two Negroes had electric lights, and there were no such things as bathtubs or commodes. There was no Negro doctor, nothing like that, and no Negroes of any wealth. The one educated Negro there was an ex-policeman from Chicago, who came back to retire. As far as the morals of the Negro community were concerned, the people did anything they wanted to do, anything they were big enough to do.

Most of the Negroes worked on farms as sharecroppers or hired hands, or as cooks, maids, and handymen for the white folks. The Negro store was only a jook, where they sold a little tobacco or snuff and soft drinks, not enough to call it a store. There was nowhere in town a Negro could eat away from home, except for one white café run by two white women, who would push a sandwich out at you through a hole in the side of the café. The teachers boarded around in the community at first, then pooled together and bought groceries and got somebody to cook for them. The three women teachers lived together in a three-room shack.

His first year there, Church got seventy-five dollars a month; his second, eighty-five dollars a month; this was the state-wide pay according to his certificate. Now he understood that the salary would be about one hundred twenty dollars a month. "One interesting thing about the white community," Church said, "was that they respected the teachers. Though most of the teachers were foreign to that section, the whites did not bother them much. Six teachers with eighty or ninety dollars a month coming in cash would spend more money in a month than the other Negroes would spend in a year. As a result, they sort of appreciated the teachers. Sometimes they even skipped up and called me Mister Church."

One of the most liberal Southern states, North Carolina furnished the grammar school books free, and the high school books at one-third of the cost. They paid a boy who had a driver's license to drive the Negro bus. When they bought new buses for the whites, they would work over the engines of the best of the discarded white buses for Negroes to use.

There were nine teachers for the Negro school, counting the principal and his wife; four taught high school and five elementary. The principal was regular his first year, then he tightened down and got really tough. The board was all white, made up of local people, and he nearly fell over backwards trying to please them and hold his job. He refused to walk on the street with any of the women teachers: though his wife was on the faculty, he didn't want to give the community the wrong impression. The Negroes in the community loved to talk about the teachers, who were outsiders and therefore doubly suspect. The young women teachers couldn't wear slacks, not even in the house.

The principal gradually changed to a little Hitler. The white board was too busy to bother with recommendations so they entrusted all of that to him, as their man Friday. At the end of the year the principal has the power to recommend and to fire, so he thinks the teachers are supposed to be his children for him to look after. This principal looked after them and, influenced by his wife, into all of their business.

"The way these Hitlers do it," said Church, "is to make their lists: this person or that one is to come back, or else his name is left off the list. The only reason needed is 'Didn't cooperate.' There is never an investigation, by all means no investigation. His first year, he gave the teachers lots of rope, and there was some tipping out. Then he got afraid of the community and clamped down. He was mortally afraid of letting anyone see him, or his teachers, taking a drink. The community would have considered that a righteous sin; meanwhile, the people of the community, white and Negro, drank their corn whiskey on the street."

Church's next two teaching ventures were in Mississippi. Perhaps because this was his native state, he insisted that Mississippi was paradoxical. "To start with the best things," he said, "Meridian has one of the most progressive high schools I've ever seen. It is heated by automatic gas, has model classrooms with adequate room space, a suite for home economics, and a modern cafeteria. The teachers range from M.A.'s on down. The white folks allow the football team to play one game in the white school stadium, always the game before Thanksgiving.

"In a nearby village, however, you will find a one-room school in a leaky shack, with teachers poorly paid and poorly prepared." Church taught for a while in one of the toughest counties in Mississippi's Black Belt. The Negroes there worked on the plantations owned by one or two companies: "I've been told people live there who've never been up to the city. As you drive through the country, you will see some pretty fine mansions, but there aren't three Negro homes with paint on them. The Negroes dare not build certain types of homes."

The school was built by the Negro community, with the help of some Rosenwald money. A Negro who owned about one hundred ninety acres gave the land. The county gave nothing.

"There was only one white man in the community. He lived openly with his Negro woman. They stayed out on a farm and reared up a whole family. All of his children that got high enough to go he sent to the Negro school. One daughter married, but most of the girls went the way of all flesh and got themselves some babies. There wasn't any ostracism. It was all right as long as it was mixed up in the community. With the exception of a few families, everybody in the community was screwing everybody else. Two or three of the trustees were tipping out with some of the teachers of the community. Some of the young girls had to come by both the principals and the trustees."

Church found that in general the young women teachers were fair game for the "educational powers." "They live in teacherages on the campus, and can't go out. Most of the fellows in the community are uneducated and sort of bad. Even if they aren't bad, the teachers can't go out with them, as they're below the teachers' level. The principal just won't hire men teachers; too much competition in different ways. So he has himself a little harem. Often he will get young girls' pictures when they make their applications. If they don't look to suit him, they don't get jobs. When they come, he starts playing around. If they don't like it, they don't come back the next year. On the report to the board: 'Lack of cooperation.' Sometimes the dismissal is verbal only. The teacher who cooperates stays. They have to come by, that's all. 'If you don't want to do it, I can get somebody who will,' is a repeated threat. Sometimes the principal's wife is in the community, sometimes on the faculty, sometimes she isn't. Often the principal had a head woman; she runs the school. He can't correct her. A lot of teachers who know the score have a saying they pass around whenever the principal got tangled up in an argument with his harem favorite: 'Huh, you didn't say that last night.' The trustees frequently go with the women teachers. Then look out; it makes no difference how inefficient they are or become, there's no getting them out. They're set, until maybe the trustees make a change in their women. They raise hell, then, to tell the truth.

"The white superintendents are guilty too. It doesn't take long before they'll approach a good-looking or just a decent-looking colored woman.

"All of the schools aren't in this mess, by any means, but too many are. Just too much power in the hands of people who are too petty to handle power. In spite of those things, the best of the teachers go out and do something. Not enough. But still there are some with the stuff in them, with ambition."

There wasn't much incentive in the region where Church taught, however. The nearest town was symbolized by Church as one "where Negro men don't wear collars and ties." More importantly, he said, "Negro men just don't go with any of the good-looking light-skinned women around here. No. Those women are just sold to those white men. They don't rate in the community; they're just about segregated from it."

One white man, brother to an important official, had a Negro common-law wife. He would bring his children to the town's school every day. Church found that "the community accepted them as just some more light-colored children. These would go out with Negro boys, either light or dark ones but it seemed that they preferred to go out with the darkest boys they could find."

At the school where Church taught, however, his strictures on the love-life of the principals didn't hold, Church insisted. The principal who was there when Church first went there was aging, and probably too decent for such carryings on anyway. He had been teaching for fifty years, after finishing the tenth grade in Columbus. He was one of the first Negroes in the section to get his first grade license. The people all agreed that he had been a crackajack teacher in his day.

When Church came, the principal was not jealous, only indifferent: "He knew my father, and seemed to like me. He thought I was too new-fangled. He used no schedule for anything. He would sit there all day with his hat on, teaching arithmetic from 8:30 to 3. The kids sat there all day with their hats on, singing out the tables. I asked him for a schedule. 'Folks ain't gonna work by that thaing,' he said. I made up a schedule, and rang a little bell at every change. It worked. A month later he said it was all right. After that he said of any plan, 'If you can make it work, work it.'"

But Church found greater hostility among the trustees: "One of them, an old handkerchief head, went to the superintendent and said, 'I could get some of my people from any town who wouldn't want all this high salary. Why some of those new people said they won't work for less than $30 a month.' There was also a tie-up with the church that didn't help any. The Baptists and Methodists fought for control of the board and of teachers. 'If you would get somebody belong to us church, us wouldn't have to bother. He could help us. But he's a Methodist. Us wants us folk.'"

But the old respected principal had recommended Church. Church asked the superintendent for his contract. He was told: "We don't even give contracts to our white teachers. We haven't made up our salary schedule yet. But you'll be paid among the highest of the colored."

Church found that to be true. He was given $30 a month, only ten dollars less than the principal. The rest of the budget for teachers was two teachers at $27.50 a month each, two at $25, and one at $22.50. The salaries of a principal and six teachers thus totaled $197.50 a month, for a school year of from four to six months. In 1933, Church's first year there, the state was so poor that it paid in script. When the certificates were cashed, 10 percent was lost: "The county superintendent said that if you held the script until the state got the money or maybe two months later, you would get full payment. But most of the teachers took them to the big store where they could be cashed at a 10 percent discount. All the whites and Negroes of the community came by this big merchant. He had it fixed so that as soon as the money came to the county he'd get his first."

The first thing Church noticed when he saw the school was a big ashpile, right out in front. None of the teachers seemed bothered about it, but he had it moved when he became principal. The town furnished nothing but teachers and registers, which are teachers' record books. Crayons, erasers, blackboards, rulers, and textbooks all had to be supplied by the Negroes themselves: "We had to put in our own windowpanes. The trustees got the wood for us. My second year there the WPA gave us a well. It was very needed; for there had been no water available; the kids would bring bottles of water to school and set them in the corner. The principal would drink from the students' bottles.

"There was a sawmill about two miles above us, and WPA got some rough lumber for some toilets. Before that the girls would use the church toilet, and the boys would run over the hill into the woods and squat. Our vocational man, who taught carpentry and agriculture, drew up plans for the toilets and supervised the building. The county had sent up some second-handed collapsible desks before I got there, but the people thought they were broken and threw them out behind the school. There weren't many, but our vocational teacher fixed them up. Then the community people brought their teams over, ploughed up the yard and fertilized it." When Church left the school it was no longer an eyesore.

Church became principal when the old man had a stroke. He planned his schedule so that his best teachers would be in the primary department. Church said, "I kept the worst teachers by me. One of them was pretty bad. I had to correct her lesson plans. They had tried to run her away. But she was one of those trustees' cousins. She had gone back to high school and had finished the eleventh and twelfth grades. In her summers she had attended the Normal School, trying to get a junior college certificate. She had a third grade license (the worst) and then got it up to the second. She didn't loaf as a teacher. She said, 'I don't want to be behind' and took all the advice and help I gave her with a willing spirit. Finally, she made a good teacher."

When Church first went to that school he was hopeful and energetic. He insisted on the students' understanding what words they were calling. He remembers that in a story about Alfred the Great, the word "conspicuous" occurred. He asked the meaning. No one knew and he told the class to look it up for the next day. He learned that one of the students, a trustee's daughter, had said of him, "He ain't gonna be here long. He's trying to be too hard. Teacher's don't do that up here in Stony Hill. They're too glad to get here." But he managed to weather the storm, and even got the word "conspicuous" over. He saw a slow improvement in the school. The white superintendent praised Stony Hill School as "one of my most progressive schools. There's a fine job up there at forty dollars a month." He became fairly well known among the whites in the neighborhood: "Some wealthy white folks had heard that I had waited in hotels in Atlanta. They wanted me to come out and wait on some of their parties, to be a part-time butler. They were very polite about it, calling me professor, and offering good money. I told them that the school work really consumed all of my time, that I was trying to do a good job there."

Church struggled to have the school stay open for a six months term, but some of his teachers kicked. They had their own farming to do. The parents generally agreed with them, and when Church left, the school went back to its average four and a half months.

In this community, Church learned, the teachers and parents tried to do what they could to keep from losing so many students: "As soon as they got to a certain age they were gone. A student would leave one year, about five or six years later their kids would be coming to the school. Healthy, strong kids, too.

"The kids were religious, but they ran wild in the woods. A boy from one grade and a girl from another would get excused from class. Then they'd meet over the hill. The best little Christian in my class, I called her the little shouting girl, was the first in the school to become pregnant.

"Each invites some young man to eat from her basket. Then she can go to the table and take anything she wants. Her boyfriend is supposed to pay for whatever she gets, if he eats out of her basket. Sometimes its five or ten dollars worth. In such a case you know something else has been going on. Otherwise they keep the expenses down. The Feast really makes money. Sometimes the trustees clear seventy or eighty dollars. All they don't sell, they carry back to the store. They get a commission of forty cents on the dollar. The preachers therefore wish to get members of their church as teachers, to help in such as this.

"They really believe in having their good homemade liquor. Nobody comes without it. The assembly room was about this high off the ground. Some of those Negroes would get drunk and walk out through the windows, taking the sashes and all. They just had to have their shooting and cutting. They would race up and down those hills, just shouting in the air.

"Yessir, they would raise torment with the teachers if they wanted to go out and have a little fun, but you could go out back of the school and find them screwing up hell. Just stumble over them.

"In the assembly they would all sit there with their hats on, men and students. Sometimes they would sing hymns and get happy. At one commencement the preacher really went to town. Then they started a song; they had tambourines and a drum for accompaniment. Sister Dumond, an old lady, but supple and limber, just skated out and started dancing. She would draw back, like a track man getting on his mark, and then start running and yelling. She told me that wasn't nothing. I told her, I'd love to see you when the spirit really hits you.

"If you were to see the people at one of these assembles, you might think they were perfectly happy. But I learned that those people are not contented; they know something is wrong, but don't know anything they can do about it. I would say that the school is doing more good than church. The young people—they will never be contented with what they have there.

"The old principal used to talk to me about education as insurance. 'These people ain't crushed,' he used to say to me, after he had felt me out. 'They just don't know which way to turn.' When I first got to know him he used to annoy me, sitting with his hat on, teaching arithmetic all day long, drinking out of the students' water bottles, and spitting in the ashes of the stove. But his little daughter was my best student. All around. She had good reasoning power. I don't know what happened to Frankie Mae, but she was a good student. Would read everything she could get her hands on. She even knew her father was off the track. She didn't know just what was wrong. But she was a long ways from satisfied."

➤ WHAT COULD FREDDIE SAY? ◄

In *Growing Up in the Black Belt,* Charles S. Johnson quotes a schoolboy who is retelling a story from his reader:

> Fred was a little boy. He went to the city to work for a man. The man told him if he worked he would pay him. Fred worked three years. The man paid him only three pennies. Fred said . . . Fred said . . . The man paid him only three pennies. Fred said . . .

Dr. Johnson blames rote-teaching for the boy's going on like a deeply grooved phonograph record. But to me the story illustrates more than the vice of learning by rote. The reciter carried Fred about as far as he could in this subversive story. After all, what could Freddie say?

The schools do not supply Freddie with answers. Freddie is supposed to like it; or if he doesn't he isn't supposed to have anything to say. To the white South, Negro education is already meaningful enough. The meaning is that Freddie shall never learn the answers.

Mississippi educators have recently been blunt on this subject. In 1940, the state legislature in Jackson amended a bill to furnish free textbooks by providing that such subjects as civics shall be taught from texts suitable "for the several types of schools," that is, that Negro children and white shall use different texts on subjects such as citizenship. The school superintendent of Meridian urged this because if uniform texts were used, Negro children would be taught "the same principles of voting, rights, and responsibilities taught white pupils." This would never do for, as a planter-senator reasoned:

> Under the Constitution the Negro is a citizen, and of course we know and accept that. But he can never expect to be given the same educational and social privileges with the white man and he doesn't expect them. The best education we can give him is to use his hands, because that's how he must earn his living. It always has and it always will be.

A further argument for different texts was that a set of books "best suited to the Negro's level of intelligence could be provided for one-third of what it costs for the white child." Insult was added to injury when a doctor urged that text books for white and Negro children be kept in separate warehouses, "because of diseases prevalent among Negroes."

What could Freddie say?

Thumbing through a few of the history primers used in the South, I found them generally weak on Lincoln but strong on Lee. Even when the books were not waving the Stars and Bars, Freddie and his fellows read such stuff as this in *Tennessee, Its Growth and Progress:*

> There were, of course, good masters and bad masters, just as there were good slaves and bad slaves. Cruel treatment of the slaves by the master was the exception rather than the rule.

Slavery wasn't bad, Freddie. It's only in freedom that the trouble begins.

The free Negro had no place in society. He could not, of course, associate with the whites. Here you come, Freddie:

> By nature the Negro is polite, he appreciates politeness in his employer. He is not disturbed about "race problems," as he is more content with his original color than he is concerned with artificial theories.

I grant you, Freddie, that *is* a poser! You theorize now, you'll lose your color.

In Tennessee there is no present or expected "race trouble." Each race understands and appreciates the place of the other, as their problems are in the main problems common to each.

Negro children attend school and profit by it.

See, Freddie, we told you. So get up early and wash behind your ears.

There is little chance that Freddie will learn anything of his rights or duties as a citizen. Just after Pearl Harbor, the schools were called on to stress democracy in education. An educational authority told me with a wry grin: "When Negro teachers were called together to work up a program, they realized that they didn't have much to teach; they hadn't seen much democracy in action. 'All men are created equal' and the Bill of Rights were dangerous doctrines where they taught. So they concentrated on discussing such problems of citizenship as hygiene and keeping the window open in their classrooms."

It is not only the beaten teachers in the backwoods who are wary around the dynamite of citizenship. Some of the better-paid, better-off teachers in the better schools warn that they have to "curve around all of that stuff. After all, we've got to live down here." Some of the largest high schools are run by men who discourage young teachers from such radicalism as teaching the meaning of the Constitution. Often these older heads exemplify how a Negro should stay in his place: one principal of a large high school in Tennessee, though he at last gets a good salary, still waits tables in the evenings at a fashionable club for whites. He brags that he is showing his students that he is not above honest toil. He is also showing white folks that his salary raise has not made him too big for his business. Another principal, a recent graduate from Harvard, is portering at a mid-Tennessee airport. "To buy bread for the family," he told me, shamefacedly. I thought this was another instance of the lowness of teachers' salaries. "No such thing," snorted an ex-teacher. "We worked ourselves to death in the fight for equalization of salaries to get that bozo decent pay. He's making a good salary now, enough to live well on. If he's got to get a second job, he can find something else other than toting bags. He's a principal. He should have some professional pride. But this won't hurt him with the white people." "They may have finer schools and buildings than we had," a middle-aged citizen of a large Tennessee town said sadly, shaking his head, "but they have no spirit. No vision. No courage. So they can't really reach the young ones."

Many of the Jeanes teachers are forward-looking. But I talked to one in Georgia, chic and well dressed, working toward her Master's degree in New York City, who surprised me. She pounced on the subject violently. "Negroes are stewing about too much," she told me. "All of them. Teachers, parents, students. Just stewing about. Stirring up ill-will. They ought not to go to court to get salaries equalized. Many of the teachers doing most of the agitating are not ready. They ought to try to get along with the white people. They'll be raised when they deserve raises. I've had no trouble myself. I've had raises. And they call me Miss. But I never stew about." She controlled the books and magazines purchased by the schools in her county. She named the periodicals that she subscribed to for her schools, but the *Journal of the Georgia Teachers' Association* was the only Negro periodical she named. I asked if she had left *The Crisis* off accidentally. "Well," she started uncomfortably, "we have only a little money. . . . My teachers probably wouldn't understand *The Crisis*." I asked her if Raper and Reid's book, *Sharecroppers All,* was recommended to her rural teachers. She was brisk here. "Of course not. It's too difficult. My teachers wouldn't be able to get its true meaning. I haven't yet read it myself, but I'm sure they wouldn't. I have to read all the controversial books first, to see if they are fit for my teachers. I want them to be objective."

I knew the power of the word objective. In Jackson, Mississippi, an educational specialist, who was to go a long way in Negro education in his state, talked with me about the inequalities in funds and facilities. I said the situation was a damned shame.

He bristled. "That is only opinion," he said.

I asked him if he didn't think the figures he reeled off to me showed an outrageous state of affairs.

"I wouldn't like to say," he said stiffly. He then rebuked me for my lack of objectivity. As I worked it out from his lecture—if you said that Negro children got for education only two bits for every dollar that white children got, you were objective, you were sticking to the facts; but if you stated an opinion that this was wrong you were not objective and shouldn't be listened to. It seems we must wait for further proof before we can be certain that injustice has been perpetrated.

There may be a day or a week dedicated by the schools to Negro history, not to showing the Negro's share in American life; what it has been, could be, should be—but something of pageantry instead: Phillis Wheatley, Booker Washington, George Washington Carver—a sort of whistling in the dark on the part of some race-conscious teacher. For these are mere names to Freddie, a murmur from the past, a ticking on the wind. Other sounds are louder, penetrate his ears more deeply: the rain beating against the loose shingles, pouring steadily in the buckets under the holes through which one sees the gray sky, dropping plop-plop in puddles under the new places. And the white superintendent, bringing visitors, walks in possessively, with his hat on, and greets the teacher whom Freddie has learned to respect: "Good afternoon, Agnes, and how is the school going?"

And even Freddie's teacher can't say anything to that, except "Fine."

✦ ONE LANGUAGE, ONE PEOPLE ✦

As the time drew near for the meeting in Atlanta of the National Council of Teachers of English, both the white local committee and the Negro teachers of English in Atlanta became anxious. Believing the membership possibilities good in the South, the Council had voted, over some protest, to come to Atlanta upon assurance that provisions would be made for Negro participation.

Unfortunately, the president of the Council, Robert C. Pooley of Wisconsin, did not ask to have the word "participation" specifically defined. A letter from Paul Farmer, chairman of the committee on arrangements, sent out a careful definition. He did this, regretting that "even a part of the privileges will be kept from the Negroes," and sincerely hoping that Negroes would "manifest a generous spirit of understanding":

> The precedent established here for Negro participation in such meetings; that is, Negroes would be admitted to all sessions with the exception of those of a social nature such as receptions, teas, breakfasts, luncheons, and the banquet; and would be seated, particularly in the large group meetings, in seats reserved for them.

To the last euphemism, Dr. Farmer added this choice equivocation:

> I have felt it unfair for the Local Committee to urge Negro registration. I believe that Negroes should be acquainted with these conditions and that if they register, the urge to do so should come from a genuine desire to benefit from the splendid sessions that are available to them.

None of this was lost on N. P. Tillman, chairman of the department of English at Atlanta University. There can certainly be no more doubt of his genuine desire to benefit from scholarly discussions than of his hostility to segregation, supported by weasel words. Characteristically, he remarked on the "several semantic somersaults" that the word "participate" had gone through. He organized a committee from the Negro teachers of English in Atlanta and drafted a letter in which he pointed out that:

> In recent years, the precedent for national educational, and for some Southern groups, has been entirely different. At meetings in Atlanta of the American Chemical Society (1930), the Association of American Colleges (1935), the Baptist World Alliance (1939), the National Physical Education Asso-

ciation (1939), Negroes had full participation in each session. A few years ago the Southern Sociological Society adopted this position as its policy and has maintained it in the three annual meetings held in Atlanta. The conduct of the meetings here of a national or sectional association has depended largely upon the stand taken by the organization itself.

The committee was "not interested in sensationalism nor in using the National Council to solve the race problem," but "in participating in the larger cultural life of our country from which Negroes are generally cut off in the South." It expected a national educational organization to take a stand in line with the best thought in our country; that is, to be anti-Nazi.

It was, of course, too late to change the place of the meeting. But letters poured in to Dr. Tillman from Negro and liberal white teachers of English all over the nation. Some were soft spoken acknowledgments, and some were fighting mad protests. One Negro scholar wisecracked, "If never the twain shall eat together, they may as well not meet together," and another, old in the teaching profession, quickened his step to come abreast:

> When that organization met in Chattanooga, Tenn., many years ago, I was allowed to attend on condition that I would take no part in any of the discussions. I attended all the meetings except those held at the Hotel. I was not segregated in the meetings attended. The Negro, now, should accept nothing short of full citizenship in that organization.

R. D. Jameson, the administrator of Consultant Services of the Library of Congress, visiting certain Southern colleges where he found "Atlanta University far and above the other colleges I have visited," wrote Dr. Pooley that "the decision of the local committee . . . to exclude all Negroes from participation in the events which are euphemistically called social, and the segregation of them in the other meetings . . . is damnable."

Some whites and a large number of Negroes boycotted the meetings, but many of those aroused came in order to see that the insult should not be repeated. As William Ellery Leonard wrote his former student Tillman: "Bear the insult with dignity . . . and join with your white colleagues in a quiet firm statement for publication that it must not happen again."

At the first meeting, a party of colleagues and friends (four Negroes and three whites) entered the Georgia Tech auditorium. After a bit of professional consultation on the part of the ushers, three polite (*noblesse oblige*) members of the Local Committee came to them and explained gently (never raise a voice to inferiors) that "Section D was reserved for colored teachers." The group, both white and colored, moved to Section D. But that was still wrong as they were still together. Soon they were joined by another party of Negroes and whites, who just about brought the sex balance even. The auditorium was confused and probably paid little attention to the speech of the superintendent of city schools. This was a pity, as he was in rare form, welcoming the convention "Damn-Yankees and all" (he was arch-Rebel, all right), regaling the visitors with several darky stories, the last about an "old nigger."

"Did you hear that?" asked one of the visitors, noted in New York for intercultural work. Dr. Tillman hadn't missed hearing him.

On the rear wall of the auditorium stage, there was a large blue velvet banner with the following emblazoned in silver letters:

"Our Defense of American Traditions"

The president's annual address was "Language in a Democracy—One People, One Language."

A panel had been planned on Intercultural Relationships. At this meeting, the Spelman-Morehouse Glee Clubs were to sing as part of the Negro contribution, but Kemper Harreld, the director, called *that* off. One of the speakers at the Intercultural Committee luncheon was to be Sidney Reedy of Lincoln University (Missouri). When Dr. Reedy heard of the type of "participation" permitted Negroes, he hastily wrote Dr. Pooley his refusal to speak. His letter crossed Dr. Pooley's letter suggesting that he "withdraw from the panel":

Political happenings in Georgia . . . have stirred anew prejudices which I sincerely hoped were dying.

(There is such a thing as tying too much on Gene Talmadge's red galluses. Recent political happenings are not needed to unsnarl the tangle of this meeting.)

In a letter to Dr. Tillman, E. A. Cross had hoped fervently that "no color line will be drawn at that luncheon," at which his friend, Dr. Reedy, was to speak. But his hope was vain. As Dr. Reedy wrote ironically, he would have been excluded from the very luncheon at which he was a featured speaker. Since he couldn't deliver his speech in person, the Intercultural Committee asked Dr. Reedy to send a phonograph recording of his speech. His voice could be allowed in the Hotel Biltmore dining room. Dr. Reedy sent over a recording, spirited and incisive, stating that his speech no longer pertained, and that "the Committee on Intercultural Relations is even now dying, having lived briefly in vain." The record was considered too hot to be played.

There was great fear that some of the protesters would get out of hand. Negroes attended many group meetings without being segregated and were treated equably, pleasantly. Herbert Agar, who had something of the license of a homeboy who had made good, did not spare sectional (and national) feelings. In one of the key speeches of the conference he described the plights of the present predicament and hypocrisy, the broken promises, especially to Negroes, promises that America had no intentions of keeping.

The next meeting of the Council will be held in Atlantic City (where, of course, a hotel problem may likewise arise). A motion put by the retiring president, Dr. Pooley, and passed by the Executive Council, stipulates that "the National Council of Teachers of English will accept invitations to hold its annual conventions only in cities which can provide equality of participation for all the members of the Council." This pronouncement, though to be considered unofficial until passed by the Board of Directors, is a victory for the forces marshaled by Dr. Tillman. He was assured by the retiring president that his action had been "becoming of a scholar and a gentleman." One might add: "and a good fighter for democracy, not easily to be fooled."

⇥ VICIOUS CIRCLE ⇤

It is not good to admit, but like many members of the teaching profession since Socrates, I have collected students' "boners." I was a party to a session discussing boners at the end of one summer school at Atlanta University. Three of us teachers gathered in the hall, near the rooms where our students were taking examinations by a sort of honor system.

"I won't stay out too long," said Tic. "I don't want them to steal too much of the wrong stuff."

"If they know where to find what I asked for in the books in one hour, they're good enough to pass," Bacote said.

I had just about decided what grade my students had reached in the six-weeks gallop, so I was also at ease.

Bacote said, "Man, I've got some howlers here. I corrected the papers last night for my American history class. Listen to these." He read excerpts. We laughed. I asked to copy down two of the answers.

One went as follows: "During the early days of history two men said they founded America and Columbus died thinking all the time that he had destroyed America. In 1492:

"The colony of S.C. was founded near Columbus, S.C. & settled during the Revolutionary War.

"The woman did all the cooking to help the men clear the land. They cooked on the fireplace. Some had brick-like stoves outdoors."

The second read: "The time pass when American want her independence from England it the mothe country disrecognized. During the year of 1600 Our County was first rule by Kings and Queens. All laws was to be obeyed.

"The Spanish was the first to came over to this country and they taught us how to build houses, cultive our soil in order that we raise our food.

"When the Indians came to America they found the Spanish already over here.

"The Spanish and the Indians could not get along after living here together for some time they begin to talk of war. During prehistoric times of war we did not have sufficient war guns to fight with & no. of men died for the want of attention."

These were written by rural teachers who were attending summer school to raise their status. We had our fun over the questions and returned to monitoring.

But the fun turned sour for me at the end of my examination. After coaxing, cajoling—"You all are keeping me from lunch. I'm a hard-working man"—sophistry—"Nothing you can write in this last minute can possibly alter your grade one way or the other"—and finally the packing of papers into the briefcase and clicking the latch, all the students had turned in their papers but one woman.

"Please, Mrs. Simmons," I said. "Please write your name on the paper and turn it in. It's ten minutes past the end of the examination period. Really I have to go." It was the last luncheon in the college dining hall; there were friends who were going to grab northbound trains and cars immediately after the luncheon, and I wanted to see them. I was as gentle as I could be, however; Mrs. Simmons had had a tough time with the course, never reciting, never saying a word; just there every day, punctual as clockwork but less audible. I walked back toward her seat. She scratched her name on the page. I noticed her hand was trembling.

"Professor," she started. "I'm sorry."

"Oh, that's all right," I said easily. "I didn't think the examination could take so long." I turned over the pages of her paper. There was very little writing on them.

"Professor," she began again. "I've got to talk to you." Her voice was husky. She was an Indian-looking woman, with wisps of iron gray in her coarse black hair. Her face looked tired but there was a firm set to her chin. Her summer dress was large and full and stiffly starched; a housewife's dress so different from the startling colorful prints of the younger girls on the campus.

"I teach down in Federal Point, South Carolina. I had to come here to get my certificate renewed. I tried awfully hard in your class. It's not your fault. I done the best I could. I'm in charge of the school down there. Down there the schools are low. I have three children. I want to send them up here to a good school under good instructors. I never had no chances myself."

Her voice was a new thing. In six weeks she had said nothing but "present" or "I don't know." Instead of the second, however, she had more often shaken her head timidly. But now the words poured out. Once the granite was out of the way, the torrent came.

"I just didn't get anything," she said. "It ain't your fault. Try as hard as I could, though, I couldn't get my mind fixed on it. But I didn't understand none of it. And this is the year my certificate comes up. I been teacher of the school for over twenty years. If I fail here I won't get my certificate."

I hemmed and hawed. "I don't want you to give me anything," she said. "I want you to give me what I make. But I want you to understand."

I was miserable just as she was, standing there. She told me how all night long, the night before, she had stayed up, studying. She had wrapped a damp towel carefully around her forehead. On one of her frequent trips to the bathroom to soak the towel, around three A.M., she had run into the younger students who were trooping into the dormitory, laughing and gossiping, some of them undoubtedly high after the summer school dance at the country club. It *had* been a bust-out, I reflected guiltily. She resented their gallivanting, but more the easy assurance of some of them before an examination. Her bitterness was mingled with the wonder that they could live so wild and know so much.

"Maybe they did just as badly as you," I ventured feebly.

"No." She was positive. "I didn't do nothing. All last night I read it, but I just see the words."

The towels had not helped. The cups of coffee at breakfast had not helped.

She pointed to the examination sheet. In one question I had asked for the author and the meaning of certain passages that I had stressed as keys to the understanding of American Romanticism. Two lines read:

> Things are in the saddle
> And ride mankind.

"I don't know who wrote it," she said. "I got some sort of idea about what it means, but I don't know how to write it down."

We talked; she talked as we came down the steps together. She did not want any favors. She had three children. She wanted to send them to good schools, someday, better than the one their mother taught. She had to pass. Her certificate was at stake. Read all she could, with a damp towel around her head, read all night long until gray daybreak, still all she could do was see the words. She had answered no questions. She wanted no favors. But she had to pass. Schools that she had attended had been low.

I promised to give her all possible consideration. "More than that, of course, you must understand, I cannot do," I said weakly.

Her gratitude was embarrassing. She walked away under the magnolias, ungainly in her house dress.

When I gave her a passing mark, I tried to discount my sentimentality and dishonesty by ridiculing the pretensions of my course. Transcendentalism for a teacher of graded schools in South Carolina, I jibed; set Walden Pond in the Congaree swamps; Snowbound in Charleston. But I knew that if the course had been based on the *Blue Back Speller* she would still, in all likelihood, have failed.

I talked about the case that afternoon to one of the campus authorities in Education with a capital E. He had worked at Columbia University toward his Ph.D. He was top-lofty about my arrant sentimentalism. "You are perpetuating the vicious circle," he said.

"Uh-huh," I said. Sure. He was right.

⇥ THE PALMER CASE ⇤

Before I got to know Lutrelle F. Palmer well, I had heard an anecdote that did him honor. It also held promise of what has happened to him since. When the white principals of Richmond's colored high schools were finally displaced by Negroes, Dr. Palmer was offered the principalship of the new Maggie Walker High School. Richmond wanted him badly, but offered him less than the principals of the white high schools were getting. Palmer naturally refused. The dickering continued; larger and larger salaries were offered. Finally Palmer stated his price, which was exactly that being paid white principals. The representative of the Richmond board spoke in aggrieved surprise: "But, Dr. Palmer, you know we can't pay you that. That's what we pay *white* principals." As the anecdote was told me at Slaughter's Café in Richmond, "The white folks offered Palmer all the way up to $3,000. 'Couldn't you take just $2,998.98, Mr. Palmer? We can't go a cent higher.' The white folks were nearly crying. Even called him *Mr.* Palmer. But Palmer wasn't coming on that deal. Not for one penny less."

Palmer admitted gravely, a bit stiffly, that the anecdote was to all intents and purposes true. I have known him for many years, having visited his model high school in Newport News, and having served with him on the staff of the Atlanta Summer School where he supervised educational workshops. About the campus he was always earnest, but in the classroom his reserve was shed and a zeal, almost that of a preacher, took its place. Years ago when I was a school kid, around Howard University I had heard him debate for Wilberforce against Howard; I remember him, even after thirty years, quiet but forceful and convincing, a man for Howard to watch. He had grown bald in the meanwhile, but the piercing, almost glaring eyes beneath the heavy rimmed glasses were the same as when he used to say "Honorable Judges, Ladies, and Gentlemen."

His home, on one of Newport News's wide streets in the better Negro section, was large and well-appointed. He introduced me to his wife, to his children, and a stream of young people—some of them soldiers—who came up on the porch as if they were completely at home. His reserve was gone as he chatted with them. And there was no reserve at all when he started talking about his case; he was full of it to overflowing. Since his being ousted from his high school principalship in Newport News, he had been appointed Professor of Education at Hampton Institute. But his heart was still in the school he had built up, and in the fight that he was waging for justice and redress.

Palmer had been in educational work in Newport News for twenty-three years. The year before he came, the agitation of the people had stirred the board to allow one teacher to do high school work for Negro children. The school was a four-room frame building, on a fifty-foot front on an unpaved road. When Palmer came, an old county school was set aside as a high school with two women teachers and Palmer as principal. Palmer had already taught seven years at Wilberforce University where the church and state politics had been too much for him, as for so many other able men. Disappointed in Negro colleges, Palmer took this little school in the Southland.

"During these twenty-three years," he said, "the people here have been all that I could ask for. From the three of us and ninety-two pupils, we have built up a school of over eight hundred pupils and thirty faculty members. Huntington High has received national recognition. In 1931, it was the first and only Negro high school to be accredited in the Southern Association of Schools and Colleges. It has been pointed to as one of the few schools in the United States that is serving as a real force for democracy in the community. Now it has a new building, its third home. In 1924, a modern structure was built, costing $150,000, a combination elementary and high school; in 1932, the high school occupied the entire building; in 1936, the present building was erected."

Huntington High School is a handsome brick building with fine laboratories, auditorium, classrooms, athletic field, and gymnasium. I knew many of its ambitious young teachers; had taught many of its graduates; and had heard its praises throughout the South. For his services in developing this high school, for his general qualities as citizen and interracial influence, Palmer had received many awards, crowned perhaps by his selection by the Richmond *Times-Dispatch* to its honor roll of eminent Virginians for the year 1938. Palmer is one of the few Negroes so to be honored.

And yet, after nearly a quarter of a century of praised services, and only a short time before retirement rights would set in (though he was far too useful and forward-looking to think of retiring), Palmer was ousted from his job without warning, without explanation, other than a vaguely muttered "for the good of the system."

He was no longer so surprised as once he had been. In the year since his dismissal he had been putting the pieces of the puzzle together; the pattern was taking form. "Saunders, the Superintendent of schools here, and I had been good friends," he said slowly, looking squarely at me. "As good friends as a white Southerner and a Negro could be in the South. He had wider contacts than most. He was on the Board of the National Education Association, was President of the State Board of Education. Under his leadership, if he had exerted his leadership, this controversy would never have arisen. But Saunders wanted to do what he called 'a magnificent thing for the South,' to show the Southern states that they did not have to obey the Supreme Court ruling.

"When we asked the city attorney if the ruling about the equalization of salaries applied—this was in the Norfolk case—we were told that according to the

Attorney General, the Supreme Court ruling applied. Salaries in Newport News would have to be equalized. Saunders thought of the idea of classifying teachers according to their ratings in a National Teachers Examination. This was originally intended for beginning teachers. Saunders spent thousands of dollars of the city's money to give these examinations to all the teachers, whites and blacks. The theory was that the whites would pass, and the Negroes fail.

"One old white lady threatened to resign, rather than take the examination. We Negroes insisted that we would take it, but that we wouldn't give it. The examination lasted for eleven hours over two days. To this day, the scores have not been released. Among Negroes, teacher after teacher has applied for his rating in this examination and can't get it. It would seem from all this that Negroes did as well as or better than whites.

"In 1940, our petition for equalizing salaries was in abeyance; there was no reply from the school board. Saunders then set up an 'equalized' salary scale, a master stroke in evasion, with a clause explaining a 'variable minimum and maximum.' The place of the teacher on this sliding scale was left to the discretion of the superintendent. This thing worked for about a year, then we decided that we were going before the board. We had meeting after meeting. These meetings resulted in some feeling, because as spokesman, I had to clash with Saunders and the board's spokesman, who was unfortunately a woman. Our teachers here were 100 percent behind our fight; they financed it right here, with not a single slacker. I was chairman of the salary equalization committee, and for eighteen years had been executive secretary of the Virginia State Teachers Association. I had spearheaded the salary equalization movement in the state.

"In 1940, the superintendent and the board showed that they were greatly displeased with what I was doing. Saunders wanted me to understand that he did not agree with the board, that he wanted to bring about changes. But by orderly means, he told me, by orderly means. The board felt that 'I was stirring up trouble unnecessarily; I was disturbing good racial relations not only in Newport News but in the State.' So Saunders wanted to exact a pledge that I would cease my activities in the equalization fight. I told him immediately that I would give no such pledge, that in the future my activities were likely to be greater, that I could not pledge to cease them or relax them. Saunders urged me not to take that stand, but to let things slide. I refused. They did elect me, however, in 1941 and 1942.

"Late in 1942 we filed suit. After two hearings we got a decision, in January 1943, a very clear-cut decision that the Newport News Board should pay equal salaries and abandon the variable scale. The court ordered a permanent injunction forbidding discrimination. After many meetings and much dissatisfied talking, the School Board adopted what they called the 'equalized scale' in the spring of 1943. The relationships between the Board, the Superintendent and myself were apparently very good. There was only one thing: our presence was no longer desired at their meetings.

"I paid no attention to that. If they don't want me as a principal, I thought, I'll go as a citizen. Every citizen has that right. But I might have known. In May, at the election of teachers, with no warning, no notice of any kind, three teachers, two elementary school principals, and myself were dropped. Why the others were fired, I don't know. The three Huntington High teachers: Miss E. E. Pannell, Eric Epps, and James Ivy, and the principals T. Roger Thompson and James Rupert Picott, were no more active in the fight than many others.

"I was on many boards with white people—the Newport News Chapter of the Red Cross, the Community Chest, the Tuberculosis Association, the Defense Recreational Committee, the War Housing Agency, the Child Care Committee, and the Peninsula County Boy Scouts of America. There was some stir; better not bother *him* is what some advised. So what they did was to seek out a Negro to find if anything was wrong in my record. Now there is a Negro in town inimical to me; he wanted places I never sought. He started a whispering campaign against me. Some of the whispers that got back to me were that my mother was a white woman, that I had clandestine relationships with white women. Friends caught a Negro circulating a paper saying that I made speeches advocating intermarriage. The man had twisted one of my talks; you know how easy that is. The club to which this fellow belonged met, and forty-four men tried him, repudiated him, and for a little would have manhandled him. It was a nasty mess.

"Then the word got to the shipyards, especially to Homer Ferguson, the president of the Peninsula Ship Company, and you know that company wields a power in this city, that I was a communist. This was because I had made a statement in Sunday School that I preferred the CIO to the PSA, a company union. So the whispering campaign went on.

"When my name didn't appear in the appointment, I thought it was an oversight. Until this day, the board has not notified us that we weren't elected. We went to the clerk of the board and asked why our names were not among the appointed teachers. 'Does that mean we're not elected?' It did. We asked why. The clerk said, 'I don't know.'

"'Weren't you there?'

"'No, I stepped out of the room.'

"'Didn't they tell you anything to tell us?'

"'Well, you weren't appointed for the good of the service.'

"The superintendent got sick at the meeting and left. He said his leaving had nothing to do with us, that he had recommended all six of us. The records show that he did, but the board didn't accept his recommendations.

"I got in touch with the NAACP. All of us did except one principal, who gave in. He knew what was going on all of the time. The woman who cooks for the Superintendent says this man had visited the Superintendent's home many nights. Though we are friends, I've never been to the Superintendent's home in my life.

"The Sunday afternoon after our dismissal there was a mass meeting of nearly two thousand people at Trinity Baptist Church. A citizen's committee was formed representing twenty-five different organizations. This committee raised money, carried the fight and the lawsuits, and is still carrying them. This was the beginning of many mass meetings. The students at Huntington High wanted to strike. I had to exert my utmost to keep them in school. I had heard that there were secret orders to throw fifty percent of the police force around the school. I didn't want the kids to get hurt, or the property damaged.

"At the second mass meeting the church was packed again. Representatives of the A.F. of L. Teachers' Union, preachers, and shipyard workers made speeches. More than a thousand dollars was raised at this meeting for a legal defense fund. In the meantime the committee asked the city council to intervene."

According to the clipping he showed me from his bulging scrapbook, the council washed its hands of the matter, certain that it had appointed "high type men" to the board, and that the council's duties were only to appoint the board and to appropriate school funds. The council went to more pressing business, writing an ordinance "that all meat, fowl, and fish sold in the city be sold by weight." The school board was also evasive, hiding behind the vague "for the good of the system."

Finally twenty-five heads of Negro families brought suits against the board for (1) exceeding authority and (2) acting corruptly. Both suits were lost in corporation court. The local law firm of Walker and Walker, father and son, one a patron of the school and the other a product, were joined by Andrew Ransom and a staff from the NAACP.

"The judge threw out my charge that in threatening me with dismissal, the board had acted corruptly. He argued that both sides seemed sincere, which I was willing to grant. He did not question my integrity but I had not established a case of their conspiring to fire me on the *basis of the salary fight*. He couldn't convince himself, he said, that fine people whom he had known all of his life could do such a dastardly thing.

"The board was quick to say that it was incorrect to tie up the dismissals with the recent suit for equalization of the pay for white and Negro teachers. 'If any such thought is entertained, it is incorrect. We have regarded that as a settled issue and it had nothing whatever to do with the Board's action.'"

But the five thousand people whose names appeared on the petition for a hearing for the dismissed teachers were not fooled by this runaround. Editorials in the white press voiced the suspicion that activity in the fight for parity pay was responsible for the dismissals. The *Norfolk Virginian-Pilot* cited the case of Aline E. Black, who was fired four years earlier by the Norfolk School Board, only to be rehired after court action, and a later "three-teacher head-chopping by the School Board of Norfolk County." "There is enough in the Newport News record . . . to warrant the suspicion that the six teachers . . . were purged for basically the same reason. . . . If it is the true explanation, the Newport News Board has committed an act shockingly contemptuous of the courts and even more shockingly contemptuous of the standards of educational decency." Later this same paper demanded that "the story of this piece of guillotining be brought into the open"—and that "school boards be taught . . . that they are executors of a public trust and not licensed executioners." Newport News papers demanded clarification. Their correspondence columns were filled with protesting letters. But the difficulty of the editorial writers in bucking some of the city fathers was illustrated by anecdote. One editor, who had written a strong protest, was talking to a Negro friend about the case. The Negro finally turned to leave, "Well, I guess I'll be going home to dinner."

"There's no dinner at home for me tonight," said the editor. "I'm in the doghouse with my wife. Just because of that editorial I wrote in this morning's paper."

Many white people of Newport News and the Peninsula did not forget their respect for Palmer, nor the honors that the state had heaped upon him and that shed some brightness on the Peninsula. Three white lawyers of the city offered to defend him; one of these, a former State Senator and Commonwealth Attorney was accepted to work on the legal staff with the NAACP lawyers.

Palmer continued his story: "In spite of the board's considering the salary issue as settled, in spite of the order of the court, the School Board resorted to a stratagem so that Negro teachers still are not paid equally with whites. The whites on a minimum salary receive an annual increment of ten years until they reach their maximum; Negroes receive an annual increment for fifteen years before they reach their maximum. So another suit was instigated, asking the court to hold the Board in contempt of court. But the original judge has died. And much has to be done again. Still it is possible for the new judge to hold all of the Board members in contempt, even to put them in jail."

Palmer was fairly confident about this fight, since it was in the capable hands of Andy Ransom and his staff. "The sad part," he said morosely, "is that they haven't been able to get a first class man for the principalship. The man whom they selected was an ex-teacher who was a Pullman porter when they offered him the job. They began him at $1,000 more than my maximum after twenty-three years. He is admittedly incompetent, a sort of negative personality. He frankly told the citizens' committee that his responsibility is not to the citizens but to the board and superintendent. The one thing that breaks my heart is that he has messed up so completely."

He spoke this without rancor, without self-satisfaction. I believe that, for all of the sharpness of the blow, Palmer is too big a man to crow, in petty spite. After all, he had spent twenty-three years in building up a school; to be happy at learning that a nonentity couldn't do his job would merely be childish revenge, and Palmer was thoughtful and ripened. "A youngster wrote me a document showing me how the school was going down. One of the things I was proudest of was the Honor System. If you have ever seen Hell's Half Acre [I had, and it was a hellhole], you will know what a job I had to get the kids of Hell's Half Acre to work with an Honor System. But it was set up, and it succeeded. Well, the first week the new principal sent out an order abolishing the Honor System. He didn't believe in it. The Student Council met to consider his action. They were ethical about it; they didn't even come to me. They wrote a very dignified statement saying that they could not abide by his order, that they had been taught to oppose dictatorship and were protesting his order. They voted that unless he could show why the honor system should be abolished he should rescind his order. Until that was done, the student council warned that the students would come to school (to abide by the law) but that they would sit in their home rooms and not go to classes. The poor fellow got scared," Palmer laughed gently, "rescinded the order, and promptly lost control. When the Senior Class dedicated the yearbook to me, he forbade it. So they didn't have a yearbook. When Picott, who was one of the principals dismissed along with me, was invited to speak by the student body, the new principal forbade that, and half the student body didn't participate in the exercises. The older teachers have left the school; only a half dozen or so remain. Incidentally, that is another way that Saunders has found to beat the law. He can get these young, inexperienced teachers at a minimum salary. At the other schools incompetent men have been placed in charge. Informers and stooges have gained a little from this affair. All of the new people have come in at excellent salaries. But the State Teachers' Association has passed a resolution, condemning them, and won't allow them to join the Association. The Parent-Teachers won't meet with them. They have no recognition in the community."

Palmer was called from the porch into his house for a telephone call. I thumbed through the last pages of his scrapbook. James Ivy, one of the ousted teachers, was quoted in the *Pittsburgh Courier*: "Only last year they tried to make Palmer sign a document in which the school board . . . had inserted clauses to the effect that he would hereafter make no mention of teachers' salaries and equalization of pay. Palmer refused to sign and the board at once threatened to fire him. But they had no grounds professionally for such a move. But you know how Southern Nazis work. First they get some Negro stooge to set up a hue and cry for the poor fellow's scalp and then you can conveniently knife him or take him for a ride. . . . We believe that a group of handkerchief-heads are behind the school board's action but we have nothing but rumor and circumstantial evidence, nothing documentary."

Well, the handkerchief-heads were decidedly in the minority at the high school commencement June 1943, at the Shipyard Community Center. Over one thousand people gave ovations to the graduating speakers, all of whom spoke on the theme "For This We Fight." The youngsters had a right to talk. Eight boys were immediately to exchange their gray caps and gowns for khaki and dungarees. Huntington High School students had bought seven jeeps in the "buy a jeep" war bond sales, more than those purchased by all of the white schools. So the youngsters talked eloquently about fighting "to protect the American job," the system of free enterprise, and our hard-earned liberties and freedom as a free people." They pledged themselves "to fight to destroy the enemies of democracy at home." In his valedictory, Palmer reviewed the twenty-three-year history of Huntington, and assured his hearers that his dismissal caused him no shame. The cheering crowd knew that.

Palmer came back to the porch. People walked by in the late afternoon sunlight: a gang of raggedy boys, a fat black woman, an earnest-faced graying old man. He spoke to them all as they waved to him. "Howdy, fellows," "Good evening," "Have you heard lately from Tom?" He had been talking to me a long time, and was slowing down. As I looked at him over the top of the scrapbooks, his expression seemed perplexed, tired. He was in the midst of a fight, and was going to make a game fight of it, I knew that. But I had the feeling that though the pieces in the pattern fit, he still could not quite believe that this had happened to him.

⤛ SIGNS OF IMPROVEMENT ⤜

With the hearty good cheer of a doctor at the bedside of a very sick patient, Virginius Dabney says, "Negro education has made tremendous strides below Mason and Dixon's line during the past several decades." I am skeptical of the word tremendous; it must have different meanings on different sides of the line. The best authorities that I could find agree that the patient has better than a fighting chance and that he is on the mend. But he is still a very sick man, and it will be long before he takes any tremendous strides.

I have been as anxious as any to see signs of improvement. I have read reports of the philanthropic foundations; it is difficult to imagine what the diagnosis of Negro education would be had it not been for their generosity. Scattered over the South are nearly six thousand Rosenwald schools, warrants to a skeptical people of what could be done. And now the Rosenwald Fund is concentrating on the realistic preparation of rural teachers. The General Education Board, the Phelps-Stokes Fund, the Slater Fund, and the Jeanes Foundation have poured millions of dollars into Southern education, especially for Negroes. This philanthropy has meant the setting up of state agents for Negro schools who have worked to raise the standards of teachers and high schools; the partial payment of Jeanes supervisors; surveys, summer workshops, publications, and scholarships.

Another sign of improvement is to be found in the increasing number of Southern white educators who are ashamed of the predicament of Negro schools and are determined to do something about it. Notable among these in the past were James Hardy Dillard of the Jeanes-Slater Fund, Jackson Davis, Fred McCuistion, and N. C. Newbold. And these have trained a number of younger men to carry on the good work.

One of the most heartening signs is that the better Negro teachers in the South have taken a firm foothold and gone to work with ingenuity and tenacity. Mrs. Elizabeth Perry Cannon of Atlanta University was one of the best of these. Before her untimely death, she was setting up model rural schools in communities near Atlanta. I visited two in Union City and Red Oak. Because of her vigor and congeniality, Mrs. Cannon was respected and loved by the people, who proudly did all they could for "teacher." As one trustee of the school said to her, "You know our school has had the best year it's ever had. I think everybody is done more for it than they is before. You see ef folks ain't ineres in your chillun, then you ain't gonna to be so ineres in them. . . . Teachers and preachers is funny. Some is ineres in de people and some ain't. Most preachers is adder house and eat. Dat preacher we had fo' dishers one sho' did like to eat. But dis year we is worked better'n we is befo' an' I think ef we try we kin raise enough money to hep ceil that school in the summer." Mrs. Cannon had the interest and knew how to get the communities to make efforts on their own. She stayed in their houses, praised their cooking and quilting, and never complained about the makeshift sleeping and the sanitary arrangements. But she quietly planted ideas about living and schooling, and these caught root quickly. She was a force that will be missed.

Her colleague at Atlantic University, Mrs. Helen Whiting, was the most optimistic of all the educators to whom I talked. A graduate of Howard and Columbia universities, she has had a long career, working with both city and rural schools. She has written textbooks that are aimed to correct the Negro child's lack of knowledge about Negro history. She has served for ten years as Special State Consultant for colored elementary schools. Her rosy view that the Georgia system of elementary schools is in advance of many surprised me. My face must have shown it, for she went on promptly to assure me that there was a democratic group of people in the state office, willing to allow people to "develop and to implement their ideas about life-related courses."

Atlanta University was quite a force for progress in teacher training, she told me, and I could agree with this. She was in charge of the Jeanes teachers of the state, most of whom had studied at Atlanta University. Jeanes teachers have to be invited by the county to serve; their salaries are paid three ways: a very small proportion comes from the Jeanes Fund, and the rest comes from the county and the state. "I just couldn't carry on without these lieutenants," she said. "Without the Jeanes teachers there would be no in-service program. For Jeanes teachers, we select people with some sort of background, both personal and educational. They really carry a weight of responsibility. Over one-third of Georgia's counties have them now."

While we were discussing "in-service" programs, I spoke of the good Rosenwald school I had seen at Union City. "That isn't a Rosenwald school," she interrupted. "Don't say Rosenwald every time you see a new school. The Rosenwald Fund is not alone responsible for the progress in Negro education. By its own admission, the Rosenwald Fund took a wrong start by merely erecting buildings. Before the schools can really develop, the community itself must be reached. The state is building new schools now, but more than that it is setting up community programs, including adult education. We teach our patrons about canning, child health, sanitary toilets, and wells. We are just social engineers," she beamed.

At Atlanta University, which Mrs. Whiting pointed to as the mecca of the educational reformers, I ran into other seriously concerned people. Benjamin F. Bullock was busy writing his book on life-related teaching in rural schools, hoping to check and reverse the flow of the most capable country youngsters to the cities. One factor worrying Bullock was that "thousands upon thousands of our rural teachers, supervisors, principals, and other rural leaders such as preachers and social workers have the city pattern of thinking and no training at all in the basic principles of food production and wholesome living on the farm." He hoped that his book would correct this.

I also talked with W. A. Robinson, principal of the Atlanta University Laboratory High School, a really outstanding school before entrenchment killed it. Robinson told me calmly of his long struggle to improve Negro high schools so that they could be accredited. Negroes were a sort of colonial people in the South, he told me, without political power and therefore really helpless. After white high schools are taken care of, there is simply not enough tax money left to give Negroes either the amount or quality of training for social efficiency. Many Negroes wanted their high schools accredited even at the cost of lower standards. Though these were outnumbered, Robinson is certain that there is still laxity in measuring high schools.

In spite of the struggle in which Robinson has had a leading role, the Negro high schools that are accredited by the Southern Association are few in number. Robinson's own state, Georgia, had little better than one Negro high school accredited out of the hundred of the total accredited high schools. He did not seem wearied or discouraged, though he was certain that only when federal funds are available will there be a decisive improvement in the schools: "The South cannot finance adequately the development of a dual system of high schools."

But Robinson was not marking time in the meanwhile. He is convinced that high schools should contribute more to their communities than preparing a handful of the smartest or luckiest for colleges. With funds from the General Education Fund, a Study of Secondary Schools for Negroes was set up at Atlanta University, and Robinson was selected as director. Sixteen schools (at least one from every Southern state) were selected for the experiments, of which two of the purposes were to discover the needs of the secondary school child, especially the Negro child, and to find out what is involved in democratic living. As a cooperative venture for school improvement, workshops were conducted, the first at Atlanta University, the second at Hampton Institute, and the third at North Carolina State College for Negroes.

At Atlanta University in a room crammed with leaflets, mimeographed materials, and charts, I talked with W. H. Brown, one of the associates in the study. Brown was ready, even eager to talk of the results of the workshop, but that day he was fairly rushed, and I needed time for full translating of the jargon that even the best of these educational specialists toss around. But from reading Brown's report, I gather that the workshop, through conferences, discussions, "visitations," audiovisual aids, and libraries, has stimulated growth on the part of the teachers, awareness of their social responsibilities, and more democratic administration. Children are being dealt with "as people." "I no longer make all choices for my pupils," one teacher wrote him, after putting into practice what she had learned at the workshop. More flexible programs were another result. The curriculum was improved, adapted, and enriched. Teachers became interested in voluntary professional reading. Community consciousness was developed, some teachers stressing the improvement of diet, health, and public behavior, others urging the registration of voters, others organizing community centers.

Robinson and his associates condemned the curriculum of Negro high schools for its meager training in health, vocation, leisure, home life, and citizenship, while securing only a limited verbal mastery of poorly understood textbooks. They believed that the job for Negro high schools in the South must be the improvement of the life of a people.

I heard this kind of talk, solemnly recited, in educational conferences. Sometimes the language stunned me as the pundits talked about it, and I "came out the same door wherein I went." Sometimes I labored over the vocabulary— "Integrations, correlations, fusions, cores, initiation, research, opportunities, whole personality rather than his intellect alone"—and thought I had the meanings until I would talk to a principal or a Jeanes teacher in a sandwich shop, and then I would be all confused again. What *they* had to tell me was something else entirely. The aims as I understood them were worthy, but the carrying them out seemed dubious. And there *was* a lot of fancy word-spinning.

Max Bond, one of the most dogged, levelheaded, and thoughtful schoolmen I met, told me an anecdote that returns too often when I think of these conferences. One of his young graduates, teaching in a very backward community, tried to high-pressure the people as soon as she got there. After repeated failures, she went to the chairman of the school board, a part-time preacher and sharecropper. He looked at her a long time and then said, "I believe you is the kind who expects to pour a thimbleful of water into the crick and make a flood."

Thinking about the kindly disposed white state agents, the Jeanes teachers, the surveys, the curriculum studies, the in-service teachers, the community programs, the model schools, I wondered if these were not thimblesful in the creek. The services these do are needed; the people performing them are humanitarian. But it is too late to patch the old framework. That has got to go.

It is not churlish, I hope, to point out that even the gifts of the philanthropists, lavish and wise as they have been, could not do the real job. As a matter of planning, the foundations did not consider it wise to attempt the job, even if it had been possible. One cannot call millions of dollars a thimbleful in a creek, but when it is realized, as Charles H. Thompson points out, that it would take two hundred million dollars more to raise Negro schools in the South to the present level of Southern white schools (which is still too low, in comparison to the entire nation), and fifty million dollars a year to keep them there, one might look on these millions donated by the foundations as priming the pump. Furthermore, now that the pump is producing some sort of a flow, the foundations are naturally withdrawing their aid.

Among all the authorities, white and Negro, the best hope lies in Federal aid to education. The politicians have kicked such bills around in stupid callousness. The bill now before Congress is inadequate, providing only three or four million dollars where conservative estimates place the minimum aid needed at around a billion dollars a year. Furthermore, the bill does not provide that present inequities in distributing state funds shall be removed, only that existing disparities shall not be increased. Only such a compromising bill seems likely of passage. Even this half-a-loaf, however, seems like manna to the starving.

Another good sign is that many white Southerners are awakening to the fact that "separate but equal" should mean what it says. It has never done so. In 1941, a Gallup Poll showed that half of the white people of the South believed that Negro children should receive equal public school advantages with white children. Much has happened in the three decades since Booker T. Washington turned off his quip that though the Negro is called inferior,

> In practice, however, the idea appears to be that he is a sort of superman. He is expected, with about one-fifth of what the whites receive for their education, to make as much progress as they are making.

And even when we read that the Kentucky Court of Appeals rules that "[Negro] pupils in an eight months' school may advance as rapidly and master the prescribed course to the same extent as those [whites] attending a nine months' school," we must recognize some kind of advancement, since now the Negro child has to be only one-eighth better, whereas once he had to be five times better.

Things are moving, not only for the Negro, but because of him. North Carolina has set up a plan to equalize salaries for teachers; Alabama has set up a less satisfactory plan. Senator Bilbo has orated that he wants good schools for Negroes, without alienating his constituency which is wedded to white supremacy. But "That Man" let the cat out of the bag when he gave his reasons for his change of face. He didn't want Negroes in *his* schools any more than he wanted them piddling in his pools. Another Mississippi fire-eater took his cue from the Supreme Court decision, handed down after much time and money were spent, that equal means equal: "The present manner of distributing the common school fund is a lie and a fraud on its face. . . . Further subterfuge or camouflage will be useless."

So the best sign of educational progress that I saw in the entire South was the aggressive campaign of the NAACP toward equalizing salaries and facilities.

The daring and sacrifice and strategy that I saw among my people did my heart good. The opposition is trying all the sifts and shunts and tricks of the trade, fighting a desperate fight from a narrowing corner. They still can make it unpleasant for a challenge, as my friend Lutrelle Palmer learned to his sorrow. But they can also be beaten, as he learned to his joy.

⇢ COLLEGES: RETREAT OR RECONNAISSANCE ⇠

THE SHADOW OF BOOKER

One of my favorite yarn-spinners in the South told me this one. He was travel-ing, as faculty director, with the Alabama State College orchestra, to play for a dance in southern Alabama. Their bus was making pretty good time on the dusty clay roads, and they passed an old jalopy filled with whites. Shouts followed them, but looking back all they could see was a cloud of orange dust. Then the jalopy roared by them, and about a hundred yards ahead turned sideways in a narrow cut and waited.

"We stopped the bus," my friend told me, "and wondered what was up. The crackers came back armed with sticks and stones. They ordered us out of the bus, and told us they were going to teach us not to give our dust to white folks. My boys were good men, all of them, but they knew what they were in for, and they didn't answer back a word. It looked pretty ugly for awhile. I noticed an old white man, just standing by, looking on. I appealed to him. He wouldn't deal with me directly, never opened his mouth. So I started talking with the loudest young cracker. He was spoiling for trouble, but so far was taking it out in talk. I told him that we had not meant any harm. He wasn't interested. I told him we were going to play at a dance for white folks and were just trying to make time as we had had to leave our school late.

"The old one looked up and said, 'Ar yawl Booker Washington's niggers?' I told him yes, that we were from Tuskegee. The old man said to the boys, 'All right, boys, you can let them go. These are Booker's niggers. Booker's a good nigger, so I been told.'

"One of the young crackers said, 'Yeah. I hearn tell of him.' The old one took over then, and said, 'When yawl git back there, you tell Booker to teach yawl some sense, 'fo he send you anywheres else. Gallivantin' over the country roads giving white people yo' dust. You be sure to tell him now.'

"I promised him that I would deliver his message. Booker had been dead for lo! these many years."

It is a sort of rough justice that Booker T. Washington, who used so many anecdotes to get over his points, should himself be the subject of many, from the time when, as my informant put it, "he swept the hell out of that Hampton class-room," all the way to his untimely end. Most of the anecdotes tell of his artful dodging, his tricks of appeasement, a sort of Br'er Rabbit cunning in a patch of wood where Br'er Bar and Br'er Fox might leap out at any moment. The figure that emerges from the legends is well summarized by Elbert Hubbard. The sage of Roycroft praised Washington as "a dictator who advances on chaos and transforms it into cosmos," "an instrument of Deity," who understood with the Southern whites, who "were forced to adopt heroic measures" to disfranchise the Negro, that "politically there was no hope for his race."

> He rides in the Jim Crow cars, and on long trips, if it is deemed expedient to use a sleeping-car, he hires the stateroom, so that he may not trespass or presume upon those who would be troubled by the presence of a colored man. . . . At hotels he receives and accepts, without protest or resentment, the occasional contumely of the inferior whites—whites too ignorant to appreciate that one of God's noblemen stands before them. For the whites of the South he has only words of kindness and respect; the worst he says about them is that they did not understand. . . . He is respected by the best people of North and South. He has the confidence of the men of affairs— he is a safe man.

Washington knew the value of protective coloration; he was something of a chameleon. Probably each of these—Armstrong of Hampton Institute, Governor Rufus Cobb of Alabama, Clark Howell of Atlanta, the president of the L&N Railroad, Andrew Carnegie, Julius Rosenwald, and Theodore Roosevelt—knew a different Booker T. Washington; and Negroes like Lewis Adams, the ex-slave commissioner of Tuskegee, T. Thomas Fortune, Emmett Scott, and Charles Anderson, customs inspector for the port of New York, each probably knew a different Booker. His many supporters deny that Washington was solely a creature of expediency and compromise. Charles Thompson, for instance, from his vast store of Washington's letters and papers, is anxious to correct such a characterization. I know how Washington courageously denounced such glaring evils as lack of educational opportunity and lynching. But an accurate psychography is not purposed here. The legend, as the white South stresses it, and as many Negroes accept it, is summed up in Hubbard's praise: "He was a safe man."

And of course, much of Washington's soft talk supports this view. One of his most recent worshippers, Anne Kendrick Walker, in *Tuskegee and the Black Belt* (*A Portrait of a Race*), paraphrases and quotes him abundantly: "Booker Washington believed that the Negro had a free field in the South, but that competition was abroad. He did not spend his time discussing the justice or injustice of the attitude of Southern white people toward the Negroes. . . . He did not eternally raise the question as to whether the Negro should be educated."

By no means, Miss Kendrick says. Instead she quotes these gems from Washington himself: "The best friend of the Negro is the Southern white man. A friend in Alabama is worth two in New York." "It is better for a man to work for nothing than not to work at all." "You white men must understand that you cannot lynch the Negro all the winter and work him all summer."

And she writes as a climax: "Holding his dusky hand high above his head, with the fingers stretched apart, he said to the white people of the South, in behalf of his race: 'In all things that are purely social, we can be as separate as the fingers, yet one as the hand in all things essential to mutual progress.' The white audience was on its feet in a delirium of applause."

In behalf of whose race? is a question that needs asking.

In spite of the delirium of the South, I believe that the Atlanta Compromise Speech does not give the full, true Washington, even of that day. Nevertheless, the fact remains that Washington bequeathed to Negro educators a strategy that may have profited them, but has not advanced Negro education.

Many practitioners of this strategy with less excuse than half a century ago, have really out-bookered Booker in the use of it. Much of what I learned of this maneuvering comes from anecdotage, sometimes apocryphal. Much comes from the direct action boys who put a bandana on the user of any tactic that is not theirs. A leading trade unionist among the transport workers of New Orleans snorted "handkerchief-head" at the name of every educator of the deep South whom I mentioned. Nevertheless, after a score of years teaching in colleges, I believe that the anecdotes present a true bill, though the factual details may be slightly off.

I give the following as I heard it; I am ready to grant that my informant strayed from the likeness a bit. "Before Pearl Harbor," he said, "they called a mass meeting in the Atlanta City Auditorium to honor Governor Talmadge. The speakers like to bust themselves wide open praising the great and good governor. When everybody thought the speechifying and shouting were over, a voice called out from the crow's nest where all the colored folks were sitting, 'Mr. Chairman, Mr. Chairman!' Finally this Negro was recognized. I was there, and I swear this is what that Negro said. Laugh all you want; he said it.

"'Mr. Chairman, I rise to praise a man who is not only the governor of the black people of this state, the wise governor of all the people of this state. I rise to speak for one hundred thousand Negroes of the great city of Atlanta.

"'I want Governor Talmadge to know that if them Japs sail in their great fleet from Tokyo to attack the state of Georgia, that one hundred thousand Negroes of Atlanta stand ready to defend it. I want the Governor to know that if them Japs sail through the Panama Canal on their way to attack the sovereign state of Georgia, that one hundred thousand black men of Georgia will arm themselves and hold themselves in readiness for the Governor's call. I want the Governor to know that if them Japs land their soldiers and sailors at Savannah and come marching up Number 80 to Macon, and from there on up here to Atlanta, one hundred thousand black men will be ready to fight and die if needs be to defend our fair city. And if them Japs march down Peachtree Street to the Governor's Mansion, I want Governor Talmadge to know that one hundred thousand black men will surround the grounds of the mansion, ready and willing to shed the last drop of the red blood in their veins to see that no harm shall come to Governor Talmadge—and, of course, to Mrs. Talmadge.'

"The white folks downstairs clapped their hands; the Negroes sat on theirs. Governor Talmadge leaned over to his secretary of state, 'Who *is* that nigger?' he asked. 'That's the first intelligent nigger I ever heard in my life. You send that nigger to me tomorrow morning.'

"So this Negro got a big job in the state library, though he hardly could read his name. Then he rose to be a high man in Georgia education. If you think this is a lie I've been telling, then you tell me how else he could have got where he is?"

Stories cluster about another henchman of Talmadge. One day he entered the anteroom of the Governor's offices, where a large number of whites were seated waiting their turns. He walked straight to the door of the sanctum, knocked, and was welcomed in. "I swear, I never thought that Gene would keep me waiting for a nigger," an old white man said. The Negro henchman stopped, turned and said, "Surely you gentlemen would not begrudge the governor the opportunity of seeing his servant?" The white farmer said, "Well, iffen you are his servant . . ." "That's exactly what I am," said the noted Negro educator, smiling. "I am His Excellency's humble servant." And he bowed, and entered His Excellency's chambers.

When Talmadge was trying to be reelected Governor by fighting against "co-education of the races," this educator was quoted in Talmadge's race-baiting *Statesman*, as disclaiming for Georgia Negroes any desire to enter the white colleges. "All we want," he said, "is a separate little university of our own." Then to sweeten even that impoliteness, he went on: "We came with the shackles of slavery about our wrists. Today we are clothed with the American ballot, which makes us citizens of the greatest republic on earth."

I heard this excerpt read with appropriate swear words from the listeners, in a barbershop in southwest Atlanta. One fellow spat and drawled, "All I can say is that if the Negro is clothed with the ballot, down here in Georgia he most certain sure is going around raggedyassed."

Al Moron, an authority on community welfare, was invited to speak at one of Georgia's state colleges. The president had sent the invitation himself, but because numerous white people were in the audience, he thought he had to take some of the wind out of Moron's sails. After Moron had talked about the tuberculosis program and slum clearance, the president made his countering speech. He said, "Now I have known a trained nurse for a long time, and she told me that when you had TB you just had it. The point I'm making is that there isn't any need in getting all stirred up about it. As far as slum clearance goes, the last time I went up to Atlanta I saw more pretty bad slums. It looks like they might do something about those slums up in Atlanta, before coming to tell us what to do about it down here." The white people, who had welcomed Moron before the meeting as a man of expert knowledge, changed after the president's speech. "Made me feel like an interloper," Al said. "Though I was invited by the school, I had to pay fifty cents for my room, and was told I would have to eat my meals off of the campus."

So the Negro presidents worry over what will get back to their white folks. They pay no mind to what gets back to their own people. They know that he who pays the fiddler calls the tune, and they keep up their repertory. One state college president, while delivering a fervent, long-winded eulogy of a member of the trustee board, was suddenly pulled back toward his seat. "All right, nigger," the trustee said, "now you sit down and let me talk." When the ambitious young president of Southern University was pleading for more funds, it is alleged that one of Louisiana's state legislators asked him, "What I want to know is, are those niggers up at Southern still singing?" On being told they were, he moved the legislature that they cut short the debate and pass the appropriation. Afterwards he said, "Now I'm coming up to the school before long, and I want those niggers of yours up there to sing me some of those good old songs."

When the trustees or legislators visit the state colleges, there is a great stir; the presidents not only out-booker Booker, but they outdo themselves. I once taught at a land grant college, and I remember how the campus hummed and how the domestic science teachers had to stay up all night getting ready for the next day's banquet for the curators. The favorite items of the fare were fried chicken, hot rolls, and the spirituals. At one state college, there was a prescribed ritual. Every member of the faculty had to perform some act of personal service for the trustees. The faculty women had to wear little lace caps and white aprons over dark dresses and wait on the trustees. One young woman, sick of the mess, refused to go along any further, and submitted her resignation. The president told her to take her time, after all he would reconsider; since she had been serving the trustees for a long time, this year all she would have to do was to write out the program, and she wouldn't have to wear an apron.

Certain of the tales told above are a sort of folklore, others were told me by actual participants. They will not surprise many Negroes who have taught in state colleges. And a large number of whites, close to Negro educators, will recognize the techniques that are used. They don't always consider what is done as flattery; sometimes they consider it merely what is fitting, what is deserved. *Five North Carolina Educators,* a book of eulogies, prepared under the direction of N. C. Newbold, finds its subjects to be most praiseworthy when they "relinquish interest in politics for much greater interest in education," when they emphasize "agricultural and mechanical arts," when they are polite and diplomatic and deferential "as he needs must be who forms a link between a State dominated by one race, and another race dwelling within it." In the character portrait of Peter Weddick Moore, who was for many years president of the Elizabeth City State Normal School, a white man who had been chairman of the school board, tells this story: "I purchased the railroad ticket and Pullman reservation for Dr. Moore. He studied [the ticket] for a moment and then handed it back to me. 'This is a Pullman ticket,' he said. 'I can't possibly use this.' I explained to him that it was his legal right. 'Understand that,' Dr. Moore replied, 'but I have made it a rule of my life never to permit myself to do anything that would be offensive to a white person. I shall be happier in the day coach.' I could not persuade him to use the sleeper."

This story is placed in climactic position in the book, as an illustration to young white and Negro students of how "Dr. Moore maintained his dignity under all circumstances."

So the shadow of Booker is lengthened and widened. Booker has definitely been out-bookered. Yet the story is not simply one of sycophancy and obsequiousness. And the manipulators vary. At one end are the abject farmers, at the other those who have to make compromises that offend their dignity, but who also have a bedrock beneath which they will not go.

There is another way, more creditable, in which these men continue Booker Washington's tradition. Like him, they have had to start from scratch to build up an educational institution, against the general ill-will of the whites and the lethargy of the Negroes. One Negro educator, unquestionably of the conciliatory sort, repeatedly told the story of how, in Reconstruction, he held a meeting in a church to lay before the community his plans to start a college in central Georgia. A tall, bearded white man sat alone on the front bench, with his double-barreled musket between his legs. He listened attentively to the educator's speech. Then, shifting his cud of tobacco, he said, "Well, puffessor, I came here to break up this meeting. I didn't hold with no truck about giving niggers extra schooling. But if that is the kind of school you're figuring on setting up, by Gawd if I ain't gonna give you some money to start it." And he handed him a greasy ten dollar bill.

No one knew better than Booker T. Washington, the tough odds against which the young teachers went out so gamely. Repeatedly he praised the faithful teacher "in some dark and neglected part of the state . . . in some wreck of a log cabin with slab seats and no backs . . . working for a salary barely sufficient to clothe and feed the body . . . bearing up under discouragements, accidents, and indifference of parents and school officials . . . completely shut out from intelligent association and from communication with the great busy progressive world." Such teachers taught terms of no more than four or five months, and were paid, as Washington said in one of his occasional barbs of wit: "about half the price received for the hire of a first class convict."

The books have been silent about their heroic story, but the communities they served have said to them, "Well done." Almost everywhere in the South, rural or urban, the gratitude of the people kept alive the names of the earlier teachers. These were some of the teachers held in beloved memory: in Roanoke, Miss Addison, prim and precise, a driver for all of her physical frailty; in Suffolk, Va., Edward Howe; in Atlanta, Principal C. L. Harper; both of them quiet-spoken, as they had to be to serve so long, but persistent workers, since inches make the foot, make the mile; in Cuthbert, Georgia, Professor Henderson, whose sons, Fletcher and Horace, went out to fame in the jazz world of America and Europe, while the old man stayed in the small town nourishing the little light. There were many others. On a motor trip from Manassas to Charlottesville, a prosperous dentist of northern Virginia talked of nothing but Jennie Deans, his schoolboy idol. He was later to write her life story in time squeezed from a busy practice; this day he was almost talking poetry.

Jennie Deans, as a domestic in Washington and Boston, had been made heartsick by the children in the slums. When she returned home to the northern neck of Virginia, she watched the bright boys and girls drawing. There was nothing to keep them in Prince William County, but she knew at bitter firsthand that there was less for them in the alleys of Washington where they were headed. The doctor remembered from his boyhood how the little woman drove her sulky, pulled by a bay mare, over the countryside, stirring interest in an industrial school for her people, collecting money, good will, and advice from local Negroes and whites (though some of the latter gave her only cold words). Money came from sources as various as Emily Howland, a leading suffragette who gave one thousand dollars in pride at a colored woman's grit; and local picnics and barbecues, where pound cakes, pies, and fried chicken were sold. Twelve years after Jennie Deans started her mission, the ground for the school was broken. Teams and laborers from Bull Run, Wellington, Sudley Springs, Sowego, and Manassas rotated in giving free labor. The doctor's grand-uncle, nearly eighty years old, worked along with the rest, tears running down his face, in thanks that he lived to see the day. In 1894, Howland Hall was dedicated before a crowd that had come by lumber wagon, oxcarts, buggies, and trains. Frederick Douglass was the orator.

Manassas Industrial School's early career was useful, but troubles came fast. The later years of the school I was familiar with, as I taught there my first summer out of college, and have kept in touch since. It was a story of bickerings, jealousies, occasionally inefficient management, lack of support among the local people, and waning funds from philanthropists. After twenty years, Oswald Garrison Villard resigned from his leadership of the board of trustees in disappointment that the Negroes themselves, many of them fairly well-to-do, supported the school so halfheartedly. In 1938, after near bankruptcy, the school was taken over by the state as a Regional High School. Several counties cooperate to provide bus transportation. The state has finally recognized its duty to the Negro schoolchildren of the area where Jennie Deans, driving her bay mare along the day roads, had dreamed her dreams.

The doctor was more interested in telling how, as a student in the school, he had worked for tuition as a carpenter on one of the new buildings, than in talking of his flourishing practice. He was curt about the sorry later years of the school. After all, he reasoned, the Regional High School might not have been there but for Jennie Deans. He cherished the memory of the little piercing-eyed lady, with her prim carriage and her pince-nez glasses on the tip of her nose, the long black string attached to her alpaca dress. She was homely, he told me, not what most people would call magnetic; but she carried herself as straight as a ramrod; she never cringed and always held her chin up.

Parallels to the story of the Manassas Industrial School are numerous. Not far away at Fredericksburg, Virginia, for instance, the Mayfield School was set up by Negroes, since the state would not provide their children a high school. Many of these people could not write their names, but they banded together, pooled their funds, and bought a farm with a large house which they used as a school building. As the enrollment increased they constructed a new building, then expanded it, and raised funds for the teaching and equipment. Several whites, even the school superintendent, chipped in some money, probably in a feeling compounded of respect and shame. A few years ago the state erected the Walker-Grant School which includes both elementary and high schools. The Mayfield School closed its doors. Throughout the South, such schools—in lodges, churches, and old mansions now on the wrong side of the tracks—have performed a dual purpose of educating both Negro schoolchildren and white school officials in the responsibilities of democracy.

Jennie Deans's story is typical of many Negro women educators—Lucy Laney, Charlotte Hawkins Brown, Mary McLeod Bethune—who, impatient at the slow-moving state departments of education, have started schools on a shoestring, a will, and a prayer. The falling off of donations is also a much repeated tale. Some of these private and denominational schools were taken over by the state, some by the foundations; those past saving died. Their ghosts stand everywhere over the South now, with windows smashed in the sedate red brick buildings, with banisters and steps stolen for kindling wood, campuses overgrown with thickets, ivy and weeds, and rats scampering in the deserted halls. Students trained in the old-fashioned schoolrooms remember them with deep affection, and feel a pang at the heart when they see the desecrated ghosts. They are pitiful now, but once they had their day of pride when the dreamers saw the cornerstone laid and the young children sang "America."

In contrast to these shades, the observer is likely to see the new, brick Negro high school with a good gymnasium and auditorium, and the new white frame county schools set back in school yards with strips of sod finally catching root, and shrubbery concealing the newness of the clearing. Centralization is paying. Negro youngsters now ride in school buses, their shrill cries louder than the engine's rumble. There are lucky chances, here and there. Kids only a few miles from their wretched cabins in the cotton and tobacco patches now gaze with awe at the gleaming white porcelain in the toilets, working at will the flushing contraption to make the water roar down, "passing out" too frequently in order to stare again at the marvelous plumbing. Or, in the new gym they almost grow sick with joy as the lanky forward, sneaking down the sidelines, makes his overhand shot and the ball drops swish into the basket: "Didn't hit nothin' but the strings!" Here a boy wears his lip out blasting on a battered golden trumpet; a kid little taller than the bass fiddle grabs its waist and saws away. Boys and girls act in plays before real footlights; this boy is a real clown, causing gales of laughter; this girl flaunting over the stage tries to prove that Lena Horne ain't got nothing she ain't got, and this one emotes heavily, a straight line from Hollywood. The cafeteria is noisy but the food comes piping hot out of gleaming containers, so unlike the heavy greens, fat meat, and bluish potatoes of home as to belong to another world. "Boy you done had six sandiges!" "These dibdabs ain't nothin'! I needs food what sticks to my ribs." "You don't need nothin' but vitamins." "Man got to have proteins, carbohydrates." "I wonder if coach would mind if I et another piece of that cherry pie." "The word is ate." "That's what I said. Et. You think you so smart."

And then there is the grand night of graduation when the buses bring extra loads of kinfolks and friends from the far-off hamlets and homes; and the preachers pray long invocations, benedictions, and in-betweens, and each of the young girls in white with a dark sash around her middle, a symbol, according to the orator, that life is due to commence, and the old people are tearful and the young ones flutter about, happy but scared.

There are other heartwarming signs. More and more the teachers are working to develop themselves, some because of the insistence of the state that they must study to renew or improve their certificate; and some because they are devoted to their youngsters and want, as they recite almost too seriously, to make the curriculum more meaningful. Constantly in the Negro press there is news of fellow teachers winning suits for equalization salaries—now Texas, now Louisiana; in all states except Mississippi, teachers have been found daring enough to buck the state officials. Mississippi is the only state where no mouse has been found willing to bell the cat.

And even Mississippi begins to see the light. Occasionally even there, good school buildings are to be found, in a few cities and where the counties have consolidated. Five years ago, the Colonel Frederick Sullins, a fire-eating editor of Jackson, called for a real crusade against the public disgrace of Negro schools in Mississippi, "hundreds of them hardly better than cattle sheds":

> We took millions of WPA money in recent years and spent practically all of it on new buildings for white schools and only a few paltry thousands here and there on Negro schools.

The crusade the Colonel called for has not yet arrived in Mississippi. But something has definitely happened there. Senator Bilbo, even while filibustering against FEPC, can orate that he wants good schools for Nigras in a calm tone, without any fear of reprisal from his white supremacy constituents. And in Louisiana, which is not so much farther up the scale, the State Survey of Education came out plainspokenly for improvement in salaries, buildings, equipment, outside resources, for increase in length of school term and number of teachers. Agitation for Federal Aid to Education is growing in strength all over the South.

So the pride of the parent-teacher associations, and the elated flush of the teachers who are winning the first rounds in their fights for justice are understandable. And yet the occasional new schools and community programs, which make the local whites say, "See what we're doing for our nigras," and the older Negroes say, "We never had such advantages when we came along," should not be cause for smugness. The random signs of progress are relative to the past, not the present.

A decade ago, Horace Mann Bond pointed out the unsavory but unanswerable conclusion:

> Not until a magnificent rural school greets the white child when he steps from his bus; not until supplies and equipment for the white school reach a level fairly comparable with existing situations in other counties and states, can the Negro child expect to receive any consideration. . . . So long as the salary of the Negro teacher must compete with the demands for a better system of transportation for white children, so long as new buildings for Negro children must be weighed in the budget along with demands for new laboratories and gymnasiums for white children, so long may we look forward to a continuation of the present inequalities.

Bond was not so sure that the progress was relative even to the past: "Left to their own devices, the *more* money the Southern states have to spend for public schools, the *less* proportionately, do they spend on Negro schools. . . . *Per pupil enrolled,* the disparity between expenditures in these 12 Southern states was (1) in 1900, 48 percent and (2) in 1930, 252 percent."

In the intervening decade, Charles H. Thompson has discovered signs of progress: the Southern states found it more and more difficult to get away legally with as much disparity as they once had done; the NAACP won several suits to equalize salaries; one or two states in the upper South began to equalize educational opportunities. Because of the Depression in the thirties, all educational expenditures were decreased, and where less money is available, it generally follows that there is less disparity, there being a sort of rock bottom beneath which expenditures cannot go. Even so, in 1940 the disparity was still 211 percent per pupil enrolled. At this rate Thompson concludes, wryly, it will take fifty-four years to achieve substantial equality, even on the common school level, to say nothing about the higher and professional educational levels where the disparity is even greater.

When I asked my mother to freshen her memories about her teaching at Sequatchie Valley over half a century ago, she wanted to know why I was going to write of that. "That is all past and gone," she said. "This is a new day." But I was thinking of the statistics that Thompson had talked to me about. And Martin Jenkins's shocking figures that Campbell Johnson had told me the Army found. And in my mind's eye I still had the picture of a late fall day only two years ago when I visited an upcountry Louisiana school. It was penmanship time for the younger children. Since they had no desks, they were kneeling in front of their benches, with their copy books spread open on the seats. They were painstakingly forming letters. But they seemed to me to be in an attitude of silent prayer, calling on the Great God Education. I wondered if he still was deaf to them as he had been to their grandparents. He was certainly still far away.

Pursuit of Happiness

Music and musicians as well as graphic arts and artists constitute the subject matter of "Pursuit of Happiness," a section devoted to African American cultural expression and the possibilities of joy in the segregated South. An aficionado of all forms of black music, Brown commits most of this section to jazz, blues, and religious music, returning, in a sense, to an earlier love of music and its ability to express both the possibilities and sobering limitations of black life. Indeed, Brown's first published essay ("Roland Hayes," *Opportunity*, June 1925) was an award-winning sketch of the world-renowned tenor, here the subject of the opening piece, "And He Never Said a Mumbalin' Word." At the height of his fame, Hayes had been the most famous stylist of black religious music on the American concert stage. Here, as the section opens, Brown finds Hayes in semi-retirement, and he delivers a poignant look at this public figure now in pursuit of personal reparations, both for himself and his local community near Rome, Georgia. Also exploring what Brown's close friend, Willis James, called the "back country," the second piece, "Song Hunter," retells many of James's experiences in the rural South collecting and recording black folk music, both religious and secular. As James stresses the importance of being close to the folk, the importance of listening and of accurate recording, he echoes Brown's own approach to folk culture, looking forward to later pieces in the section concerned with folk representation.

The middle set of pieces—"The Duke Comes to Atlanta," "Farewell to Basin Street," "Po' Wanderin' Pildom, Miserus Chile," and "Jitterbugs' Joy"—all take up jazz and blues as they describe the dance hall scene and the allure of big-band swing. Toward the end of the 1930s and through World War II, many big bands fell on hard times because of the Depression. Small ensembles were becoming more economically viable, and some were beginning to fashion a new, undanceable sound soon to be known as be-bop. But some of the big-name bands—Duke Ellington, Count Basie, and Earl "Father" Hines's groups,

251

to name a few—were able to stay afloat. Although they were subject to grueling travel schedules and unpredictable accommodations on the road, particularly in the South, these bands toured extensively and delivered upbeat dance music to a black youth culture that came of age during World War II. Brown knew many of the band members personally: Ellington, Hines, Billy Eckstine, Johnny Hodges, Dizzy Gillespie, and Miles Davis, among others. And he caught their shows in New York City and across the South, particularly in the larger cities. He observed the "cutting contests" between bands, the showmanship of the "professors" out front, and the irrepressible exuberance of black youth dancing the latest dances and donning the latest fashions.

But for Brown, the pursuit of happiness is ever incomplete as he reads the conflicted mark of race on the music and in the crowds, tempering, if not limiting, the vitality of both. As an integrated crowd pushes to catch a glimpse of Louis Armstrong backstage, Brown and his friend Cliff McKay comment on "how jazz tore down the walls. Some walls anyway." And from a balcony above the youthful crowd jitterbugging to Earl Hines's band, Brown sees this frenzied dance as an act of defiance, temporary resistance to the omnipresent cruelty of the Depression's poverty.

The section ends not with a final look at jazz, but with a gesture toward the fine arts, as "From Montmartre to Beaver Slide" reiterates a similar ambivalence over the interpretation of black life. Visiting the celebrated painter Hale Woodruff, Brown reflects on his approach to representing black Southern life. In Woodruff's choice of subject matter—the Amistad revolt or the history of Talladega College—his masterful use of colors lends a "richness and luminosity" to black faces. All serve "an important artist treating poor and ordinary Negroes with dignity and warmth," again an echo of Brown's own approach in his poetry and indeed in this collection. Thus Brown finally celebrates Woodruff as a kindred spirit dedicated to black art and life and ends a section both asserting and questioning black music and graphic art in their ability ultimately to represent African Americans in the full possession of happiness.

⤳ AND HE NEVER SAID A MUMBALIN' WORD ⤴

I

Though he preferred talking of other things, Roland Hayes was a long way from forgetting Rome. His mobile face was expressive of anger and disgust when he referred to the apologetic note in the white press that the clerk did not know who he was, as if that could serve for apology. "I know that they knew who I was," he said. "It wasn't just a little rumpus." He saw design in it. And the hush-hush campaign was bad too: "They try to put blinders on us so that we cannot see. With troubles like this all around, they tell us to keep our eyes straight ahead."

Roland Hayes is not a propagandist, and he did not want this injustice to be made into a cause célèbre, nor into mere publicity of another outrage. He wanted something definitely done, something that would stick. Just as the trouble had affected the entire group, so he felt the punishments should be far-reaching. But he wasn't talking much along that score. The affair was in the hands of his legal counsel and the NAACP. According to Cliff McKay, he promised the full details of the story in his forthcoming autobiography, but the book appeared with only this reference: "Once, not so long ago, I was beaten and thrown into jail."

Roland Hayes continues in his autobiography: "But I see no good in reciting the details of a thousand such misadventures." And he tells of a white minister who wanted "to take up with somebody" a case in Duluth of discrimination. "There is nothing you can do," Hayes said. "That is a job for me and my own people."

In that sentence probably lies the key to what perplexed several persons in Roland Hayes's comments after the case. He confronted his ordeal with what seemed to be an oriental fatalism, probably derived from Africa, which, I learned later, informed so much of his personal philosophy. Was it a Gandhi policy of passive resistance, I wondered? I was not then and am not now sure. He had stacks of letters of condolence and protest; several of them, especially from Southern white sympathizers, who praised his lack of bitterness. And the white press focused their stories more on his statement, "As for me I am not bitter toward anyone, for the humiliation is on the other side. I am only ashamed that this should happen in my native state."

There is no doubt that Roland Hayes took high ground in the case. I think it important that it be kept in mind that it was not the wanton assault of a shoe clerk and four police thugs on a world renowned artist that grieved him so deeply: it was rather that the beating was symbolic to him of the weakness of his own people and the cruel power of prejudiced whites. It was not, by any means, simply forgiving and forgetting.

And I was not certain that bitterness and humiliation did not rankle as sorely as his bruised back as he sat there talking quietly. Early words, when he was introducing his sprightly little daughter, Africa. "She's a little general," he said. "When they had me around the neck, she was right there, holding me up with her arms." He was obviously worried over what might be to her a hurt of long-recurrent pain.

He was interested in the strategies of minority groups, in all kinds of resistance and defense. "Some," he had found, "had learned to fight in such a way that nobody can tell when they've struck a blow. But the blow takes effect."

He told an oriental folktale of a man contentedly sitting under a fig tree. A more powerful man with a taste for figs came along. He made the first man pick the figs for him to eat. Then he decided that he wouldn't let the first man even sit there under the stripped tree. He explained the Southern whites' hatred of the Negro not only as a hatred of that which has been wronged: "That's not all. The Southerner says, 'I feel about a Negro like I feel about a horse I owned, and that was taken away from me without compensation. Those damn Northerners sold us the slaves and then took them away without paying us anything for them.'" He told anecdotes of a Southern white woman who applauded his concert career because she heard he was "doing this on his own, with no Yankee support," and another who refused to sign up through Northern bookers. He knew the "inside workings" of race prejudice throughout the world. Europeans, Americans, the same thing in different ways: "We are no nearer to the center of what we want to arrive at in England or France, than in America. All agree on one thing. They are never for you to the degree of allowing you to get power, the real power to get what you want, to accomplish all you can."

Inasmuch as his tragedy had clarified one thing: that, regardless of the fame a Negro might receive, he was still subject to the abuse that the entire race knew so thoroughly, he felt it would serve a good purpose.

He led the conversation away from these matters: "Let time give air to my fight." But a phrase or a sentence, dropped by the way, were reminders of what he had just gone through, and of the insight into the tragedies of race.

He told us why he had returned to Curryville. In 1926, he gave his first concert in Atlanta before a mixed audience of seven thousand. Ralph McGill, praising the performance, called Hayes one of the three great personages who had emerged from Gordon County; the others were Georgia's first governor and a Cherokee Indian chief. Roland Hayes visited his native county the next day. The District Attorney, a friend of his boyhood, accompanied him, giving the world traveler the belated news of the isolated, little known county. "He told me," Roland Hayes said, "that he had found the man who owned my mother." He was talking calmly, as he said this; he did not stress any of the words; but I do not think that

I shall ever forget the dramatic effect of the words and the expression on his face as he said "who owned my mother." It was an experience like hearing him sing the most profound spirituals.

He visited the aged slaveowner, beaten now and destitute, living in a miserable shack. He told him his intention of buying the old place, and promised to fix up a home for him and his wife. Both died, however, before that ironic circumstance could occur. The place had gone to ruin; the land was wasted and many of the buildings had sunk to the ground; nobody wanted the task of rebuilding. Roland Hayes's planning and energies and money were thrown into the rescue job. The house was renovated into the comfortable, substantial, charming home that now it is. Hayes not only restored it, but he added to it what it never had before. He is especially proud of the clapboards and hardwood floors that he put in himself with his own carpentry. The white people who had owned it in that half-a-century since Hayes knew it as a child, expressed no resentment to him for his plans. He heard that they said privately, "I don't know," but they told him, "We are glad it was rescued." The daughter wept, sitting in the yard, watching the new owners taking over. But her father comforted, "Roland is doing more for that place than I could ever do."

Roland Hayes told me how, as a little fellow, he had often delivered the washing to the back porch of this fine house (which, though not the traditional manor, was truly the big house of the community). While he stood there waiting for the money or the week's washing, the owner used to amuse himself by cracking his long whip about Roland's ankles, or by "siccing" his pack of hounds on him.

So more than an ambition for gentlemanly farming or for a retreat to the mountains after his intensive artistic life bound Roland Hayes to these acres. He has seen the farm go from nothing—when he first rented the farm out to whites "they just plundered everything"—to "a right smart possibility." I had heard in Atlanta that Hayes was just piddling at farming, but I soon discovered that the statement was unjust. He talked learnedly of his Poland China hogs, of the virtues of some of the crossings of his stock, which he had introduced in these parts. An exotic addition to Georgia farming suddenly rumbled on the scene in answer to Hayes's long melodious cry. It was a flock of Karakul sheep, long-haired and rusty brown, descended from a wealthy friend's gifts to Roland's daughter. He explained their value; when raised for commercial purposes, the lambs are killed when twelve hours old, since then the pelts are perfect in luster and curl. Past the danger mark now, these Persian sheep gamboled over these grassy hills. I did not find these Asiatics incongruous; they seemed quite consistent with Roland Hayes's own strange transplanting.

It was not transplanting, according to Roland Hayes's views; it was rather homecoming. And yet, as he remembered sadly, he and his family are strangers to many of the community, in spite of blood ties: "Many of the Negroes never come up unless they want something particular. Their attitude to us is the same as to white people. I'm one of them, but they feel their position from the economic standpoint, and some from pure envy." Both whites and blacks attend the barbecues he gives, out of curiosity, or hunger for good food and entertainment but not out of friendliness. One old codger stated that he did not want to associate with Roland Hayes, since he was getting an old age pension from the white folks. Roland Hayes was confident that he was allowed at Angelmo' on sufferance, only because the whites believe he is wealthy. The town of Calhoun, being closer and more benefited by his spendings than Rome, is more tolerant of him. Some rednecks between Curryville and Calhoun might hate him, but "you couldn't get a corporal's guard together to cause real trouble." As a matter of fact many Calhounites, especially the District Attorney, wanted something done against the people of Rome because of the beating there.

Nevertheless, even Calhoun loves his money more than his presence. One evening while giving a concert in Rome, his new 16' by 16' barn burned down; none of his fine mules were saved from the flames. Whispers came back to him of what was being said about his return to Georgia: "White folks tells us not to get too excited over what that Hayes is doin'. They is still hickory trees and hempen ropes, they says." Unable to get all the workers the place needs, Roland Hayes brought in outsiders. Before long, these outsiders told Hayes that they were leaving. They hemmed and hawed; only by accident it leaked out why they wanted to go: "You're an outsider, no business here," they had been told firmly by the powers. "Negroes and whites will fight like the devil among themselves, but they unite in wanting no outsider to come in here." A young white Canadian music student stuck it out even after shots broke the windows in his house; but eventually he too had to go. Roland Hayes gave the summary I expected: "The whites don't want the status changed; if there were more enlightened, useful Negroes, then they'd be dissatisfied. Anything bearing the slightest on that is attacked." And his bitter commentary on his Negro neighbors is that they have been cowed so long that "you just can't get the Negro here to do what he feels in his heart."

There were instances, however, when he had been welcomed. One was due to his fame. After setting up his sawmill he had approached a lumber dealer, who told him briefly that he was not in the market. (He meant, of course, for lumber cut by a Negro's sawmill. He *was* buying from everybody else who had a stick to sell.) "A buyer standing by asked who I was. 'Not Roland Hayes, the singer!' The buyer rushed over to him, saying, 'Lord, if my wife knew you were down here she'd come down right now.' " And the buyer contracted to buy all the lumber of certain dimensions that he could supply. Roland Hayes, singer of Schubert's *Lieder*, started spouting figures and terms of lumbering: 300,000 feet of pine, cross-ties, paving blocks 3 by 6, 3 by 8, sweet gum, maple, on and on he intoned.

He had hoped that the sawmill would aid in making his community self-sufficient. It had been welcomed. But from an anecdote he told, I could see that even its community service would not keep it from being another sore point. He firmly insisted on running the sawmill as a business, not as a benefaction. When a white man attempted to rent it for only a nominal sum, since the farmers in those parts were poor, Hayes stated firmly his terms, the prevailing sawmill terms. Wheedling did not budge him. Finally, when the disgruntled bargainer yielded, Roland Hayes insisted that there be inserted in the contract a clause guaranteeing payment for any harm that might come to the machinery. The bargainer signed up; but obviously this was not the way that business was done between Negroes and whites in Gordon County, Georgia.

Roland Hayes boasts that he can do anything in lumbering from stump to stack. He supplied lumber for war work in Chattanooga. He had hired both Negroes and whites, but he was quite concerned over the difficulty of obtaining labor. When he explained the high qualifications of one of the best Negro hands to the County Draft Board, he was sardonically told: "Well, well. If he can do all that, he ought to be able to shoot a gun."

II

At the Flemisters, the nearest tenants, we found the housewife flurried at meeting strangers, but Flemister, a tall brown, shrewd-faced, keen-eyed man, seemed entirely at ease. On one of the cane-bottomed chairs was a paper-bound copy of *Gospel Hymns*. Looking at the thin drizzle, he wanted to know "What is it crying about today?" and spoke of the long spell of rain. Horn Mountain, in front of us, was wreathed with low-hanging clouds; on the green flats stretching toward the far Oostanaula River, we saw a vague shower, but it did not climb the hill. Nova, the Hayeses' house dog, was frenziedly digging for something around the edge of the cotton field.

"It's good that Nova is a ratter," Hayes said. "There are a lot of rats around here. And there's a big black mole always in my watermelon patch down beneath the hill. I'm going to catch him one of these nights." He looked sardonically at Flemister.

The farmer slapped his leg and snorted, "How do you know that he's big and black?"

"You know well how I know. He sure loves watermelon. Last night he turned the biggest one over and knocked it open and ate his fill."

They laughed together, loud and long. I was surprised at the full-throated laughter of Roland Hayes. I never expected to hear a lyric tenor with such a basso profundo laugh.

But Flemister wanted his inning. "Have you fed these people?" he asked.

"Of course," Hayes answered.

"What did you give them?"

"Fried chicken and watermelon."

"Uh-uh. I'd better count my chickens," Flemister said seriously. Turning to me, "You see those two trees up there? I draw a line between them and tell my chickens, 'Chickens, any of y'all cross that line into Mr. Hayes's yard, you headed for death in the pot.'"

They cackled at the stock joke, this old codger who could barely make out to read words and letter his name, and this cultivated favorite of the great cities of America and Europe. Their bond was deep-lunged laughter.

Hayes spoke persuasively as if to swing our sympathies to him: "Don't you believe him. He's got three chickens that are always in our yard. Every time we cut a melon I believe those three chickens can smell a watermelon from here to Calhoun."

This was a new side of Roland Hayes that I saw, and it was good to hear his healthy laughter.

Flemister was the one who gave Roland Hayes sound advice about picnic grounds for a barbecue. Hayes had planned a real project, to make a "picture place," to use a tractor and scrape the roads. Flemister said, "Now, Mr. Hayes, that's all right. But don't make it too fine now. What makes us able to enjoy ourselves is here," he said, thumping the left side of his chest. "Inside us, you know, Mr. Hayes, we could enjoy ourselves on a rockpile."

Walking back to the house, Roland Hayes told me of his first plans for Angelmo', before the Depression struck. He had wanted to found a school for Negro children. He wanted to let the child know what was in himself: to teach "self-possession" and "self-reliance." The children were to be taught what they *are,* not what is *said* they are; and what they could *become.* We have accepted too long the evaluation of others. "We are all on crutches," he said. "We can't get anywhere without being helped. We are more crippled than our fathers." He doubted the validity of the present schools. "If you don't teach as they want, you don't get, or you don't keep the job. We can't do anything without asking the other fellow, 'What do you think of this!' 'Fine,' he says. But he'll do something to keep you from reaching your objective, if it's worth anything." He spoke of his mother's self-reliant grit, quoting her, "Son, if you have something to do, do it. Let the other fellow talk." He wanted to come to Georgia and set up this school with his own means; to let the founding be directly to the credit of colored people.

He felt that that would have dramatized the purpose: "If I let white philanthropists get in here, the name might have flowered, like that of Tuskegee. But it would not have been *ours.*"

He felt deeply that in spite of current undervaluation, the world wanted what the Negro had to offer, "if you make it good enough. All the Negro needs to do is to brush his wares." Many do not know the value of the wares; those who do are satisfied knowing that they have them, and do nothing about them. He mentioned that he talked over his educational theories with certain educators in Washington; he left the impression that they had given him little encouragement.

The Depression had killed his plan for the school, but he had still hoped that Angelmo' might succeed not only in giving a better living to a few impoverished families, but also as a model farm. Now he was no longer sure.

"What interests me," he said, "is why I can't leave here. It's as if I were chained. I've tried to go away. I can't go away. It must be that there's some particular duty I must perform. I've been through a great deal here. Death couldn't be as bad as some of the things."

Lounging on the back porch in the comfortable deck chairs, Cliff Mackay and I listened to Roland Hayes talk of his music. He told how he felt that the artist's vitality is bound up with his earlier experiences; how he is enriched, not so much by what he has heard or read about, but by what he has experienced. He pointed to the wide-spreading red oak a few yards away. Early formative years were the trunk; then the branches go out in all directions. Here at Curryville, Angelmo' had been his trunk; his far wanderings since had been the branches. Thus in his singing he believes that it is not so much the song, but what goes out from him *on* the song. The critics' praise for his beautiful German, he laughed off easily: "Oh, yes, so much gymnastics, so much learning." The important thing, he believed, is what the artist adds to it. He was grateful to the critic who wrote that his singing of "Waldeinsamkeit" completely rendered the true feeling, but that it was not Viennese; it was something added, a new vista. That something new, he felt, was the artist's unfoldment. He returned to the trunk of the tree to explain it. And he told, wistfully, but proudly of his mother's saying to him, "Son, you are the continuation of me."

He recalled his mother's antagonism to his career in its early stages, because the only Negro singers she knew about who sang on the stage were vaudeville minstrels. He said to her, "I don't want to be a tinkling cymbal; I want to be a great artist." He told us of his hardships, from back-breaking, perilous foundry work in Chattanooga, through the lean years at Fisk and in Boston. He was warm in praise of the support his own people in their churches gave him in the years of struggle.

Without letting his wife know, he smuggled me into the bedroom, where there was a small phonograph on a table near the valuable rosewood bed. He wanted me to listen to a few recent recordings for a new album of *Lieder* and spirituals. He was dissatisfied with the mechanical production; his acute ear picked up the flaws my dull one missed. It was certainly a rich and rare music for these hills; for a time while listening I felt that he was far from the perplexities of Georgia, in that other world where he walked so much more securely. Idly I noticed the books on the rack; his first Columbia album, a biography of Beethoven, and the *United States Department of Agriculture, Farmer's Bulletin No. 1632,* on Karakul sheep.

He was recording a few little-known spirituals in their Gordon County forms and was arranging others. The spirituals were slowly being supplanted among the rural folk by the commercialized gospel hymns of which I had seen a collection on Brother Flemister's porch. He regretted the lapse of folk musical taste toward the swingy and tinkling. Seldom would his neighbors join in with him in singing the old songs in the old way. Stemming from that same sturdy trunk that had nourished his genius, they were now shooting in a different direction.

Roland Hayes apologized for his long talking, but he knew that we were grateful to him. We left Angelmo' just before sunset; we had a good trip ahead of us that evening. He gave us directions to shorten the mileage to the highway, then he and his family spoke and waved us good-bye. As our car turned around one of the bends in the road through his front field, we saw that he was still standing there, waving under the red oak tree with the livid lightning scar. I had been struck by his sturdiness during the visit; now he seemed small and frail. Oddly, the thought came to me, "He's nearly sixty years old." And I knew that for a long time to come I should not want to hear him sing again:

> *Dey whupped him up the hill,*
> *And he never said a mumbalin' word.*

✈ SONG HUNTER ✦

I

The morning after the songfest, Willis James and I sat out on the lawn of President Bond's home, under a large, shady water oak. Barely a current of air was stirring; it was quiet and drowsy. A farm truck might cough and splutter down the red road beyond the hedge, or a mule wagon might poke along, but there wasn't much else active. Willis gave out with good talk. He was justly pleased at the showing his boys had made the night before. He wanted me to be sure to tell Kemper Harreld and Tic Tillman, his colleagues at Morehouse, and Florence Read, his boss at Spelman, just what he was doing. "I had made out all right with the fellows," he said. "They took to you O.K. Probably talking about you now over in Macon."

As we were talking, a couple of men in work clothes yelled at each other across the road. "Ssh," said Willis. "Listen."

"The bear gonna git you," said the first.

"How come he ain't got you?" the second snapped back.

Willis explained that "the bear" was the sun; the first man had meant, "The sun will get you, grab you, knock you flat." The second one meant, "How come he gonna get *me,* if he ain't got *you*? I'm as good a man as you."

"Where's Zack?" the talk went on.

"He's gone with the peaches," came to us over the hedge.

The peaches had all been picked, were gone from this section, which was famous for them. Pickers followed them in both northeasterly and southwesterly directions. Pickers' wages depended on the market; sometimes they were paid by the bushel, sometimes by the day. "It all depends on the white folks," said Willis. "They're so smart they don't standardize. The more money peaches are bringing, the more leniency they show. Only natural."

I told Willis about my inability to get a bus for Fort Valley. He said I was lucky. Buses weren't for him anymore, if he could help it. One that he was riding in the back country had a flat and ran off the road. The other Negro passengers took off their coats and pitched in to jack up and fix the tire. Willis, in a freshly cleaned summer suit, joined the white passengers on the side of the road and watched them work. The white driver asked him, "Ain't you gonna help any, Preacher?" Willis does look somewhat like a preacher: he is mild-faced, portly, with what is called "the preacher's roll" on the back of his neck. Willis gave some advice about coasting the car back to the road, since the jack wasn't getting good purchase on the soft shoulder, and the grade was downhill. There his help ended. His advice was taken and the tire changed. When they got back into the bus, a white passenger said to him: "Well, preacher, you are a lazy nigger with your hands all right, but you ain't so lazy with your head." So when Willis got to the next town with a railroad station in it, he decided that *that* was as far as he was riding on that bus.

"You couldn't win the back country," he said.

One of his friends, named Dobbins, the principal of an elementary school in Birmingham, had been driving along a country road in Alabama: "He was doing about fifty miles an hour, when a mule jumped out of the gully, right in front of the car. The car hit the mule's rear end, up around his withers, and spun him around, causing him to hit his head against the car window. The mule toppled back into the gully, out cold. Dobbins couldn't drive on; his car was nearly wrecked with its headlight broken, an axle bent, and the side stove in. Three crackers came up from nowhere. They asked him all kinds of questions and didn't want to believe the car belonged to Dobbins. But they finally let him go.

"Dobbins came back about three months later when court was being held. Don't you know that they charged him one hundred eighty dollars for that mule? In those days you could get a good mule for sixty or seventy dollars. He paid it all right. The judge told him to pay or serve it out in time on the roads."

Willis had seen his own share of trouble on the back roads. One hot day years ago, while he was traveling in southwestern Georgia with a college glee club, the bus radiator began steaming to beat hell. They came to a house unshaded and on gullied land but it had a well.

Willis told it this way:

I gave a yell. It just had to be a cracker's house. A tall redneck with a handle-bar moustache came out of the door. Barefooted, in undershirt and over-alls. Ornery looking all right. I asked him if we could get a bucket of water from the well for our radiator. He didn't say anything, but went back into the house. After a while he came back with a woman. She was barefooted too. He spit out of the side of his mouth and said, "I reckon hit's all right. But don't yawl hurt nothing." The woman just stood looking.

One of the boys started pulling up a bucket of water. The wheel was just groaning. All the time those crackers stood there glaring at us. It must have made the boy nervous because just as he got the bucket to the rim, he let it slip. That bucket went clattering down the well making the most ungodly racket.

I looked at the cracker, who was nearly purple. I thought he was about to have apoplexy, or a fit. He said something quick to his wife, and then yelled, "Gawd damn you, I tole yawl not to hurt nothing. Now you get the hell on out of here. Do it damn quick."

His wife came out of the house with a double-barreled shotgun in one hand. With the other she was holding up her apron with a few musket shells in it. "Now git," the cracker yelled. "For one word I'd shoot the hell out of you and that bus too."

We got. We didn't run, but we walked mighty fast to the bus. I looked around as I got there. He had the shotgun ready at his hip; I knew he wanted to shoot in the worst way. The woman just stood there; she hadn't opened her mouth the whole time, but she was ready too.

But Willis told another story:

On one of my trips with a glee club, I discovered that "music has charms to soothe the savage breast." The bus, which like so many belonging to the schools, was a traveling hazard, started "jumping time" when they were passing a prison camp in southern Alabama. Negro convicts in stripes were just coming in from work on the roads. I walked down to the camp's office about fifty yards away. A husky prison boss with a six-shooter on his hip, sat on a bench outside the office. As I came to the gate, the boss got up, his fingers tucked in his ammunition belt.

"What you want?"

"Captain, our bus just broke down. I'd like to call up for help. Do you have a telephone?"

"Sho we got a telephone."

"Well, would it be okay for me to use it?"

"Hell, no!" the captain shouted.

I made one or two stumbling attempts to persuade him but he was so hardboiled and frigid that I couldn't make my point. So we had to sit down in the bus and wait. We didn't know what we were going to do. It was getting toward night. When the convicts were through supper, some of them came to look at us through the stockade wire. We yelled back and forth at each other for awhile and one of the boys threw them a pack of cigarettes. Then the boss came down and told them to get away from that fence, and told us not to talk to the prisoners. I explained that we didn't mean any harm.

"Matters a damn," he said. "I run my niggers; you run yours."

I told him if he would just let me use his phone, we could get somebody to fix the bus or tow us in, and we could get away from there.

"Ain't I already told you, you cain't use my phone," he snapped.

It wasn't long before the sun had set, and darkness came on fast in those woods. Some of the boys struck up a song. Before long we could see the convicts gathering on the other side of the fence, just standing there, pressing against the wire, looking out and listening. We sang a couple of spirituals. And then we heard them singing from the other side of the fence, a sort of humming at first, low, as if they were scared. It was Nicodemus. Nicodemus, he desired to know, Lord, Lord. . . . All of a sudden a couple of voices joined in clear and strong: "How can a man be born again when he's old?"

Nobody broke it up; and after a while the convicts asked for certain songs. Most of them, we knew. Then, in the moonlight, we could see the boss and the guard standing there, a little apart from the others. They listened a few minutes, then left. Shortly afterwards, a convict yelled over the fence, "De captain say you can use the phone." One of the boys and I walked up to the office. "Go ahead and use it," the captain said, gruffly. "But it's gonna cost you two dollars." I paid the money gladly. "That was purty singing," the guard said to me as we left.

II

In Willis's forays over the state hunting songs, the experiences he ran into deepened his understanding. To really *get* the songs of the people, he said, he obviously had to be inside, to share in the humor, the irony, the melodrama, the tragedy. Cherishing the life, he soaked in all he could in every community he visited. Shocking violence, farcical upsets, prosaic detail, all were alike, grist to his mill.

A tall, strapping Negro went by the edge. "You see that fellow?" Willis said, slipping back into the lingo. "He's the only one of us in this town allowed to carry a gun. He carries the mail from the depot to the Post Office. He's licensed to shoot either white folks or colored. The people around here make him out to be really something."

"You know, Sterling, I haven't written any book, but I don't back off other collectors because of that. None of these guys can beat me at understanding Negroes."

He mentioned a Negro collector: "Hell, he's not close enough to niggers. He's a pseudo-aristocrat. He doesn't know niggers in the raw. Not the way we know them." Another Negro, high up in academic circles, was attempting to study Negro music out of a feeling of duty.

"You can't go at this stuff out of race pride. You've got to love it first, then if you want to, show what's in it. But you can't say: it's by Negroes; I'm a Negro; I'm going to love it. . . . He's my boy; we like each other and understand each other. But he doesn't know a damn thing about Negroes. And it's too late for him to start learning. He was brought up in a different environment, that's all."

A few collectors have followed his trail, knowing that the stuff he got was true and deep. He is not resentful when they publish songs that he found first, but he judges them strictly by high professional folklorist standards. Sometimes Willis would find songs in the anthologies that he felt had been tampered with. One rather famous white collector, he felt, would insert the word "nigger" when the rhythm would take it. But though Willis, in the true folkway, interspersed "nigger" throughout his talking, he felt that there was something untrue about a Negro's singing the word "nigger" before whites. Sure they might do it, but whether that is the "true" song is another matter. He also felt that when convicts were forced to sing by the warden of the penitentiary for the white collectors, the true song and the true singing somehow escaped.

"Some of these people know a few Negro expressions, but they don't know how they hang together." Willis boasted that he was of the people, and therefore knew. "My father was a cotton sampler and marker. That was a skilled labor job. He was supposed to slash a hole in the bale and take out a sample; then he would mark the bale against the sample. My mother went to high school; you know in those days that was something. She taught school; sometimes she would cook and work at day jobs. As a young one I was carried all over the lower South: Montgomery, Pensacola, Jacksonville. My daddy used to make good money.

"Both my mother and my father played the mandolin and the guitar. They would hold impromptu concerts, called them serenades. The neighbors all used to come in to play and sing. When we were living near Sandy Ridge, Alabama, I remember that Uncle Free Payne—that was the only name he had, just Free—was the champion fiddler of the country. The mandolin and violin were favorites in Alabama; in Georgia it was mainly the guitar. A band would have a fiddle, a jug, and a bass fiddle. They would blow in the top of the jug, and get the weirdest effects."

With this musical background, Willis studied music under Kemper Harreld at Morehouse College in Atlanta and at Chicago Musical College. His first teaching job was at Leland College, at Baker, Louisiana. Baker was just about on the edge of nowhere but there were a lot of Negroes near, and Willis was in a briar-patch.

"Those Negroes had a culture of their own, speaking that patois French. They worked on the riverboats, or were roustabouts on the levees. I soon learned my way around and got in with them solid. I picked up a lot of unique stuff; you can't get that kind of stuff now. I worked with children too, learning their styles of singing. Not only to collect but to pass it through my system. I wanted to learn how to sing with them; I learned by absolute participation.

"Then I started my research. I wanted to know how much is generally known. So I went through all the anthologies. Of many songs there is only one version, but I have several versions."

As a collector, on his own, and later on a Rosenwald Fellowship, he has honeycombed all of the lower South. He has hundreds of songs, and many more variants. He has been opposed to recording; and even now is in no rush to record. For over a score of years his delight has been in collecting. I accused him of hoarding, of unwillingness to share his rich finds. No, he said seriously, but he didn't like the uses that the recording companies made of the stuff. It belonged to the people; then others got hold of it and soon it wasn't the people's any longer. What the phonograph companies had done to some of the "folk" artists was a sad case in point. He was heart and soul for genuine folk festivals such as the one he had just engineered. But not for the phonies. And he had taken down the songs in words and melodies lest they be lost. Someday, he promised, he would release his book. But he wasn't in any hurry.

In the meantime, he was training glee clubs to sing these songs the true way. He wanted to imbue the youngsters with appreciation of their rich legacy. That wasn't so hard. I mentioned a fine chorus that I had heard one morning at Spelman College a few years before. Listening to one song, I told him, was an unforgettable experience: it had been a sort of burial song in which a girl's voice had soared like a clarinet above the quieted sustaining voices. "Yes," he said, "Her name was Priscilla Williams. She loved that song, and sang it beautifully. It was a pallbearers' song that I learned at a funeral in a country church." His own resonant voice sang it:

> *Now we take this feeble body*
> *And we carry it to the grave*
> *And we'll all leave it there*
> *Hallelujah*
>
> *Now we take this feeble body*
> *And we cover it with the sod*
> *But the soil will rest in God*
> *Hallelujah*
>
> *Now we take this feeble body*
> *And will dry our tear-stained eyes*
> *For in Christ we all shall rise*
> *Hallelujah*
>
> *Now we take this feeble body*
> *And we'll all march away*
> *Till we meet on the coming day*
> *Hallelujah.*

He had made an arrangement of a spiritual, "Po' Little Jesus," that was included in a book of choral songs published by Schirmer. Only two songs by Americans are in the book; the other sixteen songs are by famous composers led by Palestrina, Bach, Praetorius, and Brahms. The editor said that "although it is a Negro spiritual (and not the work of a single composer) it ought to be included, it was so effective and unique."

There weren't so many songs about the child Jesus, but he gave me one that I considered striking. It was unrhymed, but the pattern, though crude, was definite.

> *Oh look-a-yonder at Mary and Joseph*
> *And de young child, King Jesus*
> *On de journey to Jerusalem*
> *For to pay their poll taxes;*
> *On de way back dey miss de young child*
> *And dey went to Jerusalem,*
> *For to search for de young child, Jesus.*

They found him "in de temple wid de lawyers and de doctors and de elders, asking questions."

> *Den he turn to de doctor,*
> *Said, "Doctor, state and county doctor,*
> *Can you heal some sin-sick soul, suh?"*
> *Oh no, oh no, dat's a question he could not answer.*

Nor could "the state and county lawyer . . . plead some sinner's cause, suh"; nor could "the state and county judge . . . judge their righteous souls, suh."

> *Oh, no, dat's a question he could not answer.*

The congregation swelled forth in the chorus, after the state and county doctor, lawyer, and judge had each been found wanting:

> *My God is a rock in a weary lan', weary lan', weary lan'*
> *My God is a rock in a weary lan'*
> *Shelter in de time of storm.*

This union of new verses with an older chorus, a new interpretation with an older spiritual, is often to be found, Willis explained. And discovering the people's use of their own experience—the learned "doctor" becoming the state and county medical "officer"; the going to Jerusalem to "pay their poll taxes"—was one of the fascinations of collecting.

As far back as 1925, Willis James made a series of six work songs for the old Paramount Record Company, to his best knowledge the first Negro work songs ever recorded. The company released only two. His accompanist was a big fat fellow named Tiny Parham who could scarcely read music (rather he read it very inaccurately), but who did have tremendous native ability. Willis James had to lose a lot of time teaching him how these songs really went.

One song was called "River Rouster":

> *Ain't no rousters on the river*
> *Like Ace of Spades and me*
> *Rousters on the river*
> *Gwine to Memphis, Tennessee*
> *Ace of Spades and me, boy,*
> *Ace of Spades and me,*
> *Rousters on the river*
> *Gwine to Memphis, Tennessee*
> *Oh Johnny, Johnny, Johnny,*
> *Dis boat ain't rollin' right*
> *Cause Johnny boy, the fireman*
> *Is sleep tonight.*
> *Oh Johnny, Johnny, Johnny,*
> *Let dat boiler water flow*
> *In de mornin'*
> *Makin' Bayou Sara sho'.*

"He got a gal down there," said Willis, "and didn't want any playing around. But that's not a patch on this one." And he started singing in a mellow voice:

> *I'm going down, down the line*
> *Way down, down the line.*

"Down the line, not far enough," he interpolated. "Going *way* down":

> *Gotta find the gal I love*
> *To ease my mind.*

She got forty thousand diamonds
And I gave her every one
When she walks out in the morning
Lord, she looks like the rising sun.
My gal don't need no ticket
When she wants to ride the train
When she gits her mind on travelin'
She just rides on my sweet name,
Lord, Lord, on my sweet name . . .

"Lord, Lord," he breathed softly.

"You know the way I got that blues? I was coming out of Mobile one night, coming up to Montgomery; a Negro got on the train and sat in the back. He had a guitar and got to thumbing it, just hitting his thumb, harp-like. Said to me, 'Does you like to hear a box?' I told him sure, I was reared on a box. And he said, 'Well then, I'm gonna sing you some pieces.' And that was one of his songs."

Willis had also picked up one of the few love songs which expressed genuine devotion, rather than the usual free-and-easy love of the blues. It came from a lonesome boy in coal-mining Alabama. Some of the lines go:

De longes' day I ever did see
Was de day dat Roberta died
I got de news ten miles from home
An' I walked back dat road an' I cried . . .
Dis worl' is high
Dis worl' is low
Dis worl' is deep an' wide
But de longes' road I ever did see
Was de one I walked an' cried.

Of his many work songs my imagination was caught by "It Sound Like Thunder," in which a chip off of John Henry's block boasts of his prowess with a hammer:

Did yo' read it in de paper
Bout de gov'nor an' his family
Dey am 'cided to come to de new road
Jes' to hear, Lawd, my hammer fall . . .

And another is one of the censored songs about the captain "walking lak Samson . . . totin his talker (gun)," only to find that Jimbo is gone:

> De houn' dawgs come
> Oh! hab mercy
> Start to runnin'
> Dey ain't fin' you
> Oh! hab mercy
> Good ol' Jimbo
> Lawd, Lawd.

And the singer promises, that if he ever "gits de drop, Lawd, Lawd":

> Ah'm goin' on
> Lawd, Lawd,
> Dat same good way
> Lawd, Lawd
> Dat Jimbo gone
> Lawd, Lawd.

At Alabama State College, Willis experimented with the blues for choral singing: "I took the song out of the original state. It was pure blues; I didn't bother with the words and melody, I wanted to know what could be derived from the blues. But it is difficult to sing the blues in chorus. Choral blues, even by Hall Johnson, don't come up. The Negro takes his blues on a personal basis. When we think of blues, we think of personalities: Bessie Smith, Clara Smith, Lonnie Johnson. But when we think of spirituals, we think of the Hampton Singers, the Fisk Singers, and by all means the rural church.

"Folk-musicians don't have any conception of blues in the ensemble. And blues solos are personal, not social. The Negro hearing the blues is a spectator, a listener, an understander, but not a participant. I know that it has been said that Negroes dance to the blues, because they can't pay their house rent, or to express their sorrows. But I think the blues are something done *for* him, a performance *for* him, outside of himself. The Negro blues singer has to be an artist, an actress, otherwise nobody will listen to her. Of course, the Negro shares when he dances to the blues. When he takes a woman in his arms, he's as much a choreographer as Martha Graham. But his mind isn't on the house rent then, or on his sorrows. He says a whole lot more than that in his dance."

Much of the present-day stuff is only pseudo-folk. The famous choral groups, Willis feels, have done some excellent and some bad work. He praises Hall Johnson for leading the way for large professional choirs to sing folk-songs, but some of the more popular choirs have catered to the common taste, have vulgarized: "They will have to decide what they want: to reach all classes and masses with phony folk singing, or to sing the real article. Too many in the field are not really serious. Then spiritual singing has been highly colored by Hollywood. The musical scholars have produced mostly artificial arrangements, though some arrangements of course are fair: 'If you do enough, by the law of averages, or chance, you're bound to do one or two good things.' " But Willis feels that, by and large, collectors and arrangers are too far away from the proper primary sources. He feels that Hall Johnson's *Green Pastures* spirituals are first-rate examples of what he feels could be done.

"No Negro soloist can sing a spiritual like Roland Hayes," he went on. "Of course the Golden Gates are closer to the bone, as they themselves are closer to the people. They are the most authentic group singers of the spirituals. Up to recently anyway. The spirituals don't need those Mills Brothers' effects they put in. But take any of them; I can get up a festival here and show all of them how spirituals ought to be sung."

We got to talking about the strange harmony I had heard the preceding night. He didn't know whether he could make it clear for me, as I didn't know enough about music. But from his earliest collecting, he had been comparing folk singing with traditional harmony. He learned how to make "head arrangements." The folk can't write it; they make it up in their minds. So he made it up in his. And now he could sing along with them, in their style. They welcomed him.

"They sing the way they feel it. They don't know anything about doubling on the leading third and paralleling fifths, so they don't bother about avoiding these. The fact is they use the pattern of naturalness, based on nothing but pure, honest effort at expressing what they really feel. They are a folk people, with a peculiar affinity to other folk peoples, causing them to react to art forms in a similar manner. Eskimos, Africans, people over in Burma, same thing. What's the reason why they all favor drums? It's no mystery. It's like all races and peoples having bows and arrows. Same principle. They've never seen each other, but they have similar things. There's a similarity in the music of all primitive people. You take the primitive Negroes: there's a basic type of harmony in their spirituals and work songs. Basic to all primitive music. I have found it to be unfailing."

A woman in a big farm hat walked past the hedge, singing gently in the Georgia sunlight. The way she slurred the notes, the plaintive, unhurried melody, the spacing—all reminded me of the music I had heard the night before. Willis alerted as if at a listening post. "You hear that?" he said softly. "Lord, Lord, Lord . . ."

➤➤ THE DUKE COMES TO ATLANTA ◄◄

There are not many first-rate jazz bands in the South. As the musicians develop, scouts from New York and Chicago discover them and put them on big time. A group of college boys at Alabama State, with a few pick-up musicians from the vicinity, were whisked away to New York as Erskine Hawkins's band; Doc Wheeler's band, famous in southern Florida, is one of the latest to take to the national road. Negro and white jazz musicians, like many Negro and white writers, artists, professors, and scientists, are drawn away from the South to the better paying North. A few white Southern hotels may have middle-of-the-road jazz orchestras, but for most whites and Negroes, jazz comes back to its native home on radios, phonographs, juke-boxes, and one-night stands. A few years ago, I heard Duke Ellington's band play a one-night stand at the Atlanta Municipal Auditorium. The city had been agog for weeks over the Duke's appearance. The vast auditorium was packed. Half of the seats from stage right to the rear of the hall were set aside for whites; the opposite half for Negroes. The Negroes who sat there were upper and middle class: teachers, college professors, students, professional men, all of those whose compunctions about segregation or jazz let them attend. Down on the floor swarmed the Negro hoi polloi. Their garb was of all sorts: full dress, street clothing, work clothing, sweaters, and slacks. Some were cutting up frantically. On the side near the white folks, couples would put on the dog while the whites cheered their foolery and tossed down coins to them. One black Amazon, larger than her sweating partner, was clad in a low-cut, cerise silk gown, bulging and threatening to split at the seams, a cast-off from her employer, probably, who called her by name and offered advice like a fan to a baseball player. "Go to it, Marthy; oh do it!" she screamed almost hysterically, as Marthy billowed and shimmied and spun like a barge in a storm. On the side near the disapproving Negro "dicties," the showoffs checked their antics, but they resumed them when they danced back to the white folks' side and the shower of silver. No whites, of course, stepped on the dance floor, and few, if any, of the Negro middle class.

I looked at the Duke and his men, sleekly groomed, perfectly tailored. I wondered what was going on behind those impassive fronts. I looked at the fellows whose names I knew best then: Hodges, Barney Bigard, Rex Stewart, Cootie Williams, Otto Hardwicke, and Sonny Greer. Here were sophisticates, some of them expatriates from the South, who had seen the boom years of Harlem, had played before the fashionable world of the continent and even before crowned heads. I wondered if I was wrong in reading a cold disdain in their faces. And I wondered also what whites looking at these men were thinking. The whole range of complexions was there: from Juan Tizol, looking like a white man, through the more numerous light browns, to the darker Tricky Sam Nanton, Rex, and Cootie; some looked like Latins, some like Orientals. Finished artists, at the top of their bracket, suave world travelers, they seemed detached and bored, watching the show unsmiling and unfrowning, with only an occasional nod or whisper.

They gave out with good music. Even the clowning of the dancers could not stand against it, and as the musicians warmed to their job, more and more spectators banked around the footlights. When Lawrence Brown or Johnny Hodges or Tricky Sam or Cootie took their solo spots, cries of rapture rose to the girders. Ivie Anderson was the crowd's darling. She flaunted on the stage brown and slim and impudent, her body seemingly poured in a sequin-glittering sheath. I heard gasps from the high-toned folks around me. She had as much class as many of the visitors on the other side of the hall from Druid Hills or Peachtree or North Shore Drive. As she sang "It Don't Mean a Thing If You Ain't Got That Swing," the Duke's pagan challenge to an unhepped world, she swung her body slightly and the lights picked out the shimmering spangles on her gown; this and a few slightly risqué lines and gestures, archly interpolated, brought down the house. They wanted encores, but she gave only two. "When My Sugar Walks Down the Street" and "When he kisses me I sure stay kissed," she sang, and her listeners believed her. Her last number was "Solitude." Many listeners would gladly have done something for that sorrow she sang about.

The band took a long time out between numbers. Maybe it was because the bus ride had been tough, and many miles lay ahead before New York again, and that "A Train" for Harlem. Maybe they just didn't care for the high jinks on the floor. But the audience was unresentful.

Hank and I wandered backstage at the long intermission. The Duke remembered me; the old Washington home-boy stuff stood me in good stead. He had to talk to some white fans on the other side of backstage, but he promised to get that over soon. Hank and I watched the whites, especially the womenfolk, swarm all over Duke. He seemed to need protection, but was hardly likely to get the right sort from the hefty cop, who stood nearby, glowering, ill at ease. Finally we caught Duke's eye and set out into the forbidden territory for the rescue. As we came up, a smartly dressed woman was gushing: "Oh, Mister Deyook I think youah playing is just mahvelous! Couldn't you play tomorrow night for just a small party aout at my haouse? It would be wonderful, it *really* would. Just a few chosen friends?" Duke explained carefully, a bit tiredly it seemed, that he was on contract, that he was leaving Atlanta that night, that he just couldn't. But the hostess was persistent, until Duke tore himself away; he was very sorry but he was under contract, and now he really had to leave as he wanted to talk to some old friends. As we walked off with him, the large gathering of whites stared at us.

"Man, I sure was glad you came over," he said. But the intermission was about ended, so he told us to wait backstage, and he could see us when he took time out again. That plan didn't work well. The Atlanta cop came over to the wings and asked all of the Negroes what they were doing there. I told him that we were waiting to talk with Duke. He let that pass and sent all the others away. Then, after he had been on the white side of backstage he came back. "What are you all doing back here?"

"I told you, officer, we were waiting for Mr. Ellington. He told us to wait."

"Well, Duke ain't got nothing to do with this," he growled. "I got orders from the manager to clear all of you out of here."

I started to say something, but I looked at Hank, and we both looked at the cop, who had a mean glint in his narrowed eyes. So we walked offstage. We had to go through the whites crowded in the opposite wings, still oohing and ahing at the fine jazz. Some of them, however, did stop to stare at us as we picked our way through their ranks.

The cops didn't quite know how to handle this sort of turnout. I believe that they were jumpy. There was a lot of liquor flowing, and many Negroes were loudly on the loose. I saw a cop slap a colored woman who was arguing with him, and as she was pulled away from him, I saw him kick her solidly. There were many Negro men around, but they did nothing about it. The woman, swearing and crying, jerked against those trying to keep her from more trouble. I saw no cops in evidence, however, at one dangerous point. The crowd of dancers suddenly opened; one woman backed off swiftly; another slowly, almost majestically, followed her with a razor in her hand, her arm going up methodically, in long graceful curves. Men rushed toward the furious woman, then stepped back from those sweeping arcs. After the pursued had safely got out of the hall, and the steady pursuer was about at the door, I saw two cops suddenly dart through the crowd.

Toward the end of the evening, when the autograph hunt was on, the cops had to see many interracial taboos ignored. Hepcats, thrill seekers, autograph hounds, male and female, upper and lower class, white and Negro, stormed about the platform. What the cops should do when the whites left their safe perches and joined the press was not clear. They just hovered about, as protectively as they could. But they couldn't stop whites from being jostled about, their shins barked, their ribs elbowed, their toes stepped on. The whites didn't seem to mind: "It don't mean a thing; all you got to do is swing!" The Duke and his musicians had to sign slips of paper, cards, notebooks, handkerchiefs, pieces of clothing. It was like a madhouse, with the Duke and the bandsmen the only cool and sane ones as they signed their names with flourishes.

➤ FAREWELL TO BASIN STREET ◄

On my last trip to New Orleans, a sergeant got on the train at Anniston and squeezed his bulk into the seat beside me. He was a friendly sort. I learned much of his business, his chance to go to officers' training camp, his football career at Xavier University, his various jobs before Pearl Harbor. He ran over with praise of his native New Orleans. My tourist's curiosity about the Creole cuisine fired his language; he described the culinary marvels of all the various gumbos, of Jambalaya (Creole cousin of Hopping-John), of Gombo Zhèbes (a mixture of all the greens on God's earth), and of the sea foods, until the woman in front threw amused glances at us. He was hastening home on furlough; one of the jobs he anticipated was cooking up some of those fine Creole dishes. I begged off from his hymns of adoration. I had not eaten since above Spartanburg, and we were nearly in Birmingham.

I asked him about New Orleans jazz. This was another street that he walked familiarly. His brother, a clarinet player, was a friend of Barney Bigard, and had been in France with Noble Sissle when Barney was there with Duke Ellington. Yes, he knew Sidney Bechet, King Oliver, Kid Ory, Satchmo', all of them. He looked with greater favor on me; I was a bit more than a traveling schoolteacher now in his eyes. When I spoke of Kid Rena, he corrected my pronunciation but beamed. Maybe I could find Kid Raynyay. I should go to the Fern Dance Hall, on Iberville between Rampart and Burgundy, anytime late at night. Sure I could get in. Just go on in. I'd find plenty my color there, if not my race. If I didn't find him there, and Rena was known to be irregular, I might have to seek Big Eye Louie, the historic clarinetist. On Derbigny between Columbus and Kelerec, everybody would tell you where Big Eye was; not a soul in that neighborhood but would look out for Big Eye. The sergeant also named his nephew, a hot jazz cat, who could help me find Rena and Louie if these leads failed.

I could not find Kid Rena and Big Eye Louie; I did not exhaust all the sergeant's leads, though I tried some new ones. Standing across from the high school on Rampart Street, I was accosted mysteriously by a young fellow who told me, "Yes, it is true. He's dead now"; and I remembered meeting him at Paul Robeson's concert and that he was a music teacher. He had then promised that he'd help me find those remaining New Orleans jazzmen. I did not know, the school bell summoning the teacher away, whether it was Kid Rena's trumpet or Big Eye Louie's clarinet that death had finally quieted; from other people I heard that it was Big Eye. There was much more than jazz, however, that I wanted to learn about New Orleans, and after a reasonable effort I gave up the search for those musicians who stayed behind, after their compères, Louis Armstrong, Sidney Bechet, Jelly

Roll Morton, and Zutty Singleton had gone up the Mississippi to Chicago and Kansas City.

Missing these pioneers, I tried to obtain the album in which Heywood Hale Broun recorded the New Orleans jazz of Kid Rena, Big Eye, Alphonse Picou, James Robinson, and other oldsters. It came late, almost too late in their lives, this putting on wax what was probably closest to the fine old source stuff of jazz. Five music stores, including the largest in New Orleans, not only did not have the album, but had not heard of it (New York *would* be the place to get that, they cracked); and they looked quizzically at me when I asked if they knew of Rena. I should not have been surprised; my first day in New Orleans I noticed that Frankie Masters (a sweet "name-band") was playing the Hotel Roosevelt. And at a prom at Southern University up country, I had heard a Negro band from New Orleans play sweet jazz to which the collegians danced sedately, with only a bit of genteel jitterbugging. The vocalist was a chit of a girl. I could not help thinking, when she ventured a diluted blues, how Ma Rainey and Bessie Smith would have snorted at this child being sent to do a woman's work. The record shops catering to Negroes were doing a booming business in blues (Big Maceo, Yank Rachal, Bea Booze, and Lil Green) and gutter smut (*She Want to Sell My Monkey* and *Let Me Play with Your Poodle*), but they didn't stock albums, especially an album by somebody named Rena. Never heard of him.

Basin Street was another disappointment. I knew that at the very time when the famous blues came out, Basin Street already belonged to the lost past:

> That's where the light and the dark folks meet
> Heaven on earth, they call it Basin Street.

Even in its glory, it was a short street to have spread so much joy and jazz abroad. But I was not ready for its change of name to North Saratoga Street; after Canal and Rampart, what New Orleans street could be more widely known than Basin? Only a stone's throw away from the notorious section it magnetized is now the Lafitte Housing Project, trim and model. Across the iron picket fence, the Southern Railroad trains rumble "down the line," but the street itself is quiet, with warehouses and commercial buildings where the bordellos and gaudy saloons flourished. Sole memento of the vanished era of plush and lace, mahogany furniture, long mirrors, and costly paintings, is a semi-pretentious white house, graying in the railroad soot.

Behind these long arched elegant windows, boarded now, reigned that internationally known purveyor of octoroon and quadroon beauties, Lulu White, whose diamonds and other gems made her resemble "the electrical display of the Cascade at the late St. Louis exposition." This had been a show-place of Storyville, the red-light district, where over a hundred musicians, white and black, were regularly employed in the restaurants and cabarets. Many of the bandsmen later became drawing cards in the cities of America and Europe. In the "palaces," however, the piano was the favored instrument, and the pianists, so frequently Negro, were called "professors." "Professor" Tony Jackson was legendary, famed for his version of the "Naked Dance"; he is dead now, and so, more recently, is Jelly Roll Morton, who started as a mere "winin'" boy and whose memoirs recapture much of the lost re-splendence and ribaldry. A third "professor," Spencer Williams, composed *Mahogany Hall Stomp* to celebrate Lulu White's place, *Shim-Me-She-Wabble* to celebrate one of the entertainments provided there, and *Basin Street Blues* to celebrate the whole region. The last blues was elegiac even then (thirty years ago):

> *Don't you want to go with me*
> *Down the Mississippi . . .*

Rampart Street: and I thought of Ida Cox's plangent blues of the old times:

> *I want to go down to Rampart Street.*
> *I want to hear those colored jazz bands play . . .*

Across Canal to South Rampart, where Louis Armstrong, before finding harbor at the Waif's home, had sat on a coal cart scatting out his wares in what he hoped was a bass voice, where he and Sidney Bechet later played on the same advertising wagon, where Clarence Williams, backed by some of the best young musicians, played piano at the Red Onion Café, and laid up memories for *Red Onion Blues, Gravier Street Blues,* and *Baby, Won't You Please Come Home.* Gravier Street was still ramshackly enough to stir a blues feeling, but the jazz bands weren't around. Rampart was a busy street, lined with offices, perfume stands, beer-joints, clothes stores, groceries, and record stores. But it wasn't the Rampart Street of hot jazz. In one juke-joint, packed and jammed on Saturday night, the favored records were schmaltzy; one souse put nickel on top of nickel in order to hear:

> *When the lights go on again, all over the world . . .*

The sentiment was fine, but I am afraid that it was the falsetto that got him. And it was on Rampart Street that I ran into a tall white man selling a song of his composing, a hymn of which, as unbelievable as it may sound, the second line of the chorus ran, "And we shall all be as white as snow." Dr. Livingston, I presume.

On the scrap piles of the record shops, however, there were some finds: the Original Dixieland Jazz Band's *Livery Stable Blues,* a few of Clarence Williams's Red Onion Fives, and Jelly Roll's *Oh Didn't He Ramble,* that good-natured cartoon of the old funeral processions. I took this record to the house of some New Orleans friends and it quickened their memories. Chummy remembered how instead of *Home Sweet Home,* Papa Celestine would send the dancers away with *Old Man Mose Is Dead,* and Kid Rena would play *Get Out of Here.* He remembered Kid Ory's "tail-gate" trombone and Bechet's wild, free clarinet. Before Bechet would have you in his band, he told me, you would have to play *High Society* to his taste. And his taste was the way Picou had played it. Among the Creoles, Picou was remembered better than some of these others, but Perez and Robichaux were recalled, and a few light Creoles, Dave Perkins especially, who played with both colored and white bands. Everybody remembered the river steamboats, where Fate Marable assembled noted crews of jazzmen.

Both Chummy and Ferd told of the great appeal of the funeral bands. Chummy said that he would never miss a funeral; he and two others of the "second lines," the New Orleans kids who, just as kids anywhere, would stream behind the band, but who, unlike the others, had better bands to mimic. Ferd said that he would wait at Bienville and North Claiborne, and then fall in; whites and blacks and in-betweens, there was no segregation then with jazz leveling the low barriers. They remembered how after the slow funeral marches of the graveyard, on the way back the band would kick out on *I'll Be Glad When You're Dead, You Rascal You!* Mrs. Chummy recalled the tale of the funeral of a big shot, a *bon vivant,* whose respectable *cortège* was suddenly swelled when the girls from the crib houses filed out to take their mourning places.

> Bring out your rubber-tired hearses, bring out your rubber-tired hacks
> They're taking old Johnnie to the graveyard, and they ain't gonna bring
>   him back.

Most of the memories were of the funeral parades, as my informants could go to these but not to the honky-tonk dances, or Storyville *maisons de joie,* or to Antoine's, world famous restaurant, where Picou had a high class orchestra. Those funerals must have been grand experiences: the stalwart horses, plumed and decked out in nets and feathers (I learned from Mr. Geddes, one of the city's most prosperous undertakers, that his father's livery stable was famous for its fine horses). After the slow, doleful music, there was shrill or muted weeping at the tomb. And then the return: a roll of the drums, a few quick blasts on trumpet, and then the band kicking, jamming, definitely not dead. They tell me those dressed up horses pranced to the music, throwing their hooves high. I should like to have been one of that "second line" of kids.

But that too was a lost custom. At Geddes' Funeral Parlor, limousines had replaced the noble horses. Out of deep sentiment, Mr. Geddes had kept some of the stalls of the old livery stable, and his doorway was lighted by heavy carriage lamps (he was the first to use these in New Orleans, he said proudly, wistfully). I attended two wakes at his parlors. He told me that one of the deceased, a World War veteran, was to have a band at his funeral, but it would not be like the bands of old, it was a military band instead. I did not go to hear it.

There were a few good jazz combinations in town, I learned, but most of them were playing in white places where I could have gone only at the cost of problems. I found later that Bunk Johnson had recently come to town from New Iberia, and had been driven down Rampart Street between sidewalks crowded with yelling people. This was in 1942. Since then Bunk Johnson has come back to the recording studios. Jazz lovers over the nation bought him a new set of teeth; Sidney Bechet's dentist brother made them for him: "I'm glad you got your chops back, man."

Charles Smith's essay, "Land of Dreams," rebuilds his fascinating and lucky journey in search of lost New Orleans jazzmen. Better sleuths than I have discovered in contemporary New Orleans creators of jazz in the primary manner, like the clarinetist George Lewis and the trombonist Jim Robinson, and have recorded them for the Climax, Jazzman, and Jazz Information labels. Harry Lim, the cat from Java, has explored white New Orleans and has come up with a group that continues the tradition of the Original Dixielanders and the New Orleans Rhythm Kings. Stacked beside these, my search was a failure. But though my stay in New Orleans was prolonged, there was too much other than jazz that I needed to learn about. The pioneer clarinetist, Picou, I understand, is weaving his lovely melodies now at Dutches restaurant. As Dutches would be forbidden to me today, so the places where Picou played in 1942 were forbidden too, unless I was willing to *passa blanc,* which on that sojourn would have jeopardized some of my standing. In spite of the resurrection of more persistent researchers, however, I think that there still is truth in what I sensed in 1942: that in New Orleans the feeling for jazz was nostalgic, commemorative, quite different from the force that sustained the young Louis Armstrong, Sidney Bechet, Jimmy Noone, and Johnny Dodds. Bunk Johnson had to go to the coast for a real hearing. New Orleans gave jazz to the world; the world parceled bits of it back over the turntable and the airwaves.

A friend took me to see a colored Creole family in the housing project that is fringed by Basin Street. But it was far from Basin Street in a sense, for they gave us gorgeous coconut cake and ginger ale, and the music from Jimmy Dorsey's orchestra swelled dulcetly from the radio.

I left New Orleans shortly after on the Southern. As the train picked up speed rumbling "down the line," I saw Lulu White's famed house glimmering there in the dusk, a pale ghost of a place. I found myself wondering if octoroon wraiths were walking elegantly through those dusty halls, and to what delicate piano-playing . . .

⤖ PO' WANDERIN' PILDOM, MISERUS CHILE ⬿

When Horace Mann Bond and Willis James regaled me with a report on their 1942 Summer Festival of Folk Music at Fort Valley, I was struck with envy. W. C. Handy, an honored guest, had played "St. Louis Blues" on his cornet, backed by a Georgia jam band of harmonica, guitar, and washboard. Buster Ezelle had sung "Salt Water Blues" to his own guitar playing, and then had played a one-man duet on guitar and a harmonica harnessed around his neck. The prize-winner for originality had played "John Henry" on a strand of haywire strung between two bricks on a plank. An inventor, this fellow certainly was going to have *his* music. But these were curiosities, Willis assured me: the real musical value of the festival lay in the guitar playing and singing.

My unconcealed envy touched the sympathies of my informants, who put their heads together, invited me down to Fort Valley State College to give a talk, and managed to raise traveling expenses so that the two prize-winning quartets of the Festival could again drive over from Macon.

They came in uniforms. "The Middle Georgia Singers," runners-up in the Festival, wore dark blue silk shirts, with MIDDLE GA running diagonally across, and a large S over the heart. All had on blue and white polka dot bow ties and spick and span white trousers. "The Silver Moons," the Festival winners, wore lighter blue silk shirts with a silver crescent over their hearts, silver bow ties, white sashes, and white trousers. The Middle Ga's had a fifth member of their quartet, not at all a fifth wheel because their tenor was accustomed to knocking himself out. In spite of his weak heart, I was told, he sang with such fervor that he often came near dying. The quartets tried to be good sports; but like a baseball team one had out-bid the other for a star performer. Moreover, the recent contest had been very close. Their applause for each other was at first polite, but it came hard, I could see. Then as each quartet warmed up, the applause of the other got colder and finally the applauders stopped clapping and just looked at each other.

The nine fellows were keen for the cutting contest (cutting in the musical sense). Each quartet was introduced by substantially the same rite; the spokesman stepped forward, and to rhythmic humming in the background, named his team: "The fourth to my left is Mr. C. E. Smith, my second bass; give him a cheer." The audience of Fort Valley summer school students came on with this come-on: "Mr. C. L. Bell, third from my left, is my first bass; give him a cheer . . . Mr. J. W. Walker, second from my left, is first tenor; give him a cheer . . . and last but not least, yours truly, H. P. Purnell, your announcer, second tenor and manager." He omitted the "Give him a cheer," but he got a good warm one anyway.

I had never heard singing exactly like this. Once or twice they imitated the Golden Gates, but their best style (and both quartets were as close in style as in quality) was a new type of harmonizing. Willis James denied indignantly that it had any kinship to barbershop quartets, and I should have had more sense and a better ear than to have used the term. He was so irritated that I missed getting exactly his characterization of the type of singing. And, of course, words have always been weak in conveying musical qualities. There was a great deal of swinging all around the melody, or ringing changes, of all sorts of weird chords. The range of voices was extreme; the tenor reaching high and grasping the note, the bass sinking lower and lower—playing with his hearers—"Will he reach it?"—then reaching that one easily, smiling faintly, and then, after a quick breath, submerging again. It was, of course, virtuosity. But after playing around, back to the melody the quartet would come, seriously and movingly, pumping bass and leaping tenor fused again as a driving unit.

It was a sad music they sang, replete with minors, less plaintive, however, than tragic. And though we knew these young fellows were having a good time at their singing, we could also see that they understood what they were singing about; and they drove it with power into the hearts of their listeners. They were good artists.

The Middle Georgia quartet started a prayer song, "Though I walk all night long, til I find the Lord." But this mounted from prayer to a weird yelling; the singers were tense and frowning, except for their leader who took it easy, and held the reins on them:

> The soul couldn't rest contented
> Until I find my-my-my-my-Lord . . . (Hold it, boy!)

Then they sang "What a Time," repeated with about as many melodic changes as they could work out:

> Well, what a time, Lord, Lord,
> Oh, what a time, Lord, Lord,
> I mean what a time, Lord, Lord, Lord, Lord,
> Great God A'mighty
> What a time!

When they blasted this in the recording mike later the record arm jumped about and furrowed the shellac.

But they sang with restraint, too: "Please Don't Drive Yo' Children Away":

Before dis time another year
Before dis time another year
I might be dead; I'll let you know
Before I go . . .
Sometimes my heart go leakin'
And tears come streamin' down . . .
I'm bowin' on my knees . . .
Before this time another year
I might be dead . . .
Please don't drive yo' children away . . .

The Silver Moons had one of the best versions of "Tone the Bell Easy" that I have heard:

Tone the bell, I'm done made it over
Tone the bell, I'm done made it over
Tone the bell, I'm done made it over
Done made it over at last . . .

I'm gonna talk with the Father, chat with the Son,
Tell him about the worl' that I come from
I'm gonna see Joshua wave to the sun
Don't move, sun (roared out the bass)
Tone the bell, I'm done made it over . . .

"Lord, take my hand," they sang, and "I saw dat train a-comin', She was a-movin' through de land," and "I'm goin' home wid de spirit in Jesus' name." Most of their numbers told about the promise of the other world under the protection of Jesus, and the trouble of this one. "I'm des a po' wanderin' pildom, miserus chile," was a line often repeated.

The Silver Moons did a brown-skin version of "Old McDonald Had a Farm," putting on a good show with the sound effects of the hog grunting, the calf bleating, and the flivver rattling. Not to be outdone, the Middle Ga.'s did the old minstrel favorite, "Watermelon on the Vine," and made it convincing, in the Land of the Georgia rattlesnake melon. Then they swung into "Ain't It a Shame." Little Bits, the second tenor, showed that he was quite an actor, bringing the house down:

Ain't it a shame
To whip yo' wife on Sunday.

And the quartet went into the motions of beating a wife, tossing off a dram of liquor, big-mouthed gossiping and telling lies, dancing the boogie, and shooting crap. All of those shames for Sunday were done in grand pantomime. The audience was led up skillfully to a seventh sin and shame, and then disappointed. That Little Bits was a mess.

After the first shyness wore off, and after they had seen that I was a friend of Willis James, they talked with me easily. Their dialect was difficult; I asked them to repeat for me the line that was running through my head:

I'm des a po' wanderin' pildom, miserus chile.

I finally made the words out to be pilgrim and misery's. That's just what they had been saying all along, they told me. I learned that they were Macon and middle Georgia boys, drawn together by a love for harmonizing, for playing around with chords and melodic breaks and rhythms. They hadn't gone far in school; all of them knew what it was to work at hard manual labor. One of them had done a little time in jail; another had been mixed up in trouble with some ornery white men. If singing was not their business, it at least was one of the most important things in their lives. They watched in fascination while the apparatus was set up to record their voices; when they sang into it the ease of their platform manner suddenly tautened. They posed readily for photographs, but the pictures, when they came out, showed their faces set morosely, their mouths grim, their eyes intent. It wasn't all the fault of the flash bulb, I am certain. Even Little Bits, a grand comedian if there ever was one, has only the shy beginning of a smile. I guess that the photographs, as much as anything else, helped me to understand the line that they had sung with so much feeling:

I'm des a po' wanderin' pildom, miserus chile.

⤜ JITTERBUGS' JOY ⤛

Before the war ban on bus traveling, Atlanta was a good city for one-night stands. Several Negro businessmen formed an entertainment company to sponsor Negro name-bands at the municipal auditorium. Under all-Negro management the affairs had only a comparative sprinkling of whites. But they weren't missed; the Negroes came in droves. As Al Moron, the manager of the housing project, complained to me, "Atlanta Negroes will turn out in crowds for only two things: a free revival in church and a pay dance at the auditorium."

The crowds that I saw at those dances were composed largely of high school youngsters, of teen age, or in the early twenties: the boys in polo shirts and full draped trousers; the girls in flowered print dresses, or snuggling sweaters, dark skirts, bright colored socks, and low-heeled shoes. The place belonged to them those nights, and they took the lid off.

Between numbers they screamed and chased each other about, but when the music started, they either went silently into their pirouetting, stamping routine, or pressed around the footlights, staring hungrily at the famous jazzmen, anticipating time-honored riffs, applauding triumphantly at some startling improvisation, more often taut and concentrating, slaves to the harmony and the rhythm.

They knew some of the songs by heart, those the juke-boxes had plugged, and they watched for the familiar breaks and solos. Often the bandleader had only to announce the number, as Louis Jordan did with "I'm Going to Move to the Outskirts of Town," and the wild welcome pealed. Jordan's sinuous alto sax could barely be heard over the roar of recognition. And so it was with Lionel Hampton's "Flying Home." Lionel had a band of youngsters, many from the West Coast who were on their first Southern trip. The band and the crowd rivaled each other in fervor; the cheering and the brilliant brass section seemed to be on a "cutting contest," until finally the lanky young trumpeter went into a screaming spiral that shocked the noisy kids into quiet. Lionel, grinning widely, knocked the crowd out with his dexterous pommelling on the vibraphone, and nearly knocked himself out in that heat. Sweat was pouring off his face when he came backstage; the handkerchief he was mopping with was soaking. But it was worth it. "Man, that bunch out there is a killer!" And he rushed back to give them that perennial favorite "On the Sunny Side of the Street":

> "Rich as Rockefeller . . . Gold dust at my feet, On the sunny side of
> the street . . ."

His hoarse, engaging jive voice caught their mood and held it. They loved Lionel, no doubt of that. And he was solidly in the groove that night.

I heard Louis Armstrong on one of his infrequent trips back South. He wasn't as roly-poly as I had seen him in New York; he was reducing, he said, getting shed of some of that old avoirdupois, but he looked tired and drawn as well. As he delicately wrapped the large handkerchief around that famous trumpet and took a couple of brilliant solos, the crowd cheered him. But he wasn't a jukebox favorite, and only the elder generation of listeners recognized and honored him as king. His scat-singing was old stuff now, part of the idiom of the high school kids themselves. And a lot of Harry James had come to them over the airwaves. Louis sang "When It's Sleepy Time Down South" in that gravelly voice that has so much warmth in it; then he and his sidemen joshed the words a bit, but it didn't quite click. "Folks down there live a life of ease": that wasn't the way these kids had heard it.

The night that Louis Armstrong played was a grand patriotic occasion. Attorney Walden urged the need for buying bonds; his clipped, dry speaking could barely be heard in the huge auditorium and was in contrast to the floridity and extravaganza that it interrupted. Graham Jackson, home-boy of Atlanta, a good pianist and accordion player, now recruiting officer for the Navy, appeared in the gleaming white uniform of a petty officer and gave a canned recruiting spiel. Then he turned and pumped old Satchmo's hand, exchanged a bit of jive talk, went over to the piano stool that Louis Russell gladly gave over to him, and showed his virtuosity on the keyboard. He was more enthusiastic here than while making his speech, and so was the crowd.

More whites were backstage to hear Louis Armstrong than on the other nights. There were soldiers and sailors with their girlfriends, hepcats all, some of them old friends of Louie's. You could hear his rasping voice all over the place: "What do you say, Gate!" "Well, if it ain't old so-and-so himself!" "Man, where you been all this time?" There was much shaking of hands and real camaraderie. Cliff McKay and I got to talking about how jazz tore down the walls. Some walls, anyway. We saw a white youngster stand back from the water fountain and say to a Negro, "You go ahead." Then he took his drink after the Negro. "You see that?" Cliff said. By themselves, or maybe in twos, they'll act O.K. When there are more than two they're scared of being called "nigger lovers."

I butted into an argument with two Negroes who were deciding who was the greatest clarinetist in the world. I learned later how foolish I was, as these were old cronies, one a garageman, the other an electrician, who enjoyed nothing more than making fools and liars out of each other. They both had a desire to play in jazz bands, and they both collected records. Their argument concerned Artie Shaw and Benny Goodman. I asked them about other clarinetists but they had never heard of Jimmy Noone and Sidney Bechet, and they knew little of Barney Bigard's solo work. Their argument ran that if these men I named were good, they would have been heard of, they would be in the big money, wouldn't they? When I admitted that Noone and Bechet, and even Bigard, were not in the big money as Shaw and Goodman were, they looked triumphant. "They just couldn't dig me, man."

A young white fellow eavesdropped on our talk, and followed me away. He was a real hepcat from way back. He had played alto saxophone with a couple of the lesser known bands. Yes, he knew Noone's and Bechet's work, very well. He was a native of Atlanta but had been all over the country. Now he was home, getting ready to go in the Coast Guard. He told over and over his experiences in the jazz world, naming with bushleaguer's wistfulness the top men he had met there. He stopped Louie and told him where and when he had heard him play. Louie was bluff and cordial, and gladly gave the boy an autograph. Then the boy asked him to play a number and dedicate it to him; he was going in the Coast Guard soon and it would be something to remember. Louie promised, "Sure thing, man," and rushed onstage. He didn't get around to playing the number, though, and the white boy hovered in the wings, melancholy and lost, on the edge of a world that once he had had great hope of entering.

I heard the Earl Hines concert from out front up in the gallery. That night Earl was in good form, truly Father Hines, spanking the keys with all sorts of tricky rhythms and chord sequences. Finally, his white smile and his patent leather hair gleaming, he walked to the footlights, and held out his hand. The crowd knew what was coming before he announced it. It was "Skylark," their greatest juke-box favorite. Billy Eckstine, in his rich throaty voice, called "Skylark!" And hysteria broke loose.

I knew the words, straight out of the romantic books: I had wondered how they ever managed the voyage from England to Broadway, those phrases about "someone waiting to be kissed" in "some meadow in the mist," some "valley green with spring where my heart can go ajourneying;" "shadows in the rain," "blossom covered lane," "wonderful music, vague as a will-o-the-wisp, crazy as a loon, sad as a gypsy serenading the moon." The skylark is told that the lover's heart is riding on its wings: if the skylark sees those beloved things anywhere—

"Won't you take me there?"

I knew that Eckstine's deep mellow singing, coupled with a fluent saxophone solo, did much to make the song popular. At first I wondered what these kids in their zoot suit drapes, their jitterbugging costumes almost as uniform as athletic suits, had to do with valleys green with spring, or meadows in the mist, or with Keats and Shelley, even disguised in Tin Pan Alley garb. What did these kids, lost in the cramped tenements of Atlanta's Darktown, have to do with skylarks? I wondered what twist "crazy as a loon" could have for them. But as Eckstine repeated his chorus on demand, I caught what I felt to be the simple, deeper meaning. The will-of-the-wisp and "the gypsy serenading the moon," business might be foreign, but the "lonely flight," "the wonderful music in the night," those phrases were their language, and something deep in these young ones answered.

After the sentimental "Skylark," Earl Hines knocked out some jump numbers. The dancing was almost weird. The kids were seriously intent. Some of the girls were chewing gum, but all kept their faces expressionless. The wilder the gyrations, the more casual were the masks. The couples were perfect teams, apparently unconscious of anybody else on the floor. But there were no collisions, though the whirling and pirouetting were constant. A couple would embrace, swing off, the girl would be thrown away, then she would prance back, they would turn from each other, then without looking their hands would meet, clasp, and back their bodies would come into momentary embrace—all in perfect timing, a swift, clean-cut beautiful work of art. She was always there, he was always there; each anticipating the other, each knowing the other's improvising. It all seemed so effortless and easy, but I knew better. These perfectly coordinated pairs had mastered their skill, their sixth sense of each other, only after hours of practice at home to phonograph records, I knew. Many couples did not ever split up, the same boy continuing to dance with the same girl all evening long. Supple and strong, the boys still would have been awkward fielding a baseball; the girls surely had had little chance in Atlanta for swimming or tennis; this was a cheaper, more available sport, and they were winners at it. It was far from the hugging dances of the early jazz age; it was impersonal, a parade of coordinated rhythms. Each couple strove for perfection, but they seemed oblivious of attention: they seemed rather lost to the world. I saw little of the acrobatics for which entertainers are paid at New York's Savoy; it was a much simpler, but still accomplished routine that satisfied these kids. Many of the boys kept their caps on their heads; this was dancing too important for etiquette. I looked down on the dance floor from the gallery. It was a heaving sea of heads, shoulders, arms, bodies, legs and feet sweeping in irregular regular waves. I passed a white policeman who was fascinated at the spectacle; his face was a study. He was seeing frenzy, true enough, but it had discipline in it and strength. I wondered what he was thinking.

There were only a few exhibitionists. Two of these couples were pansies, with long hair and loud-colored sateen shirts, wide open at the neck, and ringed with sweat. They wanted everybody to see them and they jitterbugged with grotesque exaggerations. But most of the kids were too busy to pay them attention. As long as the music lasted, they would swing their own time.

But when the music ended, the tense preoccupation snapped, the escape was done. Back the youngsters came to high-pitched talking and laughing and quarrelling, or sullen walking about. There were some fights; knives were drawn in a few. At "Home, Sweet Home," some couples, exhausted from dancing, stupefied with drink, had to be routed out of their gallery seats. As we came down the long tunnel-like passages from the gallery, we saw liquor bottles everywhere. Drunks lurched against us. Leaving the hall, we drew in deep breaths of the cool morning air. We knew the spell was over for these kids. Just in front of us we heard raised voices, then a smack, and we saw a girl slide to the ground and a policeman forcing his way roughly in the crowd. Girlfriends and boyfriends rode in the Black Maria that night.

We got to Frank's car just a bit ahead of the pansies, who in their soprano voices were cursing each other and threatening knife play. Safe in the car, Frank wondered why I never got scared attending such affairs. "Anything could happen," he told me. "Some of these Negroes would cut you as quick as they'd look at you." Frank had been one of the most courageous athletes Morehouse had ever had and I knew he didn't scare easily. He was right. Once the music ended, these crowds could be ugly and dangerous.

Frank was wrong in implying that I wasn't scared. I was, somewhat, but it was gloom rather than fear that I felt most deeply. I thought how often I had resented the charges against my people that they were merely happy, carefree dancers. This dancing had been skillful, certainly. But it wasn't free of care, the way I saw it; it was defiant of care instead. It was a potent drug, a reefer smoke, a painkiller shot in the arm.

Tomorrow was coming for these kids with a sick thud. On their way back to their slum homes in Darktown, Ward 4, "Pittsburgh," some of them packed in jalopies, many more trudging the unlighted, unpaved streets; they knew what to look for tomorrow. The jazz and jitterbugging had warmed the damp and the darkness this night, but tomorrow had already set in: a tomorrow of crowded homes, poor food, dull work, little play and that snatched on the fly, and nothing to look forward to with any zest. Many of the boys would be in the Army soon; what they had heard of that left them cold; and who knows what the hell comes next? The girls would grow up, they'd have their babies and bring them up in the same rickety shacks with the same worries about rent and food and clothing; and then they'd get to be like their mothers whose bitter scoldings and curses were soon to greet them. They were not alone: many white kids of America, Depression's children too, knew the same hopelessness and uncertainty; they often sought the same escape. They swooned over Sinatra as these had raved over Billy Eckstine.

But these Atlanta kids weren't aware of that, and even if they had been, it wouldn't have altered their feelings. They had to grab their joy where they found it and hold on frenziedly, today. Tomorrow was another day, and from all they could see, was likely to be a hell.

➤ FROM MONTMARTRE TO BEAVER SLIDE ➤

The Writers' Project Guide to Atlanta tags on to its list of artists the name of Hale Woodruff, as the city's exponent of Negro Art. He is, of course, nothing of the kind: he is the best and best known artist in the state, and incidentally a Negro. Years ago Ralph McGill, of the *Atlanta Constitution,* spoke of Woodruff as a recent discovery only in Atlanta. It is likely that much of dominant Atlanta still is ignorant of his fine work. This is not likely to bother Hale much, in a city whose chief art treasures are the Diorama of the Battle of Atlanta, and such statues as Tom Watson pitching horseshoes in front of the State Capitol or Henry Grady reaching for something at Grady Square.

Hale isn't easily bothered anyway. When I talked with him in the dilapidated library building on Morris Brown's campus, he didn't seem abashed by the bare wreck of a place but explained to me how the dome provided ideal light for working.

Later his department was moved back to the Spelman College campus. There I found him in a makeshift studio kidding with Smitty, the superintendent of buildings, wheedling him and counterblasting. Smitty is unimpressed by Hale's international reputation, but I could see that Hale would get his walls fixed right.

Hale is a modernist painter, a careful student first of French techniques, later of Diego Rivera's. Instead of artistic jargon, however, he talks with good Midwestern and Southern pungency: "Man, I saw this gal walking down the railroad track in a red fuzzy sweater. She must have weighed about 185 or 190 lbs. She had a form-fitting sweater on those mountains and hips. Doggone if she didn't look like the back-end of a freight train."

Without "hi-falutin" language, Hale clarifies some of the difficulties of his paintings to the layman.

"Look at this arm and hand. I wanted them to suggest inner qualities of those women. I didn't want a photograph. I wanted a sort of primitive style in keeping with the nature of these people and their lives."

The fellows josh Hale when he boasts of his connoisseurship in things Parisian, reminding him that he went to Paris and stayed there on a shoestring. But the joshing has respect in it for spunk and grit. No sooner did Hale win a hundred dollar Harmon Award for Negro artists, than he sailed for Paris. He spent four tough years there as an art student. President John Hope found him stranded in 1931 and hired him for the new Atlanta University system. Five years later he jumped off again, this time for Mexico where he studied with Diego Rivera.

Hale Woodruff is most widely known for his murals in the Savery Library at Talladega College in Alabama. The first set of these frescoes celebrates the centenary of the slave revolt aboard the *Amistad*. In vivid colors, Woodruff portrays in panel one the mutinous blacks swinging wide-bladed machetes and throttling the slavers while white crewmen flee the vessel. The second panel shows the trial at New Haven with Cinque, the Mandingo leader of the revolt, and Ruiz, the Spanish buccaneer, dominating the scene. One of the slaves, quizzically scrutinizing the proceedings behind the abolitionists Arthur Tappan and Roger Baldwin, is an unflattering likeness of Hale Woodruff himself. The third panel shows the return of the freed Mandingoes to native Africa with white and Negro missionaries. The episode of the *Amistad* resulted in the formation of the American Missionary Association which founded Fisk and Atlanta universities, and Straight, Tougaloo, and Talladega colleges.

The second set of frescoes celebrates the founding of Talladega College, a less blood-stirring but no less dramatic history. The first panel shows how the American Missionary Association used its good offices between the defense of the *Amistad* captives and the Civil War. Whites are shown advising and speeding fugitive slaves on their way to the banks of the Ohio. While old Negroes huddle, frightened, one bold Negro astride a plunging horse tears down the announcement of a runaway slave, before starting after a laden coach careening to the riverbank. Far away at the top of a hill, a slave hunter is riding his horse, hell-bent for leather, following the bloodhounds.

The second panel shows the new freedmen swarming on the campus of the newly opened college, registering with the white instructors. Behind those white columns in a mansion that had once housed aristocratic scions were secrets long withheld from the ex-slaves. At their feet are strange tuition payments: sacks of potatoes, crates of chickens, bundles of cane. One old man brought a half dollar in a handkerchief. William Savery, after whom the library was named, is one of the central Negroes in the panel. Two of Savery's daughters became teachers, and his grandson was a recent student at Talladega.

The third panel shows black and white workers constructing Savery Library. Hale sketched these while they were laboring. He respects President Buell Gallagher for "sticking his chin out and hiring whites and Negroes to work side by side on the same pay basis." The panel has much to say about industrial democracy.

Hale believes modestly that the murals give the students a sense of history. One Negro educator at the dedication exercises admitted that the *Amistad* frescoes made him discard his mild speech and "give the blood and thunder one." These murals pack a heavy wallop, artistically and educationally. To youngsters whose history books never touched upon anything like a revolt of Negroes for freedom, who think of the Underground Railroad, if they have ever heard of it, as a sort of tunnel under the Ohio River, these panels of Negroes organizing and carrying through a mutiny, of grabbing their belongings and escaping to free land must come as shocks. It is important also that they see Negroes, not browbeaten, in a law court, being defended by white friends, and that they see spirited Negroes being aided by whites against a mob. It is also good that they see an important artist treating poor and ordinary Negroes with dignity and warmth. Finally, it is an educational step that these students learn that Cinque's manly defiance, the fugitives' bold determination, the ex-slaves' eagerness for learning, the draughtman's studiousness, could be discovered, without much searching, within the borders of their own lives.

Hale Woodruff has been a busy man, with his mural work, his teaching, and his frequent assignments. When I talked with him last, he was painting a portrait of Alonzo Herndon for the Atlanta Life Insurance Company. He has even done a puckishly fanciful fresco for the Yates and Milton Drug Store, where the collegians of the Atlanta University system foregather. I once overheard young Josephine and Joe College discuss the mural's manifold meanings; it would have done good to Hale's sense of humor. A social documentary small mural decorates one of Atlanta's Housing Projects for Negroes. It is rather simple propaganda. Before: An Atlanta slum, much like Beaver Slide, with drunk, impoverished people, their children growing up like weeds. After: The Housing Project is flourishing, gardens and all; plump, clean kids are at play, grown-ups look better-fed, more self-respecting. There is a big black something in this ointment, however. Under the mural is a heavy black metal piece of sculpture, caricaturing a Negro banjo-player. It looks like an ambitious hitching post. The story goes that more money went to the white artist who messed up all that metal, than to Hale Woodruff for his murals. "Where shall we put it?" asked one of the housing authorities, in embarrassment. "Put it in the toilet," said the Negro adviser.

Hale's art classes are popular and productive. Several of his students, such as Wilmer Jennings, Fred Flemister, and Albert Wells, are achieving recognition. Many of his students, however, pay him the flattery of dangerously close imitation. Hale's friends hope that his heavy teaching load and assignments will not compress too narrowly his creativeness.

Georgia opened Hale Woodruff up, as it did Jean Toomer between whose expression in prose and Woodruff's in painting there seems to me to be important similarity. After a sojourn below Macon, Hale said, "The people in deep Georgia look like they sprung right out of the ground. Like they weren't raised in houses." Hale's love of color is requited in Georgia with its clays of all shades of red, its deep green foliage, its blue and purple skies, its white massed clouds. Best known, probably, among his paintings are his heavy oil landscapes, tortuous and foreboding. Georgia shanty towns have no better interpreter. One watercolor shows shacks of all the hues of the rainbow on a red clay hillside, as colorful and troubling as sinister tropical blooms. Another shows an old woman, her arms filled with sticks of kindling, returning to her leaning box of a house, the tin porch propped by the slenderest, buckling pole. Vari-colored shacks are clustered precariously in the background. The trees are blasted, the earth eroded; in spite of the beautiful colors, the impact of barren waste and loneliness is terrifying.

Hale's early painting "The Banjo Player" was decorative, rather than interpretative. His lithograph "Ambulant Musicians" is much more deeply rooted. "Trusty on a Mule" and "Blind Musician" catch familiar Georgia scenes faithfully but with imaginative lift. "Country Church," with its swaying roof, its clapboard sides, its door awry, sums up the pathos of the weatherworn shacks so much a part of the Georgia landscape. On the top of a rise, Hale has painted an outhouse, propped by a sturdy pole. So many of his drawings have this bit of local architecture that some of his friends call it his hallmark, and he boasts of starting the Out House School, in distinction to the earlier ash-can school of American art. One of his most sardonic lithographs is "Relics": a sway-backed mule on his last legs stands beside a sway-backed stable. The mule's ribs are repeated in the ramshackle sides of the building. It tells me as much as many pages of books on the Economic Problem No. 1. A lithograph done for the anti-lynching campaign is "By Parties Unknown." A lynched Negro, the noose still around his broken neck, has been left on the wooden steps of a country church, which may have painted windows but is otherwise falling to pieces.

Hale has a flair for urban backgrounds and people too. He has fine sketches of women whose most colorful garb sometimes clashes, sometimes harmonizes with the various shades of their brown skin. He observes the parade of life down such streets as Hunter and Mason Turner with humor and sympathy. In a recent painting he tries to get deeper into Atlanta life, trying to show real religious feeling at a foot-washing ceremony. He wants the picture "to be symbolic, not cliché, not the usual religious church painting, not a snapshot of a particular church." I think he succeeds. While an old patriarch watches, his eyes partly closed, his hands folded, a woman in ceremonial garb, serving with a crooked peaceful smile, washes the feet of another massive sister, who is blissfully, quietly, caught by the spirit. Light, as if from heaven, shines in the center of the picture. The old mastery of colors, green, olive, yellow, brown, purple, white, is apparent. Hale is proud of the browns in the women's faces and arms, a sort of earthy brown. "I put a lot of red in it," he said. "I tried to give it richness and luminosity."

Hale Woodruff has taken seriously his art and the life of his people. He is generous to his fellow Negro artists, speaking critically only when he feels that they are "sitting down on their reputation as *Negro* artists." He has received honors and he deserves even more. One of his honors, however, was not an unmixed blessing.

He was invited to become a member of the Georgia Artists Association, to submit a painting and to attend the annual meeting at Athens. When Lamar Dodd, professor of art there, learned he was coming up, he invited Hale to speak to his class of thirty or forty students. Then Hale attended the meeting of the fifteen or twenty delegates. The social committee had prepared a luncheon for the out of town members. "When they were about to serve luncheon," says Hale, "and everybody was about to walk in, I was asked if I would mind eating in the kitchen. Man, you could have knocked me over with a feather. I said, 'No thanks. I have friends in the city who have invited me to eat dinner with them.' I pulled out of Athens on the next train; I don't know whether they had any afternoon meeting or not."

The way Hale saw it, Lamar Dodd seems fair when it comes to art; he would have a Negro whom he considers a first-rate painter and lithographer lecture to his class and advise his students. Yet he would ask this same Negro to eat in the kitchen. Maybe it was fear of offending his superiors at the University. "Lecturing on art: O.K." said Hale. "Drinking a glass of milk together: No."

But Hale Woodruff doesn't fret too much about this type of incident, and doesn't need to. As he says often in quite another connection, "He'll get them all on the back-raise."

Men of War

Despite more recent claims that the embrace of American political and social values by 1940s advocates of racial integration was a wrongheaded, if not a self-flagellated, vision of racial denial, Brown, in "Men of War," anticipates what many of his generation steadfastly pursued as their inherent rights, guaranteed by constitutional decree. From this angle of vision, this section might productively be considered a distilled representation of political perspectives that Brown collected at the height of World War II when the nation rallied around the cry "V for Victory." In fact, if "Out of Their Mouths" presents firsthand testimony of the varied responses of blacks to the racist conditions during World War II, "Men of War" represents Brown's interpretive record, his showcase of black patriotic efforts supporting the war effort.

No doubt the problematic reality facing Brown demanded a response that would allow for a conversation encouraging sympathetic consideration instead of antagonism and confrontation. This goal would not enable him to follow the lead established by Billie Holiday's "Strange Fruit" and Josh White's *Southern Exposure, An Album of Jim Crow Blues* (with lyrics by Richard Wright), both of which were emotionally charged works of social protest. Like the singers, he found himself opposing a mistaken but omnipresent social Darwinist view that blacks were incompetent, incapable, and indolent. However, Brown chose to expose the lie, to refute prevailing racist assumptions by using exemplary instances of black success. When the question was asked in the February 1939 *Congressional Record* "if a Negro could really fly a plane," Brown found in this ill-informed question an effective strategy for organizing "Men of War." Thus the three pieces that constitute this section resonate, thematically, with a necessary racial promotion, showcasing exemplary black talent and accomplishment. Here we find multiple examples of demonstrated black racial excellence: men flying planes, building the Tuskegee Army Air Field, and successfully managing enormous government contracts.

"Soldiers" in the title "Soldiers of Construction" is a deliberate play on the term designating the service personnel of the Army, Navy, and Air Force who were then facing enemy gunfire in the European, Northern African, and South Pacific theaters. Like their more physically threatened compatriots, the construction managers and workers sacrificed themselves to prove a point: "that the government [recognize] the Negro as part of American democracy." During the era of Jim Crow, when every instance of black achievement was cited as evidence of African American worth, the soldiers of construction established a laudable record of completing work. In addition to patriotism and racial pride, part of the incentive to do well was simply personal. Building Tuskegee Air Base meant that some black college graduates trained in engineering and related areas found themselves able, for the first time, to use their education for jobs in which they were superbly trained. Nonetheless, all workers understood what was at stake in their labor: "If the Negro proves his case down here, he'll open the doors elsewhere."

"Cubs" not only takes its name from the small Piper J-3 airplanes used to train beginning airmen; it also signifies the youthful inexperience of its trainees. Overall, the narrative, although rather brief, places the reader into the world of black pilots. In this world, safety is preached over and again, like a mantra. One crucial error might "bring down the curtain." Part of the value of this piece is the marvelous tall tale it contains. Pilots flying the cubs navigated by spotting landmarks, not by using instruments. On one occasion, a novice pilot missed the marker denoting Tuskegee and wound up flying all the way to Florida. His reception there was a combination of awe, envy, and bewilderment. Ralph Ellison would take a version of this narrative and craft a marvelous short story, "Flying Home."

In "Primary Field," Brown distills personal observation and recorded history about the establishment of the Tuskegee Army Air Field, a topic later covered at length in Robert J. Jakeman's *The Divided Skies: Establishing Segregated Flight Training at Tuskegee, Alabama, 1934–1942* (1992). From his much closer vantage point, Brown constructs a narrative that brings the human essence of this history to the reader. An article titled "Writer Visits TAAF during Tour of the South," published in the *Afro-American* (20 December 1944), contains a photograph of Brown surrounded by five members of the publicity staff at the airfield. Brown's chats with these and other airmen enabled him to locate the human side of the story of the war. "Primary Field," in brief, shows what African Americans could do, if given a chance.

Without specific mention, Brown makes this section reflect the midwar national black initiative called the "Double V Campaign." While African Americans were stubbornly seeking to participate in the nation's war effort at home and abroad, they were confronted by many resisters who fought just as tenaciously to preserve the racial status quo. African Americans understood the war as a fight to ensure a democratic way of life for all citizens of America. Thus, largely through the African American press, they launched the Double V campaign—victory abroad and victory at home. In effect, one imperative of this initiative called for a national public policy to "close ranks." However, this did not merely translate into ignoring domestic social problems in favor of a unified war effort. Instead, the Double V campaign sought to guarantee that the freedoms that African American soldiers fought for in the European, African, and Asian theaters would also be granted to them at home. Part of this struggle meant dismantling the structure of codes and practices that sustained racial separation in the armed services, in effect showing how a desegregated military could serve invaluably in desegregating American society. "Men of War" suggests something of this rich but conflicted history.

➤ SOLDIERS OF CONSTRUCTION ◄

The ten mile drive from the town of Tuskegee to the Air Base was along a typical Alabama backroad; a winding gravel and dirt road full of holes, crossing streams, some of them unbridged, and others with shaky, narrow bridges that I wondered how Army trucks could get across. There were fields of scraggly cotton, patches of underbrush, and woods, dusty near the road, and shacks and barns weather gray and askew. Chehaw was only slightly stirring from its long sleep. A few piles of Army stores, a barbed wire enclosure of gas and oil tanks, the Primary Field laying over to the right, none too prominent; these were the only signs of the new activity.

But at the bridge over the winding creek, the end of one world came, and another world began. On this side of the creek was a typical rural church, unshaded in a bare plot of ground. On the other was the guard post with smart military police stopping cars and trucks and then waving them on.

Looking at the air base, I wondered how in the back hills of Alabama such a perfect site for a camp could have been discovered. I was to learn later that the site was man-made. Light yellow buildings with green roofs centering about a large building with streets radiating off as spokes from a wheel were clustered on a slope; at the foot stretched the buildings, hangars, and towers of the line and the long concrete runways. A couple of planes looking like silver fish were aloft, glinting in the sun.

A phone call cleared my entering. The well-built highway, so different from the backroad we had traveled, stretched on newly made, newly leveled land, still raw clay, up the hill, past another MP station to the hub of the camp, the headquarters building.

One of my first interviews was with Calvin McKissack, whose firm had been responsible for the construction of the base, the largest building job that had been granted to Negro builders by the Defense Program.

Calvin McKissack called the soldiers at the air base, whether officers, non-coms, or privates, an exceptionally fine group of fellows. "It is more of a university system than an Army camp," he said. And so I found it. From the moment of my arrival there, when Hayden Johnson, adjutant of the 99th Squadron, now overseas in the Mediterranean Theater, called out of the window, "Well, if it ain't the Flying Dutchman himself," I found the warmest welcome. There were bull sessions, group gatherings, private confabs; I saw ex-students, ex-colleagues, old friends; I made new friends. Almost everyone had a tale to tell, or a job he wanted me to inspect. I got badly trounced at ping-pong in one of the soldiers' recreation halls; I heard some odd homegrown boogie-woogie trounced out by a determined buck private, who was more interested in his own left hand than in my yarns about Pete Johnson, Al Ammons, and Meade Lux. Officers or enlisted men, they wouldn't let me use my nickels in the fascinating machine that threw Coca-Cola bottles out at you. I drank so many Cokes that I felt that I would fizz away in that August heat.

The building job was in the last stretch, and McKissack was not too busy to show me around. I found him to be the same quiet, philosophical friend I had known years ago in Nashville. He is grayer now, but he seems no less vigorous. Unlike his brother Moses, who is a fountain of jests and whopping tall tales, Calvin McKissack talks little and then slowly and carefully. The cast of his face is brooding and sad, that of a man who has seen a great deal and has thought about it a long time.

He told me that really to appreciate what was there now, I should have seen the place before the bulldozers came. He pointed to the surrounding countryside and said that the camp had had the same rolling contours, similar hills and woods and thick undergrowth. There had been a cemetery on a hill, dating back before the Civil War, apparently a mixed graveyard with both white and colored buried there. He traced some designs on the sand, showing me where a swamp had been and how the course of a stream had been changed.

Yes, it had been quite different. And now, in the core of the Alabama hills, the post was about completed, and had of course been in service for months. So many million yards of dirt moved, shifted; waterworks, sewage disposal works, electrical distributors constructed; streets laid out, and what would be miles of pipe, miles of wiring, and many, many miles of highway if the runways and streets were laid end to end. It was an interesting growth, and he had seen it from the first bulldozers nuzzling into the hills, to the present. We heard a faint roar back on the line; a P-45 was zooming down the long runway; up above, three planes were skimming along against the bright blue sky.

A sweaty Negro near the sewage disposal plant looked up as we came by. "Hullo," Calvin said in his bass voice. "Do you have a match?" The man gave him a dirty packet; Calvin crumpled off some of his homespun twist into his corncob pipe, and lighted it. He talked briefly to the man. "Yassuh," the respectful fellow said over and over. "You welcome." The big boss was obviously well liked.

"It does a fellow good sometimes to be working for his own folks," Calvin said, cannily figuring out what I was thinking. Then he told me how the job gave openings that were all but closed throughout the nation: "Even cities like Washington or New York City don't have Negroes working at skilled jobs in public utilities. So I wanted you to see this." In the sewage plant, testing the sludge for bacteria content, there was a young fellow whose face and whose name I remembered. He was a graduate of the Howard University Engineering School, only a few years out of school. It was an ill-smelling job, and he wouldn't shake my hand, but I could see that he was happy. He was having a chance to do what he had been trained to do; much responsibility for the health of the base depended on his scientific knowledge. He explained the Imholl Tank, the Dosing Chamber, the Filter Bed, the functions of chlorines with learned pride; he was glad to see another Howardite, but he excused himself to go back to his analyzing.

He was a good signpost to the future, Calvin McKissack told me. The average Negro boy in college couldn't see a future in this kind of work: "It's a bread and meat proposition with them. They don't see any chance for these skills, so they crowd into medicine, the ministry, and teaching. Colored boys had such hard going getting into the Defense Program. They have always had trouble in getting a chance to handle big affairs on their own. They want a feeling of belonging, want something of the say-so about how things are being run." He took pride, quite reasonably, I thought, in the openings that this construction job had afforded trained Negro personnel. From general superintendent down to foremen and unskilled laborers, the job was all colored. "If the Negro proves his case down here, he'll open the doors elsewhere.

"The Negro has all along been saying, 'I can do it, I can do it.' But what the government really wants to hear is 'See what I've done.'

"A year ago, nobody would talk cold turkey on a job like this; some didn't want Negroes, others didn't believe that Negroes could lay out plans and then carry them out. Can Negroes build an air base; can Negroes operate it once it's built?

"We never became uneasy. They were curious about steam fitting, for instance. Well, we put a crew of Negro steam fitters on the job. When the first engines kicked off, we didn't have any trouble then or ever since. They asked us how many white mechanics we would need. We said, none. The Army was not sure we could do the job, and sent in a lot of inspectors. They were always sitting down watching, expecting to see a bunch of lazy Negroes. We went right ahead. One high Army officer was asked 'When are you coming down to see how we are getting along?' He said, 'Well I'll tell you, I was down last week. I flew down. It looks like you're doing all right.' Nobody expected Negroes to finish such a job on time."

We stood watching a gang of men "pouring a wall" at a far end of the line. They were scurrying about, pushing loads of cement in wheelbarrows equipped with fat rubber tires. "So that's where the rubber goes," I said. "Those are the first Georgia buggies I ever saw with tires on them." Calvin and the foremen chuckled. The men would dump a load and race back to the loaders with their empty barrows bouncing. There was much yelling and laughter. I wondered if their speed was due to the presence of the big boss, but when I looked at the foreman I reckoned not. He was an able man, I could see that. He boasted that from nine to four-thirty, in one day, his men would pour eight hundred foot of wall. They looked fast enough to do it.

"Well the work has gone along on schedule; there is no kick about the quality; the cost has fallen within the estimated amount. We haven't ripped out ten feet of lumber. The Mayor of Tuskegee had been skeptical, but he called it a feat nothing short of miraculous. We're satisfied with our job, but we are most satisfied that the government recognizes the Negro as part of American democracy."

The area engineer, a captain of the United States Engineers, had told me something of the difficulties. The McKissacks had sublet the land operations, being primarily builders, without the bulldozers, draglines, clam shells, power shovels, etc., that were necessary to clear a swamp, change a river's course, clip off a hill here, and grade another there. Besides the natural engineering problems, much of the construction was done during the winter when the weather had to be fought. The engineer gave me figures on the average amount of dirt moved in one day, and one record twenty-four hours of removal; he was obviously impressed at a good job done.

He praised Calvin McKissack as a man "who knew how to play his cards smart." At the peak of the job there were three thousand white and colored employed; at one time the McKissacks had twenty-five hundred of their own workers employed. Men were drawn from all over the Southeast, from as far off as Memphis and lower Florida. There had been no labor and no race difficulties. The safety record was a very good one; for four months they had held the safety banner, and he named a staggering number of man hours in which there had been no loss of time due to injury. He insisted that I make no specific references to his figures.

The Tuskegee Air Post was as Army posts go, but it was equal in quality to any other, answering exactly the high Army engineering qualifications. The runways were as good as could be found anywhere; and so were the sewage disposal, the waterworks, the layout, the buildings (hangars, observation towers, barracks, mess halls, kitchens, administrative buildings, hospital, the chapels, the Post Exchanges, the technical buildings, the theatres, etc.). The captain praised it as a model job of construction.

The McKissack and McKissack Company, certainly unusual in America, is the outgrowth of a family business in existence over seventy-five years. The grandfather of the McKissacks was a master builder far back in slavery days; their father was a prominent builder in his day and time; their uncle was a brick man in Athens, Ga. The whole family is involved in the building profession; Moses junior is a registered architect, and Calvin's wife is the daughter of another builder. The concern, licensed in all Southern states, has done much work all over the South, including many public buildings. It is not so well known as might be. "Religiously," said Calvin, "Moses and myself have stayed out of the public eye as much as we can. The less newspaper publicity, the better for all concerned. We are ready, however, for our friends to see what we have done."

The single white employee whom I ran across was the office manager. He was spoken of as a job organizer who brought great experience to the McKissacks, part of which he had gained as secretary of Caldwell and Co., the large, well-known firm in Nashville. "We have to make use of all the other fellows' risks and experiences," Calvin explained. This manager was valuable as contact man also; working chiefly in the deep South, the McKissacks knew the minority technique. He was affable and voluble; he advertised McKissack and McKissack as "a contracting organization with the talent, resources, facilities required to design, layout, and construct Government Defense Projects and other diversified construction, supplying both architectural and engineering services." By that time I knew all that myself.

John D. Reed, the personnel manager, had been a protégé of Booker T. Washington. He stayed so busy that he was called "the whirling Dervish." Calvin McKissack said that one of his problems had been that of housing, though it had not proved to be so grave since many of the workers from the neighboring sections had been living in doghouses anyway. But Reed had done a good job in getting this large labor force into sanitary quarters and in keeping morale high.

I walked around with Reed, finding it hard under the blazing August sun to keep up with his swift walking and enthusiastic talking. He introduced me to a few key workers. One whom I remember was named Jenkins. He was a huge brick-red Negro, six feet three inches tall, with a pleasant freckled face shaded by a sun helmet. He weighed over two hundred, and looked to be solid muscle, a good chip off of John Henry's block. When not working as foreman for the McKissacks, he was preacher of a Baptist church in a small Florida town. Calvin McKissack had just given him a leave to go to the Baptist Convention in Memphis.

"Have I anything to say about Mr. McKissack?" he answered my question. "I don't know what to say about him. I just don't have any words to tell you. He's a great man, that's all. Only way he can get shed of me is to fire me.

"I'll tell you something. I'm pastor of a little church. When I got my letter from Mr. McKissack, I asked my church for a leave of absence. If they hadn't give it to me I was going to resign. You know when a preacher is willing to give up his church, he really must have heard a call."

Reed asked me to say a few words to the men at their meeting that afternoon at quitting time. I sat on the small platform with them and the office manager; their talks were on keeping the safety record, on buying bonds for victory. I forget what I said except that I was surprised and happy at the grand job of construction that they had done, and that the world outside looked on them, just as it did on the boys servicing the planes and flying them, as showing what we could do, once given a chance. I repeated Reed's name for them: "Soldiers of Construction." My talk was floundering, but those fellows, old and young, dirty and sweaty, veteran hands at construction, and college boys, illiterate and educated, gave me cheer on cheer. Many crowded about the platform and wrung my hands. I know it wasn't because the speech was any good; it was rather their own pride in a hard job well done and their hope that somehow the good news of it would reach out to other parts of the world.

➤➤ CUBS ◄◄

Without difficulty Lieutenant Marchbanks, medical officer of the primary field at Tuskegee, obtained permission for me to hang around the headquarters room. There was a board indicating times of flight and records of the flyers. A placard read: "Don't forget that aviation is not unsafe, but like the sea is terribly unforgiving of any carelessness or neglect." A cartoon showing a torn-up house, its chimney off, and the tail of an airplane sticking out of it, told of "A Very Hot Pilot":

> *A very hot pilot was Henry Hightowers*
> *Who boasted of having three hundred hours*
> *To prove it he dove on his girl's house one day*
> *They would have been married the fifteenth of May.*

In spite of these warnings, the flyers had made some mistakes, as indicated by gold stars beside their names. Mistakes were inevitable. Nevertheless, as instructor Charley Woods told me, it didn't take but one mistake to bring down the curtain. Extra severity in marking the cadets might save trouble later. Charley was a tall, slim, nonchalant chap, with whom I could talk easily, especially when he recited a few stanzas of my Slim Greer poems. He had the reputation of being one hell of a fine pilot.

Through the window I watched the cadets in their parachute harnesses and goggled helmets walking toward their training planes, or dismounting from them, the propellers making a last few tired spins. They strode toward the building, feeling good, I guess because of the additions to their total hours in the air. Quite a group finally got together in the room. They were as courteous as I found all officer material at the camps; they said "Sir" in a way that made me feel vaguely uncomfortable, outside of their real concerns. When they identified themselves they stood up like school boys reciting. Things warmed up after we discovered people and places that we knew in common.

Most of them were college chaps; one young fellow had heard me talk at Morgan College, and others had studied under friends of mine. They were typically young Brown America, a few were ruddy and tan, a few were dark, most were brown. Three had been drafted and had worked their way up to being recommended for the Air Corps. One, a school teacher, had been attempting all along to get in the Air Corps, but he had been told and retold: "There is no place for the Negro in the Air Corps." Now he had his chance. Another had had his leg broken when a bulldozer snapped over on it; when his leg mended he went to Chanute Field and served as airplane mechanic, then he was sent here to qualify as pilot. One, though young, had been a coal miner; he had left a wife and kid back in Birmingham; he had built them a house and was now concerned about "keeping all those little wolves away from my door."

As a plane roared down to a landing and taxied to the ramp, their eyes would follow it, and the talk would stop abruptly. But soon they took up the slack and were in the middle of kidding and tall tales. One was joked about his dancing; he explained it simply, "She was trying to do an Immermann, and I was doing a Chandelle." They told me that they didn't like clouds; there were too many P-40's flying around here, ripping through the air at 300 miles an hour. There had been no mid-air crashes, which nearly always proved fatal. In the clouds you don't know up from down. They fly by field contact, with no air speed indicator. Everybody gets lost at some time or other in his training.

The best yarn on being lost was told by a young cadet without too much embarrassment, and I imagine with some garnishing. He had been attempting to spot Tuskegee by its white water tower, but as he got closer to the first tower he couldn't see other distinctive landmarks so he kept on. Another tower, same thing. He kept flying, heading for a white water tower. Finally, the trail of water towers (he didn't know this was a distinctive mark of many Southern towns) carried him all the way to Florida. He was forced to land in a cow pasture. As he bounced to a stop, wondering where he was and what he was going to do, a little white boy stuck his head over the wing of the plane and barked out, "Are you a Jap?" The cadet proved to the little boy, and to all the gathering crowd, that he was an American. Everybody turned out to see the marvel. One old colored woman looked disapprovingly at the plane. "Humph," she said, "Never get me in one of those thaings."

For a forced landing, the order was to set your plane down and stick with it. The cadet did this, and got word back to the primary field. The next day, a rescue plane reached him. His buddies added details that they said they learned from the rescuing lieutenant and pilot. When they found their lost sheep, he was seated in his plane, with a picnic spread out on the wing: a thermos bottle with lemonade, sandwiches, cake, everything. And some young white ladies were waiting on him. He brought the leftovers, some canned goods and sandwiches, back in his plane.

The cadet was a bit sheepish at the enlargements his mates made on his story, but he admitted the general truth.

John Pinkett and Charley Woods told me how the cadets concentrated their working hours and perhaps their sleeping hours on the tough job they were mastering. "They say 'Allah' as they walk by a plane, and salaam slightly. They are models of military decorum, saluting all the time and saying 'Sir' to every-body before they get their wings. But once they get them, they're hell in britches."

(*Brown's note*: All of these cubs who made it—and most did—have now seen service in the Mediterranean Theater. In all probability their success is well-known to readers of *Phylon*.)

➤➤ PRIMARY FIELD ◄◄

John circled low over a patch of woods, landed on a large field, and jockeyed to the large hangar. Since it was Sunday, there weren't many people about, but I met several mechanics, electricians, and a licensed parachute rigger. John named the planes for me: a Howard, nicknamed DGA for "damned good aeroplane"; a dismantled Stinson, a rugged, reliable load carrier; several Luscombes, Wacos, and small yellow Cubs for pilot training. John showed me the Link trainer for blind flying and described it: "They put you in, pull down the hood, and you get every sensation of flying. You're supposed to learn to fly entirely by instruments."

At the field, cadets receive primary training under civilian instructors furnished by Tuskegee Institute under contract with the Army. The training is supervised by the Army, the maintenance by Tuskegee Institute. The general manager is G. L. Washington, formerly director of mechanical industries at Tuskegee. He told me a great deal of the history and purposes of the field.

He had corralled Negroes from all over the country from Boston to Texas: pilots, airplane engineers, men trained in Civil Aeronautics, mechanics, all the many technicians needed not only for teaching flying but also to service engines, aircraft, and manage the multiple duties connected with aeronautics. The staff met all the standards. The prevailing attitude had been that of the skeptic who asked in the *Congressional Record* for February 1939 "if a Negro could really fly a plane," though at that time there were approximately three hundred licensed Negro pilots. The Army naturally made frequent investigations to see that the field met the strict stipulations, and, every time, maintenance and training came up to snuff.

On January 16, 1941, the radio announced that pursuit pilot training was to be set up for Negroes at Tuskegee. This historic decision came only after many trips to Washington, conferences, and investigations. There were also conflicts. Judge Hastie, then civilian aide to the Secretary of War, was firmly opposed to the establishment of a separate unit. He insisted that Negroes should be included in other training units all over the country. Washington stated that Hastie had kept his clear-cut stand all down the line; Washington had less respect for some other opposing forces who were willing to accept a segregated base, but merely wanted it in their locality. President Patterson had been doggedly determined to have a primary field at Tuskegee, in spite of all the blasts about segregation. His trustees backed him up, and since such a project demanded sponsorship of the kind that Tuskegee could afford, and since Tuskegee was in a good weather area where training could be given for twelve months, the Air Forces gave the contract to Tuskegee. President Patterson kept his closest touch with the activities of the field. He had just flown with some of the guests of Tuskegee in the Howard plane which I had seen outside the hangar.

At first an unsure gamble, the field is now on a firm business basis, with a half million dollar payroll. The 99th Flying Squadron can be said to be an offshoot of the Primary Field, which is steadily feeding pilots to the basic training at the Air Flying School. The number of washouts, once the cadets are passed from primary to basic, is not great, although it is quite a jump for green cadets, used only to cubs, to go to those high-powered ships with their intricate instrument boards. There may be some schools doing a better job, Washington confided, but not many.

Yet pursuit training is one of the most difficult types. Solo flying in these high-powered fighter planes is a sneaky thing. It's not a Tinker to Evers to Chance teamwork, as with a crew; it's a sort of Joe Louis affair, out there alone, on one's own. All the primary field can do is to try to give the best of training in the best facilities that the Army affords them. He mentioned casually that the boys of the 99th had taken the track meet at Chanute Field, Illinois.

Washington found many white people cooperative with the attempts to establish the primary field. One story had it that a white Tuskegeean said that the whites downtown were getting peeved; the major is reported to have called it a lie: "Old so-and-so drinks so much liquor that he gets ideas." In the early days of flying around Tuskegee, a request was made for permission to use the field at Alabama Polytechnic Institute at nearby Auburn. It was decided to put the matter up to a vote of the white cadets. During the conference, the Dean of Women at Auburn is alleged to have said, "I pity the boy that doesn't vote for it." The vote was 100 percent for permission.

"You know your race contends for a lot of things it's not ready for," an Army man said. "Now is a chance to prove what you can do, with a lot of eyes watching." The day that the first Negro pilot was to land on the Auburn field was a special occasion. White people and Negroes were swarming about the field. The Auburn cadets were up in their cub planes until the time scheduled for the Negro to arrive.

"Then Civilian Pilot Anderson came in with his Waco. It was a hair raiser, the most powerful motor that had been heard so far at Auburn, where they had only cubs. You know a Waco takes a lot of beating. Anderson did some acrobatics, a lazy eight, some slow rolls and snap rolls. A cracker at the fences yelled, 'Migard but that darky can fly!'

"Anderson drove right up to the hangar, to let the boys really see it. 'Here she is. Go over and have a look at her.' Nobody moved. Suddenly one man started, and then all went to the plane. They sat in it, and felt it all over.

"Our boys used that field all summer. It was just a show place, with crowds out on Sunday. It was that way at many airports which had never seen a Negro pilot in an airplane before. At Anniston, a Negro pilot about to land saw a car scurrying along in clouds of dust, trying to get to the airport. When he landed, a man ran out of the car toward him. It was the sheriff. 'Well, I'll be damned,' he said, 'I heard about it but I just wanted to see it: a nigger flying a plane!' "

The Negroes made a good reputation as flyers, and on the professional level, met the other flyers as equals. Of course they didn't insist on eating with them, Washington added.

At the Civilian Pilot Training Field, another adjunct to the training program at Tuskegee, there is a crew consisting not only of Negroes, but also of Italians, Jews, Southern whites, Yankees, and Brooklyners, all under a Negro chief pilot. It was from here that Pilot Anderson flew Mrs. Roosevelt, a trip she publicized in her column. Many white Southerners take lessons here; one brought his daughter regularly for a Negro pilot to train. One might think that this might add to the natural hazards of flying, but the safety record is high here, as it is at the primary field and at the air base.

Much of what Washington told me had to stay off the record. But I saw and heard enough to realize that what was once a quip at Maxwell Field, "How's your nigger unit coming?" no longer has any point. Negroes have answered the Congressman's skepticism, not with words but with planes serviced on the ground and soaring in the skies.

Epilogue

It is appropriate that we place Brown's "Count Us In" as the conclusion to *A Negro Looks at the South*. Rhetorically, this essay signifies at different levels to express most cogently, although at times polemically, Brown's reflections on the polyvocal observations he recorded of the black South. As a self-contained text, it consists of anecdotes, personal testimony, reportage, transcriptions of meetings, and other forms of "talk." Its rhetorical power derives from a strong, insistent voice that functions as a narrative guide, combining the various texts into a composite racial portrait. As a statement declaring the African American spirit of the age—that most African Americans felt an urgent need to end the divisive, dehumanizing policies and practices of Jim Crow— "Count Us In" contributes mightily to the forum published in *What the Negro Wants* (1944), a collection of essays that attempted to survey the political mood of African Americans at the height of World War II. As a mode of scientific investigation, its participant observation critiques some of the most disturbing conclusions reached in *An American Dilemma*, an inquiry, unprecedented in breadth and scope, into United States race relations, funded by the Carnegie Foundation and written principally by the Swedish sociologist and moral philosopher Gunnar Myrdal.

Read only as a self-contained text, "Count Us In" still does much to confirm the significance of "talk" or, as B. A. Botkin called it, "living-people-lore." Brown, like Jonathan Daniels before him, attempted to redeem the image of the South through its people. For Brown, this meant assembling a shifting blend of factual data, reportage, anecdotes, personal experience, and more into credible testimony that refuted the prevailing representations that denied the humanity of African Americans. By reporting and commenting on their words, Brown gave voice to a people that social conditions either marginalized or silenced. He was not content with just offering expressions of the racial problem, with providing evidence of grousing; in a collective narrative voice, he sets forth a strong, declamatory solution to the forces creating the racial divide.

And yet, as participant observation, this essay offers, rather ingeniously, a critique of the most ambitious inquiry to date of those relations. *An American Dilemma*, an imposing study of 1,482 pages separated into eleven sections containing forty-five chapters and ten appendices, interrogated the black-white racial divide by continually returning to a moral issue: the conflict between the professed belief in the American Creed and its practice as applied to the nation's African American citizens. Among its many conclusions, the study's notion that American Negro culture, as Myrdal wrote, was "a distorted development, or a pathological condition, of the general American culture" was deeply disturbing to Brown. Instead of ignoring or fretting about this conclusion, Brown sought to educate the supposedly "objective" Myrdal about the error of his social science.

In a cleverly inventive gesture, Brown appropriates the actual Myrdal and makes him a character in "Count Us In." Before setting about the task of reviewing the published literature about black-white relations, Myrdal spent from October to November 1938, his first two months in the country, on a whirlwind fact-finding tour of the South. The essay opens with this figure, characterized as naive, uninformed, incredulous, and distrustful of what his own eyes have allowed him to see, just returning from his trip South. Rhetorically, the essay's narrator asserts his own authority and sits him down for a lecture confirming and expanding what the traveler saw. In effect, the lessons taught also become a commentary on "ways of knowing" or "ways of seeing." As a social scientist, Myrdal would proceed down an epistemological path that privileged dispassionate, unbiased, "objective" study. He would fail to understand the merits of Brown's proposal of subjective, intimate, humanistic experiences as viable means for divining blacks' racial experiences. Perhaps their methodologies point, then, to an important distinction. When Myrdal takes his trip South, he comes back with a dilemma; Brown, on his many trips, returns with unambiguous confirmation of a people who, despite the efforts of Jim Crow, emerge as healthy, happy, and whole.

As an articulation of Southern black zeitgeist, "Count Us In" locates the South both as source or symbol of racial discrimination and as site of salvation. These twin motifs testify to the contradictory, ambiguous nature of enforced racial difference. When the University of North Carolina Press via its publisher, William Terry Couch, encouraged historian Rayford W. Logan to gather conservative, moderate, and liberal black voices to conduct a forum on the status and future of the Negro, what resulted was *What the Negro Wants* (1944), a book that proved personally and intellectually embarrassing to Couch.

By the standards of that day, Couch would have been considered politically liberal, since he had publicly voiced his opposition to Jim Crow transportation and accommodations. But however progressive his thought, Couch remained a gradualist and expected the pace of social change to be evolutionary. Thus he was horrified when every contributor responded to the question "What does the Negro want?" with "We want complete racial integration, and we want it now!" Couch had thought the forum contributors would agree with him that blacks preferred segregation in housing and the indefinite maintenance of separate schools. This act of defiance caused Couch to make an unprecedented gesture: he wrote a "Publisher's Introduction" to the collection. In it, Couch set out to absolve himself from culpability in the Logan essay collection by defending white racial superiority. He theorized that the Negro's own social condition was produced by inferiority but an inferiority that could be overcome and that the prejudice that resulted from it could be cured. Eliminating the worst excesses of this condition, he maintained, required a slow, patient program of social change. Certainly change was possible, he argued, but both races, for the present, had to accept as fact that the values inherent in "civilization" and "culture" clearly made Euro-Americans vastly superior to African Americans. Simply put, the white race stood closer than blacks to the storehouse of values that made up civilization. Such positioning, in his view, established the racial superiority of white people.

Writing in *The War Within: From Victorian to Modernist Thought in the South, 1919–1945*, Daniel Joseph Singal put Couch's argument in perspective. Oddly, the target of Couch's ire was not *What the Negro Wants* but the source he felt inspired the supposedly mistaken position expressed in Logan's book: *An American Dilemma*. Couch firmly believed that Myrdal had misled the forum contributors by encouraging an adherence to the concept of cultural relativism, which espoused the belief that all cultures must be judged equal in value. To shore up his position of white racial superiority, Couch embarked on a torturous rhetorical path in which he argued civilization as the sum of all cultures and culture as the equivalent of race. An equilibrium would be achieved, he felt, after gradualism became the accepted speed of interracial change.

Conceptually, "Count Us In" provided little support for Couch's premise. It did, however, reaffirm an idea implicit in his argument: that the struggle to resolve these issues would take place on the South's embattled turf. The South as site of contentiousness points directly to one of Brown's basic tenets: that although racial segregation was omnipresent in the nation, in the South, Jim Crow represented the "gravest denial of democracy." Thus, he concludes: "It goes without saying that what happens to the Negro in the South has great bearing on what participation the Negro will attain in American democracy."

As the Epilogue of *A Negro Looks at the South*, "Count Us In" provides both context and coda for Brown's thinking. It is the longest piece he intended to include in this collection, making it the most comprehensive statement of his efforts to demonstrate the life, vitality, and vigor of Southern black life. It also becomes his best effort to mirror in prose the magnificence of his poetry. Reading the disparate pieces leading up to this one should stand as proof that "Count Us In" is an appropriate climax for this important book.

⇥ COUNT US IN ⇤

⇥ Counted Out

A young European scholar, back from a swift trip through the South, picked up from my desk a copy of Hal Steed's *Georgia: Unfinished State*. A passage on the last page confused him. It read: "I would not say that the Anglo-Saxon is superior to other races, but that this race makes up nearly one hundred percent of the population of the South augurs well for unity—unity in political beliefs, in religion, in social problems." The European was amazed at the figure—nearly one hundred percent Anglo-Saxon. "But I saw so many Negroes there," he said.

I could have mentioned other oddities in the enumerating of the Negro, from the adoption of the Constitution when a Negro slave counted as three-fifths of a man, to the present when a Negro is counted as a unit, a fraction, or a zero, according to the purpose of the counter. Instead I assured him that the evidence of his eyes could be trusted: the gatherings at one side of the depot to see the train go through, the hordes in the ramshackly slums of the cities, the crammed Jim Crow waiting rooms and coaches. Negroes were there all right. Even the publicists who excluded Negroes as part of the population would admit that they were there. Too much so, some might say ruefully, pointing out the large numbers of Negroes as the cause of the poverty and backwardness of the South, apologizing for the belt of swarming cabins engirdling the cities, hoping that the stranger might soften his verdict on the town until the business section around the depot slowly came into view. Too numerous, therefore Negroes had to be kept in their places, the argument might run. Such spokesmen would have a glib reply to reconcile the statistics of "nearly one hundred percent Anglo-Saxon" with the patent reality: "Oh, that's easy to understand. By population, we mean the people that count."

I knew that longer study of the South would convince the visitor that in certain respects, Negroes definitely counted. He might learn how it was that one scholar called them "the central theme of Southern history" running constantly through the record of the section. It would be easy for him to see how the presence of Negroes was chiefly responsible for the political "solidifying" of a region, so far from solid in many other respects. Fear of Negroes voting had been the primary cause for a poll tax peculiar to the region, resulting in the disfranchisement of ten millions of American citizens, half again as many whites as Negroes. This disfranchisement, he might learn, exerts more than a sectional influence, since it has been estimated that one poll tax vote is worth more than five votes in states with no poll tax. Many poll tax Congressmen seem to have a permanent tenure on their seats in Congress, and their resulting seniority gives them a power disproportionate to the number of people who voted them into office, to say the least. The European might learn that the Federal ballot for soldiers was most forcefully opposed by those who feared that Negro soldiers might vote; that Federal aid to education was defeated because the race issue was raised; that the "G.I. Bill of Rights" providing unemployment insurance for returning soldiers was jeopardized because of what the Senator in charge of the bill calls the "hatred of certain Congressmen for the colored portion of our armed forces." He might learn how a program of social reform—the Farm Security Administration—though it aided Southern whites as much as Negroes, was in danger of being scuttled by those who feared it meant that the Negro would "get out of his place."

Just how the Negro counted might be clarified should the visitor read Lillian Smith's "Two Men and a Bargain: A Parable of the Solid South," in which the rich white man says to the poor white man:

> There's two big jobs down here that need doing: Somebody's got to tend to the living and somebody's got to tend to the nigger. Now, I've learned a few things about making a living you're too no-count to learn (else you'd be making money same way I make it): things about jobs and credit, prices, hours, wages, votes, and so on. But one thing you can learn easy, any white man can, is how to handle the black man. Suppose now you take over the thing you can do and let me take over the thing I can do. What I mean is, you boss the nigger, and I'll boss the money.

The visitor would thus learn that the Negro counted, and still counts in this "Anglo-Saxon" section. But he would learn also what the Southern spokesmen mean by "people that count."

Negroes have lived too long with this paradox, as with so many others, to be confused by it; they understand the reality behind it. They have been counted out for so long a time.

"Sure, the Negro is all out for the war," my friend the sociologist told me. "He's 72 percent all out for it." Some might consider this estimate to be cynicism, others optimism. The general conclusion is hardly to be disputed: that for all of its high promise, this war has not summoned 100 percent of the Negro's enthusiasm and energies.

Before attacking this apathy as short-sighted, it might be wise to look for its causes. They are unfortunately too ready at hand to require much searching. On a six months' stay in the deep South of wartime I saw my fill of them; even casual observations in a border city and on trips to the North have heaped the measure to overflowing.

Documentation of the refusal to count the Negro in the war effort is hardly needed. Discrimination in industry was so flagrant, North and South, East and West, that Executive Order 8802 was issued to ban discrimination in wartime industrial jobs, and the President's Committee on Fair Employment Practices was set up to investigate cases of alleged discrimination. While Negro employment was definitely aided, progress has not been in a straight line. All sorts of obstacles have been in the way: Congressmen and pressure groups continue to snipe and blast at the Committee; the governor of a Southern state openly violated the Executive Order; the railroads have defiantly challenged a showdown. The integration of Negroes into industry has been opposed even with violence; strikes have been called because Negro workers were upgraded; and one of the causes of the Detroit riot is said to be the influx of Negro workers. In spite of welcome gains, Negroes are far from convinced that fullest use is being made of Negro manpower, North or South.

A powerful symbol to the Negro of his "not belonging" was the refusal of the Red Cross to accept Negro donors to the blood bank. Against the medical authorities who stated that there was no such thing as Negro blood, that blood from the veins of whites and Negroes could not be told apart, the Red Cross sided officially with Congressman Rankin, who saw, in the proposal that Negroes too might contribute much needed blood, a communist plot to "mongrelize America": "They wanted to pump Negro or Japanese blood into the veins of our wounded white boys regardless of the dire effect it might have on their children." The establishment of a segregated blood bank—needless, complicated, and irrational—did not help matters much. Nor did the fact, publicized by the recent Spingarn Award, that one of the most important men in the successful establishment of the blood bank was Dr. Charles Drew, a Negro.

In the armed forces, advances have certainly been made over World War I. Drafted to their full quota, Negroes are supposed to be serving in all branches of the Army. Only recently it was reported that Negro paratroopers in Atlanta proved to white paratroopers that they really belonged to the dare-devil's branch. Except in training for pursuit piloting, Negro officers are trained along with white. There are more Negro officers than in the last war, several officers of the rank of colonel and one brigadier general. Negro airmen are now being trained as bombardiers and navigators. Negro squadrons have seen action in the hot fighting in the Mediterranean theater, and have been highly commended by military authorities. The long-closed ranks of the Marine Corps are now open, and Marine officers praised Negro Marines as "good Marines," to be used everywhere and exactly as other Marines. In the Navy, Negroes have finally been admitted to other capacities than messboys. Some are to serve as seamen on patrol boats and destroyer escorts. The first ensigns have been commissioned. The record of the Coast Guard toward Negroes has been a good one, and the Merchant Marine, with its Negro officers and mixed crews, is looked upon as an achievement in democracy.

Advances have been made, but the Negro was so far behind in opportunity that he does not let his glance linger on the gains; he looks ahead along the road to full participation. This is good Americanism rather than ingratitude. The gains are not unmixed: there still seem to be, for instance, a ceiling on Negro officers and an opposition to having white officers serve under Negro officers. Negroes are dubious about the large number of Negro troops in the service and non-combat units; when the famous Tenth Cavalry, a source of historic pride, was assigned to service duties, Negroes were disturbed in spite of the assurance that military necessity required the transfer. And the Negro still looks askance at the Navy.

In the South, I met on every hand the sense of not belonging. On a bus near Baton Rouge, conversation had hardly started with my seat-mate, a little fellow who looked like a black Frenchman, when he offered me a sure way of staying out of the Army: I was to roll a piece of "actican" (Octagon) soap in a pellet of bread and eat it just before the physical examination. He himself knew it would work, he said in his patois. He didn't have nothing against the Germans or Japs, neither one, but he did know some enemies over here. I found the same embittered spirit in a young Negro lieutenant who wanted to get overseas, anywhere, where he could find an enemy *to shoot at*. At the Negro section of an air base, segregated from the rest by a marker reading "Beale Street," I found the men not proud of belonging to the Air Corps, but disgruntled at the type of menial labor they were called on to perform. I talked with a well-educated young Negro corporal, who had felt that some meaning might be given to his work in the Army when he learned that he was to be sent to an "area and language" school, but who on the eve of going was told that the school had suddenly been closed to Negroes. I talked with Negro pilots, who in the long hours of the day were learning the intricacies of high-powered P-40's, reading the involved instrument boards, soaring into the "wild blue yonder," with their lives and planes dependent on split-second judgments, developing the aggressiveness and self-reliance necessary for combat pilots. At night, these men were forbidden by curfew to be seen in the downtown section of Tuskegee. This kind of thing, and so much else, rankled.

With a few honorable exceptions, newspapers, radio programs, and motion pictures (omitting, of course, Negro newspapers and newsreels for Negro theaters only) have done little to convince Negro soldiers of belonging. Some Northern periodicals, *PM* outstandingly, may publicize Negro military service. But in practically all Southern newspapers, the daily row on row of native sons with the armed forces never showed a dark face. I should have known better, perhaps, than to look for one: pictures of Negroes in these papers were traditionally confined to those of prizefighters or recently deceased ex-slaves. In the North, the practice is little better. In a Northern railroad station, a picture, "blown up" by marvelous photographic technique, showed departing soldiers what they were fighting for: a sea of American faces looking out, anxiously, proudly. All were white. An observer saw a contingent of Negro troops entraining; they gave the eye-catching picture a swift glance, and then snapped their heads away, almost as if by command. He wondered, he told me, what thoughts coursed through their minds.

"The Negro Soldier" is a first-class picture, wisely aimed at offsetting some of this indifference and ignorance concerning one-tenth of our armed forces. But only when the picture reaches American white people will Negroes believe its real service to be achieved.

The situation that I found in the South was not solely that of whites refusing to count Negroes in, and of Negroes sensing that they did not and could not belong. It would be inaccurate to omit the friendliness that undoubtedly exists in the South between many whites and many Negroes. Though exaggerated by sentimentalists into a mystical cult of mutual affection instead of a human attachment, certain Southern whites have for a long time protected "their Negroes" and have cherished them with a fondness that has been gratefully received. But, as is frequently pointed out, this has generally been on a basis of master and underling. It has been affection rather than friendship, patronage returned by gratefulness, not the meeting of friends on a plane of mutual respect. It has been Santa Claus and the child. In certain phases—in the courts for instance—when a white man protects *his* Negro regardless of innocence or guilt, the relationship is dangerous. Kindness can kill as well as cruelty, and it can never take the place of genuine respect. Those who boast of the affection between the races below the Mason-Dixon line must be brought up sharp when they realize that one of the worst insults to a Southern white is to be called "nigger-lover," and one of the worst to a Negro is to be called "white-folks nigger."

Genuine respect between whites and Negroes can be found in the South, though to a smaller degree than paternalistic affection and dependent gratefulness. It would be a serious omission to fail to recognize undoubted services rendered by many white people, not in the spirit of "Christmas gift," but at the price of social ostracism, loss of preferment, and even physical violence. Sheriffs have braved mobs to protect their prisoners; women have leagued against lynching; preachers, editors, professional men, scholars and authors have spoken and acted against flagrant abuses; trade union organizers have risked life and limb in efforts to establish industrial democracy. Many people, less dramatically, have been generous and courageous in treating Negroes in the spirit of brotherhood. People like Frank Graham, Arthur Raper, Thomas Sancton, Lillian Smith, and Paula Snelling, to name a conspicuous few, are warrants that there are white Southerners who believe that a New South of justice is attainable, or at the least, worth fighting for.

These exceptions must be noted. Yet what I found most apparent among Southern Negroes—civilians and military men, upper and lower class, conservatives and radicals—was a sense of not belonging, and protest, sometimes not loud but always deeply felt. It is a mistake to believe that this protest in the South is instigated by Negroes from the North, or other "furriners," as Eugene Talmadge called them. I found a large degree of militancy in Negroes who were Southern born and bred, some of whom have never been out of the South. I talked with sharecroppers, union organizers, preachers, schoolteachers, newspapermen, and bankers who spoke with bitter desperation and daring. Clinton Clark, certainly among the sturdiest fighters, was born in one of the back country parishes of Louisiana; when he was arrested for organizing in a parish nearby, the planters refused to believe him a native of the section. The protest I heard ranged from the quietly spoken aside, through twisted humor and sarcasm, to stridency. Time and time again I heard the anecdote, which spread like a folktale, of the new sort of hero—the Negro soldier who, having taken all he could stand, shed his coat, faced his persecutors and said: "If I've got to die for democracy, I might as well die for some of it right here and now." Some of the protest, undoubtedly, is chip-on-the-shoulder aggression, like that of the Negro woman who, in a jammed bus lumbering through the Louisiana night, suddenly raised her voice, seemingly apropos of nothing, to say: "I had my Texas jack with me, and I told that white man I would cut him as long as I could see him."

At Columbus, Georgia, buses marked "K.O. for Tokyo" roared past Negro soldiers, who had to wait for special buses to take them to Fort Benning. It was not only the boys from Harlem or Jersey who griped. The Negro train passengers who, standing in the aisle, wisecracked at the flushed conductor seated in his "office" in the Jim Crow coach, and then belabored the Negro porter for being a good man Friday, were not Northerners. It was not a Northern waiter who told the Negro sitting in the diner after lavish and ostentatious service: "Man, I was afraid you weren't coming back here." They were not Northern Negroes who repeated the refrain, whether called for or not, "That ain't no way to win the war."

I found this protest natural, since the Southern Negro is where the grip is tightest and the bite goes deepest and most often. The legend of Negro docility was always exaggerated. The novelists and poets, "befo' de war," wrote soothingly of contented slaves, but many of their readers lived in dread of insurrections, and applauded the politicians who, fuming about the loss of their property via the Underground Railroad, sought anxiously to put teeth into the fugitive slave bill and to set up a code of *verbotens* to prevent slave uprisings. Printers, whose presses busily ran off stories of docile Mose and Dinah, kept handy the stereotype of a

Negro with a bundle on a stick, loping toward free land. The image of docility was cherished as a dream, but the hard actuality of furtiveness, truculence, rebelliousness, and desperation gave other images to the nightmares. The praises of old massa that white men wrote in "Negro" speech and "Negro" melody ring falsely when set beside "I been rebuked and I been scorned," "Go Down Moses, tell old Pharaoh, let my people go," and "I thank God, I'm free at last."

"When a man's got a gun in your face, ain't much to do but take low or die," a sharecropper in Macon County told Charles S. Johnson. In that setting he was talking sense, not docility. Southern Negroes too often have seen the gun in their faces; but many, all along, have asserted their manhood as far as they were able, walking as close to the danger line as they could and still survive. Some edged over, some were dragged over, and some found the line a shifting one; many of these last paid the penalty. This has been true through the long years, and now, when fine-sounding talk of freedom and democracy comes to them from the newspapers and sermons, tales swapped around the cracker-barrels of country stores, letters from their boys in camps, and speeches over the radio, Negroes begin putting in stronger, though still modest, claims. Talk about freedom did not reveal a new discovery; true freedom was something they had long been hankering for. I do not believe that they were so naïve that they expected full values for all of the promissory notes. Freedom was a hard-bought thing, their tradition warned them; the great day of "jubilo" had been followed by gloomy days; but the talk sounded good and right, and perhaps a little more freedom *was* on its way. Through the radios—many of them the battery sets which fill needs in small shacks once filled only by phonographs and guitars—booming voices told them of the plans for a new world. Over the airwaves came the spark, lighting and nursing small fires of hope; the glow and the warmth were good in the darkness. "One of the worst things making for all this trouble," a Mississippi planter told me, with frank honesty, "is the radio. Those people up in Washington don't know what they're doing down here. They ought to shut up talking so much."

Evidence of the Negro's not belonging is readier at hand in the South. But the North is by no means blameless in its race relations. According to an alleged folk anecdote, a Negro said he would prefer to be in a race riot in Detroit than in a camp meeting in Georgia. And orators repeatedly urge, "Come North, young man," as the only solution. Nevertheless, the folklore that the North is a refuge, a haven, has met up with the hard facts of unemployment, discrimination, and tension. Paradise Valley in Detroit is as badly misnamed as Ideal, Georgia. The mobs that wrecked that Negro section of Detroit showed a crazed lust for bloodshed and destruction that was no Southern monopoly. Harlem has been fondly spoken of as a Mecca for Negroes; but the rioting Negroes who smashed the windows and looted the stores reveal that Negroes have found causes there for desperation and fury. In Northern cities that cradled abolitionism, Negroes are to be found cramped in ghettos, still denied a chance to earn decent livelihoods, to make use of their training, to develop into full men and women.

Though convinced that the Negro is "thoroughly Jim Crowed all over the North—considering Jim Crow in its deepest aspects," Thomas Sancton writes:

> And yet it is true that the main body of the race problem lies within the boundaries of the Southern states, because some three-fourths of America's 13,000,000 Negroes live there. . . . The Negro is oppressed in many ways in the North, and certainly economically, but the long anti-slavery tradition has at least given him some basic civil and social rights which the white South continues to deny him and would like to deny him forever.

Since the problem of the Negro in America is of national scope, steps to integrate the Negro into American democracy must be taken everywhere. Nevertheless, it remains true that the gravest denial of democracy and the greatest opposition to it are in the South. It goes without saying that what happens to the Negro in the South has great bearing on what participation the Negro will attain in American democracy. If a Negro is allowed only second- or third-class citizenship in Tupelo, Mississippi, his Harlem brother's citizenship is less than first-class. And if America has more than one class of citizenship, it is less than a first-class democracy.

⤳ No Trespassing

What are the chances that freedom is really on its way, that the Negro may finally be "counted in"? Some signs are none too propitious. For instance, Negro soldiers are indoctrinated to believe that they are to fight for the four freedoms, but what they run up against daily is confusing, rather than reassuring. Fraternization between Negro soldiers and white soldiers is largely discouraged; it seems to be considered un-American for soldiers of different color, though fighting for the same cause, to be brothers-in-arms. A bulletin from headquarters may attack the subversiveness of race hostility, but part of the bulletin will warn Negro soldiers that dissatisfaction with Jim Crow is tantamount to subversiveness. Democracy to many seems to be symbolized by this message, printed under a large red "V" on a bus in Charleston, South Carolina:

Victory Demands Your Cooperation

If the peoples of this country's races do not pull together, Victory is lost. We, therefore, respectfully direct your attention to the laws and customs of the state in regard to segregation. Your cooperation in carrying them out will make the war shorter and Victory sooner. Avoid friction. Be patriotic. White passengers will be seated from front to rear; colored passengers from rear to front.

Looking about them, especially in the South but also in the North, Negroes see convincing proof of these implications: that patriotism means satisfaction with the *status quo ante* Pearl Harbor, that cooperation really does not mean pulling together but rather the Negro's acceptance of the subservient role; that friction otherwise threatens.

A current anecdote tells of a white officer who, seeing a Negro officer eating in the diner, exclaimed: "I'd rather see Hitler win the war than for niggers to get out of their place like that!" Negroes do not believe the attitude to be exceptional.

With all of the commendable efforts of the Army to improve the morale of Negro troops and to investigate and iron out the difficulties, Negro soldiers still find too many violations of democracy, ranging from petty irritations to rank injustices. Negroes may lose precious hours of leave because they can find no place to ride on the buses. Negro officers may find a studied refusal on the part of white soldiers to salute. Negro soldiers may be manhandled, cursed, and even killed by civilian officers of the law. Living the rough, exacting life on maneuvers, driving a jeep, manning a tank or machine gun, servicing or flying a fighter plane, the Negro soldier is expected to be a man doing a man-size job. In contact with civilian life, however, the Negro soldier is expected to be something else again.

There are signs elsewhere that do not reassure. That Negroes were given jobs at a steel plant "that have always been filled by white men," that Negro veterans of World War I were filing legal action "to force the American Legion in Alabama to charter Negro posts," that Tuskegee officials were demanding that pistols be restored to Negro military police in Tuskegee—these frightened and angered Horace Wilkinson of Bessemer, Alabama, into urging the foundation of a "League to Maintain White Supremacy." He was shocked at the impertinence of the Fair Employment Practices Committee in coming to Birmingham and recording proof that Southern industrialists and labor unions discriminated against Negro labor and thereby hampered the war effort. Mr. Wilkinson's efforts have reached some success; the "League to Maintain White Supremacy" has been set up. A race-baiting sheet, *The Alabama Sun*, is being published. The first issue has a picture of

Mrs. Roosevelt greeting a Negro Red Cross worker, back from service in England, with the caption "Mrs. Roosevelt Greets Another Nigger."

Mr. Wilkinson is playing an old game, of course, and is a member of a large squad. Mrs. Roosevelt, because of her genuine and gracious democracy, has long been the target of abuse in the South. Years ago, in order to aid the election of Eugene Talmadge, the *Georgia Woman's World* published a picture of the first lady escorted by two Negro cadet officers on her visit to a Negro university. Recent rumormongering has built up a folklore of mythical Eleanor Clubs, dedicated to getting Negro women out of the kitchens, and white women into them. The smear campaign was indecently climaxed when a Mississippi editor, hardly concealing his satisfaction at the Detroit riots, blamed Mrs. Roosevelt for the massacre. The editorial impressed Representative Boykin of Alabama so favorably that he had it inserted in *The Congressional Record*. It closed:

> In Detroit, a city noted for the growing impudence and insolence of the Negro population, an attempt was made to put your preachments into prac-
> tice . . . blood on your hands, Mrs. Roosevelt, and the damned spots won't
> wash out, either.

According to a Gallup Poll, many white Southerners believe that the Negro has been made "unruly and unmanageable" because "large scale reforms have been undertaken too swiftly." Writing from his winter home in Florida, Roger Babson lectured his friends—"the several millions of colored people"—about their "lazy, wasteful, saucy moods." White workers may "strike when they shouldn't, but they are not lazy nor do they throw away money."

In all likelihood, "sauciness," rather than laziness or wastefulness, is the chief cause of the present wide race-baiting. Any symbol of the Negro's getting out of "his place"—a lieutenant's shoulder bars, or even a buck private's uniform; a Negro worker at a machine, or a Negro girl at a typewriter, or a cook's throwing up her job—these can be as unbearable as an impudent retort, or a quarrel on a bus, or a fight.

The demagogues have had and are having a field day. Running for reelection as governor in 1942 against strong opposition, Eugene Talmadge of Georgia preached race prejudice from Rabun Gap to Tybee's shining light. He ordered his state constabulary to be vigilant against Northern Negroes and other "furriners" and warned Southern womanhood to arm. His opponent was not above race-baiting himself; it seemed that he had to do it to win. In neighboring states in the Deep South, the demagogues may have been less spectacular, but they were busy. Results were soon forthcoming. Three Negroes, two of them boys, were lynched within a week in Mississippi. Negroes were beaten and thrown off buses and trains in all sections of the South. Crises have followed close on crises. A riot stopped work in a Mobile shipyard because Negroes were upgraded; a pogrom laid waste the Negro section of Beaumont, Texas, because of a rape charge, later discredited; and murder ran wild in Detroit.

Any concessions to Negroes—any guaranteeing of democratic rights—set the demagogues off full steam. Sometimes they cry "wolf," as in the instance of the voluminous report of the Office of Education which, among other recommendations, urged cooperation between Negro and white colleges "in the interest of national welfare." Congressman Brooks of Louisiana equated this cooperation to "forcible co-mingling of students of the two races in the South . . . unthinkable . . . leading to the producing of a mongrel race in the United States."

When two anthropologists published a pamphlet, *The Races of Mankind*, to give wide circulation to the scientific proof of the brotherhood of man, and to help bring it about that "victory in this war will be in the name, not of one race or another, but of the universal Human Race," Congressman May of Kentucky was enraged. He was especially irked to read that Northern Negroes scored higher on the A.E.F. Intelligence Test than Southern whites (of his native state, for instance), although the authors advised that the statistics meant only that "Negroes with better luck after they were born, got higher scores than whites with less luck." As Chairman of the House Military Affairs Committee, Congressman May decided that these scientific facts had "no place in the Army program," and promised to keep his eyes open lest the soldiers be contaminated with such doctrine. The pamphlets went to an Army warehouse.

Coincidental with the fight waged by the National Association for the Advancement of Colored People to equalize teachers' salaries in South Carolina, the South Carolina House of Representatives resolved:

> We reaffirm our belief in and our allegiance to establish white supremacy as now prevailing in the South and we solemnly pledge our lives and our sacred honor to maintaining it. Insofar as racial relations are concerned, we firmly and unequivocally demand that henceforth the damned agitators of the North leave the South alone.

Shortly after the Negro teachers of South Carolina won the fight to equalize salaries, a Charleston judge stated that many Negroes "would be better off carrying a load of fertilizer rather than a bunch of school books. . . . I am going to break up some of this education."

The perennial demagogues of Mississippi, Senator Bilbo and Representative Rankin, hold the limelight. Senator Bilbo recently held up for the admiration of his constituents his old scheme for deporting Negroes to Africa. One of the first steps he planned as chairman of the Senate Committee for the District of Columbia was clearing Negroes out of the alleys of Washington: "I want them to get into the habit of moving so as to be ready for my movement to West Africa." Until the day of that migration, Senator Bilbo promises alley dwellers of Washington that they can find places to stay in the basements of city homes, and on farms in neighboring states, where the need for cooks and farmhands is acute. Senator Bilbo also threatens to repeat his record-making filibuster against the repeal of the poll tax.

Representative Rankin also stays busy: attacking the President's Committee on Fair Employment Practices as subversive of democracy, since white and Negro sailors in the National Maritime Union are assigned to the same ship; threatening with lynching "that gang of communistic Jews and Negroes that . . . tried to storm the House restaurants, and went around arm in arm with each other"; attacking the Federal ballot for soldiers; and raging at every specter of "social equality."

Both Senator Bilbo and Congressman Rankin, as so many other demagogues, protest that they act in the interests of the Negro. Senator Bilbo says, "I am the best friend the Negro has." And Representative Rankin blames "communistic Jews" for causing "the deaths of many good Negroes who never would have got into trouble if they had been left alone."

So run the warnings from the demagogues. But it is not only among the demagogues and their Gestapos—the frontier thugs, the state constabularies, the goon squads and the lynchers—that violent aversion to change is found. Many of the intellectuals speak lines that sound like Talmadge and Rankin. A decade ago, *The American Review*, now defunct, published their ideas. Donald Davidson viewed with dire misgivings "a general maneuver, the object of which is apparently to set the Negro up as an equal, or at least more than a subordinate member of society. The second, or unavowed, program was the new form of abolitionism, again proposing to emancipate the Negro from the handicap of race, color, and previous condition of servitude." Mr. Davidson considered this program (he was talking chiefly of a program of ownership of small farms by Negroes) to be "unattainable as long as the South remains the South," and its sponsors he called ruthless. The only possible solution, he thought, is "to define a place for the American Negro as special as that which they [the American people] defined for the American Indian." Allen Tate, condemning the reformers "who are anxious to have Negroes sit by them on street cars," wrote:

> I argue it this way: the white race seems determined to rule the Negro race in its midst; I belong to the white race; therefore I intend to support the white rule. Lynching is a symptom of weak, inefficient rule; but you can't

destroy lynching by *fiat* or social agitation; lynching will disappear when the white race is satisfied that its supremacy will not be questioned in social crises.

Tempting the Negro to question this supremacy, he believes, is irresponsible behavior.

Frank Owsley called the agitation to free the Scottsboro boys the "third crusade." More important to him than the defendants' innocence or guilt was the fact that some Negroes were going to get hurt: "The outside interference with the relationship of the whites and blacks in the South can result in nothing but organizations like the Ku Klux Klan and in violent retaliation against the Negroes—themselves often innocent."

It is to be expected that the die-hards should interpret Negro aspirations to democracy as incendiarism. But there are Southern liberals who do the same. Some congressmen, noted for their support of New Deal reforms, have been recently forced into race-baiting, in order to prove that they are not "nigger-lovers." Some of the liberals protest with David Cohn that they view the position of the American Negro with "a sore heart, a troubled conscience, and a deep compassion." A few of these have shown genuine sympathy with the Negro's progress. Nevertheless, by and large, they are defeatists. Mark Ethridge, one of the leaders of Southern white liberals, stated flatly: "There is no power in the world—not even in all the mechanized armies of the earth, Allied and Axis—which could now force the Southern white people to the abandonment of the principle of social segregation."

Since the Negro hardly would count upon the armies of the Axis as friends in any case, the prophecy is all the more direful. Mr. Ethridge warns that "cruel disillusionment, bearing the germs of strife and perhaps tragedy" will result from exacting the abolition of social segregation as the price of participation in the war. It is inaccurate to say that the Negroes were exacting this: Negroes at the time of Mr. Ethridge's prophecy were in all likelihood participating as fully as they were allowed to participate.

It is the gravity of the fear, however, rather than the accurate description of its cause, that concerns us here. Howard Odum also sees the net results of outside agitation in the affairs of the South to be "tragedy of the highest order, tragedy of the Greek, as it were, because it was the innocent Negro who suffered." Virginius Dabney sees the two races edging nearer and nearer "to the precipice," if the Negro continues his demands.

David Cohn echoes Mr. Ethridge. As so many Southern intellectuals do, he finds comfort in William Graham Sumner's adage that you cannot change the mores of a people by law. Segregation is "the most deep-seated and pervasive of the Southern mores"; Negroes and whites who would break it down by Federal fiat had therefore better beware. "I have no doubt," Mr. Cohn writes, "that in such an event every Southern white man would spring to arms and the country would be swept by civil war." Patience, goodwill, and wisdom (wisdom meaning acceptance of segregation without protest) are needful, otherwise the question will be delivered out of the hands of decent whites and Negroes "into the talons of demagogues, fascists, and the Klu Kluxers, to the irreparable harm of the Negro."

It is significant that Southern spokesmen, reactionaries and liberals alike, are exercised over the harm that may come to Negroes. Watch out, the warning goes, or *Negroes* will get hurt. This is an old refrain; over a century ago the first proslavery novelist threatened, when Garrison's blasts were sounding off from Boston, that the "mischievous interference of abolitionists would involve the negro in the rigor which it provokes." And the latest demagogue expresses this threat and this tenderness.

The whites and Negroes who hope for a democratic solution to the problem must learn that the problem is insoluble, warns Mr. Cohn: "It is at bottom a blood or sexual question." Southern whites are determined that "no white in their legal jurisdiction shall marry a Negro" and "white women shall not have physical relations with Negro men except, when discovered, upon pain of death or banishment inflicted upon one or both parties to the act." And John Temple Graves takes his stand on two bedrock "facts": "The unshakable belief of Southern whites that the problem was peculiarly their own and that attempts to force settlement from outside were hateful and incompetent. The absolute determination that the blood of the two races should not be confused and a mulatto population emerge."

Negroes have long recognized this as the hub of the argument opposing change in their status. A chief recruiting slogan for the Ku Klux Klan of Reconstruction, when Negroes were "getting out of their place" by voting, buying farms and homes, and attending schools, was that Southern white womanhood must be protected. "The closer the Negro got to the ballot-box, the more he looked like a rapist," is the quip of a Negro who has studied the period closely. Thomas Nelson Page wrote that the barbarities of Reconstruction were based upon "the determination to put an end to the ravishing of their women by an inferior race, or by any race, no matter what the consequence." Though a later Southern student, W. J. Cash, has estimated that "the chance [of the Southern white woman's being violated by a Negro] was much less . . . than the chance that she would be struck by lightning," it is Page rather than Cash whose opinions are most followed. Political campaigns still seem to be waged not so much to get into office as to protect women. In his last campaign, Eugene Talmadge reported "an unusual number of assault cases and attempts to assault white ladies" (though newspaper reporters could not find them), and he denounced the Rosenwald Fund, noted for its benefactions to the South, as being determined to make a "mulatto South." Senator Ellender, in one of his attacks on an anti-lynching bill, revealed the train of thought of so many filibusters when he promised that if the bill should pass, he would propose three amendments—all prohibiting intermarriage. If mobs were forbidden by Federal law to lynch Negroes, white people were at least not going to be allowed to marry Negroes. Instances of such reasoning make up a sorry tale.

For all of their protesting of decency and good will, the intellectuals do not talk very differently from Gerald L. K. Smith, a spellbinder generally considered to be of the native fascist variety. The Reverend Smith inherited one of Huey Long's mantles; he is certain that he knows what people want or at least that he can rouse them into wanting what he wants. Immediately after the Detroit riot, the Reverend Smith wrote in *The Cross and the Flag* that most white people would not agree to any of the following: intermarriage of blacks and whites; mixture of blacks and whites in hotels and restaurants; "intimate relationships" between blacks and whites in the school system; "wholesale mixture of blacks and whites in residential sections"; "promiscuous mixture" of blacks and whites in streetcars and on trains, "especially when black men are permitted to sit down and crowd in close to white women and vice versa." The Reverend Smith added generously, "I have every reason to believe black women resent being crowded by white men." Mixture in factories was also offensive, "especially when black men are mixed with white women closely in daily work."

It is true that the Reverend Smith is no longer tilling Southern fields, but he learned his demagoguery in the South, and many of his audience were transplanted Southerners. It is also undeniable that his words struck responsive chords in many Northerners. But he expresses a cardinal tenet of the Southern creed that social mixture must be forbidden, or else as John Temple Graves puts it, "a mulatto population will emerge."

Negroes know well that that horse has been out of the stable too long a time for the lock to be put on the door now. Even the race purists must realize the large amount of mixture in the American Negro, that hybrid of African, Indian, and Caucasian stock. And though, as the anthropologist Montague Cobb says, the Caucasian component is "the most apparent and the least documented," race purists must realize how the Negro got that way.

Fears that lowering the barriers of segregation will lower the level of civilization are often expressed. If these fears are not lies, one consequence might be that civilization in such Southern cities as Atlanta, Birmingham, Memphis, and Vicksburg will decline to the level of that in unsegregated Boston, New York, Iowa City, and Seattle. According to these fears, intermarriage will result when Negroes and whites eat in the same restaurants or in a diner without a little green curtain; when they stop in the same hotels, and ride the same streetcars and buses without wooden screens, or other separating devices. Negroes laugh at the suggestion that crowded buses and streetcars and cafeterias are marriage bureaus. They know that intermarriage is not widespread in the states where there are no segregation laws and no laws forbidding intermarriage. They believe with great reason that there are more illicit sexual relations between the races in the states whose laws forbid intermarriage than there are mixed marriages elsewhere.

Intermarriage is hardly a goal that Negroes are contending for openly or yearning for secretly. It is certainly not a mental preoccupation with them and scarcely a matter of special concern. Nevertheless, they do not want laws on the statute books branding them as outcasts. They do not want governmental sanction of caste, however long they have seen it hardened about them. They know how prophetic were the words of the anguished heroine of George Washington Cable's story of the last century: "A lie, Père Jerome! Separate! No! They do not want to keep us [white men: colored women] separate: no, no! But they *do* want to keep us despised!"

It is likely, of course, that friendships will develop where Negroes and whites meet on a basis of respect and where people can be drawn together by kindred interests. It is likely that some of these friendships might ripen into love and marriage. That certainly should be left as a private matter, the affair of the persons involved, as it is now in most civilized lands. An individual's choice of a mate should hardly be considered as a chief cause of the downfall of Western, or American, or even Southern civilization. A more grievous cause for alarm, a more dangerous omen of ruin, is the contempt for personality based on skin color and hair texture. Negroes laugh a bit ruefully at the dread that one-tenth of a nation's population will corner the marital market of the nine-tenths. They know to what a degree in the past the opposite has prevailed, though the market could not with accuracy be termed marital. They could scarcely consider laws banning intermarriage to be protective of their own women. And they do not share the Southern white man's fear that the white women of the South are so weak and easily misled that they cannot be trusted to select their own husbands. They agree instead with the numerous white women of the South who have publicly stated that they do not need lynching or special legislation to protect them.

The black herring of intermarriage has been dragged too often across the trail to justice. "Would you want your sister to marry a nigger?" is still the question that is supposed to stun any white man who sponsors rights for Negroes. It stirs Negroes to ironic laughter, although on all levels they recognize the white man's fear of intermarriage as deep-seated. From the jokes of the people—of Negroes talking to Negroes, where "Miss Annie's" name is changed to "Miss Rope" or "Miss Hemp"—to the satire of the publicists, this awareness is to be found. A Negro editor, fighting a covenant restricting housing, was asked point blank: "Do you believe in intermarriage?" to stop his guns of logic and facts. Some Negro public speakers, faced with the question, dodge behind statements like "Well, I'm married already myself." Some take refuge in Kipling's line, "Never the twain shall meet," without sharing Kipling's assurance or hope. The twain have met and the twain will meet. But Negroes are not convinced thereby that they must give up their struggle to share in American democracy.

Though David Cohn warns that irony and reason cannot answer what he calls "blood-thinking," the "biological" fear of "a chocolate-colored American people," Negroes wonder if that fear is as real among Southerners as the determination to keep the Negro in his place economically. Certain Southern liberals have stated their willingness for Negroes to have the rights of voting, good schools, sanitation, paved and lighted streets, justice in the courts, and equitable employment. But Negroes wonder if the possibilities of these—merely these without intermarriage—do not stir great and widespread fears, real instead of spectral. They wonder if the smokescreen of intermarriage is not raised to frighten Southerners from conceding any of these rights, which are fraught with more danger to privilege and exploitation. Some Negroes wonder if maintaining a cheap labor reservoir is not as important a motive as preventing Negroes from crowding whites on buses and proposing marriage to them. Pointing to a group of poor whites and poor Negroes, a planter said to Ira Reid and Arthur Raper: "As long as these whites keep those Negroes humble, we'll keep them both poor."

Many Negroes are sardonic about the oddities of segregation. The white patron, who is willing to eat soup prepared in the kitchen by black hands and served by a black waiter who may get his thumb in it, but who nearly faints when he discovers a Negro eating at another table in the same restaurant; a man's fulsome worship of the black nurse in whose lap he was rocked to sleep, and his horror at sitting next to a black man on a streetcar (it might be the nurse's son); the preservation of white supremacy on a diner by a little green curtain, or on a streetcar by a screen or a rope, in a Jim Crow coach by a chalk line beyond which the overflow from the white coach may not roll, in a government office by setting a Negro's desk catercornered, slightly off the line of the other desks—these afford ribald amusement. They do not make sense; they do not add to respect for the rationality of Southern whites. Such instances are recognized as sprouting from deep roots, certainly; but other superstitions have been uprooted. Maybe these can be.

Some Negroes, of course, realize that a logic does lie behind the apparent oddities. This is the time-hallowed logic of dividing and ruling—the playing off of underprivileged whites against Negroes to prevent a real democratic union— a practice that has paid the oligarchs well. Northern industrialists in the South have done their full share of capitalizing on race hostility, exciting it by talk of

Negroes "getting out of their places." Some Negroes, therefore, see segregation as more than a superstition; but they are convinced that it can, and must be uprooted.

Negroes are not contending for wholesale entree into drawing rooms. They see no contradiction in democracy that people shall select their own friends, cliques, husbands, and wives. They do see as contradictory that false fears of social intermingling should be raised to jeopardize honest aspirations to full citizenship. What segregationists denounce as "wanting to be with white folks," Negroes think of as participating in the duties and enjoying the privileges of democracy. This means being with white folks, undoubtedly, since whites have nearly monopolized these duties and privileges. But it means being with them in fields and factories, in the armed forces, at the voting booths, in schools and colleges, in all the areas of service to democracy.

⤞ Count Us In

Negroes want to be counted in. They want to belong. They want what other men have wanted deeply enough to fight and suffer for it. They want democracy. Wanting it so much, they disregard more and more the warnings: "This is not the time." "The time isn't ripe." "Take your time, take your time." Nearly a hundred years ago, in desperation at the plight of the slaves, Herman Melville wrote, "Time must befriend these thralls." And in crucial moments since, time has been pointed to as the solvent. Patience, urges David Cohn, rules out the emotional and irrational and then the burden will rest "upon the whites to do for the Negro what they have not done at all, or only in part." But the Negro has difficulty in finding the guarantees of this hope that so many Negro and white spokesmen have promised to him. Southern Negroes are not of one mind with Southern whites that "outside interference is hateful and incompetent." They do not see democracy as a commodity to be quarantined at the Potomac and Ohio Rivers, as a sort of a Japanese beetle to be hunted for in the luggage before travelers are allowed to go on. Negroes are glad whenever democratic ideas circulate through the South, whether by means of liberal weeklies, *PM*, the speeches of labor organizers, pamphlets, sermons, radio forums, books, Negro newspapers and magazines, or letters from the boys in service. They know, of course, that if democracy is to be achieved in the South, where it is least found, the greatest work must be done by Southerners, whites and Negroes together. But they welcome whatever help they can get from any sources.

And they know, furthermore, that the agencies working for democracy are not necessarily "outside agitators." The National Association for the Advancement of Colored People may have its headquarters in New York, but, as its name suggests, it is a *national* association. Many of its leaders are Southerners by birth and training. Many of its courageous workers are living in the South. The Negro teachers who risk their jobs and even worse in the struggle for equalization of salaries are Southern born and bred. Negro journalists in the deep South generally speak out uncompromisingly for justice. Southern Negroes have not needed Northern agitators to stir up dissatisfaction with discrimination and abuse. As pointed out earlier, they have learned the hard way, and the lessons have sunk in deeply.

They have heard the threats. Against their democratic aspirations they see a concerted lineup: college professors as well as hoodlums; congressmen as well as vigilantes; Rotarians as well as manual laborers; cotton planters as well as cotton hands. Negroes expect that some of them are going to get hurt before they get what they want. This is no new experience for them; they have been getting hurt in this country since 1619. But getting hurt in a stand-up struggle for justice is one thing; getting hurt merely because of the color of your skin, while lying down, is quite another.

On trips through the South, I have talked with several who had been hurt. With Roland Hayes, for example, shortly after he had been savagely beaten by the policemen of Rome, Georgia. With Hugh Gloster, a young college professor, who had been thrown off a train in Tupelo, Mississippi, because he asked the conductor to let Negroes who were standing in the aisles of the Jim Crow coach overflow into a white coach, only partly filled. With Clinton Clark, who had been beaten, arrested, jailed and threatened with the rope time and time again for organizing the cane-cutters and cotton hands of Louisiana into a union. Roland Hayes talked broodingly; Hugh Gloster, sardonically; Clinton Clark, stoically, without any surprise: "You try to organize people to get out of slavery, may as well expect the big planters and their boys—the sheriffs and deputies—to get tough." But all of these, and others who told me their stories of abuse, knew the shock of the sudden oath, the blow, the murderous look in the eye.

They had been hurt, no doubt of that. But it is unlikely that they, or many other Negroes, merely because of the violence, will become reconciled to what caused it. Many Negroes are still going to protest rough language to their wives, as Roland Hayes did; or unfair travel accommodations, as Hugh Gloster did; or exploitation in the cane and cotton fields, as Clinton Clark did. "Get out and stay out of this parish," the jailer in Natchitoches told Clark. "I'll be back," said Clark, "I'll have a stronger organization behind me the next time."

Some of the victims do not forget the lessons that the rubber hose, the fist, the long black hours in the smelly cell fix so deeply. But from as many other victims comes this: "And if I had it to do all over, I'd do the same thing again."

Negroes who profess faith, whether real or not, in passively waiting for decent whites to take up their burden are losing that faith. Negroes who feared that asking for democracy would lead to some Negroes getting hurt, are losing that fear. But losing the passive faith is not defeatism, and losing the fear is not bravado.

There are many Negroes who are not convinced, as some forlorn liberals are, that democracy is a doomed hope in the South. They see heart-warming signs. They see the opponents of the poll tax gathering strength. The filibusters may rant so long or maneuver so craftily that the repeal may not pass this year, but the struggle against the poll tax will continue. Negroes applaud the Supreme Court decisions outlawing the white primary as a private club's election. They see the FEPC holding on, a symbol of the hope to abolish discrimination in industry, though challenged on many sides, flouted occasionally, and hard beset. They hear native white South Carolinians disclaim the "white supremacy" resolution of their House of Representatives in humiliation "because it is white people who have thus held up the state to scorn. . . . The only white supremacy which is worthy of the name is that which exists because of virtue, not power." White supremacy is not the issue, they say, but that Negroes should serve on juries; that they should be allowed representation on boards which administer affairs involving Negro citizens and their property; that Negro policemen should be provided in Negro residential districts; that the disfranchisement of all Negroes in South Carolina cannot endure indefinitely; these are some of the pressing issues. Negroes are aware of the importance of such words from representative citizens, neither interracialists nor "radicals," in Cotton Ed Smith's bailiwick.

Of course, many Negroes keep their fingers crossed. They expected Congressman Rankin's blast at the Supreme Court vote, which ran true to form: "I see that the parlor pinks in the Department of Justice are already starting to harass the Southern states as a result of the blunder of the Supreme Court. The Negroes of the South are having their hope of peace and harmony with their white neighbors destroyed by these pinks." Canny through long experience with the politicos, Negroes realize that the road from outlawing white primaries and the poll tax to widespread voting may be long and rocky. "Let 'em try it," said the *Jackson Daily News*; "There are other ways of preserving Southern tradition," the *Birmingham Post* said; "We will maintain white supremacy; let the chips fall where they may," said the Governor of South Carolina.

It may be a long and rocky road. But it is the right road. Some Negroes may remain lethargic about their rights and duties as citizens. Some Negroes may get hurt; some may be timorous; the overpraised "harmony" may go off-key. As a sign that they are being "counted in" Negroes see several Southern editors applauding the decision. One called it "a much-needed political safety valve" instead of a threat. Virginius Dabney writes that Tennessee, Kentucky, North

Carolina, and Virginia, all of them without the white primary, have never seen white supremacy endangered. More significantly, he writes: "No society . . . is truly democratic . . . which shuts out anywhere from a quarter to a half of its people from all part in the choice of the officials under whom they must live and work."

Another cheering signpost, indicating that some mileage has been covered on the long journey, is the work of certain Southern white liberals. Virginius Dabney performed a historic act in advocating the abolition of Jim Crow on Virginia street-cars and buses. It is true that he had to surrender his proposal; though numerous white Virginians applauded it, Mr. Dabney became convinced that the time was not right. But it was a first step that may count, and the proof that Virginia white opinion was not unanimous for Jim Crow is worth recording. Hoping that Negro leadership will rest in Atlanta (not so coincidentally Walter White's native city) rather than in New York, Mr. Dabney realizes that steps toward democracy must be taken *in the South*. This realization is quite as honest as his fear of trouble.

Southern white liberals deplore the demands of outsiders, and then come out themselves for many of the same reforms. The Atlanta Conference of representative white Southerners praised the Southern Negro Conference at Durham for frankness and courage. Among so much else the Atlanta Conference conclusions stated: "No Southerner can logically dispute the fact that the Negro, as an American citizen, is entitled to his civil rights and economic opportunities"; and "we agree . . . that it is 'unfortunate that the simple efforts to correct obvious social and economic injustices continue, with such considerable popular support, to be interpreted as the predatory ambition of irresponsible Negroes to invade the privacy of family life. . . . ' We agree also that 'it is a wicked notion that the struggle by the Negro for citizenship is a struggle against the best interest of the nation.' "

Negroes look with hope to the continuing conference, composed of several Southern Negro leaders who met in Durham and Southern whites who met in Atlanta. The conference is "to convene together for better cooperation, more positive and specific action, and for enduring ways and means for carrying out the recommendations." They have reason for confidence in the two co-chairmen, Guy Johnson of the University of North Carolina and Ira Reid of Atlanta University. Many Negroes deplore the isolation of the problem as a Southern regional affair, but they want the results that such a conference may achieve. They notice the stress on good manners and good will and on the absence of "any suggestion of threat and ultimatum," and may wonder just how these terms are defined; but they suspect that this forward step would not have been taken without the activity of organizations like the NAACP. "We want those fellows to keep the heat on," a quiet Southern Negro preacher said to me.

On the national scene, wherever significant work is done to integrate the Negro into the war effort—in industry, in agriculture, in community planning, in the armed services—Negroes are cheered, and their morale rises accordingly. Sometimes discounted as drops in the bucket, these instances of integration might also be considered leaks in the levee, straws in the wind, or as the signposts I have frequently called them. If signposts, Negroes know that the longer, perhaps rougher journey lies ahead. They are therefore not in the mood for stopping, for laying over, for slowing up, or for detouring. And they do not want to be mere passengers, a sort of super-cargo, hitchhikers being given a lift, guests being sped along. They want to do some of the map-reading and some of the driving. Thomas Sancton, a white Southerner who recognizes this truth, writes: "The real liberal knows that the Negro is never going to win any right he doesn't win for himself, by his own organization, courage, and articulation."

The sticking point in the cooperation of Negro and Southern white liberals is segregation. The Atlanta Conference stepped gingerly about it: "We do not attempt to make here anything like a complete reply to the questions raised. . . . The only justification offered for [segregation] laws . . . is that they are intended to minister to the welfare and integrity of both races."

However segregation may be rationalized, it is essentially the denial of belonging. I believe that Negroes want segregation abolished. I realize that here, as so often elsewhere, it is presumptuous to talk of what *the* Negro wants. I understand that Negroes differ in their viewpoints toward segregation: the half-hand on a back county farm, the lost people on Arkansas plantations, the stevedore on Savannah docks, the coal miner in Birmingham, the cook-waitress-nurse in Charleston, the man-on-the-street in Waco, Los Angeles, New York, Boston, the government workers, the newspaper editors, the professional men, the spokesmen for pressure groups—all see segregation from different angles. An illiterate couple on Red River may differ greatly in attitude from their children on River Rouge. On the part of many there has been a long accommodation to segregation, but I believe that satisfaction with it has always been short.

An old railroad man in Birmingham, directing me to the FEPC hearings in the Federal Building, told me that whites and Negroes entered the court room by the same door (there was only one), but that they did not sit together. "No," he said. "They sits separate; whites on one side, the colored on the yother." Then he added, "And that's the way I'd ruther have it, too, ef'n I had my druthers. Of course I don't believe in scorning nobody, but—." He might have had memories of whites and Negroes "mixing socially," where the gains had all fallen to the whites, or where insult or violence had followed. But he knew, in spite of his "druthers," that segregation and scorn were bedfellows.

During Mr. Talmadge's campaign against the coeducation of the races, one Georgia Negro college president gave white folks the assurance that "Negroes didn't want to attend the University of Georgia; all they wanted was a little school of their own." I found a young Negro Army doctor who sharply opposed the setting up of mixed military units, especially a mixed hospital. Only in an all-Negro hospital, according to his experience, could a Negro physician function to the best of his ability, realize his full development, and be free from insult. He was nevertheless violently opposed to Jim Crow in transportation and public services.

I heard varying defenses of segregation, but I still did not find many supporters of it, even in the South. Of the many who had gained from it in safety, comfort, wealth, and prestige, I found some who were candid enough to admit that in segregated schools, churches, lodges, banks, and businesses, they had risen higher than they might have risen in competition with whites. Many were fighting to improve their side of the biracial fence, to equalize teachers' salaries, to obtain buses for students, and for similar ends. But the fighting was not to buttress biracialism, but to make the most of a bad thing, to lessen the inferiority that segregation always seemed to mean. The young flyers at the segregated Tuskegee base trained rigorously to become first-rate fighting men, to prove that Negroes should be piloting planes; but their most fervent admirers, however proud of their achievement, would not say that they would have made a poorer record at an unsegregated base. And they would not deny that there were indignities at the segregated base.

A sign in Atlanta read: "This line marks the separation of the races which were [sic] mutually agreed to by both." My friend, certainly no hot-head but long "accommodated," interpreted it: "Mutual agreement. You know: a man puts his gun in your ribs and you put your pocketbook in his hands."

When the conference in Durham excluded Northern Negroes, many white Southerners (and Negroes, for that matter) were led to expect a conservative set of principles. As Benjamin Mays, an important member of the conference, states: "They were Negroes the whites of the South knew. They were not radicals. They were Negroes the South says it believes in and can trust." Yet the Durham charter went on record as fundamentally opposed to segregation, and Walter White considered the recommendations to be almost identical in language and spirit with those of the NAACP and the March-on-Washington movement.

A chief difference between Southern and Northern Negro spokesmen is not that one group defends and the other condemns segregation, but that Southern leaders, in daily contact with it, see it as deeply rooted; Northern leaders, not seeing it to be so widespread and knowing that occasionally it can be ripped out, do not see the long, sturdy tentacles. The dangers are that Southern Negroes will believe it ineradicable and that Northern Negroes will believe it can be easily uprooted by speeches and governmental decree.

At Negro mass meetings in the North, demands that racial segregation should be abolished, "that the Negro and the white must be placed on a plane of absolute political and social equality," have been roundly applauded. It is doubtful if even the orators themselves envisaged that their demands would be immediately or even soon forthcoming. Delegates from the South knew that on the return trip home, at St. Louis or Cincinnati or Washington, they would be herded into the inferior Jim Crow coach; that if they wished to travel by bus they would be lucky even to get on, into the rear seats; that once home, Jim Crow would be all about them wherever they turned. Even Northern delegates knew where Jim Crow had caught hold in their communities.

Negroes know that more than stirring speeches will be needed to remove Jim Crow. But they also know another thing, on all levels and in all callings—whether an illiterate sharecropper comparing the one-room ramshackly school for his children with the brick consolidated school for the white children, or a college president who knows, in spite of the new brick buildings, how unequal a proportion of state funds has come to his school—Negroes recognize that Jim Crow, even under such high-sounding names as "biracial parallelism," means inferiority for Negroes. And most American whites know this too, and that is the way that many prefer it. As the beginning of one kind of wisdom, Negroes recognize that the phrase "equal but separate accommodations" is a myth. They have known Jim Crow a long time, and they know Jim Crow means scorn and not belonging.

What Negroes applauded from their orators, many recognized as a vision, the vision of a good thing. Though a dream, and difficult of achieving, it still was not wild and illogical. It made more sense than the reality: that in the world's leading democracy, democratic rights were withheld from one man out of every ten, not because he had forfeited his right to them, but because his skin was darker and his hair of a different texture from those of the other nine. The reality was that in a war against an enemy whose greatest crimes are based on spurious race thinking, this democracy indulged in injustice based on race thinking is just as spurious.

This war is the Negro's war as much as it is anybody's. If the Axis were victorious, Negroes would be forced from the present second-class citizenship to slavery. Hitler's contempt for Negroes as apes and his sadistic treatment of Jews and all the conquered peoples, and Japan's brown Aryanism, similarly ruthless and arrogant, offer far less hope than America's system of democracy, bumbling though it may be, but still offering opportunity for protest and change. Even at the cost of the preservation of the *status quo*, this is still the Negro's war.

These are truisms. But they do not incite high morale. Indeed, they are somewhat like telling a man with a toothache that he should consider himself fortunate, since he might have a broken back. True, but his tooth still aches, and he wants something done for it.

This is even more the Negro's war, if it is truly a people's war, a war of liberation, aimed at establishing the Four Freedoms, ushering in the century of the common man, as the fine slogans have it. The Negro could do well with the Four Freedoms, especially the Freedoms from want and fear, for these two Freedoms have long been strangers to him. This is all the more the Negro's war if, as Michael Straight hopes, the peace will "guarantee to all of its citizens the right to constructive work at fair wages; to good low-cost housing; to minimum standards of nutrition, clothing, and medical care; to full opportunities for training and adult education; to real social security."

There is more cleverness than wisdom in the remark of John Temple Graves that asking for complete democracy at home is as logical as saying "that because America's house was on fire America must take the occasion for renovating the kitchen or putting Venetian blinds in the parlor." The trouble with the house is more serious than that; it really has much to do with the foundation. Wendell Willkie warns that:

> We cannot fight the forces and ideas of imperialism abroad and maintain any form of imperialism at home. . . . We must mean freedom for others as well as ourselves, and we must mean freedom for everyone inside our frontiers as well as outside.

and Pearl Buck points out:

> Our democracy does not allow for the present division between a white ruler race and a subject colored race. If the United States is to include subject and ruler peoples, then let us be honest about it and change the Constitution and make it plain that Negroes cannot share the privileges of the white people. True, we would then be totalitarian rather than democratic.

Daily reports of the violations of democracy crowd upon the Negro, breeding cynicism. Nevertheless, while denouncing them, he does so in the framework of democracy. He continually relies on America's professions of democracy as having some validity; he has not yet descended to the hopeless view that America prefers totalitarianism.

As has been so often stated: If America is to indoctrinate the rest of the world with democracy, it is logical to expect that the American Negro will share it at home. It may take a long time, but segregation must be abolished before there will be true democracy at home. True democracy will mean the right and opportunity to win respect for human worth. It can have no truck with Nazi concepts of race-supremacy, with Nazi contempt for people because of race. Democracy will mean equal pay for equal labor, equal employment opportunities, opportunities to learn and use technical skills and to advance according to mastery of them, and the right to join and participate fully in trade unions. The tentative beginning made by FEPC must be developed. Democracy will mean equal educational opportunities, equalized salaries for teachers, and equalized facilities in the schools. The spread of the segregated system of education must be checked and eventually abolished as wasteful and unjust. Democracy will mean that the Federal Government will go on record against mob violence, for, in spite of the decline in lynching, threats of mob violence are still powerfully coercive. Democracy will mean the discouraging of police brutality, will mean justice in the courts rather than patronizing clemency or cruel intolerance. Negroes will serve on the police force, at the lawyers' bar, in the jury docks, and on the judges' bench. Democracy will mean the franchise, with elimination of the poll tax and the subterfuges and intimidations that keep qualified Negroes from the polls. It will mean training Negroes to fulfill the duties of free citizens. Democracy will mean the strengthening and extension of the social legislation begun by the New Deal in such agencies as the Farm Security Administration and the Federal Housing Authority; and the opportunity not only to share in the benefits of such agencies but also in their planning and operation. Democracy will mean the opportunity to qualify for service in the armed forces in all its branches, the opportunity for whites and Negroes to fight side by side in mixed commands. Democracy will mean simply the opportunities for all Americans to share to the full extent of their capacities in the defense of America in war and the development of America in peace.

This is not much to ask for, since it is essentially what America guarantees to every white citizen. Only when viewed from the angle that these opportunities are to be extended to Negro citizens, does the list seem staggering, outrageous to some, foolishly idealistic and unattainable to many.

I think that most Negroes are not so optimistic that they foresee the overnight arrival of these opportunities. No group should know better that perfectly functioning democracy in the United States has always been a hope, rather than an actuality. Even in those sections where one undemocratic practice—legal segregation—has been missing, democracy—to whites as well as to Negroes—has not been simon-pure. The poverty of the South would be oppressive on both whites and Negroes even if segregation laws were stricken from the books, and discrimination from the practices, tomorrow. The Negro's plight in the South will be lightened substantially only when the plight of the poor white is enlightened; when these cannot be pitted against each other in contempt and hatred; when genuine democracy replaces the fictitious (and fictitious not only in the matter of race relations). Nevertheless, however Herculean the task, Negroes are not so defeatist that they think democracy to be unattainable. They are good Americans in nothing more than in their faith that "democracy *can* happen here." Worth fighting for in Europe, it is worth working for here. But since time does not stand still, all America—black and white—had better start to work for it. President Roosevelt, speaking of the Four Freedoms, has said: "Magna Carta, the Declaration of Independence, the Constitution of the United States, the Emancipation Proclamation and every other milestone in human progress—all were ideals which seemed impossible of attainment—yet they were attained."

Negroes should not want fundamental rights of citizenship donated to them as largesse, and should not consider them as barter for loyalty, or service. American whites should not consider Negroes as beneficiaries, being accorded gifts that to men of different complexion are rights. Nor should they think of Negroes as passive objects of humanitarianism, since Negroes can really be allies in a common struggle for democracy. Even after Hitler and Tojo are defeated, democracy is going to need all of its strength to solve grave problems. The strength of the Negro will be as much needed and as useful in the coming economic and political crises as it is needed and should be useful now.

I believe that many Negroes realize this and wish to be allowed to share in the sacrifice and travail and danger necessary to attain genuine democracy. Wendell Willkie's world trip excited him with "fresh proof of the enormous power within human beings to change their environment, to fight for freedom with an instinctive awakened confidence that with freedom they can achieve anything." In times of frustration, Negroes would do well to recognize that power, and to understand that it fights on their side.

Negroes know they have allies. There are the numerous colored peoples of the world, the millions of yellow, brown, and black men in China, India, the Philippines, Malaysia, Africa, South America, the Caribbean, all over the globe, where hope for democracy is stirring a mighty ferment. Almost all are concerned with their own perplexities, but they agree in their fight against color prejudice. The success of the Soviet Union in destroying race prejudice gives hope and courage. And there are other allies abroad, in the smaller as well as the larger, the conquered as well as the unconquered nations, who are tied, not by a common urge to abolish race prejudice, but by the determination to be free. And in America there are allies too. It does not seem over-optimistic to believe them on the increase, although still outnumbered by the indifferent or the hostile. Negroes must join with these American allies, in the North and in the South, in a truly interracial program, or better, a democratic program. The minority must work with the men of good will in the majority. Negroes recognize their allies here without difficulty, and their affection for them runs strong and deep.

Americans, Negroes and whites, may believe that to achieve full democracy is arduous. It may well take a slow pull for a long haul. But it can no longer be postponed. American dreams have been realized before this, however difficult they seemed to the faint-hearted and skeptical. Americans, Negro and white, have mustered the doggedness and courage and intelligence needed. I have confidence in my own people that they will help achieve and preserve democracy, and will prove worthy of sharing it. But we must be counted in.

Annotations

INTRODUCTION

FEDERAL WRITERS' PROJECT The Federal Writers' Project (FWP) was one of Franklin D. Roosevelt's Works Progress Administration (WPA) programs designed to provide useful work for thousands of writers displaced by the Depression. A primary goal of the FWP was to write and to publish a series of local, state, and federal guidebooks, combining the features of a tour book with historical facts and data. These books took their impetus from the famous Baedeker Travel Guides, which made tourist information and attractions into absolute necessities for travelers. Sterling A. Brown held the position of editor on Negro affairs for the national FWP office. His duties included guarding against misrepresentations of African Americans in the various guidebooks.

BENJAMIN BOTKIN'S *LAY MY BURDEN DOWN* (1945) A collection of oral testimonies on the experiences of African American folk in the South. Brown was interested in what the narratives revealed about black life, character, and language, and about the social character that shaped them. Benjamin Botkin worked closely with Brown on folklore projects, including this book.

VIRGINIA PROJECT A state project under the auspices of the Federal Writers' Project. Under the direction of Eudora Richardson, this project produced what many feel was the first state history of the Negro ever published, *The Negro in Virginia* (1940). Unique in approach, its use of anecdote, interview, and documents serves as a good example of social history. The actual research was conducted by a group of project workers led by Roscoe E. Lewis. The cogent advice Brown offered to the project has led some people to the mistaken conclusion that he was the study's sole author. To commemorate their friendship and working relationship, Brown dedicated his poem "Remembering Nat Turner" to Lewis.

JAMES WELDON JOHNSON (1871–1938) A leading figure of the New Negro Renaissance, Johnson was a distinguished poet, novelist, teacher, critic, diplomat, and NAACP official. He is perhaps most often remembered as the lyricist for "Lift Every Voice and Sing," often referred to as the Black National Anthem. Johnson wrote a compelling introduction to Brown's *Southern Road* (1932) in which he modified his criticism of poetry written in black dialect.

THE NEGRO CARAVAN (1941) An anthology of African American literary and cultural expression. With Arthur P. Davis and Ulysses Lee as coeditors, Brown set out to present a more accurate and revealing story of the Negro writer than had ever been told. The anthology presented a body of writing by African American authors and a number of folk sources that revealed a "truthful mosaic" of black character, thought, and experience and that, through perceptive literary interpretations and critical evaluations, attested to the rich diversity of black writing and cultural expression. It remains one of the most useful and comprehensive anthologies of African American writing ever published and continues to be important for establishing the basis for modern criticism of black literature.

NATIONAL COUNCIL OF TEACHERS OF ENGLISH The NCTE is an organization devoted to improving the teaching and learning of English and language arts at all levels of education. Since 1911, NCTE has provided a forum for the profession, an array of opportunities for teachers to continue their professional growth throughout their careers, and a framework for cooperation to address issues that affect the teaching of English.

JULIUS ROSENWALD (1862–1932) An American businessman and philanthropist, he served as president and chairman of the board of Sears, Roebuck, and Company. Rosenwald was committed to social reform and the improvement of race relations. In 1917, he established the Julius Rosenwald Fund; it was largely used to establish rural schools for blacks. It later offered fellowships to scholars, writers, and artists; Brown was a recipient of a Rosenwald fellowship in 1942.

VIRGINIA SEMINARY AND COLLEGE Originally known as the Virginia Baptist Seminary, Virginia Theological Seminary and College was the first post–Civil War college in Lynchburg. It was incorporated in 1888. Along with theological instruction, the seminary offered college preparatory work, teacher training, vocational education, and liberal arts courses. It was to this school that Rev. Sterling Nelson Brown and Dr. Carter G. Woodson sent Sterling A. Brown after his graduation from Harvard in 1923. No doubt the senior Brown hoped his son would "hear the call," become a seminarian, and succeed him as a theologian and pastor. But from 1923 to 1926, Brown would heed a different calling, one that embraced the lives, lore, and language of black folk. These became important sources of his evolving poetic sensibility.

MRS. BIBBY AND CALVIN "BIG BOY" DAVIS Among those people Brown met while teaching at Virginia Seminary, two were crucial to his development of a folk-based aesthetic: Mrs. Bibby and Calvin "Big Boy" Davis, both of whom figure significantly in *Southern Road* (1932), his first published collection of poems. Mrs. Bibby, the mother of the one of his students, typified in many ways the tough-mindedness and strength that Brown admired in the folk. She is represented in "Virginia Portrait" and "Sister Lou." Calvin "Big Boy" Davis, an itinerant worker and guitar player, provided him excellent instruction in the spirituals and "gut bucket" blues for a few coins to keep him going. Poems such as "Odyssey of Big Boy" and "When de Saints Go Ma'chin' Home" preserve the memory of those wonderful experiences.

LINCOLN UNIVERSITY More than $6,000 raised by the black fighting men of the 62nd and 65th U.S. Colored Infantry constituted the initial endowment for a 22-foot-square room in which classes first began in 1866 at what is now Lincoln University in Jefferson City, Missouri. Known then as Lincoln Institute, the school began receiving state aid in 1870 in order to expand its teacher training program. It became a state institution nine years later and implemented college-level courses in 1887. It has been known as Lincoln University since 1921. As a faculty member in the English Department and part-time language instructor at Lincoln Academy from 1926 to 1928, Brown used to outrage his more staid colleagues by hanging out in "The Foot," one of the more colorful parts of the black community. There he learned from such artful storytellers as Slim Greer and Revelations.

FISK UNIVERSITY A private liberal arts college, Fisk was founded in 1866 in Nashville, Tennessee, by the American Missionary Association. Faltering from economic woes, the school turned to a strategy that had gained popularity since the mid-1800s. Many black institutions of higher education fielded a group of jubilee singers or a vocal quartet to sing spirituals in concerts for fund-raising. The Jubilee Singers of Fisk was one of the most successful. In 1871, this small group set out to raise money for the financially strapped school. Over the next decade, the singers toured most of the Northern states and much of Europe, performing for such dignitaries as England's Queen Victoria. Georgia Gordon, a cousin of Sterling A. Brown's mother, Adelaide Allen, was an original member of the Fisk Singers. Both of Brown's parents were graduates of Fisk.

IDA B. WELLS (1862–1931) A fearless antilynching crusader, suffragette, women's rights advocate, journalist, and speaker. Wells-Barnett courageously sued the Chesapeake, Ohio, and Southwestern Railroad Company for forcefully removing her from a train when she refused to give up her seat to a white man. As editor of the Memphis *Free Speech*, she wrote a scathing denunciation of the lynching of three black store owners whom white store owners saw as competitors for business. A mob looted and destroyed the newspaper in response; Wells-Barnett's life was spared because she was in Chicago at the time.

ANNE SPENCER (1882–1975) A well-known poet during the New Negro Renaissance. Spencer's verse was noted for its enigmatic, allusive quality and privacy of vision. She lived in Lynchburg, Virginia, with her husband, Edward, both of whom graduated from Virginia Seminary. Her reputation was further enhanced by her intricate flower gardens. Brown was a frequent visitor to their home, where they discussed their different poetic styles.

SOUTHERN ROAD (1932) Sterling Brown's first book of poems. It was published during his doctoral studies at Harvard University. In introducing this collection, James Weldon Johnson recanted his valedictory that black vernacular speech had but two stops: pathos and humor. Instead, he found that Brown had infused his poetry "with genuine characteristic flavor by adopting as his medium the common, racy, living speech of the Negro in certain phases of *real* life." Even the eminent critic Alain Locke was moved to proclaim that these poems "hail[ed] a new era in Negro poetry, for such is the deeper significance of this volume."

OPPORTUNITY MAGAZINE The periodical of the National Urban League. In its 1925 literary contest, Brown won second prize for his essay "Roland Hayes." His poem "When de Saints Go Ma'chin' Home" won him the first-place prize in its 1927 contest. Beginning in 1931, until the end of the decade, Brown wrote a regular column for *Opportunity* with variations on the title "The Literary Scene: Chronicle and Comment."

BOLL WEEVILS An insect that feeds on cotton plants. The years 1914 and 1917 marked a sharp decline in Southern agricultural production, in part because of the spread of the boll weevil. One result of this devastation was the series of migrations of blacks to the North.

GERTRUDE "MA" RAINEY (1886–1939) Born in Columbus, Georgia, as Gertrude Malissa Nix Pridgett, Ma Rainey emerged as one of the most important "blues queens" in the 1920s. This success took place after a career of owning her own musical group, the Rabbit Foot Minstrels. Poet-journalist Frank Marshall Davis once described her as "commanding a big, deep, fat-meat-and-greens voice, rich as pure chocolate, and her words told of common group experiences. It was like everybody was shaking out his heart. Way, way low down it was and hurting good." Brown shares much of this feeling in a poetic homage titled "Ma Rainey."

DAVID WALKER (1785–1830) An abolitionist, an orator, and a writer. Walker's fame rests primarily on a small but explosive pamphlet titled *David Walker's Appeal to the Colored Citizens of the World* (1829–30). It was circulated clandestinely but widely throughout the antebellum South, proposing to incite slave uprisings as the only possible solution to ending slavery. After his *Appeal* was published, his life was threatened. He refused to flee to Canada and, instead, vowed to fight on. He died shortly thereafter in circumstances that led many abolitionists to believe he had been murdered.

FREDERICK DOUGLASS (1818–95) One of the foremost leaders of the abolitionist movement. A brilliant speaker, Douglass was asked by the American Anti-Slavery Society to engage in a tour of lectures and so became recognized as one of America's great speakers. His fame increased when his first autobiography was published in 1845. After the Civil War, he engaged in a vigorous struggle for black civil rights and an equally impassioned fight for women's suffrage.

HARRIET JACOBS (1813–97) The author of *Incidents in the Life of a Slave Girl: Written by Herself* (1861), the most well-known slave narrative by an African American woman.

WILLIAM WELLS BROWN (1814–84) Novelist, playwright, and historian. He was the son of a slave woman and a white relative of her owner. Brown escaped from slavery in January 1834. During his flight, he received aid from an Ohio Quaker named Wells Brown, whose name he subsequently adopted in the course of defining his new identity as a free man. An active abolitionist, he also became a prolific author, producing a body of work that includes *Narrative of William W. Brown, A Fugitive Slave* (1847); *Three Years in Europe, or Places I Have Seen and People I Have Met* (1852); a novel, *Clotel; or the President's Daughter: A Narrative of Slave Life in the United States* (1853); and the melodramatic play *The Escape; or a Leap for Freedom* (1858).

W. E. B. DU BOIS (1868–1963) Scholar, critic, poet, novelist, editor, political activist. Du Bois emerged at the turn of the century as the leading opponent within the black community of Booker T. Washington's accommodationist approach to securing civil rights for African Americans, advocating instead organized political and legal resistance to segregation. To this end, he helped to launch the Niagara Movement in 1905 and in 1909 cofounded the National Association for the Advancement of Colored People (NAACP). His *The Souls of Black Folk* (1903) remains important for a number of reasons, not the least of which is the profound statement it prophesied: "The problem of the Twentieth Century is the problem of the color line."

SOUTH ON THE MOVE

JOHN L. LEWIS (1880–1969) The leader of the United Mine Workers of America from 1920 to 1960. A very influential union organizer, he helped to organize the Congress of Industrial Organizations in the 1930s, which, for the first time, allowed African American membership.

ROARK BRADFORD (1896–1948) A white author who wrote pseudo–African American folklore, often versions of stories from the Bible. He is best known for *Ol' Man Adam an' His Chillun* (1928) from which the play *Green Pastures* was adapted. Brown was especially critical of his characterizations of blacks, which appeared to Brown as so many clowns and buffoons.

DONALD DAVIDSON (1893–1968) A diehard member of the Fugitive Movement, which took its name from a short-lived publication *The Fugitive,* originating at Vanderbilt University during the 1920s. This group, which included John Crowe Ransom, Allen Tate, and Robert Penn Warren among its members, held fast to agrarian ideals, even when industrialization had become important to redefining the Southern way of life. Thus when Davidson describes himself as a "throwback," he acknowledges his poetry that romanticizes "Old South" traditions.

SAM FRANKLIN Franklin participated in a farm experiment near Hillhouse in Bolivar County, Mississippi. Ultimately named the Delta Farm Cooperative, this farm consisted of little more than twenty-one hundred acres. The impetus for this collective came from the Southern Tenant Farmers Union, whose attempts at unionization were thwarted in Northeast Arkansas and whose members were run off the land, beaten, or killed. A comparatively safer place was located in Mississippi, although the interracial makeup of the members caused the collective to be circumspect and to follow somewhat the racial rules governing African American and white relations. Franklin served as "the social administrator," in other words, its resident director. All members belonged to a producers' and a consumers' cooperative. Politically, the collective vacillated between socialist and Christian principles, no doubt much more of the latter than the former. Franklin was the subject of a chapter in Jonathan Daniels's *A Southerner Discovers the South*.

ERSKINE CALDWELL (1903–87) Playwright, novelist, essayist. With Margaret Bourke-White, a New York photographer, Caldwell collaborated on *You Have Seen Their Faces* (1937), a photographic record of the Depression-era South that specifically addresses the ways the South's racial apartheid made the Depression even more intolerable for blacks. A prolific writer, Caldwell published a number of works, including *Tobacco Road* (1932), *God's Little Acre* (1933), and *Kneel to the Rising Sun and Other Stories* (1935).

JOHN P. DAVIS (1905–73) A graduate of Harvard Law School, Davis helped lobby for the fair inclusion of blacks in New Deal Programs. Along with Ralph Bunche, he founded the National Negro Congress in the 1930s to advance the social, political, and economic status of both black and white workers. He was known to be a member of Roosevelt's "Black Cabinet."

MARY McLEOD BETHUNE (1875–1955) Cofounder of Bethune-Cookman College, Bethune served as its president in 1945. From 1936 to 1944, she served as the director of the Negro Division of the National Youth Administration and, between 1935 and 1944, as President Roosevelt's Special Adviser on Minority Affairs. She was one of the founders in 1935 and the first president of the National Council of Negro Women (NCNW). In 1939, she organized what became the Federal Council on Negro Affairs. This network of twenty-seven men and three women, many of whom worked with the Works Progress Administration (WPA), became known as the "Black Cabinet."

HUEY LONG (1893–1935) A Democrat who served as governor of Louisiana from 1928 to 1932 and U.S. senator from 1932 to 1935. As governor, Long (nicknamed "the Kingfish") consolidated a powerful political machine. Considered a radical populist by some, Long enacted many reforms that made him popular with the rural poor. He championed the little man against the rich and privileged and was an outspoken enemy of Wall Street bankers and big business. As senator, he opposed Franklin D. Roosevelt's New Deal programs, proposing instead his Share Our Wealth program. He wanted the federal government to guarantee every family in the nation an annual income of $5,000 and to provide an old-age pension for everyone over sixty. He also proposed limiting private fortunes to $50 million, legacies to $5 million, and annual incomes to $1 million. Long announced plans to run for the presidency shortly before his assassination in Baton Rouge in September 1935.

OUT OF THEIR MOUTHS

HERMAN EUGENE TALMADGE (1913–2002) Talmadge served six years as governor of Georgia and twenty-four years as U.S. senator. During that time, he skillfully rode the tide of Southern racial politics, evolving from a staunch segregationist to a powerful committee chairman who championed economic development in appealing to black and white voters.

BOB CONSIDINE (1907–75)   A well-known political correspondent and syndicated columnist, Considine was one of the nationally syndicated white sportswriters who, through the 1940s, pushed for the desegregation of baseball.

WESTBROOK PEGLER (1894–1969)   As a sports journalist in the early 1930s, he was initially sympathetic to Franklin Roosevelt and the New Deal. However, later in the 1930s, he became a controversial right-wing newspaper columnist for the *Chicago Daily News* and the *Washington Post*; in 1936, he wrote an article praising a lynching that took place in California. His targets were the Roosevelts, labor leaders, intellectuals, poets, and others. In the 1950s, he became an avid supporter of McCarthyism, providing McCarthy with information on "left-wing" writers and artists.

OLD BUCK

SLIM GREER   One of many outstanding "liars" or storytellers from whom Brown learned, Slim Greer was a sometimes waiter, train car porter, and barber. Brown met him in "the Foot," an area of Jefferson City, Missouri, held in disrepute by Brown's colleagues at Lincoln University. Under Brown's artful transformations, Slim Greer is the protagonist in a series of poems noted for their use of tall tales to satirize the absurdities of racism.

NATIONAL YOUTH ADMINISTRATION   The NYA provided relief for the youth of America during the Second World War. Under Aubrey Williams, a white Mississippian, the NYA set up a program to benefit African American youth. In the out-of-school programs, 13 percent of those enrolled were blacks, and they learned a variety of trades that were to be beneficial in the war emergency. African Americans all the way from grade school to graduate school found it possible to continue their education by means of the benefits obtained by the NYA.

OLD MAN McCORKLE

PATTERROLLERS   A militia established to enforce slavery. The members of the militia were in charge of patrolling areas to guard against slaves escaping or otherwise committing infractions of the laws. Hence the name "patrollers," which, in the vernacular of many slaves, was pronounced "patterrollers."

RETURN OF THE NATIVE

CANE BIÉRE A beer made from sugar cane.

EVANGELINE In Longfellow's "Evangeline," a more idyllic version of the poem, Evangeline wanders through much of the United States before finding her lover in a Philadelphia almshouse just before his death.

BARBUS PATASA A kind of fish that seems to be a combination of brim or perch with catfish. The "barbus" refers to the "whisker-like" protrusions, as are found on catfish.

COURBILLION Brown's spelling of "court bouillon," a fish broth made with water, white wine, spices, and butter.

"QUE TOUTES MES HONNÊTES DETTES SOIENT PAYÉES" French for "so that all my honest debts be paid."

CHARLES SPURGEON JOHNSON (1893–1956) Scholar, editor, and social activist. Johnson studied sociology at the University of Chicago where he was greatly influenced by Robert Park. One of the first black academics to secure major funding for his research, he worked tirelessly to demonstrate the connection between socioeconomic and historical factors and the plight of Southern race relations. In 1923, as director of the National Urban League's Department of Research and Investigations, Johnson also assumed the position of editor of its *Opportunity Magazine*.

ON THE GOVERNMENT

COFFEE-POT MILLS Slang for a small lunchroom or diner, also known as "greasy spoons."

FARM SECURITY ADMINISTRATION (FSA) A program that in 1937 took over the work of the Resettlement Administration. African Americans received benefits, though infrequently in proportion to their numbers or their needs. Those who managed to secure loans through the FSA did so largely because of the capable leadership of Will W. Alexander. Alexander insisted that there be no discrimination between white and black farmers. His policy came under such fire that, in 1942, the enemies of the FSA managed to cut appropriations so drastically that the greater part of its program was ended.

JAMES MONTGOMERY FLAGG (1877–1960) An artist and illustrator particularly involved with wartime recruitment posters. His most famous poster is the 1917 picture of Uncle Sam with the caption "I Want You for the U.S. Army." Flagg and his second wife, Dorothy, honeymooned by driving across the country and back. From this trip, he published and illustrated a light, humorous report, *Boulevards All the Way—Maybe*, in 1925. Perhaps it was this text or illustrations from this cross-country romp that Brown alluded to here. When World War II began, Flagg resumed poster painting, and his 1917 classic was re-released.

JIM CROW SNAPSHOTS

DEADHEADING A railroad term for riding the train on a free pass given to workers.

AND/OR

DICTY An African American vernacular pejorative that describes behavior believed to be stuck-up, over refined, or too upper class.

I LOOK AT THE OLD SOUTH

ROSCOE E. LEWIS (1904–61) An editor of *The Negro in Virginia* (1940), the best-known and most outstanding publication to come out of the Virginia project. This book represented the collective efforts of fifteen black writers and research-ers and included the narratives of ex-slaves.

MAX BOND Educator and diplomat who earned his doctorate by successfully de-fending, in 1936, "The Negro in Los Angeles," his doctoral dissertation. Bond served as a sociology professor at Dillard University and Tuskegee University during the 1930s. He was the founder and president of the University of Liberia. Bond was the uncle of Julian Bond and the father of well-known architect J. Max Bond Jr.

BARBARA FRIETCHIE (1766–1862) Civil War heroine. Her valor was commemo-rated by poet and abolitionist John Greenleaf Whittier in a poem bearing her name.

SUNKEN ROAD (OR THE "BLOODY LANE") Part of the location for the Battle of Antietam, the bloodiest one-day battle of the Civil War, which took place on

September 17, 1862, near Sharpsburg, Maryland. The road acquired its name because it was worn down by years of wagon travel, which formed a natural trench and gave an advantage to the soldiers positioned on top of its ridges. Historians estimate that the "Bloody Lane" experienced more than five thousand casualties alone in four hours. Even though neither side gained a decisive advantage, President Lincoln seized what bit of significance the battle held for the North to announce his Emancipation Proclamation.

THE BLOODY ANGLE Also known as the "Mule Shoe" salient, this battle was one of the bloodiest of the Civil War, and it was part of the ongoing battle for the Spotsylvania Court House in Spotsylvania, Virginia. The Confederate salient, or line of defense, was a prime target. Soldiers fought in hand-to-hand combat for twenty hours on May 12, 1864, across a large pile of logs. Casualties on both sides reached more than 7,000. A particular angle in the Confederate army east of the salient apex, called Bloody Angle, was an area of intensive fighting. Confederate soldiers gained confidence after intense battle, but both sides were heavily battered. Despite the bloodshed of the Bloody Angle, the fighting continued for Spotsylvania. After eleven days, Grant withdrew toward Fredericksburg.

SEVEN PINES BATTLE (OR BATTLE OF FAIR OAKS) The Seven Pines Battle, fought at a road junction by that name six miles east of the Confederate capital of Richmond, was the culmination of an offensive up the Virginia Peninsula by Union forces. The counter-offensive launched by the Confederates fell apart almost immediately because the orders were issued verbally. Poor organization thus led to the Confederates' withdrawal. The battle, fought May 31 and June 1, 1862, is also known as the Battle of Fair Oaks because it occurred near the Fair Oaks railroad station.

MALVERN HILL The Battle of Malvern Hill occurred on July 1, 1862. It was the culmination of the Seven Days battles. As a result of confusion among Confederate army troops, the battle began before Robert E. Lee intended. The Confederates were defeated by massive Union firepower. The Union army suffered a loss of 3,007 men, and the Confederates 5,650. Though Lee was defeated at this particular battle, the Union army was forced to retreat from the Confederate capital.

COLD HARBOR A battle fought on June 3, 1864, near a small tavern by that name less than ten miles from Richmond. The battle, part of the 1864 campaign that included the Battle of the Wilderness and a second battle at Spotsylvania Court House, was disastrous for the Union side and forced a change in Union military tactics. Grant ordered a frontal attack against Confederates who, having had time to prepare, were well entrenched. The Union lost 7,000 men in the battle, and the Confederates lost 1,500. From then on, the Army of Potomac was wary of attacking fortified positions.

CARTER'S GROVE Located near Williamsburg, this plantation was begun in 1750 by Carter Burwell and restored in 1928 when it was purchased by Archibald McCrea and his wife. The plantation was a significant center for social life in eighteenth-century Virginia, and in one of its rooms, the "Refusal Room," both George Washington's and Thomas Jefferson's proposals of marriage were refused by different women. The land is the site of an English settlement that was destroyed in the spring of 1622 by Native Americans. A century after the raid, it was bought by Carter Burwell's grandfather, Robert "King" Carter.

WESTOVER Built in 1730 by Richard Byrd II, founder of Richmond. Named for Henry West, fourth Lord Delaware, who was the son of Thomas West, the governor of Virginia.

BERKELEY On December 4, 1619, English settlers came ashore here and observed the first official Thanksgiving. The mansion was built in 1726. It is the birthplace and property of the Harrison family, whose sons were instrumental in early American government. Benjamin Harrison signed the Declaration of Independence and governed Virginia for several terms. His brother, William Henry Harrison, became the ninth president of the United States in 1840. The latter's grandson Benjamin Harrison would become the twenty-third American president.

SHIRLEY Shirley was founded in 1613, only six years after the Jamestown settlement. It was well known for its hospitality in colonial Virginia. It was also associated with the Carter family who owned Carter's Grove. During the American Revolution, it was a British army supply center. Later, it became part of Civil War history: Anne Hill Carter, Robert E. Lee's mother, was born there, and Lee received some of his early schooling there. Nevertheless, after the Battle of Malvern Hill, Union troops were fed by the homeowners.

SISTER CITIES

MILES BREWTON (1731–75) The Miles Brewton House was designed by builder/architect Ezra Waite. Because of the house's immense size, it was occupied twice during both the Revolutionary and Civil Wars.

WILLIAM RHETT (1666–1723) Rhett came to South Carolina in 1698 and soon successfully gained high social status as a colonial leader. Colonel Rhett was dispatched in 1706 to command a flotilla to fight off a Franco-Spanish attack on Charleston. His reputation was further enhanced when he captured the infamous "gentleman pirate" Major Stede Bonnet. After acquiring a sugar plantation, he completed work on a new house in 1716. Following his death, this marvel of architecture passed through numerous hands and was renovated many times over.

JOHN RUTLEDGE (1739–1800)   Born in Charleston, South Carolina, Rutledge was a member of the First Continental Congress and one of the main authors of the South Carolina constitution in 1776.

MANIGAULT   The Manigault mansion was built in approximately 1790 for Joseph Manigault by his brother Gabriel, an architect. Both were successful merchants during the American Revolution.

GONE WITH WHAT WIND

STONE MOUNTAIN SCANDAL   Situated some sixteen miles east of Atlanta, Stone Mountain has been hailed as the largest body of granite in the world. In 1915, the United Daughters of the Confederacy (UDC) leased the land and commissioned Gutzon Borghum to create the "Lost Cause" memorial. Actual carving began on June 23, 1923. His work came to an abrupt halt in early 1925 when the prospect of raising $2.5 million precipitated a distasteful episode of double-dealing, dishonor, and hatred. Borghum's refusal to compromise on a temporary solution to a long-term stone-cutting problem got caught up in an attempt by new members of the UDC to take control of the incoming funds. At loggerheads with them, Borghum destroyed his own models of the memorial, fearing they would be used in an attempt to complete his artistic vision. The price of his models was fixed at fifty dollars, which made his "crime" a felony and therefore extraditable should he flee the state. He managed to escape to North Carolina, where he posted bond; however, the state of Georgia never pursued extradition, although it left the warrant for his arrest in place. In between periods of dormancy, work was eventually completed on the memorial around 1972. Along the way, though, the primary goal of an homage to the Lost Cause gave way, to a diversity of programs that appealed to a broader segment of the population.

SYMBOL OF THE OLD SOUTH

NATCHEZ DANCEHALL FIRE   On April 23, 1940, the Rhythm Night Club in Natchez, Mississippi, held a one-night-only dance, featuring Walter Barnes and his Orchestra. Spanish moss was used throughout the corrugated iron building for decoration. The boarded-up windows were intended to prevent patrons from entering and avoiding the fifty-cent admission. Estimates vary, but as many as 300 people were inside or trying to gain entry to the dance when a careless smoker set fire to the dry moss by the front door. Because the front entrance was the only way in and out, musicgoers had little chance to escape. Between 150 and 200 people died in the tragedy.

HARMAN BLENNERHASSETT (1764–1831) An Irish immigrant. He is known best for his tangled and unsuccessful schemes with Aaron Burr. Harman and his wife, Margaret, left Ireland in 1796 for the United States. They bought 170 acres on an island near what is now Parkersburg, West Virginia. In the spring of 1805, Burr convinced the Blennerhassetts to support and invest in his scheme for a campaign against the Spanish empire in Mexico. His neighbors suspected treason and stormed his island home. Blennerhassett and Burr were arrested later in Kentucky. Neither one was convicted. The Blennerhassett mansion and island were destroyed by fire in 1812 but later renovated.

JOSEPH HERGESHEIMER (1880–1954) In *Quiet Cities*, published in 1928, Hergesheimer writes several romantic short stories praising antebellum American virtues. Brown's "Negro Character as Seen by White Authors" specifically attacks Hergesheimer for his romanticizing of antebellum Southern life.

GOAT CASTLE In August 1932, Jane "Jennie" Merrill, an aging recluse from a prominent family, was murdered mysteriously at her home, Glenburnie, in Natchez, Mississippi. The prime suspects accused of the killing were her equally eccentric next-door neighbors, Dick Dana and Octavia Dockery, who shared a home called Glenwood. As children and young adults, these three and Duncan Minor had been the closest of friends and the shining jewels of Southern aristocracy. Beginning sometime in the mid-1890s, their friendships deteriorated. Dick and Octavia never again got along with Jennie and Duncan. In the ensuing years, each became either reclusive, depressed, or "strange." While Glenburnie maintained a degree of respectability, Glenwood suffered from want of care and became squalid. Animals, including goats, wandered freely in and out of the house, which caused it to be nicknamed "Goat Castle." Jennie's death not only shed light on Dick and Octavia's destitution, but it also made Glenwood a perverse attraction for tourists who paid fifty cents each for an almost carnivalesque sideshow tour in which Octavia spun antebellum tales and Dick accompanied her with off-kilter music he played on the piano. According to local legend, Jennie's ghost haunted the woods separating the properties, looking for vengeance for her murder.

BARATARIANS The Baratarians were an elaborate smuggling ring that operated from a base near the Gulf Coast of Louisiana. These men, who represented various nationalities, met as an association of privateers in 1805. In total, they numbered between three thousand and five thousand men, led by the Lafitte brothers, Pierre and Jean. Before the War of 1812, the Baratarians disregarded naval laws and attacked American, English, Spanish, and neutral ships. With tensions over naval control rising on all sides, the U.S. Navy and Baratarians fought minor conflicts from 1812 to 1814. The Baratarians were a power to be reckoned with, and both the British and U.S..forces recognized a formidable enemy and possible ally. The British offered Jean Lafitte land in British North America, protection of his property and person, thirty thousand dollars in cash, and the rank of captain in their navy. Lafitte requested and was granted time to consider the offer. In the meantime, he approached the governor of Louisiana with proof of the British proposal and offered to help the Americans in return for a pardon for himself and his men. Even though the governor knew of Jean Lafitte's value, the United States destroyed Barataria. For not resisting the American onslaught, the governor recommended clemency for Lafitte and his men. When the British began their invasion of New Orleans, General Andrew Jackson sought and received the services of Jean Lafitte and his men, who fought valiantly in turning back the invading British.

A TOUR OF HISTORY: OLD NEW ORLEANS

BENJAMIN FRANKLIN BUTLER (1818–93) A provocative political force before, during, and following the Civil War. From the state of Massachusetts, Butler was promoted to brigadier general of the state's militia in 1855, a rank closely associated with his political position and certainly not military prowess. In 1861, while commanding Fort Monroe in Virginia, he refused to return to their owners slaves who had crossed Union lines on the grounds that their labor for the North made them "contraband," thus originating the term as applied to African Americans. In 1862, he earned such nicknames as "Beast," "Brute," and "Spoons" (for his habit of stealing silverware) when, as commander of the forces occupying New Orleans, he seized $800,000 from the Dutch consulate, hanged a man for ripping the Union flag down from the United States Mint, and declared women who insulted Union soldiers to be treated as prostitutes. Following the war, as a Democratic member of Congress who supported the Radical Republican policies during Reconstruction, he wrote the 1871 Ku Klux Klan Act, which outlawed the Klan.

BIENVILLE Known formally as Jean-Baptiste Le Moyne, Sieur de Bienville (1680–1767). Born in Montreal, he and his brother were part of the expedition that founded the colony of Louisiana. In 1701, Bienville became its acting commandant. He served as governor of the Louisiana colony in 1701–12, 1718–26, and 1733–40. He is credited with founding New Orleans, in 1718.

GEORGE WASHINGTON CABLE (1844–1925) Cable is most noted for his work on Creole society in Louisiana. He had an extensive literary career totaling fourteen novels and short-story collections. Cable had a complex if not contradictory relationship with the South. Though he was a Confederate soldier, he later wrote essays calling for a reformed South. He was horrified by slavery, yet he was quite enamored with romantic notions of the antebellum South.

CHARLES ETIENNE GAYARRE (1805–95) New Orleans lawyer, novelist, essayist, and historian who wrote in both French and English. His best-known work was the four-volume *History of Louisiana* published between 1854 and 1866.

GRACE KING (1852–1932) Novelist and short story writer who portrayed the pre–Civil War South at least sympathetically (some critics say romantically). Offended by George Washington Cable's more realistic portrayals of old Southern life, King began writing in response to him. She also became one of the first women to write histories of the South; *New Orleans: The Place and the People* (1895) is her first history.

PERRY YOUNG A Yale graduate and editor of *World Ports Magazine*, Young connected with S. P. Walmsley to devise themes for the Mystic Club, which sponsored the Mistick Krewe of Comus for Mardi Gras. In 1925 Young and Walmsley began a collaboration that was to lead to a history of the club. It was published in 1931 as *The Mistick Krewe* by Young. Walmsley died before the project was completed.

LYLE SAXON (1891–1946) Writer of fiction, biography, and history who also championed the romance and tradition of Old New Orleans. Saxon became the director of the Louisiana Federal Writers' Project. He also compiled and contributed to *Gumbo Ya-Ya*, a collection of Louisiana folktales and valuable guides to New Orleans and other parts of Louisiana.

ANTOINE DE LA MOTHE CADILLAC (1658–1730) In 1701, this French explorer, trader, and all-around colorful figure founded the settlement of Fort Ponchartrain du Detroit, which later became the city of Detroit. Historians agree that his background as a member of royalty is dubious; however, they disagree on the year of his appointment as governor of Louisiana, then an almost unknown wilderness. Reports vary from 1710 to 1711 to 1713. In all likelihood, his tenure can be dated from 1712, when French merchant Antoine Crozat was granted a monopoly over Louisiana. He appointed Cadillac governor of Louisiana and Jean Baptiste de Bienville "commander of the Mississippi and its tributaries" or lieutenant governor, second in line to Cadillac. In 1717, Cadillac returned to France, thus making it possible for Bienville to reclaim the governorship he previously held from 1701 to 1712.

ESTEBAN MIRO (1744–1802) Third Spanish governor of Louisiana, from 1785 to 1791.

ANTOINE DE ULLOA (1716–95) First Spanish governor of Louisiana (or "La Florida Occidental"), from 1766 to 1768, after France willingly ceded Louisiana to Spain in 1762 through the Treaty of Fontainebleau. Ulloa was expelled by French settlers who revolted against Spanish rule.

GENERAL ALEXANDER O'REILLY (1722–94) A descendant of an old Irish family that migrated to Spain, O'Reilly was sent to Louisiana to serve the colony as its second Spanish governor and to reestablish Spanish control over the dissidents who had resisted the domination of the Spaniards. His tenure lasted from 1767 to 1769, in part because his rule was virtually despotic.

JOHN LAW (1671–1729) Scottish financier who founded the first French bank (Banque Générale, 1716), issued paper money, and organized the Company of the Indies, which in 1717 was granted a twenty-five-year monopoly over colonization in Louisiana. His "Mississippi Scheme" ruined many of his investors, but it also brought thousands of French and German settlers to Louisiana.

BAMBOULA AND CALINDA Although both dances probably had roots in West African cultural expression, their origins are generally ascribed to West Indian blacks during the eighteenth century. The Calinda (Fr.) or Calenda (Span.) has been described as a dance of multitude or a sort of vehement cotillion. Both men and women danced making sexual gestures by rhythmically striking their own thighs together and thrusting the pelvis and gyrating the hips. The Bamboula also probably had African roots, but it became a form of entertainment in Congo Square, in antebellum New Orleans. Musicians sat in a circle while women formed a chorus. A male dancer would enter the ring and begin a solo performance before seeking the hand of a woman to join him. The woman apparently played the role of coquette, rotating her hips while keeping the upper body immobile, while the man pursued and enticed. Slowly, other couples entered the ring to participate in a music that was frantic and sensual.

OSCAR DUNN (1826–71) An African American who served as lieutenant governor of Louisiana during Reconstruction, from 1868 until his death.

C. C. ANTOINE (1836–1921) An African American who served as lieutenant governor of Louisiana during Reconstruction, from 1872 until 1876.

P. B. S. PINCHBACK (1837–1921) An African American who served as lieutenant governor of Louisiana from 1871 to 1872 and as acting governor from December 9, 1872, until January 17, 1873, after the state legislature impeached Governor Henry Warmoth. In 1876, Pinchback was elected U.S. senator by the Louisiana State Legislature, but the U.S. Senate denied him a seat.

PIERRE GUSTAVE TOUSANT BEAUREGARD (1818–93) Louisiana-born, West Point–trained Confederate general, Beauregard led the attack on Fort Sumter that began the Civil War. Put in charge of defending the South Carolina and Georgia coasts, he repelled a Union assault on Charleston in September 1863 and took part in the defense of Richmond in the spring of 1864.

BAGASSE MILLS Bagasse is the matted cellulose fiber residue left over after juice is extracted from sugar cane. It is traditionally burned as fuel by sugar mills.

GEE'S BEND

T. M. CAMPBELL (1883–1956) Thomas Monroe Campbell of Tuskegee Institute's School of Agriculture worked with George Washington Carver to develop agricultural extension programs at Tuskegee Institute. Their purpose was direct teaching of scientific agriculture to area farmers. The Tuskegee Institute program influenced Federal Extension Programs, and Campbell became the first U.S. extension agent.

JOHN HAMMOND (1910–87) A jazz record producer and critic whose contribution to the development of American jazz has yet to be fully determined. As a record producer, he brought out recordings by Fletcher Henderson, Benny Carter, Benny Goodman, and Teddy Wilson, among many other jazz notables. In 1938 and 1939, he organized the two historic "Spirituals to Swing" concerts in Carnegie Hall.

DR. WILL W. ALEXANDER (1884–1956) Executive director of the Commission on Interracial Cooperation (CIC), which was founded in Atlanta in 1919 to address the racial tension growing out of World War I. Through the 1920s, the CIC worked to combat the Ku Klux Klan and lynchings. During the 1930s, Alexander headed a CIC committee that worked to ensure the inclusion of blacks in Franklin D. Roosevelt's New Deal programs and to persuade government agencies to hire black advisors on minority affairs. It is significant that the CIC never attacked segregation itself; rather, the agency's strategy was to work to improve conditions for blacks under segregation. The CIC merged with the Southern Regional Council in 1944. See Farm Security Administration (FSA) under "On the Government."

TAKE YOUR COAT OFF, GENE!

CLARK HOWELL (1863–1936) Succeeded Henry Grady as editor-in-chief of the *Atlanta Constitution* in 1897. He considered himself an enlightened conservative and generally opposed racial demagoguery; however, like Grady, he maintained the paper's "separate but equal" political stance. He wrote an editorial praising Booker T. Washington's Atlanta Exposition speech, but he criticized Washington when he sought to go beyond the compromise position expounded in that speech.

RALPH McGILL (1898–1969) Columnist for the *Atlanta Constitution*. He became its editor-in-chief in 1938. McGill opposed the Klan, racial terrorism, and, eventually, segregation, thus placing the *Constitution* in the vanguard of New South journalism. He was awarded the Pulitzer Prize in 1959 for courageous editorial leadership.

INSURANCE EXECUTIVE

DEAN WILLIAM PICKENS (1881–1954) Educator, writer, editor, and social activist. A graduate of Yale in 1904, William Pickens was the second black to receive a Phi Beta Kappa key from the institution. For the next sixteen years, he taught classics and sociology at Negro colleges. In 1915, Pickens accepted the position of dean of Morgan College in Baltimore, and he was the first African American in the school's history to hold this job. He remained at Morgan for five years, the last two of which he spent as vice president. Although his tenure as dean was brief, his administrative title essentially was used as his given name. In 1920, he moved to New York and became field secretary of the NAACP. A dynamic speaker, Pickens also served as contributing editor to the Associated Negro Press (1919–40). Taking leave from the NAACP in 1941, he assumed the directorship of the Interracial Section of the U.S. Treasury Department's Savings (later War) Bonds division. His autobiography, *Bursting Bonds* (1923), was reissued in 1991.

ANGELO HERNDON (1913–?) A political activist born in Wyoming, Ohio, Eugene Angelo Braxton Herndon was arrested in 1932 in Atlanta for trying to organize poor and unemployed black and white workers. Under an 1866 Georgia statute, Herndon was charged with attempting to incite a riot. The usual penalty was death, but, mercifully, he was given only eighteen to twenty years. He was released on bond in 1934, largely because of the national and international attention his case drew. The U.S. Supreme Court, in a split decision, overturned the decision, on the grounds it violated the Fourteenth Amendment. Careful historians have deduced that his real "crime" was that he belonged to the Communist Party.

HENRY GRADY (1850–89) Became managing editor and part-owner of the *Atlanta Constitution* in 1880. Known for progressive proposals, Grady coined the term "New South" in an 1886 speech. Specifically, he argued that plantation agriculture should be replaced by industrialization; that the South was sick of sectionalism and in need of Northern capital to support industrialization; and that race relations in the South had changed so that blacks could become partners in the New South. He championed his New South proposals in the pages of the *Constitution* and on speaking tours in Boston and New York.

FRANK STANTON (1857–1927) A writer for the *Atlanta Constitution*. He wrote one of the first daily columns, "Just from Georgia." Stanton also published several volumes of poetry and was sometimes called the Poet Laureate of Georgia.

MRS. MALONE (1869–1957) Founder of Poro College. Annie Minerva Turnbo Malone was one of the most successful black entrepreneurs of the early twentieth century; some cite her as the first black millionaire. She made her fortune through the development of such products as nondamaging hair straighteners, hair growers, and hair conditioners, and her company had international operations in Africa, the Caribbean, and the Philippines. Mrs. Malone established Poro College in St. Louis in 1917 to train black beauticians in the correct application of Poro cosmetics and hair products and to instruct salespersons on how to market the products; the college also trained barbers, secretaries, and bookkeepers. The blocklong campus housed a manufacturing plant, sales operations, and the school itself. Madam C. J. Walker was a salesperson for Mrs. Malone before she started her own line of products.

HEMAN PERRY (1873–1929) An Atlanta businessman. He completed only the seventh grade, but he rose from cotton sampling to establish the Standard Life Insurance Company in 1913. By 1918, it had $8.2 million insurance in force and premium income of $339,327. With Standard as his base, Perry opened an array of businesses, including a bank, a discount corporation, an engineering and construction company, a laundry, and a real estate firm.

E. FRANKLIN FRAZIER (1894–1962) African American sociologist and educator. Edward Franklin Frazier is best known for his extensive, groundbreaking studies of the African American family, including *The Negro Family in the United States* (1939), a classic in sociology, and *Black Bourgeoisie* (1957), considered his most controversial book. Frazier was no stranger to controversy. His 1927 essay published in *Forum*, "The Pathology of Race Prejudice," evoked quite a stir, even though it dissected racial bigotry from within the authoritative, scholarly perspective of a new social science approach. He went on to earn a doctorate in sociology from the University of Chicago in 1931; he became chairman of the sociology department at Howard University in 1934 and taught there for the next twenty-five years.

HOWARD THURMAN (1900–1981) African American theologian and educator. Howard Thurman served as director of religious life and professor of religion at Morehouse and Spelman Colleges in Atlanta from 1929 to 1932; dean of Rankin Chapel and professor of theology at Howard University from 1932 to 1944. In 1944 he cofounded the Church for the Fellowship of All Peoples in San Francisco and served as the church's pastor until 1953. Thurman authored more than twenty books. He studied nonviolent resistance to oppression and led the first African American delegation to meet Mohandas Gandhi in India. Thurman was a professor from 1953 to 1964 at Boston University, where he was a mentor to Martin Luther King Jr. and often discussed Gandhi's teachings with him.

RAYFORD W. LOGAN (1897–1982) African American historian and author. Receiving his Ph.D. from Harvard University in 1936, Logan taught history at Atlanta University from 1933 to 1938 and at Howard University from 1938 until he retired in 1965. He was the editor of the *Journal of Negro History* and the author or editor of several books, including *Diplomatic Relations of the United States with Haiti* (1941), *What the Negro Wants* (1944), and *The Betrayal of the Negro: From Rutherford B. Hayes to Woodrow Wilson* (1965).

WALTER WHITE (1893–1955) African American writer and activist, White produced a well-documented history of lynching, *Rope and Faggot: A Biography of Judge Lynch,* in 1929. He became executive secretary of the NAACP in 1931; during the twenty-four years in which he held that position, he lobbied for antilynching legislation and against job discrimination, poll taxes, white primaries, and unequal education. He tried without success to persuade Franklin Roosevelt to support an antilynching bill. His investigations into the treatment of black soldiers during World War II were documented in his book *A Rising Wind* and provided one of the bases for President Truman's executive order desegregating the U.S. armed services.

NO TIES THAT BIND

GENERAL NATHAN BEDFORD FORREST (1821–77) Confederate general and cofounder of the Ku Klux Klan. He ordered the slaughter of African American troops at Fort Pillow on April 12, 1864, in one of the worst atrocities of the Civil War. Fort Pillow was held by six hundred Union troops, half of whom were African American. The fort was attacked by fifteen hundred Confederate cavalrymen under General Forrest. The Confederate troops essentially murdered surrendering African American soldiers. Reportedly, black sergeants were singled out; several were nailed to logs before they were set on fire. Of the Union soldiers at the fort, 226 survived: 168 white soldiers and 58 black soldiers. The Confederates denied any wrongdoing, saying they officially viewed captured black soldiers as slaves. In later testimony, Confederate soldiers reported that General Forrest had ordered the carnage. A slave dealer in Memphis before the war, Forrest became one of the organizers of the Klan after the war.

THE LITTLE GRAY SCHOOLHOUSE

DOXEY ALPHONSO WILKERSON (1905–93) Educator and Communist Party official. Wilkerson, born in Excelsior Springs, Missouri, grew up in Kansas City, Missouri. He earned an A.B. at the University of Kansas in 1926 and an A.M. from the same school in 1927. He joined the Communist Party, USA, in 1943 as education director for Maryland and the District of Columbia. In the mid-1940s, he moved to New York, where he was executive director of the Communist-led Harlem newspaper, *The People's Voice*, and a columnist for the *Daily Worker*, the official newspaper of the party.

HORACE MANN BOND (1904–72) Teacher and administrator. Bond wrote a major scholarly work, *The Education of the Negro in the American Social Order* (1934), that argued that the poor quality of education among African Americans was directly linked to their lack of political and economic power. Bond did not recommend the abolition of segregated schools; instead, he called for the equalization of resources given to black and white children. In 1939, he published his dissertation, *Negro Education in Alabama: A Study of Cotton and Steel*, which is considered to be an important challenge to established scholarship on Reconstruction. Bond argued that Reconstruction was a significant step forward for black Americans, particularly because of the educational institutions established during that period. Bond published a number of discussions which demanded that American society recognize the intellectual abilities and accomplishments of African Americans, and he was particularly forceful in criticizing racially biased interpretations of intelligence tests, which conveyed the notion that African Americans were inherently inferior. Brown and Bond worked together on many occasions when Brown taught at Fisk University, from 1928 to 1929, and when he worked for the Federal Writers' Project, from 1936 to 1940.

DAVID COHN (1894–1960) White Southern writer from Mississippi and a firm believer in racial segregation. Cohn believed that though it would be possible for Southern blacks to gain voting rights, justice in the courts, and equitable shares of tax money for health, education, and public services, on segregation there could be no compromise. Cohn insisted that if the federal government interceded to end segregation, "every Southern white man would spring to arms and the country would be swept by civil war."

ONE LANGUAGE, ONE PEOPLE

NATHANIEL "TIC" TILLMAN (1898–1965) An old friend of Brown's, Tillman served Atlanta University as chairman of the English department and dean of the graduate school. He was a founding member of the College Language Association.

WILLIAM ELLERY LEONARD (1876–1944) American poet, essayist, teacher, and scholar. He was born in Plainfield, N.J., and was educated at Boston University, Harvard, Gottingen, and Columbia, where he obtained his Ph.D. in 1904. From 1906 to 1944, he was a teacher at the University of Wisconsin. Of his numerous volumes of poetry, the most famous is *Two Lives* (1922), a sonnet sequence relating the tragic story of his first marriage, which ended in his young wife's suicide. His psychological autobiography, *The Locomotive God* (1927), describes his distance phobia; like his life, his writing was marked by psychic defeat.

SIDNEY REEDY Educator and scholar. Reedy taught at Lincoln University (Missouri) and was a member of the National Council of Teachers of English and its Intercultural Relations Committee. Among his publications was "Higher Education and Desegregation in Missouri," which appeared in the *Journal of Negro Education* (Summer 1958).

E. A. CROSS Educator and scholar. Cross was the head of the Division of Literature and Languages at Colorado State College. His *Fundamentals in English: A Textbook for Teachers Colleges Treating the Subject-Matter of Formal English from the Professional Point of View* appeared in 1926. His *Teaching English in High Schools*, written with Elizabeth Carney, was published in 1939. Especially in the latter book, he pays homage to the National Council of Teachers of English as "the most efficiently active organization of teachers in the country today."

HERBERT AGAR (1897–1980) The English-born editor of the Louisville *Courier-Journal* and a white liberal. During World War II, he noted that the war had "ordained" the United States with the responsibility of "taking the lead in bringing a spiritual sense of equality to the world." He added apprehensively that Southern Negroes lived so far from "equality" with white Americans that to them the very word was a joke. He was one of the writers whom Virginius Dabney accused, along with Pearl S. Buck and John Temple Graves, of "stirring up the Negroes" during World War II.

SIGNS OF IMPROVEMENT

SLATER FUND A foundation to support black industrial education. John Fox Slater, a Connecticut industrialist, created the Slater Fund in 1882, when he donated $1 million for the schooling of former slaves and their children in the South. He was motivated by the belief that education was vital if African Americans were to become responsible participants in the American economy and political process. Board members of the fund believed that manual training would best provide blacks with useful skills and would instruct them in moral discipline and social conformity. Between 1891 and 1911, the New York–based fund supported a few model industrial schools, such as Hampton Institute and Tuskegee Institute, eventually giving these schools one half of its annual appropriations. After 1911, the fund pursued its interest in manual training by preparing black teachers in county training schools; it helped build 384 such schools in the South over the next two decades. The Slater Fund joined with the Jeanes Fund, the Peabody Education Fund, and the Virginia Randolph Fund in 1937 to form the Atlanta-based Southern Education Fund, which still exists.

PHELPS-STOKES FUND Nonprofit foundation established in 1911 by New York philanthropist Caroline Phelps-Stokes to support the education of African Americans, Native Americans, Africans, and poor whites. Between 1911 and 1944, it made numerous small grants and produced landmark reports: *Negro Education in the United States* (1916), *Education in Africa* (1922), *Education in East Africa* (1924), and *The Problem of Indian Administration* (1928). The organization's proficiency in administering grants and delivering services was greatly enhanced during the 1950s and 1960s under the leadership of Frederick Douglas Patterson. Deeply committed to historically black colleges, Patterson organized the cooperative college development program, which dispensed more than $6 million in federal aid to improve facilities and to upgrade funding capabilities. His initiative ultimately resulted in the formation of the United Negro College Fund.

JEANES FOUNDATION   The Negro Rural School Fund, which later became known as the Anna T. Jeanes Fund, was the first fund established for the sole purpose of improving rural public education for African American children in the South. Anna Thomas Jeanes donated $1 million to create the fund in 1907. The Philadelphia-based organization accomplished its goal by employing dedicated, experienced, and talented teachers from black schools, then providing them with money and training to become "master teachers." The "Jeanes teachers," later called "Jeanes supervisors," operated on a countywide basis over fifteen Southern states. Assistance included developing curricula, introducing new subjects, acting as principals and superintendents, and training teachers. The Jeanes teachers also served as community advocates, raising money to build new schools and playing an essential role in the overall educational, economic, cultural, and social development for countless rural communities in the South. The Jeanes Fund was distinctive because it was one of the first white philanthropic organizations in which African Americans had real power and authority. Anna T. Jeanes entrusted Booker T. Washington of Tuskegee Institute and Hollis Frissell, president of Hampton Institute, to oversee the initial $1 million donation. In 1937, the Jeanes Foundation, along with the George Peabody Foundation, the John F. Slater Fund, and the Virginia Randolph Fund, merged into the Southern Education Fund.

GENERAL EDUCATION BOARD   Philanthropic organization founded in 1902 with a $1 million donation from industrialist John D. Rockefeller Sr. Its goal was the promotion of education in the United States without regard to race, sex, or creed. From 1902 until it ceased operations in 1960, the General Education Board awarded $325 million in grants to various educational efforts across the nation, particularly in the South. Of this amount, approximately $63 million went toward improving the education of African Americans.

VIRGINIUS DABNEY (1901–95)   White Southern liberal reporter who campaigned against racial intolerance in the South. He started his career as a frequent contributor to many national magazines, and, from 1939 to 1969, was editor of the influential *Richmond Times-Dispatch*. Dabney's racial liberalism never quite moved beyond a highly articulate—and undoubtedly sincere—"separate but equal" position. In fact, his position on blacks serving in the Second World War was described as an effort "to reaffirm their commitment to a concept of inter-racial cooperation that did not challenge segregation itself."

COLLEGES: RETREAT OR RECONNAISSANCE

EMMETT J. SCOTT (1873–1957) Author and administrator. Because his views were generally close to those of Booker T. Washington, Scott was asked by Washington to become his personal secretary. He was elected secretary of Tuskegee Institute in 1912. After Washington's death in 1915, Scott became special assistant to the U.S. Secretary of War in charge of Negro affairs at the start of World War I. From 1919 until 1939, Scott held positions as secretary, treasurer, or business manager at Howard University in Washington, D.C. In the business community, Scott became the principal organizer of the National Negro Business League. Like Washington, Scott believed that African Americans who achieved business success and property ownership would be given political and civil rights. His views are set forth in works such as *Tuskegee and Its People* (1910); *The American Negro in the World War* (1919); and a biography of his mentor, *Booker T. Washington, Builder of a Civilization* (1916).

T. THOMAS FORTUNE (1856–1928) Editor, reporter, and social activist. Before Booker T. Washington's ascent as a national figure began in 1895, Fortune was acknowledged as a major spokesperson for black America. His leadership role in the late-nineteenth-century civil rights movement was instrumental in shaping the debate over how African Americans would respond to their legal and social oppression in the decades to come. He started the *New York Freeman*, which later became known as the *New York Age*. The *New York Age* became a leading black newspaper primarily because of Fortune's editorials, which denounced racial discrimination and demanded full equality for African Americans.

PEACHTREE STREET A major artery in Atlanta running more than nine miles from the center of downtown northward to the elite enclave of Buckhead. Atlanta boasts a veritable orchard of peach trees. There are more than a hundred thoroughfares with peach trees in their names, in addition to a bounty of buildings. In the post–Civil War period, Peachtree Street developed its mystique as an elite residential address. Beginning in the 1920s, its residential status was supplanted by retail, office, and entertainment uses. The building boom of the 1960s to 1990s turned the downtown section of Peachtree Street into the only one in Atlanta that is the concrete canyon usually associated with twentieth-century cities.

DRUID HILLS Affluent white community in the eastern part of Atlanta. While trying to regulate black movement in the city, white officials also worked to keep Atlanta a majority white city by annexing the burgeoning predominantly white suburbs. The major absorption came in 1952 with annexations that increased Atlanta's size from 37 to 118 square miles.

COUNT US IN

FRANK GRAHAM (1886–1972) Educator, scholar, and university president. A native of Fayetteville, Graham grew up in Charlotte, North Carolina, where his father, as superintendent of public instruction, tried to see that black schools received a just share of funds. Aside from his father's efforts on behalf of Negro education, the major influences on Graham's racial liberalism were America's professed democratic heritage and Christianity. In 1915, he joined the faculty of the University of North Carolina, where he drew more attention for his liberal views than for his scholarship. In 1930, he became president of the university, which he presided over until 1948, when he was appointed to the U.S. Senate. But Graham, for all his liberal passions, was not yet ready to violate the Jim Crow laws openly.

CLINTON CLARK Brown probably became acquainted with Clark on one of his trips to New Orleans to do research for *A Negro Looks at the South*. The relationship between Brown and Clark is captured in Brown's unfinished manuscript titled *Saga of an Organizer*. Clark, in an unpublished memoir titled "The Autobiography of Clinton Clark," recounts their relationship, which Elizabeth Davey has marvelously analyzed in her introduction to the text.

LILLIAN SMITH (1897–1966) American writer and champion of racial equality, who is best known for *Strange Fruit* (1944), a controversial novel dealing with the tragic outcome of an interracial love affair in the Deep South. Born in Jasper, Florida, she taught music at a mission school in China during the early 1920s, directed a girls' camp in Clayton, Georgia, from 1925 to 1949, and, with Paula Snelling, edited *Pseudopodia* (1936), which became the *North Georgia Review* (1937–41) and, later, *The South Today* (1942–45). Her active support of the civil rights movement evoked racist anger. Her papers were destroyed by arson in 1955, and two novella manuscripts were lost; *One Hour* (1959) was her only published novel other than *Strange Fruit*. Her nonfiction books include *Killers of the Dream* (1949), *The Journey* (1954), *Now Is the Time* (1955), and *Our Faces, Our Words* (1964).

PAULA SNELLING (1899–?) Employed by Lillian Smith to oversee the Laurel Falls Camp for Girls, a summer camp, Snelling became Smith's lifelong companion and friend. Their approach to the South's problems was different from that of most Southern liberals. They saw most Southern liberals' efforts to come to grips with the region's injustices as amounting only to "scratching the topsoil."

FOUR FREEDOMS A formulation of American post–World War II hopes made by President Roosevelt in his State of the Union address of January 6, 1941.

Speaking eleven months before the United States officially entered the war, Roosevelt set forth the freedoms in these words:

> The first is freedom of speech and expression—everywhere in the world. The second is freedom of every person to worship God in his own way—everywhere in the world. The third is freedom from want—which translated into world terms means economic understandings which will secure to every nation a healthy peacetime life for its inhabitants—everywhere in the world. The fourth is freedom from fear—which translated into world terms means a worldwide reduction of armaments to such a point and in such a thorough fashion that no nation will be in a position to commit an act of physical aggression against any neighbor—anywhere in the world.

ARTHUR FRANKLIN RAPER (1899–1979) In 1926, Arthur F. Raper, a native of Winston-Salem, North Carolina, was recruited as research director of the Commission on Interracial Cooperation. The commission was a Southern organization in which blacks could be members and were allowed to voice complaints. Prevention of violence between the two races remained a prime objective of the body. Supporters of the commission argued that promotion of "better understanding" between the two races was also vital. Raper, unlike his predecessor, M. Ashby Jones, never thought that segregation was good or that it would last indefinitely. While with the commission, Raper produced such works as the *Tragedy of Lynching* in 1933 and, three years later, *Preface to Peasantry*, an account of the severe problems of white and black sharecroppers in two rural Georgia counties.

CONGRESSMAN JOHN RANKIN (1882–1960) Rankin, from the state of Mississippi, served in the U.S. House of Representatives from 1921 to 1953. A committed segregationist and states' rights advocate, he was consistently vituperative in denouncing efforts to accord blacks the constitutional guarantees of life, liberty, and the pursuit of happiness. During the mid-1940s, he often found conspiracy theory to be an effective means for attacking racial integration. For instance, he vilified the Fair Employment Practices Commission for subverting democracy and threatened to lynch "communistic Jews and Negroes" who attempted to integrate the House of Representatives cafeteria. He posed a similar xenophobic argument in a diatribe against the American Red Cross, whose efforts to collect blood from blacks he characterized as a communist plot to mongrelize America.

FEDERAL EMPLOYMENT PRACTICES COMMISSION (FEPC) On June 25, 1941, President Roosevelt issued executive order 8802, establishing this committee to prevent discrimination based on race, creed, color, or national origin in defense-related work. It was issued in response to a threatened mass march by blacks on Washington, organized by civil and labor rights leader A. Phillip Randolph.

THOMAS SANCTON (1915–?) Louisiana native and Southern liberal who wrote for the *New Republic*. In October 1942, a group of Southern blacks met in Durham, North Carolina, and drafted a statement in which they called for equal pay, opportunities for blacks in industry, a federal antilynching law, equality in public services, the hiring of Negroes by Southern police departments, and the abolition of poll taxes and white primaries. They also suggested that it was a "wicked notion" to suggest that the struggle for Negro rights contradicted the best interests of a nation at war. Sancton was one of the white liberals who enthusiastically supported the Durham Statement.

SCOTTSBORO BOYS On April 9, 1931, Haywood Patterson, Olen Montgomery, Clarence Norris, Willie Roberson, Andrew Wright, Ozie Powell, Eugene Williams, and Charlie Weems were sentenced to death for the alleged rape of two known white prostitutes. After perfunctory trials in the mountain town of Scottsboro, Alabama, all-white juries convicted eight of the youths. The case of the ninth defendant, thirteen-year-old Leroy Wright, ended in a mistrial after a majority of the jury refused to accept the prosecution's recommendation for life imprisonment because of his extreme youth. The repercussions of the Scottsboro case were felt throughout the 1930s; by the end of the decade, it had become one of the great civil rights cases of the twentieth century. The nine young men were sentenced to die on July 10, 1931, but worldwide protests as well as demonstrations around the country delayed any action. The NAACP and the International Labor Defense of the Communist Party intervened. The U.S. Supreme Court, on November 7, 1932, reversed decisions reached by the Alabama courts, on the grounds that the defendants had been denied the right of counsel, which was a violation of due process as guaranteed by the Fourteenth Amendment. The cases were remanded to the lower courts. Over the years, ending finally in 1976, the men were either paroled, freed, or pardoned.

Index